Political Science 150
American Political Institution
Professor Ross Pugia
California State University, Channel Islands

Table of Contents

American Government

Power and Purpose

CORE
EIGHTH
EDITION

Theodore J. Lowi
Cornell University

Benjamin Ginsberg
The Johns Hopkins University
and

Kenneth A. Shepsle
Harvard University

W • W • NORTON & COMPANY NEW YORK • LONDON

W. W. Norton & Company has been independent since its founding in 1923, when William Warder Norton and Mary D. Herter Norton first published lectures delivered at the People's Institute, the adult education division of New York City's Cooper Union. The Nortons soon expanded their program beyond the Institute, publishing books by celebrated academics from America and abroad. By mid-century, the two major pillars of Norton's publishing program—trade books and college texts—were firmly established. In the 1950s, the Norton family transferred control of the company to its employees, and today—with a staff of four hundred and a comparable number of trade, college, and professional titles published each year—W. W. Norton & Company stands as the largest and oldest publishing house owned wholly by its employees.

The text of this book is composed in Berling Roman
with the display set in Bawdy.
Composition by TSI Graphics
Manufacturing by Quebecor World Versailles
Book designer: Sandra Watanabe
Production manager: Diane O'Connor
Editor Stephen P Dunn
Manuscript editor Carol Flechner
Managing editor, college· Marian Johnson
Editorial assistant Susan Cronin

Library of Congress Cataloging-in-Publication Data

Lowi, Theodore J
    American government: power and purpose / Theodore J Lowi, Benjamin Ginsberg,
and Kenneth A Shepsle.—Core 8th ed
      p cm
    Includes bibliographical references and index
    ISBN 0-393-92482-3 (pbk)
    1 United States—Politics and government I Ginsberg, Benjamin II Shepsle,
Kenneth
A III Title

    JK276 L69 2004
    320 473—dc22

2003070212

W W Norton & Company, Inc
500 Fifth Avenue, New York, NY 10110
www wwnorton com
W W Norton & Company Ltd
Castle House, 75/76 Wells Street, London W1T 3QT
1 2 3 4 5 6 7 8 9 0

CHAPTER

2

Constructing a Government: The Founding and the Constitution

"**N**o taxation without representation" were words that stirred a generation of Americans long before they even dreamed of calling themselves Americans rather than Englishmen. Reacting to new English attempts to extract tax revenues to pay for the troops that were being sent to defend the colonial frontier, protests erupted throughout the colonies against the infamous Stamp Act of 1765. This act required that all printed and legal documents, including newspapers, pamphlets, advertisements, notes and bonds, leases, deeds, and licenses be printed on official paper stamped and sold by English officials. To show their displeasure with the act, the colonists conducted mass meetings, parades, bonfires, and other demonstrations throughout the spring and summer of 1765. In Boston, for example, a stamp agent was hanged and burned in effigy. Later, the home of the lieutenant governor was sacked, leading to his resignation and that of all of his colonial commission and stamp agents. By November 1765, business proceeded and newspapers were published without the stamp; in March 1766, Parliament repealed the detested law. Through their protest, the nonimportation agreements that the colonists subsequently adopted, and the Stamp Act Congress that met in October 1765, the colonists took the first steps that ultimately would lead to war and a new nation.

The people of every nation tend to glorify their own history and especially their nation's creation Generally, through such devices as public-school texts and national holidays, governments encourage a heroic view of the nation's past as a way of promoting national pride and unity in the present. Great myths are part of the process of nation building and citizenship training in every nation, and America is no exception. To most contemporary Americans, the revolutionary period represents a brave struggle by a determined and united group of colonists against British oppression. The Boston Tea Party, the battles of Lexington and Concord, the winter at Valley Forge—these are the events that we emphasize in our history. Similarly, the American Constitution—the document establishing the system of government that ultimately emerged from this struggle—is often seen as an inspired, if not divine, work, expressing timeless principles of democratic government. These views are by no means false. During the founding era, Americans did struggle against misrule. Moreover, the American Constitution did establish the foundations for over two hundred years of democratic government.

To really understand the character of the American founding and the meaning of the American Constitution, however, it is essential to look beyond the myths and rhetoric.

The men and women who became revolutionaries were guided by principles, to be sure, but they also had interests. Most of them were not political theorists, but were hard-headed and pragmatic in their commitments and activities. Although their interests were not identical, they did agree that a relationship of political and economic dependence on a colonial power, one that did not treat them as full-fledged citizens of the empire, was intolerable. In the end, the decision to break away and, over the succeeding decade, to fashion institutions of self-governance was the consequence.

Many of those most active in the initial days of the Revolution felt pushed into a corner, their hands forced. For years, the imperial center in London, preoccupied by a war with France that spread across several continents, had left the colonists to their own devices. These were years in which colonists enjoyed an immense amount of local control and home rule. But suddenly, as the war with France drew to a close in the 1760s, the British presence became more onerous and intrusive. This historical experience incited the initial reactions to taxes. Nearly a century of relatively light-handed colonial administration by London had produced a set of expectations in the colonists that later British actions unmistakably violated.

This is where we begin our story in the present chapter. We will first assess the political backdrop of the American Revolution. Then we will examine the Constitution that ultimately emerged— after a rather bumpy experience in self-government just after the Revolution—as the basis for America's government. We will conclude with a reflection upon the founding period by emphasizing a lesson to be learned from the founding that continues to be important throughout American history. This lesson is that politics, as James Madison said in *The Federalist*, generally involves struggles among conflicting interests. In 1776, the conflict was between pro- and anti-revolutionary forces. In 1787, the struggle was between the Federalists and the Antifederalists. Today, the struggle is between the Democrats and the Republicans, each representing competing economic, social, and sectional interests. Often, political principles are the weapons developed by competing interests to further their own causes. The New England merchants who cried "no taxation without representation" cared more about lower taxes than expanded representation. Yet, today, representation is one of the foundations of American democracy

What were the great principles that emerged from the conflicts during the founding period? How do these principles continue to shape our lives long after the Constitution's framers completed their work? These are the important questions that will be addressed in this chapter.

PREVIEWING THE PRINCIPLES

All five principles of politics come into play in this chapter. The framers of the Constitution, in addition to being guided by underlying values, also had conflicting interests that were ultimately settled in the rules and procedures set forth in the Constitution. The Constitution not only provides a framework for government, but often acts as a brake on the policy process—even to this day.

History Principle

The American colonists, used to years of self-governance, believed that the Stamp Act of 1765 threatened their autonomy.

THE FIRST FOUNDING:
INTERESTS AND CONFLICTS

Competing ideals and principles often reflect competing interests, and so it was in revolutionary America. The American Revolution and the American Constitution were outgrowths and expressions of a struggle among economic and political forces within the colonies. Five sectors of society had interests that were important in colonial politics: (1) the New England merchants; (2) the southern planters; (3) the "royalists"—holders of royal lands, offices, and patents (licenses to engage in a profession or business activity); (4) shopkeepers, artisans, and laborers; and (5) small farmers. Throughout the eighteenth century, these groups were in conflict over issues of taxation, trade, and commerce. For the most part, however, the southern planters, the New England merchants, and the royal office and patent holders—groups that together made up the colonial elite—were able to maintain a political alliance that held in check the more radical forces representing shopkeepers, laborers, and small farmers. After 1750, however, by seriously threatening the interests of New England merchants and southern planters, British tax and trade policies split the colonial elite, permitting radical forces to expand their political influence, and set into motion a chain of events that culminated in the American Revolution.[1]

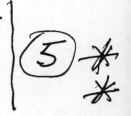

British Taxes and Colonial Interests

Beginning in the 1750s, the debts and other financial problems faced by the British government forced it to search for new revenue sources. This search rather quickly led to the Crown's North American colonies, which, on the whole, paid remarkably little in taxes to the mother country. The British government reasoned that a sizable fraction of its debt was, in fact, attributable to the expenses it had incurred in defense of the colonies during the recent French and Indian wars, as well as to the continuing protection that British forces were giving the colonists from Indian attacks and that the British navy was providing for colonial shipping. Thus, during the 1760s, England sought to impose new, though relatively modest, taxes upon the colonists.

Like most governments of the period, the British regime had at its disposal only limited ways to collect revenues. The income tax, which in the twentieth century has become the single most important source of governmental revenue, had not yet been developed. For the most part, in the mid-eighteenth century, governments relied on tariffs, duties, and other taxes on commerce, and it was to such taxes, including the Stamp Act, that the British turned during the 1760s.

---

[1] The social makeup of colonial America and some of the social conflicts that divided colonial society are discussed in Jackson Turner Main, *The Social Structure of Revolutionary America* (Princeton: Princeton University Press, 1965).

The Stamp Act and other taxes on commerce, such as the Sugar Act of 1764, which taxed sugar, molasses, and other commodities, most heavily affected the two groups in colonial society whose commercial interests and activities were most extensive—the New England merchants and southern planters. Under the famous slogan "no taxation without representation," the merchants and planters together sought to organize opposition to the new taxes. In the course of the struggle against British tax measures, the planters and merchants broke with their royalist allies and turned to their former adversaries—the shopkeepers, small farmers, laborers, and artisans—for help. With the assistance of these groups, the merchants and planters organized demonstrations and a boycott of British goods that ultimately forced the Crown to rescind most of its new taxes. It was in the context of this unrest that a confrontation between colonists and British soldiers in front of the Boston customshouse on the night of March 5, 1770, resulted in what came to be known as the Boston Massacre. Nervous British soldiers opened fire on the mob surrounding them, killing five colonists and wounding eight others. News of this event quickly spread throughout the colonies and was used by radicals to fan anti-British sentiment.

From the perspective of the merchants and planters, however, the British government's decision to eliminate most of the hated taxes represented a victorious end to their struggle with the mother country. They were anxious to end the unrest they had helped to arouse, and they supported the British government's efforts to restore order. Indeed, most respectable Bostonians supported the actions of the British soldiers involved in the Boston Massacre. In their subsequent trial, the soldiers were defended by John Adams, a pillar of Boston society and a future president of the United States. Adams asserted that the soldiers' actions were entirely justified, provoked by a "motley rabble of saucy boys, negroes and mulattoes, Irish teagues and outlandish Jack tars." All but two of the soldiers were acquitted.[2]

Despite the efforts of the British government and the better-to-do strata of colonial society, it proved difficult to bring an end to the political strife. The more radical forces representing shopkeepers, artisans, laborers, and small farmers, who had been mobilized and energized by the struggle over taxes, continued to agitate for political and social change within the colonies. These radicals, led by individuals like Samuel Adams, cousin of John Adams, asserted that British power supported an unjust political and social structure within the colonies, and they began to advocate an end to British rule.[3]

Organizing resistance to the British authorities, however, required widespread support. Collective action, as we saw in the previous chapter, may emerge

[2]George B. Tindall and David E. Shi, *America A Narrative History*, 5th ed (New York W. W. Norton, 1999), p 218

[3]For a discussion of events leading up to the Revolution, see Charles M. Andrews, *The Colonial Background of the American Revolution Four Essays in American Colonial History* (New Haven Yale University Press, 1924)

spontaneously in certain circumstances, but the colonists' campaign against the British imperial power in late eighteenth-century America was a series of encounters, maneuvers, and, ultimately, confrontations that required planning, coalition building, bargaining, compromising, and coordinating, all elements of the give-and-take of politics. Conflicts among the colonists had to be solved by bargaining, persuasion, and even force. Cooperation needed cultivation and encouragement. Leadership was clearly a necessary ingredient

Collective Action Principle

The colonists required strong leaders to resolve differences and to organize resistance to British authority

Political Strife and the Radicalizing of the Colonists

The political strife within the colonies was the background for the events of 1773–1774. In 1773, the British government granted the politically powerful East India Company a monopoly on the export of tea from Britain, eliminating a lucrative form of trade for colonial merchants. To add to the injury, the East India Company sought to sell the tea directly in the colonies instead of working through the colonial merchants. Tea was an extremely important commodity in the 1770s, and these British actions posed a mortal threat to the New England merchants. The merchants once again called upon their radical adversaries for support. The most dramatic result was the Boston Tea Party of 1773, led by Samuel Adams.

This event was of decisive importance in American history. The merchants had hoped to force the British government to rescind the Tea Act, but they did not support any demands beyond this one. They certainly did not seek independence from Britain. Samuel Adams and the other radicals, however, hoped to provoke the British government to take actions that would alienate its colonial supporters and pave the way for a rebellion. This was precisely the purpose of the Boston Tea Party, and it succeeded. By dumping the East India Company's tea into Boston Harbor, Adams and his followers goaded the British into enacting a number of harsh reprisals. Within five months after the incident in Boston, the House of Commons passed a series of acts that closed the port of Boston to commerce, changed the provincial government of Massachusetts, provided for the removal of accused persons to England for trial, and, most important, restricted movement to the West—further alienating the southern planters who depended upon access to new western lands. These acts of retaliation confirmed the worst criticisms of England and helped radicalize Americans.

The choice of this course of action by English politicians looks puzzling in retrospect, but at the time it appeared reasonable to those who prevailed in Parliament that a show of force was required. The toleration of lawlessness and the making of concessions, they felt, would only egg on the more radical elements in the colonies to take further liberties and demand further concessions. The English, in effect, drew a line in the sand. Their repressive reactions served as a clear point around which dissatisfied colonists could rally. Radicals like Samuel Adams had been agitating for more violent measures to deal with England. But ultimately they needed Britain's political repression to create widespread support for independence.

Thus, the Boston Tea Party set into motion a cycle of provocation and retaliation that in 1774 resulted in the convening of the First Continental Congress—an assembly consisting of delegates from all parts of the country—that called for a total boycott of British goods and, under the prodding of the radicals, began to consider the possibility of independence from British rule. The eventual result was the Declaration of Independence.

The Declaration of Independence

In 1776, the Second Continental Congress appointed a committee consisting of Thomas Jefferson of Virginia, Benjamin Franklin of Pennsylvania, Roger Sherman of Connecticut, John Adams of Massachusetts, and Robert Livingston of New York to draft a statement of American independence from British rule. The Declaration of Independence, written by Jefferson and adopted by the Second Continental Congress, was an extraordinary document both in philosophical and political terms. Philosophically, the Declaration was remarkable for its assertion that certain rights, called "unalienable rights"—including life, liberty, and the pursuit of happiness—could not be abridged by governments. In the world of 1776, a world in which some kings still claimed to rule by divine right, this was a dramatic statement. Politically, the Declaration was remarkable because, despite the differences of interest that divided the colonists along economic, regional, and philosophical lines, the Declaration identified and focused on problems, grievances, aspirations, and principles that might unify the various colonial groups. The Declaration was an attempt to identify and articulate a history and set of principles that might help to forge national unity.[4]

The Articles of Confederation

Articles of Confederation and Perpetual Union America's first written constitution. Adopted by the Continental Congress in 1777, the Articles of Confederation and Perpetual Union was the formal basis for America's national government until 1789, when it was supplanted by the Constitution.

Having declared their independence, the colonies needed to establish a governmental structure. In November of 1777, the Continental Congress adopted the *Articles of Confederation and Perpetual Union*—the United States' first written constitution. Although it was not ratified by all the states until 1781, it was the country's operative constitution for almost twelve years, until March 1789.

The Articles of Confederation was a constitution concerned primarily with limiting the powers of the central government. The central government, first of all, was based entirely in Congress. Since it was not intended to be a powerful government, it was given no executive branch. Execution of its laws was to be left to the individual states. Second, Congress had little power. Its members were not much more than delegates or messengers from the state legislatures. They were chosen by the state legislatures, their salaries were paid out of the state

---

[4] See Carl L Becker, *The Declaration of Independence A Study in the History of Political Ideas* (New York Vintage, 1942)

treasuries, and they were subject to immediate recall by state authorities. In addition, each state, regardless of its size, had only a single vote.

Congress was given the power to declare war and make peace, to make treaties and alliances, to coin or borrow money, and to regulate trade with the Native Americans. It could also appoint the senior officers of the United States Army. But it could not levy taxes or regulate commerce among the states. Moreover, the army officers it appointed had no army to serve in because the nation's armed forces were composed of the state militias. Probably the most unfortunate part of the Articles of Confederation was that the central government could not prevent one state from discriminating against other states in the quest for foreign commerce.

In brief, the relationship between Congress and the states under the Articles of Confederation was much like the contemporary relationship between the United Nations and its member states, a relationship in which virtually all governmental powers are retained by the states. It was properly called a "confederation" because, as provided under Article II, "each state retains its sovereignty, freedom, and independence, and every power, jurisdiction, and right, which is not by this Confederation expressly delegated to the United States, in Congress assembled." Not only was there no executive, there was also no judicial authority and no other means of enforcing Congress's will. If there was to be any enforcement at all, it would be done for Congress by the states.[5]

THE SECOND FOUNDING: FROM COMPROMISE TO CONSTITUTION

The Declaration of Independence and the Articles of Confederation were not sufficient to hold the nation together as an independent and effective nation-state. From almost the moment of armistice with the British in 1783, moves were afoot to reform and strengthen the Articles of Confederation.

International Standing and Balance of Power

There was a special concern for the country's international position. Competition among the states for foreign commerce allowed the European powers to play the states against each other, which created confusion on both sides of the Atlantic. At one point during the winter of 1786–1787, John Adams of Massachusetts, a leader in the independence struggle, was sent to negotiate a new treaty with the British, one that would cover disputes left over from the war. The British government responded that, since the United States under the Articles of Confederation was unable to enforce existing treaties, it would negotiate with each of the thirteen states separately.

[5]See Merrill Jensen, *The Articles of Confederation* (Madison: University of Wisconsin Press, 1963)

At the same time, well-to-do Americans—in particular the New England merchants and southern planters—were troubled by the influence that "radical" forces exercised in the Continental Congress and in the governments of several of the states. The colonists' victory in the Revolutionary War had not only meant the end of British rule, but it also significantly changed the balance of political power within the new states. As a result of the Revolution, one key segment of the colonial elite—the royal land, office, and patent holders—was stripped of its economic and political privileges. In fact, many of these individuals, along with tens of thousands of other colonists who considered themselves loyal British subjects, left for Canada after the British surrender. And while the pre-revolutionary elite was weakened, the pre-revolutionary radicals were now better organized than ever before and were the controlling forces in such states as Pennsylvania and Rhode Island, where they pursued economic and political policies that struck terror into the hearts of the pre-revolutionary political establishment. In Rhode Island, for example, between 1783 and 1785, a legislature dominated by representatives of small farmers, artisans, and shopkeepers had instituted economic policies, including drastic currency inflation, that frightened businessmen and property owners throughout the country. Of course, the central government under the Articles of Confederation was powerless to intervene.

Institution Principle

Institutional arrangements matter, but there is no guarantee that they will be perfect, as the Articles of Confederation make apparent.

The Annapolis Convention

The continuation of international weakness and domestic economic turmoil led many Americans to consider whether their newly adopted form of government might not already require revision. Institutional arrangements are experiments in governance, and they don't always work out. Nearly a decade under the Articles had made amply clear the flaws it contained. In the fall of 1786, many state leaders accepted an invitation from the Virginia legislature for a conference of representatives of all the states. Delegates from five states actually attended. This conference, held in Annapolis, Maryland, was the first step toward the second founding. The one positive thing that came out of the Annapolis Convention was a carefully worded resolution calling on Congress to send commissioners to Philadelphia at a later time "to devise such further provisions as shall appear to them necessary to render the Constitution of the Federal Government adequate to the exigencies of the Union."[6] This resolution was drafted by Alexander Hamilton, a thirty-four-year-old New York lawyer who had played a significant role in the Revolution as George Washington's secretary and who would play a still more significant role in framing the Constitution and forming the new government in the 1790s But the resolution did not necessarily imply any desire to do more than improve and reform the Articles of Confederation.

[6]Reported in Samuel Eliot Morrison, Henry Steele Commager, and William E Leuchtenburg, *The Growth of the American Republic*, 6th ed , vol 1 (New York· Oxford University Press, 1969), p 244

Shays's Rebellion

It is possible that the Constitutional Convention of 1787 in Philadelphia would never have taken place at all except for a single event that occurred during the winter following the Annapolis Convention: Shays's Rebellion. Like the Boston Tea Party, this was a focal event. It concentrated attention, coordinated beliefs, produced widespread fear and apprehension, and thus convinced waverers that "something was broke and needed fixing." In short, it provided politicians who had long been convinced that the Articles were flawed and insufficient with just the ammunition they needed to persuade a much broader public of these facts [7]

Daniel Shays, a former army captain, led a mob of farmers in a rebellion against the government of Massachusetts. The purpose of the rebellion was to prevent foreclosures on their debt-ridden land by keeping the county courts of western Massachusetts from sitting until after the next election. The state militia dispersed the mob, but for several days, Shays and his followers terrified the state government by attempting to capture the federal arsenal at Springfield, provoking an appeal to Congress to help restore order. Within a few days, the state government regained control and captured fourteen of the rebels (all were eventually pardoned). In 1787, a newly elected Massachusetts legislature granted some of the farmers' demands.

Although the incident ended peacefully, its effects lingered and spread. Washington summed it up: "I am mortified beyond expression that in the moment of our acknowledged independence we should by our conduct verify the predictions of our transatlantic foe, and render ourselves ridiculous and contemptible in the eyes of all Europe."[8]

Congress under the Confederation had been unable to act decisively in a time of crisis. This provided critics of the Articles of Confederation with precisely the evidence they needed to push Hamilton's Annapolis resolution through the Congress. Thus, the states were asked to send representatives to Philadelphia to discuss constitutional revision. Delegates were eventually sent by every state except Rhode Island.

> **History Principle**
>
> Shays's Rebellion focused attention on the flaws of the Articles of Confederation, leading to the Constitutional Convention.

The Constitutional Convention

Twenty-nine of a total of 73 delegates selected by the state governments convened in Philadelphia in May 1787, with political strife, international embarrassment, national weakness, and local rebellion fixed in their minds. Recognizing that these issues were symptoms of fundamental flaws in the Articles of Confederation, the delegates soon abandoned the plan to revise the Articles and committed themselves to a second founding—a second, and ultimately successful, attempt to create a legitimate and effective national system. This effort occupied the convention for the next five months.

---

[7] For an easy-to-read argument that supports this view, see Keith L. Dougherty, *Collective Action under the Articles of Confederation* (New York Cambridge University Press, 2001)

[8] Morrison et al, *The Growth of the American Republic*, p 242

A Marriage of Interest and Principle   For years, scholars have disagreed about the motives of the founders in Philadelphia. Among the most controversial views of the framers' motives is the "economic" interpretation put forward by historian Charles Beard and his disciples.[9] According to Beard's account, America's founders were a collection of securities speculators and property owners whose only aim was personal enrichment. From this perspective, the Constitution's lofty principles were little more than sophisticated masks behind which the most venal interests sought to enrich themselves.

Contrary to Beard's approach is the view that the framers of the Constitution *were* concerned with philosophical and ethical principles. Indeed, the framers sought to devise a system of government consistent with the dominant philosophical and moral principles of the day. But, in fact, these two views belong together; the founders' interests were reinforced by their principles. The convention that drafted the American Constitution was chiefly organized by the New England merchants and southern planters. Though the delegates representing these groups did not all hope to profit personally from an increase in the value of their securities, as Beard would have it, they did hope to benefit in the broadest political and economic sense by breaking the power of their radical foes and establishing a system of government more compatible with their long-term economic and political interests. Thus, the framers sought to create a new government capable of promoting commerce and protecting property from radical state legislatures. They also sought to liberate the national government from the power of individual states and their sometimes venal and corrupt local politicians. At the same time, they hoped to fashion a government less susceptible than the existing state and national regimes to populist forces hostile to the interests of the commercial and propertied classes.

The Great Compromise   The proponents of a new government fired their opening shot on May 29, 1787, when Edmund Randolph of Virginia offered a resolution that proposed corrections and enlargements in the Articles of Confederation. The proposal, which showed the strong influence of James Madison, was not a simple motion. It provided for virtually every aspect of a new government. Randolph later admitted it was intended to be an alternative draft constitution, and it did in fact serve as the framework for what ultimately became the Constitution. (There is no verbatim record of the debates, but Madison was present during virtually all of the deliberations and kept full notes on them.)[10]

This proposal, known as the "Virginia Plan," provided for a system of representation in the national legislature based on the population of each state or the

[9]Charles A Beard, *An Economic Interpretation of the Constitution of the United States* (New York Macmillan, 1913)

[10]Madison's notes along with the somewhat less complete records kept by several other participants in the convention are available in a four-volume set See Max Farrand, ed , *The Records of the Federal Convention of 1787*, rev ed , 4 vols (New Haven Yale University Press, 1966)

proportion of each state's revenue contribution, or both. (Randolph also proposed a second branch of the legislature, but it was to be elected by the members of the first branch.) Since the states varied enormously in size and wealth, the Virginia Plan was thought to be heavily biased in favor of the large states.

While the convention was debating the Virginia Plan, additional delegates were arriving in Philadelphia and were beginning to mount opposition to it. Their resolution, introduced by William Paterson of New Jersey and known as the "New Jersey Plan," did not oppose the Virginia Plan point for point. Instead, it concentrated on specific weaknesses in the Articles of Confederation, in the spirit of revision rather than radical replacement of that document. Supporters of the New Jersey Plan did not seriously question the convention's commitment to replacing the Articles. But their opposition to the Virginia Plan's scheme of representation was sufficient to send its proposals back to committee for reworking into a common document. In particular, delegates from the less populous states, which included Delaware, New Jersey, Connecticut, and New York, asserted that the more populous states, such as Virginia, Pennsylvania, North Carolina, Massachusetts, and Georgia, would dominate the new government if representation were to be determined by population. The smaller states argued that each state should be equally represented in the new regime regardless of its population.

The issue of representation was one that threatened to wreck the entire constitutional enterprise. Delegates conferred, factions maneuvered, and tempers flared. James Wilson of Pennsylvania told the small-state delegates that if they wanted to disrupt the union they should go ahead. The separation could, he said, "never happen on better grounds." Small-state delegates were equally blunt. Gunning Bedford of Delaware declared that the small states might look elsewhere for friends if they were forced. "The large states," he said, "dare not dissolve the confederation. If they do the small ones will find some foreign ally of more honor and good faith, who will take them by the hand and do them justice." These sentiments were widely shared. The union, as Oliver Ellsworth of Connecticut put it, was "on the verge of dissolution, scarcely held together by the strength of a hair."

The outcome of this debate was the Connecticut Compromise, also known as the *Great Compromise.* Under the terms of this compromise, in the first branch of Congress—the House of Representatives—the representatives would be apportioned according to the number of inhabitants in each state. This, of course, was what delegates from the large states had sought. But in the second branch—the Senate—each state would have an equal vote regardless of its size; this was to deal with the concerns of the small states. This compromise was not immediately satisfactory to all the delegates. Indeed, two of the most vocal members of the small-state faction, John Lansing and Robert Yates of New York, were so incensed by the concession that their colleagues had made to the large-state forces that they stormed out of the convention. In the end, however, both sets of forces preferred compromise to the breakup of the union, and the plan was accepted.

Great Compromise Agreement reached at the Constitutional Convention of 1787 that gave each state an equal number of senators regardless of its population, but linked representation in the House of Representatives to population.

The Question of Slavery: The Three-fifths Compromise The story so far is too neat, too easy, and too anticlimactic. If it were left here, it would only contribute to American mythology. After all, the notion of a bicameral (two-chambered) legislature was very much in the air in 1787. Some of the states had had this for years. The Philadelphia delegates might well have gone straight to the adoption of two chambers based on two different principles of representation even without the dramatic interplay of conflict and compromise. But a far more fundamental issue had to be confronted before the Great Compromise could take place: the issue of slavery.

Many of the conflicts that emerged during the Constitutional Convention were reflections of the fundamental differences between the slave and the non-slave states—differences that pitted the southern planters and New England merchants against one another. This was the first premonition of a conflict that was almost to destroy the Republic in later years. In the midst of debate over large versus small states, Madison observed:

> The great danger to our general government is the great southern and northern interests of the continent, being opposed to each other. Look to the votes in Congress, and most of them stand divided by the geography of the country, not according to the size of the states[11]

Over 90 percent of all slaves resided in five states—Georgia, Maryland, North Carolina, South Carolina, and Virginia—where they accounted for 30 percent of the total population. In some places, slaves outnumbered nonslaves by as much as 10 to 1. If the Constitution were to embody any principle of national supremacy, some basic decisions would have to be made about the place of slavery in the general scheme. Madison hit on this point on several occasions as different aspects of the Constitution were being discussed. For example, he observed:

> It seemed now to be pretty well understood that the real difference of interests lay, not between the large and small but between the northern and southern states. The institution of slavery and its consequences formed the line of discrimination. There were five states on the South, eight on the northern side of this line. Should a proportional representation take place it was true, the northern side would still outnumber the other but not in the same degree, at this time; and every day would tend towards an equilibrium.[12]

Three-fifths Compromise
Agreement reached at the Constitutional Convention of 1787 that stipulated that for purposes of the apportionment of congressional seats, every slave would be counted as three-fifths of a person.

Northerners and southerners eventually reached agreement through the **Three-fifths Compromise.** The seats in the House of Representatives would be apportioned according to a "population" in which five slaves would count as three persons. The slaves would not be allowed to vote, of course, but the num-

[11]Ibid., I, p 476
[12]Ibid., II, p 10

ber of representatives would be apportioned accordingly. This arrangement was supported by the slave states, which obviously included some of the biggest and some of the smallest states at that time. It was also accepted by many delegates from nonslave states who strongly supported the principle of property representation, whether that property was expressed in slaves or in land, money, or stocks. The concern exhibited by most delegates was over how much slaves would count toward a state's representation rather than whether the institution of slavery would continue The Three-fifths Compromise, in the words of political scientist Donald Robinson, "gave Constitutional sanction to the fact that the United States was composed of some persons who were 'free' and others who were not, and it established the principle, new in republican theory, that a man who lives among slaves had a greater share in the election of representatives than the man who did not. Although the Three-fifths Compromise acknowledged slavery and rewarded slave owners, nonetheless, it probably kept the South from unanimously rejecting the Constitution."[13]

The issue of slavery was the most difficult one faced by the framers, and it nearly destroyed the Union. Although some delegates believed slavery to be morally wrong, an evil and oppressive institution that made a mockery of the ideals and values espoused in the Constitution, morality was not the issue that caused the framers to support or oppose the Three-fifths Compromise. Whatever they thought of the institution of slavery, most delegates from the northern states opposed counting slaves in the distribution of congressional seats. Wilson of Pennsylvania, for example, argued that if slaves were citizens they should be treated and counted like other citizens. If on the other hand, they were property, then why should not other forms of property be counted toward the apportionment of Congress? But southern delegates made it clear that if the northerners refused to give in, they would never agree to the new government. William R. Davie of North Carolina heatedly said that it was time "to speak out." He asserted that the people of North Carolina would never enter the Union if slaves were not counted as part of the basis for representation. Without such agreement, he asserted ominously, "the business was at an end." Even southerners like Edmund Randolph of Virginia, who conceded that slavery was immoral, insisted upon including slaves in the allocation of congressional seats. This conflict between the southern and northern delegates was so divisive that many came to question the possibility of creating and maintaining a union of the two. Pierce Butler of South Carolina declared that the North and South were as different as Russia and Turkey. Eventually, the North and South compromised on the issue of slavery and representation. Indeed, northerners even agreed to permit a continuation of the odious slave trade to keep the South in the union. But, in due course, Butler proved to be correct, and a bloody war was fought when the disparate interests of the North and South could no longer be reconciled.

Collective Action Principle
The framers preferred compromise to the breakup of the union, and thus accepted the Great Compromise and the Three-fifths Compromise.

---

[13]Donald L Robinson, *Slavery in the Structure of American Politics, 1765–1820* (New York Harcourt Brace Jovanovich, 1971), p. 201

Were the Framers Rational Actors?

How can we use the five principles of politics to interpret events that occurred centuries ago? The strategic decision making at the American Constitutional Convention has been a fertile area of study.

Many of the basic ingredients for a strategic politics analysis are present. The historical record is detailed and seemingly very accurate. The entire Constitutional Convention took place in secret, and the delegates took pains to ensure that the media and mass public were not aware of the decisions being made, the alternatives that were rejected, or the process that was being utilized.

In line with Principle 2, keeping the group small and homogeneous increased the chance of successful collective action. Participation was restricted to those delegates who were directly appointed by the state legislatures. By keeping the proceedings closed, it reduced the likelihood that outside parties could influence the discussion or that new issues could be introduced that would complicate the process.

At the same time, the convention allowed for extensive internal discussion. Most participants knew the preferences of the other participants. In the language of rational choice, the setting was close to "full information." In situations where every player knows the goals and options of every other player, it is far easier to predict everyone's behavior.[14]

In a famous article and book, historian Charles Beard advocated the view of the founders as strategic actors by making the provocative argument that the Constitution is a document written by wealthy elites to preserve their own economic and political power.[15] Beard focused on the secretive and elite-centered nature of the convention and the limited franchise found throughout the process. In Beard's analysis, the Constitution is not the grand design of political philosophers, but instead the product of hard-nosed political bargaining and self-interests. An infamous example of this is the "three-fifths" rule for counting slaves. This was the result of a bargain between pro-slavery, anti-tariff southerners and northerners who were opposed to slavery yet wanted to retain protective tariffs.

William Riker similarly shows how delegates, such as Gouverneur Morris, delegate from Pennsylvania, manipulated the procedures at the convention in order to obtain his desired outcome. According to Riker, Morris and a few other Pennsylvanians were the only opposition to the "Virginia Plan," whereby the executive would be elected by the national legislature (the two houses of Congress). If adopted, the Virginia Plan would have rendered states wholly subservient to the national government because the plan also allowed the national legislature to abrogate state laws.[16] In essence, Morris was able to change the order in which various provisions of the Virginia Plan were considered such that it became apparent that endorsing the Virginia Plan was tantamount to endorsing a lifetime presidency.[17] As Principle 3 indicates, rules and procedures—particularly agenda control—matter.

Still, this approach to the founding remains controversial. Americans revere the founders as angels and brilliant philosophers. Many object to this self-interested interpretation. Historian Robert Brown disputes Beard's account of the convention.[18] What Beard fails to appreciate, Brown argues, is that American society as a whole was in favor of the democratic changes enshrined in the Constitution. Americans did not perceive the Constitution as an elite vehicle being foisted upon them. Brown argues that agrarian, commercial, and mercantile interests felt that they were well represented by the delegates

Regardless if you believe that the founders "truly" were strategic or not, rational choice can help you understand how the convention proceeded the way it did. Keep the group small (Principle 2), keep control of rules and procedures (Principle 3), and you can readily control the outcome. Even when actors are motivated by altruistic concerns, institutional rules and procedures can be used to obtain a preferred outcome

---

[14]These types of situations are rare in everyday life Substantial research in political science and economics has focused on how individuals make do with "limited" information

[15]Charles A Beard, *An Economic Interpretation of the Constitution of the United States* (New York Macmillan, 1913)

[16]This was precisely the goal of the supporters of the Virginia Plan. They believed that state legislatures were incompetent and that states should be governed by a national elite.

[17]The specifics are laid out in more detail in Chapter 4 of William H. Riker's *The Art of Political Manipulation* (New Haven. Yale University Press, 1986).

[18]Robert E Brown, *Charles Beard and the Constitution A Critical Analysis of "An Economic Interpretation of the Constitution"* (New York W W. Norton, 1965)

THE CONSTITUTION

The political significance of the Great Compromise and Three-fifths Compromise was to reinforce the unity of the mercantile and planter forces that sought to create a new government. The Great Compromise reassured those who feared that the importance of their own local or regional influence would be reduced by the new governmental framework. The Three-fifths Compromise temporarily defused the rivalry between the merchants and planters. Their unity secured, members of the alliance supporting the establishment of a new government moved to fashion a constitutional framework consistent with their economic and political interests.

In particular, the framers sought a new government that, first, would be strong enough to promote commerce and protect property from radical state legislatures such as Rhode Island's. This became the constitutional basis for national control over commerce and finance, as well as the establishment of national judicial supremacy and the effort to construct a strong presidency. Second, the framers sought to prevent what they saw as the threat posed by the "excessive democracy" of the state and national governments under the Articles of

bicameralism
Having a legislative assembly composed of two chambers or houses.

Confederation. This led to such constitutional principles as ***bicameralism*** (division of the Congress into two chambers), checks and balances, staggered terms in office, and indirect election (selection of the president by an electoral college rather than by voters directly). Third, the framers, lacking the power to force the states or the public at large to accept the new form of government, sought to identify principles that would help to secure support. This became the basis of the constitutional provision for direct popular election of representatives and, subsequently, for the addition of the Bill of Rights to the Constitution. Finally, the framers wanted to be certain that the government they created did not use its power to pose even more of a threat to its citizens' liberties and property rights than did the radical state legislatures they feared and despised. To prevent the new government from abusing its power, the framers incorporated principles such as the separation of powers and federalism into the Constitution.

 **Rationality Principle**
The framers of the Constitution were guided by principles, but they also had interests.

The framers provided us with a grand lesson in instrumental behavior. They came to Philadelphia united by a common distaste for government under the Articles and animated by the agitation following Shays's Rebellion. They didn't always agree on what it was they disliked about the Articles. They certainly didn't agree on how to proceed—hence the necessity for the historic compromises we have just described. But they did believe that the fostering of commerce and the protection of property could better be served by an alternative set of institutional arrangements than that of the Articles. They agreed that the institutional arrangements of government mattered for their lives and those of their fellow citizens. They believed that both too much democracy and too much governmental power were threats to the common good, and they felt compelled to find instruments and principles that weighed against these. Let us assess the major provisions of the Constitution's seven articles to see how each relates to these objectives.

 Institution Principle
The constitutional framework promoted commerce, protected property, prevented "excessive democracy," and limited the power of the national government.

The Legislative Branch

The first seven sections of Article I of the Constitution provided for a Congress consisting of two chambers—a House of Representatives and a Senate. Members of the House of Representatives were given two-year terms in office and were to be elected directly by the people. Members of the Senate were to be appointed by the state legislatures (this was changed in 1913 by the Seventeenth Amendment, which instituted direct election of senators) for six-year terms. These terms, moreover, were staggered so that the appointments of one-third of the senators would expire every two years. The Constitution assigned somewhat different tasks to the House and Senate. Though the approval of each body was required for the enactment of a law, the Senate alone was given the power to ratify treaties and approve presidential appointments. The House, on the other hand, was given the sole power to originate revenue bills.

The character of the legislative branch was directly related to the framers' major goals. The House of Representatives was designed to be directly responsible to the people in order to encourage popular consent for the new Constitution and to help enhance the power of the new government. At the same time, to guard against "excessive democracy," the power of the House of Representatives was checked by the Senate, whose members were to be appointed for long terms rather than be elected directly by the people. The purpose of this provision, according to Alexander Hamilton, was to avoid "an unqualified complaisance to every sudden breeze of passion, or to every transient impulse which the people may receive."[19] Staggered terms of service in the Senate, moreover, were intended to make that body even more resistant to popular pressure Since only one-third of the senators would be selected at any given time, the composition of the institution would be protected from changes in popular preferences transmitted by the state legislatures. This would prevent what James Madison called "mutability in the public councils arising from a rapid succession of new members."[20] Thus, the structure of the legislative branch was designed to contribute to governmental power, to promote popular consent for the new government, and at the same time to place limits on the popular political currents that many of the framers saw as a radical threat to the economic and social order.

The issues of power and consent were important throughout the Constitution. Section 8 of Article I specifically listed the powers of Congress, which include the authority to collect taxes, to borrow money, to regulate commerce, to declare war, and to maintain an army and navy By granting it these powers, the framers indicated very clearly that they intended the new government to be far more influential than its predecessor. At the same time, by defining the new government's most important powers as belonging to Congress, the framers sought to promote popular acceptance of this critical change by reassuring citizens that their views would be fully represented whenever the government exercised its new powers

As a further guarantee to the people that the new government would pose no threat to them, the Constitution implied that any powers not listed were not granted at all. This is the doctrine of **expressed power**. The Constitution grants only those powers specifically *expressed* in its text. But the framers intended to create an active and powerful government, and so they included the **necessary and proper clause**, sometimes known as the elastic clause, which signified that the enumerated powers were meant to be a source of strength to the national government, not a limitation on it. Each power could be used with the utmost vigor, but no new powers could be seized upon by the national government without a constitutional amendment. In the absence of such an amendment, any power not enumerated was conceived to be "reserved" to the states (or the people).

The Executive Branch

The Constitution provided for the establishment of the presidency in Article II. As Alexander Hamilton commented, the presidential article aimed toward "energy in the Executive." It did so in an effort to overcome the natural stalemate

expressed power
The notion that the Constitution grants to the federal government only those powers specifically named in its text.

necessary and proper clause
Article I, Section 8, of the Constitution, which enumerates the powers of Congress and provides Congress with the authority to make all laws "necessary and proper" to carry them out; also referred to as the "elastic clause."

[19]E M Earle, ed , *The Federalist* (New York. Modern Library, 1937), No 71.
[20]Ibid , No 62

that was built into the bicameral legislature as well as into the separation of powers among the legislative, executive, and judicial branches. The Constitution afforded the president a measure of independence from the people and from the other branches of government—particularly the Congress.

In line with the framers' goal of increased power to the national government, the president was granted the unconditional power to accept ambassadors from other countries; this amounted to the power to "recognize" other countries. He was also given the power to negotiate treaties, although their acceptance required the approval of the Senate. The president was given the unconditional right to grant reprieves and pardons, except in cases of impeachment. And he was provided with the power to appoint major departmental personnel, to convene Congress in special session, and to veto congressional enactments. (The veto power is formidable, but it is not absolute since Congress can override it by a two-thirds vote.)

The framers hoped to create a presidency that would make the federal government rather than the states the agency capable of timely and decisive action to deal with public issues and problems. This was the meaning of the "energy" that Hamilton hoped to impart to the executive branch.[21] At the same time, however, the framers sought to help the president withstand (excessively) democratic pressures by making him subject to indirect rather than direct election (through his selection by a separate electoral college). The extent to which the framers' hopes were actually realized will be the topic of Chapter 6.

The Judicial Branch

In establishing the judicial branch in Article III, the Constitution reflected the framers' preoccupations with nationalizing governmental power and checking radical democratic impulses, while guarding against potential interference with liberty and property from the new national government itself.

Under the provisions of Article III, the framers created a court that was to be literally a supreme court of the United States and not merely the highest court of the national government. The most important expression of this intention was granting the Supreme Court the power to resolve any conflicts that might emerge between federal and state laws. In particular, the Supreme Court was given the right to determine whether a power was exclusive to the federal government, concurrent with the states, or exclusive to the states. The significance of this was noted by Justice Oliver Wendell Holmes, who observed:

> I do not think the United States would come to an end if we lost our power to declare an act of Congress void. I do think the union would be imperilled if we could not make that declaration as to the laws of the several states.[22]

[21] Ibid., No. 70
[22] Oliver Wendell Holmes, *Collected Legal Papers* (New York: Harcourt Brace, 1920), pp. 295–96

In addition, the Supreme Court was assigned jurisdiction over controversies between citizens of different states. The long-term significance of this was that as the country developed a national economy, it came to rely increasingly on the federal judiciary, rather than on the state courts, for resolution of disputes.

Judges were given lifetime appointments in order to protect them from popular politics and from interference by the other branches. This, however, did not mean that the judiciary would actually remain totally impartial to political considerations or to the other branches, for the president was to appoint the judges and the Senate to approve the appointments. Congress would also have the power to create inferior (lower) courts, to change the jurisdiction of the federal courts, to add or subtract federal judges, even to change the size of the Supreme Court.

No direct mention is made in the Constitution of *judicial review*—the power of the courts to render the final decision when there is a conflict of interpretation of the Constitution or of laws between the courts and Congress, the courts and the executive branch, or the courts and the states. Scholars generally feel that judicial review is implicit in the very existence of a written Constitution and in the power given directly to the federal courts over "all Cases . . . arising under this Constitution, the Laws of the United States, and Treaties made, or which shall be made, under their Authority" (Article III, Section 2). The Supreme Court eventually assumed the power of judicial review. Its assumption of this power, as we shall see in Chapter 8, was not based on the Constitution itself but on the politics of later decades and the membership of the Court.

judicial review
Power of the courts to declare actions of the legislative and executive branches invalid or unconstitutional. The Supreme Court asserted this power in *Marbury v. Madison.*

National Unity and Power

Various provisions in the Constitution addressed the framers' concern with national unity and power, including Article IV's provisions for comity (reciprocity) among states and among citizens of all states.

Each state was prohibited from discriminating against the citizens of other states in favor of its own citizens, with the Supreme Court charged with deciding in each case whether a state had discriminated against goods or people from another state. The Constitution restricted the power of the states in favor of ensuring enough power to the national government to give the country a free-flowing national economy.

The framers' concern with national supremacy was also expressed in Article VI, in the *supremacy clause,* which provided that national laws and treaties "shall be the supreme Law of the Land." This meant that all laws made under the "Authority of the United States" would be superior to all laws adopted by any state or any other subdivision, and the states would be expected to respect all treaties made under that authority. This was a direct effort to keep the states from dealing separately with foreign nations or businesses. The supremacy clause also bound the officials of all state and local as well as federal governments to take an oath of office to support the national Constitution. This meant that every action taken by the United States Congress would have to be applied within each state as though the action were in fact state law.

supremacy clause
Article VI of the Constitution, which states that all laws passed by the national government and all treaties are the supreme laws of the land and superior to all laws adopted by any state or any subdivision.

Amending the Constitution

The Constitution established procedures for its own revision in Article V. Its provisions are so difficult that Americans have availed themselves of the amending process only seventeen times since 1791, when the first ten amendments were adopted. Many other amendments have been proposed in Congress, but fewer than forty of them have even come close to fulfilling the Constitution's requirement of a two-thirds vote in Congress, and only a fraction have gotten anywhere near adoption by three-fourths of the states. The Constitution could also be amended by a constitutional convention. Occasionally, proponents of particular measures, such as a balanced-budget amendment, have called for a constitutional convention to consider their proposals. Whatever the purpose for which it was called, however, such a convention would presumably have the authority to revise America's entire system of government.

It should be noted that any body of rules, including a national constitution, must balance the need to respond flexibly to changes, on the one hand, with the caution not to be too flexible, on the other. An inflexible body of rules is one that cannot accommodate major change. It risks being rebelled against, a circumstance in which the slate is wiped clean and new rules designed, or ignored altogether. Too much flexibility, however, is disastrous. It invites those who lose in normal everyday politics to replay battles at the constitutional level. If institutional change is too easy to accomplish, the stability of the political system becomes threatened.

Ratifying the Constitution

The rules for ratification of the Constitution of 1787 were set forth in Article VII of the Constitution. This provision actually violated the amendment provisions of the Articles of Confederation. For one thing, it adopted a nine-state rule in place of the unanimity required by the Articles of Confederation. For another, it provided that ratification would occur in special state conventions called for that purpose rather than in the state legislatures. All the states except Rhode Island eventually did set up state conventions to ratify the Constitution.

Constitutional Limits on the National Government's Power

separation of powers The division of governmental power among several institutions that must cooperate in decision making.

federalism System of government in which power is divided by a constitution between a central government and regional governments

Bill of Rights The first ten amendments to the U.S Constitution, ratified in 1791. They ensure certain rights and liberties to the people

As we have indicated, although the framers sought to create a powerful national government, they also wanted to guard against possible misuse of that power. To that end, the framers incorporated two key principles into the Constitution—the *separation of powers* and *federalism* (see Chapter 3). A third set of limitations, in the form of the *Bill of Rights,* was added to the Constitution to help secure its ratification when opponents of the document charged that it paid insufficient attention to citizens' rights

The Separation of Powers   No principle of politics was more widely shared at the time of the 1787 founding than the principle that power must be used to balance power The French political theorist Baron de Montesquieu (1689–1755)

FIGURE 2.1

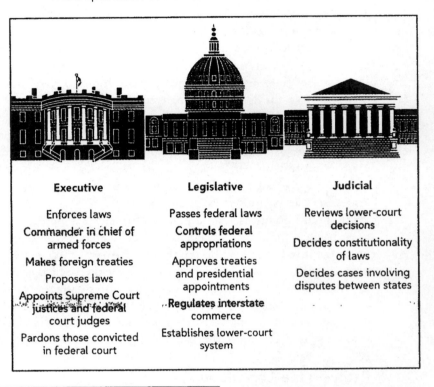

The Separation of Powers

Executive	Legislative	Judicial
Enforces laws	Passes federal laws	Reviews lower-court decisions
Commander in chief of armed forces	Controls federal appropriations	Decides constitutionality of laws
Makes foreign treaties	Approves treaties and presidential appointments	Decides cases involving disputes between states
Proposes laws		
Appoints Supreme Court justices and federal court judges	Regulates interstate commerce	
Pardons those convicted in federal court	Establishes lower-court system	

believed that this balance was an indispensable defense against tyranny, and his writings, especially his major work, *The Spirit of the Laws*, "were taken as political gospel" at the Philadelphia convention.[23] The principle of the separation of powers is nowhere to be found explicitly in the Constitution, but it is clearly built on Articles I, II, and III, which provide for the following:

1. Three separate and distinct branches of government (see Figure 2.1).
2. Different methods of selecting the top personnel, so that each branch is responsible to a different constituency. This is supposed to produce a "mixed regime," in which the personnel of each department will develop very different interests and outlooks on how to govern, and different groups in society will be assured some access to governmental decision making.

[23]Max Farrand, *The Framing of the Constitution of the United States* (New Haven: Yale University Press, 1962), p 49

FIGURE 2.2

Checks and Balances

Executive over Legislative

Can veto acts of Congress

Can call Congress into a special session

Carries out, and thereby interprets, laws passed by Congress

Vice president casts tie-breaking vote in the Senate

Legislative over Judicial

Can change size of federal court system and the number of Supreme Court justices

Can propose constitutional amendments

Can reject Supreme Court nominees

Can impeach and remove federal judges

LEGISLATIVE

Legislative over Executive

Can override presidential veto

Can impeach and remove president

Can reject president's appointments and refuse to ratify treaties

Can conduct investigations into president's actions

Can refuse to pass laws or to provide funding that president requests

Judicial over Legislative

Can declare laws unconstitutional

Chief justice presides over Senate during hearing to impeach the president

JUDICIAL

Executive over Judicial

Nominates Supreme Court justices

Nominates federal judges

Can pardon those convicted in federal court

Can refuse to enforce Court decisions

Judicial over Executive

Can declare executive actions unconstitutional

Power to issue warrants

Chief justice presides over impeachment of president

EXECUTIVE

checks and balances
Mechanisms through which each branch of government is able to participate in and influence the activities of the other branches. Major examples include the presidential veto power over congressional legislation, the power of the Senate to approve presidential appointments, and judicial review of congressional enactments

3. *Checks and balances*—a system under which each of the branches is given some power over the others. Familiar examples are the presidential veto power over legislation, the power of the Senate to approve presidential appointments, and judicial review of acts of Congress (see Figure 2.2).

One clever formulation of the separation of powers is that of a system not of separated powers but of "separated institutions sharing power,"[24] and thus diminishing the chance that power will be misused.

[24]Richard E Neustadt, *Presidential Power The Politics of Leadership* (New York Wiley, 1960), p 33

Federalism   Compared to the confederation principle of the Articles of Con-federation, federalism was a step toward greater centralization of power The delegates agreed that they needed to place more power at the national level, without completely undermining the power of the state governments. Thus, they devised a system of two sovereigns—the states and the nation—with the hope that competition between the two would be an effective limitation on the power of both.

The Bill of Rights   Late in the Philadelphia convention, a motion was made to include a bill of rights in the Constitution. After a brief debate in which hardly a word was said in its favor and only one speech was made against it, the motion to include it was almost unanimously turned down Most delegates sincerely believed that since the federal government was already limited to its expressed powers, further protection of citizens was not needed. The delegates argued that the states should adopt bills of rights because their greater powers needed greater limitations. But almost immediately after the Constitution was ratified, there was a movement to adopt a national bill of rights. This is why the Bill of Rights, adopted in 1791, comprises the first ten amendments to the Constitution rather than being part of the body of it. We will have a good deal more to say about the Bill of Rights in Chapter 4.

THE FIGHT FOR RATIFICATION: FEDERALISTS VERSUS ANTIFEDERALISTS

The first hurdle faced by the new Constitution was ratification by state conventions of delegates elected by the people of each state. This struggle for ratification was carried out in thirteen separate campaigns. Each involved different men, moved at a different pace, and was influenced by local as well as national considerations. Two sides faced off throughout all the states, however, calling themselves Federalists and Antifederalists (see Table 2.1)[25]. The Federalists (who more accurately should have called themselves "Nationalists," but who took their name to appear to follow in the revolutionary tradition) supported the Constitution and preferred a strong national government. The Antifederalists opposed the Constitution and preferred a federal system of government that was decentralized; they took on their name by default, in reaction to their better-organized

---

[25]An excellent analysis of these ratification campaigns, based on a quantitative assessment of the campaigners' own words as found in campaign documents, pamphlets, tracts, public letters, and the eighteenth-century equivalent of op-ed pieces (like the individual essays that comprise the *Federalist Papers*) is William H. Riker, *The Strategy of Rhetoric Campaigning for the American Constitution* (New Haven. Yale University Press, 1996)

TABLE 2.1

Federalists versus Antifederalists

	FEDERALISTS	ANTIFEDERALISTS
Who were they?	Property owners, creditors, merchants	Small farmers, frontiersmen, debtors, shopkeepers
What did they believe?	Believed that elites were best fit to govern; feared "excessive democracy"	Believed that government should be closer to the people; feared concentration of power in hands of the elites
What system of government did they favor?	Favored strong national government; believed in "filtration" so that only elites would obtain governmental power	Favored retention of power by state governments and protection of individual rights
Who were their leaders?	Alexander Hamilton James Madison George Washington	Patrick Henry George Mason Elbridge Gerry George Clinton

opponents. The Federalists were united in their support of the Constitution, while the Antifederalists were divided as to what they believed the alternative to the Constitution should be.

During the struggle over ratification of the proposed Constitution, Americans argued about great political issues and principles. How much power should the national government be given? What safeguards were most likely to prevent the abuse of power? What institutional arrangements could best ensure adequate representation for all Americans? Was tyranny to be feared more from the many or from the few?

In political life, of course, principles—even great principles—are seldom completely divorced from some set of interests. In 1787, Americans were divided along economic, regional, and political lines. These divisions inevitably influenced their attitudes toward the profound political questions of the day.

 **Rationality Principle**

The debate over ratification revealed the conflicting interests of the Federalists and Antifederalists

Many well-to-do merchants and planters, as we saw earlier, favored the creation of a stronger central government that would have the capacity to protect property, promote commerce, and keep some of the more radical state legislatures in check. At the same time, many powerful state leaders, like Governor George Clinton of New York, feared that strengthening the national government would reduce their own influence and status. Each of these interests, of course, justified its position with an appeal to principle.

Principles are often important weapons in political warfare, and seeing how and by whom they are wielded can illuminate their otherwise obscure implications. In our own time, dry academic discussions of topics such as "free trade" become easier to grasp once it is noted that free trade and open markets are generally favored by low-cost producers, while protectionism is the goal of firms whose costs of production are higher than the international norm.

Even if a principle is invented and initially brandished to serve an interest, however, once it has been articulated it can take on a life of its own and prove to have implications that transcend the narrow interests it was created to serve. Some opponents of the Constitution, for example, who criticized the absence of a bill of rights in the initial document did so simply with the hope of blocking the document's ratification. Yet, the Bill of Rights that was later added to the Constitution has proven for two centuries to be a bulwark of civil liberty in the United States.

Similarly, closer to our own time, support for the extension of voting rights and for massive legislative redistricting under the rubric of "one man, one vote" during the 1960s came mainly from liberal Democrats who were hoping to strengthen their own political base since the groups that would benefit most from these initiatives were overwhelmingly Democratic. The principles of equal access to the ballot and one man, one vote, however, have a moral and political validity that is independent of the political interests that propelled these ideas into the political arena.

These examples show us that truly great political principles surmount the interests that initially set them forth. The first step in understanding a political principle is understanding why and by whom it is espoused. The second step is understanding the full implications of the principle itself—implications that may go far beyond the interests that launched it. Thus, even though the great political principles about which Americans argued in 1787 *did* reflect competing interests, they also represented views of society, government, and politics that surmount interest and so must be understood in their own terms. Whatever the underlying clash of interests that may have guided them, the Federalists and Antifederalists presented important alternative visions of America.

During the ratification struggle, thousands of essays, speeches, pamphlets, and letters were presented in support of and in opposition to the proposed Constitution. The best-known pieces supporting ratification of the Constitution were the eighty-five essays written, under the name of "Publius," by Alexander Hamilton, James Madison, and John Jay between the fall of 1787 and the spring of 1788. These *Federalist Papers*, as they are collectively known today, defended the principles of the Constitution and sought to dispel fears of a national authority. The Antifederalists published essays of their own, arguing that the new Constitution betrayed the Revolution and was a step toward monarchy. Among the best of the Antifederalist works were the essays, usually attributed to New York Supreme Court justice Robert Yates, that were written under the name of "Brutus" and published in the *New York Journal* at the same time the *Federalist Papers* appeared. The Antifederalist view was also ably presented in the pamphlets and letters written by a former delegate to the Continental Congress and future U.S. senator, Richard Henry Lee of Virginia, using the pen name "the Federal Farmer." These essays highlight the major differences of opinion between Federalists and Antifederalists. Federalists appealed to basic principles of government in support of their nationalist vision. Antifederalists cited equally fundamental precepts to support their vision of a looser confederacy of small republics.

The two sides engaged in what was almost certainly the very first nationwide political campaign in the history of the world. Though each side was itself only loosely organized, a rudimentary form of coordination and cooperation was manifest—especially in the division of labor between Hamilton, Madison, and Jay as they alternately wrote under the "Publius" pseudonym on different aspects of the newly drafted Constitution in an effort to affect its ratification in the state of New York.

Representation

One major area of contention between the two sides was the question of representation. The Antifederalists asserted that representatives must be "a true picture of the people, . . . [possessing] the knowledge of their circumstances and their wants."[26] This could only be achieved, argued the Antifederalists, in small, relatively homogeneous republics such as the existing states. In their view, the size and extent of the entire nation precluded the construction of a truly representative form of government.

The absence of true representation, moreover, would mean that the people would lack confidence in and attachment to the national government and would refuse to obey its laws voluntarily. As a result, according to the Antifederalists, the national government described by the Constitution would be compelled to resort to force to secure popular compliance. The Federal Farmer averred that laws of the remote federal government could be "in many cases disregarded, unless a multitude of officers and military force be continually kept in view, and employed to enforce the execution of the laws, and to make the government feared and respected."[27]

[26]Melancton Smith, quoted in Herbert J Storing, *What the Anti-Federalists Were For The Political Thought of the Opponents of the Constitution* (Chicago University of Chicago Press, 1981), p 17
[27]"Letters from the Federal Farmer," No 2, in *The Complete Anti-Federalist*, ed. Herbert J Storing, 7 vols (Chicago University of Chicago Press, 1981)

Federalists, for their part, did not long for pure democracy and saw no reason that representatives should be precisely like those they represented. In their view, government must be representative *of* the people, but must also have a measure of autonomy *from* the people. Their ideal government was to be so constructed as to be capable of serving the long-term public interest even if this conflicted with the public's current preference.

Federalists also dismissed the Antifederalist claim that the distance between representatives and constituents in the proposed national government would lead to popular disaffection and compel the government to use force to secure obedience. Federalists replied that the system of representation they proposed was more likely to produce effective government. In Hamilton's words, there would be "a probability that the general government will be better administered than the particular governments."[28] Competent government, in turn, should inspire popular trust and confidence more effectively than simple social proximity between rulers and ruled.

The Threats Posed by the Majority

A second important issue dividing Federalists and Antifederalists was the threat of *tyranny*—unjust rule by the group in power. Both opponents and defenders of the Constitution frequently affirmed their fear of tyrannical rule. Each side, however, had a different view of the most likely source of tyranny and, hence, of the way in which the threat was to be forestalled.

From the Antifederalist perspective, the great danger was the tendency of all governments—including republican governments—to become gradually more and more "aristocratic" in character, where the small number of individuals in positions of authority would use their stations to gain more and more power over the general citizenry. In essence, the few would use their power to tyrannize the many. For this reason, Antifederalists were sharply critical of those features of the Constitution that divorced governmental institutions from direct responsibility to the people—institutions such as the Senate, the executive, and the federal judiciary. The latter, appointed for life, presented a particular threat: "I wonder if the world ever saw . . . a court of justice invested with such immense powers, and yet placed in a situation so little responsible," protested Brutus.[29]

The Federalists, too, recognized the threat of tyranny. They were not naive about the motives and purposes of individuals and took them to be no less opportunistic and self-interested than the Antifederalists did. But the Federalists believed that the danger particularly associated with republican governments was not aristocracy, but instead, majority tyranny. The Federalists were concerned that a popular majority, "united and actuated by some common impulse of passion, or of interest, adverse to the rights of other citizens," would endeavor

tyranny
Oppressive government that employs the cruel and unjust use of power and authority.

---

[28]*The Federalist*, No. 27.
[29]"Essays of Brutus," No 15, in *The Complete Anti-Federalist*

to "trample on the rules of justice."[30] From the Federalist perspective, it was precisely those features of the Constitution attacked as potential sources of tyranny by the Antifederalists that actually offered the best hope of averting the threat of oppression. The size and extent of the nation, for instance, was for the Federalists a bulwark against tyranny. In Madison's famous formulation,

> The smaller the society, the fewer probably will be the distinct parties and interests . . . the more frequently will a majority be found of the same party; and the smaller the number of individuals composing a majority, and the smaller the compass within which they are placed, the more easily will they concert and execute their plans of oppression. Extend the sphere, and you take in a greater variety of parties and interests; you make it less probable that a majority of the whole will have a common motive to invade the rights of other citizens; or if such a common motive exists, it will be more difficult for all who feel it to discover their own strength, and to act in unison with each other.[31]

The Federalists understood that, in a democracy, temporary majorities could abuse their power. The Federalists' misgivings about majority rule were reflected in the constitutional structure. The indirect election of senators, the indirect election of the president, the judicial branch's insulation from the people, the separation of powers, the president's veto power, the bicameral design of Congress, and the federal system were all means to curb majority tyranny. These design features in the Constitution suggest an awareness on the part of the framers of the problems of majority rule and the need for institutional safeguards. Except for the indirect election of senators (which was changed in 1913), these aspects of the constitutional structure remain in place today.[32]

Governmental Power

A third major difference between Federalists and Antifederalists, and the one most central to this book, was the issue of governmental power. Both the opponents and proponents of the Constitution agreed on the principle of limited government. They differed, however, on the fundamentally important question of how to place limits on governmental action. Antifederalists favored limiting and enumerating the powers granted to the national government in relation both to the states and to the people at large To them, the powers given the national gov-

[30]*The Federalist*, No 10

[31]Ibid

[32]A classic development of this theme is found in James M Buchanan and Gordon Tullock, *The Calculus of Consent Logical Foundations of Constitutional Democracy* (Ann Arbor University of Michigan Press, 1962) For a review of the voting paradox and a case study of how it applies today, see Kenneth A. Shepsle and Mark S Bonchek, *Analyzing Politics Rationality, Behavior, and Institutions* (New York W W Norton, 1997), pp 49–81

ernment ought to be "confined to certain defined national objects."[33] Otherwise, the national government would "swallow up all the power of the state governments."[34] Antifederalists bitterly attacked the supremacy clause and the necessary and proper clause of the Constitution as unlimited and dangerous grants of power to the national government [35]

Antifederalists also demanded that a bill of rights be added to the Constitution to place limits upon the government's exercise of power over the citizenry. "There are certain things," wrote Brutus, "which rulers should be absolutely prohibited from doing, because if they should do them, they would work an injury, not a benefit to the people."[36] Similarly, the Federal Farmer maintained that "there are certain unalienable and fundamental rights, which in forming the social compact . . . ought to be explicitly ascertained and fixed."[37]

Federalists favored the construction of a government with broad powers. They wanted a government that had the capacity to defend the nation against foreign foes, guard against domestic strife and insurrection, promote commerce, and expand the nation's economy. Antifederalists shared some of these goals but still feared governmental power. Hamilton pointed out, however, that these goals could not be achieved without allowing the government to exercise the necessary power. Federalists acknowledged, of course, that every power could be abused but argued that the way to prevent misuse of power was not by depriving the government of the powers needed to achieve national goals. Instead, they argued that the threat of abuse of power would be mitigated by the Constitution's internal checks and controls As Madison put it, "the power surrendered by the people is first divided between two distinct governments, and then the portion allotted to each subdivided among distinct and separate departments. Hence a double security arises to the rights of the people. The different governments will control each other, at the same time that each will be controlled by itself."[38] The Federalists' concern with avoiding unwarranted limits on governmental power led them to oppose a bill of rights, which they saw as nothing more than a set of unnecessary restrictions on the government.

The Federalists acknowledged that abuse of power remained a possibility, but felt that the risk had to be taken because of the goals to be achieved. "The very idea of power included a possibility of doing harm," said the Federalist John Rutledge during the South Carolina ratification debates. "If the gentleman would show the power that could do no harm," Rutledge continued, "he would at once discover it to be a power that could do no good."[39]

---

[33]"Essays of Brutus," No 7
[34]"Essays of Brutus," No 6
[35]Storing, *What the Antifederalists Were For,* p 28
[36]"Essays of Brutus," No 9
[37]"Letters from the Federal Farmer," No 2
[38]*The Federalist,* No 51
[39]Quoted in Storing, *What the Antifederalists Were For,* p 30

CHANGING THE INSTITUTIONAL FRAMEWORK: CONSTITUTIONAL AMENDMENT

The Constitution has endured for two centuries as the framework of government. But it has not endured without change. Without change, the Constitution might have become merely a sacred relic, stored under glass.

Amendments: Many Are Called, Few Are Chosen

The need for change was recognized by the framers of the Constitution, and the provisions for amendment incorporated into Article V were thought to be "an easy, regular and Constitutional way" to make changes, which would occasionally be necessary because members of Congress "may abuse their power and refuse their consent on the very account . . . to admit to amendments to correct the source of the abuse."[40] Madison made a more balanced defense of the amendment procedure in Article V: "It guards equally against that extreme facility, which would render the Constitution too mutable; and that extreme difficulty, which might perpetuate its discovered faults."[41]

 Institution Principle

The procedures for amending the Constitution are difficult. As a result, the amendment route to political change is extremely limited.

Experience since 1789 raises questions even about Madison's more modest claims. The Constitution has proven to be extremely difficult to amend. In the history of efforts to amend the Constitution, the most appropriate characterization is "many are called, few are chosen." Between 1789 and 1993, 9,746 amendments were formally offered in Congress. Of these, Congress officially proposed only 29, and 27 of these were eventually ratified by the states. But the record is even more severe than that. Since 1791, when the first 10 amendments, the Bill of Rights, were added, only 17 amendments have been adopted. And two of them—Prohibition and its repeal—cancel each other out, so that for all practical purposes, only 15 amendments have been added to the Constitution since 1791. Despite vast changes in American society and its economy, only 12 amendments have been adopted since the Civil War amendments in 1868.

Four methods of amendment are provided for in Article V:

1. Passage in House and Senate by two-thirds vote; then ratification by majority vote of the legislatures of three-fourths (thirty-eight) of the states.
2. Passage in House and Senate by two-thirds vote; then ratification by conventions called for the purpose in three-fourths of the states.
3. Passage in a national convention called by Congress in response to petitions by two-thirds of the states, ratification by majority vote of the legislatures of three-fourths of the states.

---

[40]Observation by Colonel George Mason, delegate from Virginia, early during the convention period Quoted in Farrand, *The Records of the Federal Convention of 1787*, I, pp 202–3
[41]Clinton Rossiter, ed , *The Federalist Papers* (New York New American Library, 1961), No 43, p 278

FIGURE 2.3

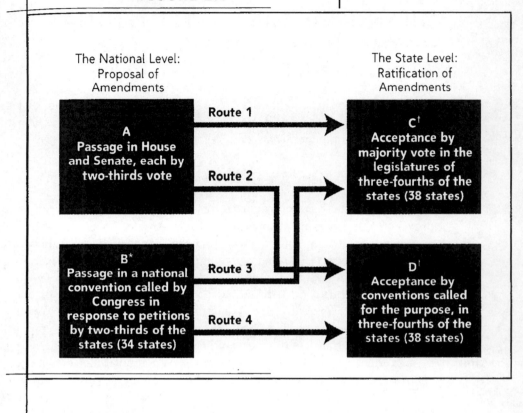

The National Level:
Proposal of
Amendments

The State Level:
Ratification of
Amendments

A
Passage in House and Senate, each by two-thirds vote

Route 1

Route 2

C†
Acceptance by majority vote in the legislatures of three-fourths of the states (38 states)

B*
Passage in a national convention called by Congress in response to petitions by two-thirds of the states (34 states)

Route 3

Route 4

D‡
Acceptance by conventions called for the purpose, in three-fourths of the states (38 states)

4. Passage in a national convention, as in method 3; then ratification by conventions called for the purpose in three-fourths of the states.

(Figure 2.3 illustrates each of these possible methods.) Since no amendment has ever been proposed by national convention, however, methods 3 and 4 have never been employed. And method 2 has only been employed once (the Twenty-first Amendment, which repealed the Eighteenth, or Prohibition, Amendment). Thus, method 1 has been used for all the others.

Now we should be better able to explain why it has been so difficult to amend the Constitution. The main reason is the requirement of a two-thirds vote in the House and the Senate, which means that any proposal for an amendment in Congress can be killed by only 34 senators *or* 146 members of the House. What is more, if the necessary two-thirds vote is obtained, the amendment can still be killed by the refusal or inability of only thirteen state legislatures to ratify it. Since each state has an equal vote regardless of its population, the thirteen holdout states may represent a very small fraction of the total American population.

Constitutional Amendment   **65**

The Twenty-seven Amendments

Despite difficulties of the process, the Constitution has been amended twenty-seven times since the framers completed their work. The first ten of these amendments, known as the Bill of Rights, were added to the Constitution shortly after its ratification. As we saw, Federalists feared that a bill of rights would weaken the new government, but they were forced to commit themselves to the principle of an enumeration of rights when the Antifederalists charged that the proposed Constitution was a threat to liberty.

Most of the Constitution's twenty-seven amendments share a common characteristic. all but two are concerned with the structure or composition of government. This is consistent with the dictionary, which defines *constitution* as the makeup or composition of a thing, anything. And it is consistent with the concept of a constitution as "higher law," because the whole point and purpose of a higher law is to establish *a framework within which government and the process of making ordinary law can take place.* Even those who would have preferred more changes in the Constitution would have to agree that there is great wisdom in this principle. A constitution ought to enable legislation and public policies to take place, but it should not determine what that legislation or those public policies ought to be.

The purpose of the ten amendments in the Bill of Rights was basically structural, *to give each of the three branches clearer and more restricted boundaries.* The First Amendment clarified the jurisdiction of Congress. Although the powers of Congress under Article I, Section 8, would not have justified laws regulating religion, speech, and the like, the First Amendment made this limitation explicit: "Congress shall make no law. . . ." The Second, Third, and Fourth Amendments similarly spelled out specific limits on the executive branch. This was seen as a necessity given the abuses of executive power Americans had endured under British rule.

The Fifth, Sixth, Seventh, and Eighth Amendments contain some of the most important safeguards for individual citizens against the arbitrary exercise of government power. And these amendments sought to accomplish their goal by defining the judicial branch more concretely and clearly than had been done in Article III of the Constitution. Table 2.2 analyzes the ten amendments included in the Bill of Rights.

Five of the seventeen amendments adopted since 1791 are directly concerned with expansion of the electorate (see Table 2.3). These occasional efforts to expand the electorate were made necessary by the fact that the founders were unable to establish a national electorate with uniform voting qualifications. Stalemated on that issue, the delegates decided to evade it by providing in the final draft of Article I, Section 2, that eligibility to vote in a national election would be the same as "the Qualifications requisite for Electors of the most numerous Branch of the State Legislature." Article I, Section 4, added that Congress could alter state regulations as to the "Times, Places and Manner of holding Elections for Senators and Representatives." Nevertheless, this meant that any

TABLE 2.2

The Bill of Rights: Analysis of Its Provisions

AMENDMENT	PURPOSE
I	*Limits on Congress:* Congress is not to make any law establishing a religion or abridging the freedom of speech, press, assembly, or the right to petition freedoms.
II, III, IV	*Limits on Executive:* The executive branch is not to infringe on the right of people to keep arms (II), is not to arbitrarily take houses for a militia (III), and is not to engage in the search or seizure of evidence without a court warrant swearing to belief in the probable existence of a crime (IV).
V, VI, VII, VIII	*Limits on Courts:* The courts are not to hold trials for serious offenses without provision for a grand jury (V), a petit (trial) jury (VII), a speedy trial (VI), presentation of charges, confrontation of hostile witnesses (VI), immunity from testimony against oneself (V), and immunity from trial more than once for the same offense (V). Neither bail nor punishment can be excessive (VIII), and no property can be taken without just compensation (V).
IX, X	*Limits on National Government:* All rights not enumerated are reserved to the states or the people.

important *expansion* of the American electorate would almost certainly require a constitutional amendment.

Six more amendments are also electoral in nature, although not concerned directly with voting rights and the expansion of the electorate (see Table 2.4). These six amendments are concerned with the elective offices themselves (the Twentieth, Twenty-second, and Twenty-fifth) or with the relationship between elective offices and the electorate (the Twelfth, Fourteenth, and Seventeenth).

Another five amendments have sought to expand or to delimit the powers of the national and state governments (see Table 2.5).[42] The Eleventh Amendment

[42]The Fourteenth Amendment is included in this table as well as in Tables 2 2 and 2 3 because it seeks not only to define citizenship but *seems* to intend also that this definition of citizenship included, along with the right to vote, all the rights of the Bill of Rights, regardless of the state in which the citizen resided A great deal more will be said about this in Chapter 4

TABLE 2.3

Amending the Constitution to Expand the Electorate

AMENDMENT	PURPOSE	YEAR PROPOSED	YEAR ADOPTED
XIV	Section I provided national definition of citizenship*	1866	1868
XV	Extended voting rights to all races	1869	1870
XIX	Extended voting rights to women	1919	1920
XXIII	Extended voting rights to residents of the District of Columbia	1960	1961
XXIV	Extended voting rights to all classes by abolition of poll taxes	1962	1964
XXVI	Extended voting rights to citizens aged 18 and over	1971	1971

*In defining *citizenship*, the Fourteenth Amendment actually provided the constitutional basis for expanding the electorate to include all races, women, and residents of the District of Columbia Only the "eighteen-year-olds' amendment" should have been necessary since it changed the definition of citizenship The fact that additional amendments were required following the Fourteenth suggests that voting is not considered an inherent right of U.S citizenship Instead it is viewed as a privilege

protected the states from suits by private individuals and took away from the federal courts any power to take suits by private individuals of one state (or a foreign country) against another state. The other three amendments in Table 2.5 are obviously designed to reduce state power (Thirteenth), to reduce state power and expand national power (Fourteenth), and to expand national power (Sixteenth). The Twenty-seventh put a limit on Congress's ability to raise its own salary

The two missing amendments underscore the meaning of the rest: the Eighteenth, or Prohibition, Amendment and the Twenty-first, its repeal. This is the only instance in which the country tried to *legislate* by constitutional amendment In other words, the Eighteenth is the only amendment that was designed to deal directly with some substantive social problem. And it was the only amendment ever to have been repealed. Two other amendments—the Thirteenth, which abolished slavery, and the Sixteenth, which established the power to levy an income tax—can be said to have had the effect of legislation. But the purpose of the Thirteenth was to restrict the power of the states by forever for-

TABLE 2.4

Amending the Constitution to
Change the Relationship between
Elected Offices and the Electorate

AMENDMENT	PURPOSE	YEAR PROPOSED	YEAR ADOPTED
XII	Provided separate ballot for vice president in the electoral college	1803	1804
XIV	Section 2 eliminated counting of slaves as "three-fifths" citizens for apportionment of House seats	1866	1868
XVII	Provided direct election of senators	1912	1913
XX	Eliminated "lame duck" session of Congress	1932	1933
XXII	Limited presidential term	1947	1951
XXV	Provided presidential succession in case of disability	1965	1967

bidding them to treat any human being as property. As for the Sixteenth, it is certainly true that income-tax legislation followed immediately; nevertheless, the amendment concerns itself strictly with establishing the power of Congress to enact such legislation. The legislation came later; and if down the line a majority in Congress had wanted to abolish the income tax, they could also have done this by legislation rather than through the arduous path of a constitutional amendment repealing the income tax.

For those whose hopes for change center on the Constitution, it must be emphasized that the amendment route to social change is, and always will be, extremely limited. Through a constitution it is possible to establish a working structure of government; and through a constitution it is possible to establish basic rights of citizens by placing limitations and obligations on the powers of that government. Once these things have been accomplished, the real problem is how to extend rights to those people who do not already enjoy them. Of course, the Constitution cannot enforce itself. But it can and does have a real influence on everyday life because a right or an obligation set forth in the Constitution can become a *cause of action* in the hands of an otherwise powerless person

Constitutional Amendment   **69**

TABLE 2.5

	Amending the Constitution to Expand or Limit the Power of Government		
AMENDMENT	**PURPOSE**	**YEAR PROPOSED**	**YEAR ADOPTED**
XI	Limited jurisdiction of federal courts over suits involving the states	1794	1798
XIII	Eliminated slavery and eliminated the rights of states to allow property in persons	1865*	1865
XIV	(Part 2) Applied due process of Bill of Rights to the states	1866	1868
XVI	Established national power to tax incomes	1909	1913
XXVII	Limited Congress's power to raise its own salary	1789	1992

*The Thirteenth Amendment was proposed January 31, 1865, and adopted less than a year later, on December 18, 1865

Private property is an excellent example. Property is one of the most fundamental and well-established rights in the United States; but it is well established not because it is recognized in so many words in the Constitution, but because legislatures and courts have made it a crime for anyone, including the government, to trespass or to take away property without compensation.

REFLECTIONS ON THE FOUNDING: PRINCIPLES OR INTERESTS?

The final product of the Constitutional Convention would have to be considered an extraordinary victory for the groups that had most forcefully called for the creation of a new system of government to replace the Articles of Confederation. Antifederalist criticisms forced the Constitution's proponents to accept the addition of a bill of rights designed to limit the powers of the national government. In general, however, it was the Federalist vision of America that triumphed. The Constitution adopted in 1789 created the framework for a powerful national government that for more than two hundred years has defended the nation's interests, promoted its commerce, and maintained national unity. In one notable instance, the national government fought and won a bloody war to prevent the nation from breaking apart.

Though the Constitution was the product of a particular set of political forces, the principles of government it established have a significance that goes far beyond the interests of its authors. As we have observed, political principles often take on lives of their own. The great political principles incorporated into the Constitution continue, more than two centuries later, to shape our political lives in ways that the Constitution's framers may not always have anticipated. For example, when they empowered the Congress of the United States to regulate commerce among the states in Article I, Section 8, of the Constitution, the framers could hardly have anticipated that this would become the basis for many of the federal government's regulatory activities in areas as diverse as the environment and civil rights.

Two great constitutional principles, federalism and civil liberties, will be discussed in Chapters 3 and 4. A third important constitutional principle that has affected America's government for the past two hundred years is the principle of *checks and balances*. As we saw earlier, the framers gave each of the three branches of government a means of intervening in and blocking the actions of the others. Often, checks and balances have seemed to prevent the government from getting much done. During the 1960s, for example, liberals were often infuriated as they watched Congress stall presidential initiatives in the area of civil rights. More recently, conservatives were outraged when President Clinton thwarted congressional efforts to enact legislation promised in the Republican "Contract with America." At various times, all sides have vilified the judiciary for invalidating legislation enacted by Congress and signed by the president.

Over time, checks and balances have acted as brakes on the governmental process. Groups hoping to bring about changes in policy or governmental institutions seldom have been able to bring about decisive and dramatic transformations in a short period of time. Instead, checks and balances have slowed the pace of change and increased the need for compromise and accommodation.

Policy Principle

The constitutional framework, such as the principle of checks and balances, can act as a brake on the policy process.

Groups able to take control of the White House, for example, must bargain with their rivals who remain entrenched on Capitol Hill. New forces in Congress must reckon with the influence of other forces in the executive branch and in the courts. Checks and balances inevitably frustrate those who desire change, but they also function as a safeguard against rash action. During the 1950s, for example, Congress was caught up in a quasi-hysterical effort to unmask subversive activities in the United States, which might have led to a serious erosion of American liberties if not for the checks and balances provided by the executive and the courts. Thus, a governmental principle that serves as a frustrating limitation one day may become a vitally important safeguard the next.

As we close our discussion of the founding, it is also worth reflecting on the Antifederalists. Although they were defeated in 1789, the Antifederalists present us with an important picture of a road not taken and of an America that might have been. Would we have been worse off as a people if we had been governed by a confederacy of small republics linked by a national administration with severely limited powers? Were the Antifederalists correct in predicting that a government given great power in the hope that it might do good would, through "insensible progress," inevitably turn to evil purposes? Two hundred plus years of

Rationality Principle	Collective Action Principle	Institution Principle	Policy Principle	History Principle
The framers of the Constitution were guided by principles, but they also had interests.	The colonists required strong leaders to resolve differences and to organize resistance to British authority	Institutional arrangements, such as the Articles of Confederation, can be flawed.	The constitutional framework, such as the principle of checks and balances, can act as a brake on the policy process	The American colonists, used to years of self-governance, believed that the Stamp Act of 1765 threatened their autonomy
The debate over ratification revealed the conflicting interests of the Federalists and Antifederalists	The framers preferred compromise to the breakup of the union, and thus accepted the Great Compromise and the Three-fifths Compromise	The constitutional framework promoted commerce, protected property, prevented "excessive democracy," and limited the power of the national government		Shays's Rebellion focused attention on the flaws of the Articles of Confederation, leading to the Constitutional Convention
		The procedures for amending the Constitution are difficult As a result, the amendment route to political change is extremely limited		

government under the federal Constitution are not necessarily enough to definitively answer these questions. Only time will tell.

SUMMARY

Political conflicts between the colonies and England, and among competing groups within the colonies, led to the first founding as expressed by the Declaration of Independence. The first constitution, the Articles of Confederation, was adopted one year later (1777) Under this document, the states retained their sovereignty The central government, composed solely of Congress, had few powers and no means of enforcing its will The national government's weakness soon led to the Constitution of 1787, the second founding.

In this second founding the framers sought, first, to fashion a new government sufficiently powerful to promote commerce and protect property from radical state legislatures. Second, the framers sought to bring an end to the "excessive democracy" of the state and national governments under the Articles of

Confederation. Third, the framers introduced mechanisms that helped secure popular consent for the new government. Finally, the framers made certain that their new government would not itself pose a threat to liberty and property.

The Constitution consists of seven articles. In part, Article I provides for a Congress of two chambers (Sections 1–7), defines the powers of the national government (Section 8), and interprets the national government's powers as a source of strength rather than a limitation (necessary and proper clause). Article II describes the presidency and establishes it as a separate branch of government. Article III is the judiciary article. While there is no direct mention of judicial review in this article, the Supreme Court eventually assumed that power. Article IV addresses reciprocity among states and their citizens. Article V describes the procedures for amending the Constitution. Thousands of amendments have been offered, but only twenty-seven have been adopted. With the exception of the two Prohibition amendments, all amendments were oriented toward some change in the framework or structure of government. Article VI establishes that national laws and treaties are "the supreme Law of the Land." And finally, Article VII specifies the procedure for ratifying the Constitution of 1787.

The struggle for the ratification of the Constitution pitted the Antifederalists against the Federalists. The Antifederalists thought the proposed new government would be too powerful, and they fought against the ratification of the Constitution. The Federalists supported the Constitution and were able to secure its ratification after a nationwide political debate.

FOR FURTHER READING

Bailyn, Bernard. *The Ideological Origins of the American Revolution* Cambridge: Harvard University Press, 1967.

Beard, Charles A. *An Economic Interpretation of the Constitution of the United States*. New York: Macmillan, 1913.

Farrand, Max, ed. *The Records of the Federal Convention of 1787*. Rev. ed. 4 vols. New Haven: Yale University Press, 1966.

Hamilton, Alexander, James Madison, and John Jay. *The Federalist Papers*. Edited by Isaac Kramnick. New York: Viking Press, 1987.

Lipset, Seymour M. *The First New Nation: The United States in Historical and Comparative Perspective*. New York: Basic Books, 1963.

Main, Jackson Turner. *The Social Structure of Revolutionary America*. Princeton: Princeton University Press, 1965

Riker, William H. *The Strategy of Rhetoric: Campaigning for the American Constitution*. New Haven: Yale University Press, 1996.

Storing, Herbert J., ed. *The Complete Anti-Federalist*. 7 vols. Chicago: University of Chicago Press, 1981.

Wood, Gordon S. *The Creation of the American Republic, 1776–1787*. New York: W. W. Norton, 1982.

Burning the Flag and the Constitution

Given New Legs, an Old Idea Is Back

By SHERYL GAY STOLBERG

Anyone who doubts the appeal of the American flag need only wander through the basement corridors of the Capitol. There, thousands of boxed flags that have flown over the building await pickup by members of Congress, who send them to constituents by request. Last year alone, nearly 124,000 were sent, up from 97,401 the year before.

The Republican-controlled House understands that these are good times for Old Glory, as Americans respond to the threat of terrorism and the war in Iraq. So today, when the House considered a perennial legislative favorite—a constitutional amendment that would give Congress the power to bar desecration of the American flag—it came as no surprise that the measure passed handily, 300 to 125.

This was the fifth time the House had passed the measure. But it has always died in the Senate, where opponents, mainly Democrats, argue that it would infringe on the First Amend-

ment. Now the question is whether the surge of patriotism will overcome those objections and carry the measure to passage.

The White House backs the bill, and proponents say it has support from the legislatures of all 50 states. If ever there were a chance to outlaw burning the flag, they say, this is it.

But with the Senate majority leader, Bill Frist, focused on pressing matters like a Medicare prescription drug benefit, the amendment may not come up for a Senate vote until next year. So its backers were unwilling to make any predictions today.

"It's always an uphill battle," said the amendment's Senate sponsor, Orrin G. Hatch of Utah, the Judiciary Committee chairman. "But we're hoping we can get it done this year. Well, maybe not this year, but probably next year."

Much has changed in the Senate since the last time the bill was considered there, in March 2000. There are 10 new senators, 8 of them Republicans.

New York Times, 4 June 2003, p. A28

Some, like John Cornyn of Texas, Norm Coleman of Minnesota and Saxby Chambliss of Georgia, said today that they would support the amendment. Others, like Lamar Alexander of Tennessee, were more circumspect "What flag amendment?" Mr Alexander said. "I haven't seen one yet."

The measure, which requires a two-thirds majority in each house and ratification by three-fourths of the states, is intended to circumvent two Supreme Court rulings. In 1989, the court struck down a Texas law prohibiting flag burning. Congress responded with federal legislation. But in 1990, by a 5-to-4 vote, the justices overturned that measure, too.

The amendment's chief sponsor, Representative Randy Cunningham, Republican of California, complained today that the court had reversed "200 years of tradition." He added, "I'm not proposing this, but in the Civil War it was a penalty of death to desecrate the flag."

The House debate today was marked by fiery exchanges over whether there should be limits on freedom of speech, and whether opposition to the amendment was unpatriotic. One opponent, Representative Alcee L. Hastings, Democrat of Florida, thundered, "All of us are superpatriots in the sense that we provide service for our country, each in our way!"

Lawmakers fought as well over whether it would be wise to alter the Constitution for a problem that, after all, is virtually nonexistent.

"We're amending the Constitution for a noncrisis," said Representative Ron Paul of Texas, one of 11 Republicans voting against the bill. . . .

Still, there have been just 100 cases or so of flag burning in the United States since the 1960's, according to David White, executive director of the National Flag Foundation, a Pittsburgh-based group that takes no position on

ESSENCE OF THE STORY

- The surge of patriotism after the terrorist attacks of September 11, 2001, encouraged the Republican-led House of Representatives to attempt to pass a constitutional amendment banning desecration of the flag.

- An amendment has passed the House five times but has always died in the Senate. Recent Court decisions and turnover in the Senate has also emboldened the supporters.

- There is disagreement over whether flag burning is serious enough to merit a constitutional amendment.

POLITICAL ANALYSIS

- Some suggest that voting for the flag amendment in the House is a strategic no-brainer, even for someone who opposes amending the Constitution in this way. A member can wear the patriotic mantle while being assured that the amendment will fail in the Senate.

- The different procedures of the House and Senate mean that politically popular but controversial legislation such as the flag amendment often passes the House, only to be stopped by a filibuster in the Senate.

- Some believe that the amendment procedure is too cumbersome, making it too hard to change the Constitution on matters such as flag burning. Others believe that the Constitution represents our most basic laws and should be amended only in the most weighty circumstances.

the amendment, instead promoting education as a way to counter desecration of the flag.

For all the battling, there is one instance in which flag burning is accepted by all. If a flag is old and tattered, Mr. White noted, the proper way to dispose of it is to burn it, "in a dignified manner." The rules are detailed, he said, in the Flag Code, guidelines for flag etiquette that were adopted by many patriotic organizations in 1923 and passed by Congress in 1942.

"Isn't that ironic?" Mr. White asked.

CHAPTER

3

The Constitutional Framework: Federalism and the Separation of Powers

Replacement of the Articles of Confederation by the Constitution is a classic case study of political realism. As an instrument of government, the Articles of Confederation had many virtues. Many considered it the second greatest constitution ever drafted. But as a confederation, it left too much power to the states, whose restrictions and boundaries interfered with national and international markets being sought by new economic interests. The Articles of Confederation had to be replaced, and a stronger national power had to be provided for, if the barriers to economic progress were to be lowered.[1]

To a point, political realists are correct. Everything in politics revolves around interests; a constitution must satisfy those interests or it will not last long as a governing instrument. But just as pure force is an inadequate foundation for government, so is pure interest, despite its immediate importance. Interests must be

[1]For two important realist interpretations of the rejection of the Articles in favor of the Constitution, see John P Roche, "The Foundıng Fathers: A Reform Caucus in Action," *American Political Science Review* 55 (December 1961): 799–816, and the discussion of Charles Beard's economic interpretation in the text.

translated into higher principles, and there will be no loyalty or support for any government unless most of the powerful as well as the powerless accept the principles as *legitimate*.

A government can be considered legitimate when its actions appear to be consistent with the highest principles that people already hold. The American approach to legitimacy is based on *contract*. A contract is an exchange, a deal. The contract we call the American Constitution was simply this: *the people would give their consent to a strong national government if that government would in turn accept certain strict limitations on its powers*. In other words, power in return for limits, or *constitutionalism*.

Three fundamental limitations were the basis of the contract between the American people and the framers of the Constitution: *federalism*, the *separation of powers*, and *individual rights*. Nowhere in the Constitution were these mentioned by name, but we know from the debates and writings that they were the primary framework of the Constitution. We can call them the *framework* because they were to be the structure, the channel through which governmental power would flow.

Federalism sought to limit government by dividing it into two levels—national and state—each with sufficient independence, or **sovereignty**, to compete with the other, thereby restraining the power of both.[2]

The *separation of powers* sought to limit the power of the national government by dividing government against itself—by giving the legislative, executive, and judicial branches separate functions, thus forcing them to share power.

Individual rights as embodied in the Bill of Rights sought to limit government by defining the people as separate from it—granting to each individual an identity in opposition to the government

constitutionalism
A system of rule in which formal and effective limits are placed on the powers of the government.

sovereignty
Supreme and independent political authority.

CHAPTER OUTLINE

Federalism and the Separation of Powers as Political Institutions

Who Does What? The Changing Federal Framework

- Federalism in the Constitution

- The Slow Growth of the National Government's Power

- Cooperative Federalism and Grants-in-Aid

- Regulated Federalism and the National Standards

- New Federalism and the National-State Tug-of-War

The Separation of Powers

- Checks and Balances

- Legislative Supremacy

- The Role of the Supreme Court

Altering the Balance of Power: What are the Consequences?

---

[2]The notion that federalism requires separate spheres or jurisdictions in which lower and higher levels of government are uniquely decisive is developed fully in William H. Riker, *Federalism: Origin, Operation, Significance* (Boston: Little, Brown, 1964). This American version of federalism is applied to the emerging federal arrangements in the People's Republic of China during the 1990s in a paper by Barry R. Weingast, "The Economic Role of Political Institutions: Market-Preserving Federalism and Economic Development," *Journal of Law, Economics & Organization* 11 (1995): 1–32.

Although this chapter refers to all five principles of politics, the most salient principle is that institutions matter—that is, rules and procedures shape politics. As we learned in Chapter 1, institutions are part "script" and part "scorecard." Throughout American political history, the institutional script has determined whether states or the national government would exercise influence in a given policy area. Similarly, at the national level, the separation-of-powers system that delineates the role and authority of members of Congress, the president, and the courts provides the scorecard that allows political actors to predict who will be influential on a given political issue. And, in that they are consequential, these institutional structures channel and constrain the actions of political actors as they pursue their different goals.

itself. Individuals are given rights, which are claims to identity, to property, and to personal satisfaction or "the pursuit of happiness," that cannot be denied except by extraordinary procedures that demonstrate beyond doubt that the need of the government or the "public interest" is more compelling than the claim of the citizen.

This chapter will be concerned with federalism and the separation of powers. The purpose here is to look at the evolution of each in order to understand how we got to where we are and what the significance of each in operation is. Together federalism and the separation of powers constitute a script and a scorecard for the exercise of governmental power. They characterize the way the different fragments of governmental machinery mesh together into a whole, and they provide a list and a description of the players in the game of politics. We will conclude by reviewing the question "How do federalism and the separation of powers limit the power of the national government?" Individual rights will be the topic of the next chapter. But all of this is for introductory purposes only. All three elements form the background and the context for every chapter in this book.

FEDERALISM AND THE SEPARATION OF POWERS AS POLITICAL INSTITUTIONS

The great achievement of American politics is the fashioning of an effective constitutional structure of political institutions. Although it is an imperfect and continuously evolving "work in progress," this structure of law and political practice has served its people well for more than two centuries by managing conflict, providing inducements for bargaining and cooperation, and facilitating collective action. There has been one enormous failure—the cruel practice of slavery, which ended only after a destructive civil war. But the basic configuration of institutions first formulated in Philadelphia in 1787 survived these debacles, though severely scarred by them, and has otherwise stood the test of time.

As we noted earlier, institutional arrangements like federalism and the separation of powers are part *script* and part *scorecard*. As two of the most important features of the constitutional structure, federalism and the separation of powers serve to channel and constrain political agents, first by limiting their jurisdictional authority and second by pitting them against one another as political competitors.

One of the ingenious features of the constitutional design adopted by the framers is the principle of dividing and separating. Leaving political authority unobstructed and undivided, it was thought, would invite intense competition of a winner-take-all variety. The winners would then be in a position to tyrannize, while the losers would either submit or, with nothing else to lose, be tempted to violent opposition. By adopting the divide-and-separate principle—implemented as federalism and the separation of powers, and consisting of checks and balances—the framers of the Constitution created *jurisdictional arrangements*. The Constitution reflects this in two distinct ways. First, it encourages diversity in the political actors occupying the various institutions of government by requiring that they be selected at different times, from different constituencies, by different modes of selection (chiefly various forms of election and appointment). This, it was believed, would prevent a small clique or narrow slice of the political elite from dominating all the institutions of government at the same time. Second, the Constitution allocates the consideration of different aspects of policy to different institutional arenas. Some explicitly mentioned activities, like the coinage of money or the declaration of war, were assigned to Congress. Matters relating to the execution and implementation of the law were delegated to the president and the executive bureaucracy. Other activities, like adjudicating disputes between states, were made the preserve of the judicial branch. Those activities not explicitly mentioned in the Constitution were reserved to the states. In short, through a jurisdictional arrangement, the Constitution sought a balance in which there was the capacity for action, but in which power was not so concentrated as to make tyranny likely.

The amazing thing about these American political institutions is that they are not carved in granite (even if the official buildings that house them are!). While the Constitution initially set a broad framework for the division of authority between the national government and the states, and the division of labor among the branches of the national government, much adaptation and innovation took place as these institutions themselves were bent to the purposes of various political players. Politicians, remember, are goal-oriented and are constantly exploring the possibilities provided them by their institutional positions and political situations. Another political player that has helped shape the current jurisdictional arrangements and sharing of power is worth remembering as well. This is the United States Supreme Court. As former Supreme Court Justice Charles Evans Hughes once remarked, "We are under a Constitution, but the Constitution is what the judges say it is."[3] As we shall see in this chapter, the Court has been a

Institution Principle

The Constitution created jurisdictional arrangements by encouraging diversity in the elected leaders occupying office and allocating the consideration of different aspects of policy to different institutional arenas.

Rationality Principle

As political institutions, federalism and the separation of powers have adapted to the purposes of various political players.

History Principle

Since the time of the founding, federalism has been shaped strongly by the Supreme Court.

[3]Charles Evans Hughes, speech at Elmira, New York, 3 May 1907.

central player in settling the ongoing debate over how power should be divided between the national government and the states and between Congress and the president.

WHO DOES WHAT? THE CHANGING FEDERAL FRAMEWORK

federalism
System of government in which power is divided by a constitution between a central government and regional governments.

Federalism can be defined with misleading ease and simplicity as the division of powers and functions between the national government and the state governments.

Federalism sought to limit national and state power by creating two sovereigns—the national government and the state governments, each to a large extent independent of the other. As we saw in Chapter 2, the states had already existed as former colonies before independence, and for nearly thirteen years they were virtually autonomous units under the Articles of Confederation. In effect, the states had retained too much power under the Articles, a problem that led directly to the Annapolis Convention in 1786 and to the Constitutional Convention in 1787. Under the Articles, disorder within states was beyond the reach of the national government (see Shays's Rebellion, Chapter 2), and conflicts of interest between states were not manageable. For example, states were making their own trade agreements with foreign countries and companies that might then play one state against another for special advantages. Some states adopted special trade tariffs and further barriers to foreign commerce that were contrary to the interest of another state.[4] Tax and other barriers were also being erected between the states.[5] But even after the ratification of the Constitution, the states continued to be more important than the national government. For nearly a century and a half, virtually all of the fundamental policies governing the lives of Americans were made by the state legislatures, not by Congress.

Federalism in the Constitution

The United States was the first nation to adopt federalism as its governing framework. With federalism, the framers sought to limit the national government by creating a second layer of state governments. American federalism recognized two sovereigns in the original Constitution and reinforced the principle in the Bill of Rights by granting a few *"expressed powers"* to the national government and reserving all the rest to the states.

expressed powers Specific powers granted to Congress under Article 1, Section 8, of the Constitution.

The Powers of the National Government As we saw in Chapter 2, the "expressed powers" granted to the national government are found in Article I, Sec-

---

[4]For good treatment of these conflicts of interests between states, see Forrest McDonald, *E Pluribus Unum: The Formation of the American Republic, 1776–1790* (Boston: Houghton Mifflin, 1965), Chapter 7, especially pp. 319–38.

[5]See David M. O'Brien, *Constitutional Law and Politics*, 3rd ed., 2 vols. (New York: W. W. Norton, 1997), I, pp. 602–3.

tion 8, of the Constitution. These seventeen powers include the power to collect taxes, to coin money, to declare war, and to regulate commerce (which, as we will see, became a very important power for the national government). Article I, Section 8, also contains another important source of power for the national government: the *implied powers* that enable Congress "to make all Laws which shall be necessary and proper for carrying into Execution the foregoing Powers." Not until several decades after the founding did the Supreme Court allow Congress to exercise the power granted in this *necessary and proper clause,* but, as we shall see later in this chapter, this doctrine allowed the national government to expand considerably the scope of its authority, although the process was a slow one. In addition to these expressed and implied powers, the Constitution affirmed the power of the national government in the supremacy clause (Article VI), which made all national laws and treaties "the supreme Law of the Land."

The Powers of State Government   One way in which the framers sought to preserve a strong role for the states was through the Tenth Amendment to the Constitution. The Tenth Amendment states that the powers that the Constitution does not delegate to the national government or prohibit to the states are "reserved to the States respectively, or to the people." The Antifederalists, who feared that a strong central government would encroach on individual liberty, repeatedly pressed for such an amendment as a way of limiting national power. Federalists agreed to the amendment because they did not think it would do much harm, given the powers of the Constitution already granted to the national government. The Tenth Amendment is also called the *reserved powers* amendment because it aims to reserve powers to the states.

The most fundamental power that is retained by the states is that of coercion—the power to develop and enforce criminal codes, to administer health and safety rules, to regulate the family via marriage and divorce laws. The states have the power to regulate individuals' livelihoods; if you're a doctor or a lawyer or a plumber or a barber, you must be licensed by the state. Even more fundamentally, the states had the power to define private property—private property exists because state laws against trespass define who is and is not entitled to use a piece of property. If you own a car, your ownership isn't worth much unless the state is willing to enforce your right to possession by making it a crime for anyone else to drive your car. These are fundamental matters, and the powers of the states regarding these domestic issues are much greater than the powers of the national government, even today.

A state's authority to regulate these fundamental matters is commonly referred to as the *police power* of the state and encompasses the state's power to regulate the health, safety, welfare, and morals of its citizens. Policing is what states do—they coerce you in the name of the community in order to maintain public order. And this was exactly the type of power that the founders intended the states to exercise.

In some areas, the states share *concurrent powers* with the national government, wherein they retain and share some power to regulate commerce and to

implied powers
Powers derived from the necessary and proper clause of Article I, Section 8, of the Constitution. Such powers are not specifically expressed but are implied through the expansive interpretation of delegated powers.

necessary and proper clause
From Article I, Section 8, of the Constitution, it provides Congress with the authority to make all laws "necessary and proper" to carry out its expressed powers.

reserved powers
Powers, derived from the Tenth Amendment to the Constitution, that are not specifically delegated to the national government or denied to the states.

police power
Power reserved to the government to regulate the health, safety, and morals of its citizens.

concurrent powers
Authority possessed by *both* state and national governments, such as the power to levy taxes.

affect the currency—for example, by being able to charter banks, grant or deny corporate charters, grant or deny licenses to engage in a business or practice a trade, and regulate the quality of products or the conditions of labor. This issue of concurrent versus exclusive power has come up from time to time in our history, but wherever there is a direct conflict of laws between the federal and the state levels, the issue will most likely be resolved in favor of national supremacy.

State Obligations to One Another   The Constitution also creates obligations among the states. These obligations, spelled out in Article IV, were intended to promote national unity. By requiring the states to recognize actions and decisions taken in other states as legal and proper, the framers aimed to make the states less like independent countries and more like parts of a single nation.

Article IV, Section I, calls for "Full Faith and Credit" among states, meaning that each state is normally expected to honor the "public Acts, Records, and judicial Proceedings" that take place in any other state. So, for example, if a couple is married in Texas—marriage being regulated by state law—Missouri must also recognize that marriage, even though they were not married under Missouri state law.

full faith and credit clause
Provision from Article IV, Section 1, of the Constitution requiring that the states normally honor the public acts and judicial decisions that take place in another state.

This *full faith and credit clause* has recently become embroiled in the controversy over gay and lesbian marriage. In 1993, the Hawaii Supreme Court prohibited discrimination against gay and lesbian marriage except in very limited circumstances. Many observers believed that Hawaii would eventually fully legalize gay marriage. In fact, after a long political battle, Hawaii passed a constitutional amendment in 1998 outlawing gay marriage. However, in December 1999, the Vermont Supreme Court ruled that gay and lesbian couples should have the same rights as heterosexuals. The Vermont legislature responded with a new law that allowed gays and lesbians to form "civil unions." Although not legally considered marriages, such unions allow gay and lesbian couples most of the benefits of marriage, such as eligibility for the partner's health insurance, inheritance rights, and the right to transfer property. The Vermont statute could have broad implications for other states. More than thirty states have passed "defense of marriage acts" that define marriage as a union between men and women only. Anxious to show its disapproval of gay marriage, Congress passed the Defense of Marriage Act in 1996, which declared that states will *not* have to recognize a same-sex marriage, even if it is legal in one state. The act also said that the federal government will not recognize gay marriage—even if it is legal under state law—and that gay marriage partners will not be eligible for the federal benefits, such as Medicare and Social Security, normally available to spouses.[6]

Because of this controversy, the extent and meaning of the full faith and credit clause is sure to be considered by the Supreme Court. In fact, it is not clear that the clause requires states to recognize gay marriage because the

[6]Ken I. Kersch, "Full Faith and Credit for Same-Sex Marriages?" *Political Science Quarterly* 112 (Spring 1997): 117–36; Joan Biskupic, "Once Unthinkable, Now under Debate," *Washington Post*, 3 September 1996, p. A1.

Court's past interpretation of the clause has provided exceptions for "public policy" reasons: if states have strong objections to a law, they do not have to honor it. In 1997 the Court took up a case involving the full faith and credit clause. The case concerned a Michigan court order that prevented a former engineer for General Motors from testifying against the company. The engineer, who left the company on bad terms, later testified in a Missouri court about a car accident in which a woman died when her Chevrolet Blazer caught fire. General Motors challenged his right to testify, arguing that Missouri should give "full faith and credit" to the Michigan ruling. The Supreme Court ruled that the engineer could testify and that the court system in one state cannot hinder other state courts in their "search for the truth."[7]

Article IV, Section 2, known as the "comity clause," also seeks to promote national unity. It provides that citizens enjoying the ***Privileges and Immunities*** of one state should be entitled to similar treatment in other states. What this has come to mean is that a state cannot discriminate against someone from another state or give special privileges to its own residents. For example, in the 1970s, when Alaska passed a law that gave residents preference over nonresidents in obtaining work on the state's oil and gas pipelines, the Supreme Court ruled the law illegal because it discriminated against citizens of other states.[8] This clause also regulates criminal justice among the states by requiring states to return fugitives to the states from which they have fled. Thus, in 1952, when an inmate escaped from an Alabama prison and sought to avoid being returned to Alabama on the grounds that he was being subjected to "cruel and unusual punishment" there, the Supreme Court ruled that he must be returned according to Article IV, Section 2.[9] This example highlights the difference between the obligations among states and those among different countries. Recently, France refused to return an American fugitive because he might be subject to the death penalty, which does not exist in France.[10] The Constitution clearly forbids states from doing something similar.

States' relationships to one another are also governed by the interstate compact clause (Article I, Section 10), which states that "No State shall, without the Consent of Congress . . . enter into any Agreement or Compact with another State." The Court has interpreted the clause to mean that states may enter into agreements with one another, subject to congressional approval. Compacts are a way for two or more states to reach a legally binding agreement about how to solve a problem that crosses state lines. In the early years of the Republic, states turned to compacts primarily to settle border disputes. Today they are used for a wide range of issues but are especially important in regulating the distribution of

privileges and immunities clause Provision from Article IV, Section 2, of the Constitution that a state cannot discriminate against someone from another state or give its own residents special privileges.

---

[7]Linda Greenhouse, "Supreme Court Weaves Legal Principles from a Tangle of Legislation," *New York Times*, 30 June 1988, p. A20

[8]Hicklin v. Orbeck, 437 U.S. 518 (1978).

[9]Sweeny v Woodall, 344 U.S. 86 (1953)

[10]Marlise Simons, "France Won't Extradite American Convicted of Murder," *New York Times*, 5 December 1997, p. A9.

river water, addressing environmental concerns, and operating transportation systems that cross state lines.[11]

Local Government and the Constitution   Local government occupies a peculiar but very important place in the American system. In fact, the status of American local government is probably unique in world experience. First, it must be pointed out that local government has no status in the American Constitution. *State* legislatures created local governments, and *state* constitutions and laws permit local governments to take on some of the responsibilities of the state governments. Most states amended their own constitutions to give their larger cities *home rule*—a guarantee of noninterference in various areas of local affairs. But local governments enjoy no such recognition in the Constitution. Local governments have always been mere conveniences of the states.[12]

Local governments became administratively important in the early years of the Republic because the states possessed little administrative capability. They relied on local governments—cities and counties—to implement the laws of the state. Local government was an alternative to a statewide bureaucracy.

The Slow Growth of the National Government's Power

As we have noted, the Constitution created two layers of government: the national government and the state governments. This two-layer system can be called *dual federalism.* The consequences of dual federalism are fundamental to the American system of government in theory and in practice. They have meant that states have done most of the fundamental governing. Table 3.1 is a listing of the major types of public policies by which Americans were governed for the first century and a half under the Constitution. We call it the "traditional system" because it prevailed for three-quarters of our history and because it closely approximates the intentions of the framers of the Constitution. The contrast between national and state policies, as shown by the table, demonstrates the difference in the power vested in each. The list of items in column 2 could actually have been made much longer. Moreover, each item on the list is only a category made up of laws that fill many volumes of statutes and court decisions for each state.

Questions about how to divide responsibilities between the states and the national government first arose more than two hundred years ago, when the framers wrote the Constitution to create a stronger union. But they did not solve the issue of who should do what. There is no "right" answer to that question;

home rule   Power delegated by the state to a local unit of government to manage its own affairs.

dual federalism   The system of government that prevailed in the United States from 1789 to 1937 in which most fundamental governmental powers were shared between the federal and state governments.

Institution Principle
In answering "Who does what?" federalism determines the flow of government functions and through that, the political development of the country.

[11]Patricia S. Florestano, "Past and Present Utilization of Interstate Compacts in the United States," *Publius* 24 (Fall 1994): 13–26.

[12]A good discussion of the constitutional position of local governments is in York Y. Willbern, *The Withering Away of the City* (Bloomington: Indiana University Press, 1971). For more on the structure and theory of federalism, see Thomas R. Dye, *American Federalism: Competition among Governments* (Lexington, Mass.: Lexington Books, 1990), Chapter 1, and Martha Derthick, "Up-to-Date in Kansas City: Reflections on American Federalism" (the 1992 John Gaus Lecture), *PS: Political Science & Politics* 25 (December 1992): 671–75

TABLE 3.1

The Federal System: Specialization of Governmental Functions in the Traditional System (1789–1937)		
NATIONAL GOVERNMENT POLICIES (DOMESTIC)	**STATE GOVERNMENT POLICIES**	**LOCAL GOVERNMENT POLICIES**
Internal improvements	Property laws (including slavery)	Adaptation of state laws to local conditions ("variances")
Subsidies	Estate and inheritance laws	Public works
Tariffs	Commerce laws	Contracts for public works
Public lands disposal	Banking and credit laws	Licensing of public accommodations
Patents	Corporate laws	Assessable improvements
Currency	Insurance laws	Basic public services
	Family laws	
	Morality laws	
	Public health laws	
	Education laws	
	General penal laws	
	Eminent domain laws	
	Construction codes	
	Land-use laws	
	Water and mineral laws	
	Criminal procedure laws	
	Electoral and political parties laws	
	Local government laws	
	Civil service laws	
	Occupations and professions laws	

each generation of Americans has provided its own answer. In recent years, Americans have grown distrustful of the federal government and have supported giving more responsibility to the states.[13] Even so, they still want the federal government to set standards and promote equality.

Institution Principle

The national-state tug-of-war is an institutional feature of the federal system.

Political debates about the division of responsibility often take sides: some people argue for a strong federal role to set national standards, while others say the states should do more. These two goals are, not necessarily at odds. The key is to find the right balance. During the first 150 years of American history, that balance favored state power. But the balance began to shift toward Washington in the 1930s. Since the mid-1990s, there have been efforts to shift the balance back toward the states.

Having created the national government, and recognizing the potential for abuse of power, the states sought through federalism to constrain the national government. The "traditional system" of weak national government prevailed for over a century despite economic forces favoring its expansion and despite Supreme Court cases giving a pro-national interpretation to Article I, Section 8, of the Constitution.

commerce clause
Article I, Section 8, of the Constitution, which delegates to Congress the power "to regulate Commerce with foreign Nations, and among the several States, and with the Indian Tribes." This clause was interpreted by the Supreme Court in favor of national power over the economy.

That article delegates to Congress the power "to regulate commerce with foreign nations, and among the several States and with the Indian tribes." This *commerce clause* was consistently interpreted *in favor* of national power by the Supreme Court for most of the nineteenth century. The first and most important case favoring national power over the economy was *McCulloch v. Maryland*.[14] The case involved the Bank of the United States and the question of whether Congress had the power to charter a bank since such an explicit grant of power was nowhere to be found in Article I, Section 8. Chief Justice John Marshall answered that the power could be "implied" from other powers that were expressly delegated to Congress, such as the "powers to lay and collect taxes; to borrow money; to regulate commerce; and to declare and conduct a war." The constitutional authority for the implied powers doctrine is a clause in Article I, Section 8, which enables Congress "to make all Laws which shall be necessary and proper for carrying into Execution the foregoing Powers." By allowing Congress to use the "necessary and proper" clause to interpret its delegated powers, the Supreme Court created the potential for an unprecedented increase in national government power.

A second historic question posed by *McCulloch* was whether a state had the power to tax the Baltimore branch of the U.S. Bank since it was a national agency. Here Marshall again took the side of national supremacy, arguing that an agency created by a legislature representing all the people (Congress) could not be put out of business by a state legislature (Maryland) representing only a small portion of the people (since "the power to tax is the power to destroy"). Marshall

[13]See the poll reported in Guy Gugliotta, "Scaling Down the American Dream," *Washington Post*, 19 April 1995, p. A21.
[14]McCulloch v Maryland, 4 Wheaton 316 (1819).

concluded that whenever a state law conflicted with a federal law, the state law would be deemed invalid since "the laws of the United States . . . 'shall be the supreme law of the land.'" Both parts of this historic case were "pro-national," yet Congress did not immediately attempt to expand the policies of the national government.

This nationalistic interpretation of the Constitution was reinforced by another major case, that of *Gibbons v. Ogden* in 1824. The important but relatively narrow issue was whether the state of New York could grant a monopoly to Robert Fulton's steamboat company to operate an exclusive service between New York and New Jersey. Ogden had secured his license from Fulton's company, while Gibbons, a former partner, secured a competing license from the U.S. government. Chief Justice Marshall argued that Gibbons could not be kept from competing because the state of New York did not have the power to grant this particular monopoly. In order to reach this decision, it was necessary for Chief Justice Marshall to define what Article I, Section 8, meant by "Commerce . . . among the several States." Marshall insisted that the definition was "comprehensive," extending to "every species of commercial intercourse." He did say that this comprehensiveness was limited "to that commerce which concerns more states than one," giving rise to what later came to be called "interstate commerce." *Gibbons* is important because it established the supremacy of the national government in all matters affecting interstate commerce.[15] What would remain uncertain during several decades of constitutional discourse was the precise meaning of interstate commerce, notwithstanding John Marshall's expansive reading of "commerce among the several states."

Article I, Section 8, backed by the "implied powers" decision in *McCulloch* and by the broad definition of "interstate commerce" in *Gibbons,* was a source of power for the national government as long as Congress sought to improve commerce through subsidies, services, and land grants. But later in the nineteenth century, when the national government sought to use those powers to *regulate* the economy rather than merely to promote economic development, the concept of interstate commerce began to operate as a restraint on rather than as a source of national power. Any effort of the federal government to regulate commerce in such areas as fraud, the production of impure goods, the use of child labor, or the existence of dangerous working conditions or long hours was declared unconstitutional by the Supreme Court as a violation of the concept of interstate commerce. Such legislation meant that the federal government was entering the factory and workplace, and these areas were considered inherently local because the goods produced there had not yet passed into commerce. Any effort to enter these local workplaces was an exercise of police power—the power reserved to the states for the protection of the health, safety, and morals of their citizens. No one questioned the power of the national government to regulate certain kinds of businesses, such as railroads, gas pipelines, and waterway

[15]Gibbons v Ogden, 9 Wheaton 1 (1824).

transportation, because they intrinsically involved interstate commerce.[16] But well into the twentieth century, most other efforts by the national government to regulate commerce were blocked by the Supreme Court's interpretation of federalism, which used the concept of interstate commerce as a barrier against most efforts by Congress to expand the national government's power.

After 1937, the Supreme Court threw out the old distinction between interstate and intrastate commerce, converting the commerce clause from a source of limitations to a source of power. The Court began to refuse to review appeals challenging acts of Congress protecting the rights of employees to organize and engage in collective bargaining, regulating the amount of farmland in cultivation, extending low-interest credit to small businesses and farmers, and restricting the activities of corporations dealing in the stock market, and many other laws that contributed to the construction of the "welfare state."

Cooperative Federalism and Grants-in-Aid

If the traditional system of two sovereigns performing highly different functions could be called dual federalism, the system since the 1930s could be called *cooperative federalism*—which generally refers to supportive relations, sometimes partnerships, between national government and the state and local governments. It comes in the form of federal subsidization of special state and local activities; these subsidies are called *grants-in-aid*. But make no mistake about it: although many of these state and local programs would not exist without the federal grant-in-aid, the grant-in-aid is also an important form of federal influence. (Another form of federal influence, the mandate, will be covered in the next section.)

A grant-in-aid is really a kind of bribe, or "carrot," whereby Congress appropriates money for state and local governments with the condition that the money be spent for a particular purpose as defined by Congress. Congress uses grants-in-aid because it does not have the political or constitutional power to command cities to do its bidding. When you can't command, a monetary inducement becomes a viable alternative. Grants-in-aid are also mechanisms that help to coordinate the separate activities of all those state and local governments around a common set of standards or policy principles in circumstances when a multiplicity of these things would undermine the purposes of the policy.

The principle of the grant-in-aid goes back to the nineteenth-century land grants to states for the improvement of agriculture and farm-related education. Since farms were not in "interstate commerce," it was unclear whether the Constitution would permit the national government to provide direct assistance to agriculture. Grants-in-aid to the states, earmarked to go to farmers, presented a way of avoiding the constitutional problem while pursuing what was recognized in Congress as a national goal.

[16]In Wabash, St. Louis, and Pacific Railway Company v. Illinois, 118 U.S. 557 (1886), the Supreme Court struck down a state law prohibiting rate discrimination by a railroad; in response, Congress passed the Interstate Commerce Act of 1887 creating the Interstate Commerce Commission (ICC), which was the first federal administrative agency.

FIGURE 3.1

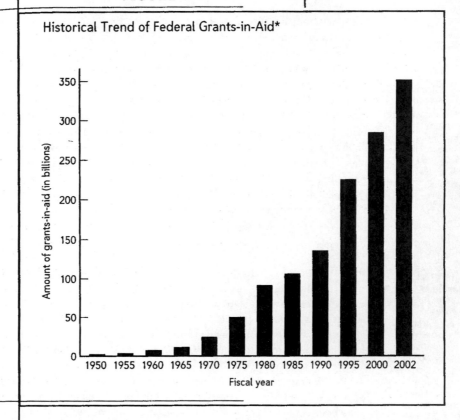

Historical Trend of Federal Grants-in-Aid*

*Excludes outlays for national defense, international affairs, and net interest.

SOURCE: Office of Management and Budget, *Budget of the United States Government, Fiscal Year 2004, Analytical Perspectives* (Washington, D.C.: Government Printing Office, 2003), Table 10-2, p 255.

Beginning in the late 1930s, this same approach was applied to cities. Congress set national goals such as public housing and assistance to the unemployed and provided grants-in-aid to meet these goals. World War II temporarily stopped the distribution of these grants. But after the war, Congress resumed providing grants for urban development and lunches in the schools. The value of such *categorical grants-in-aid* increased from $2.3 billion in 1950 to $350 billion in 2002 (see Figure 3.1). Sometimes Congress requires the state or local government to match the national contribution dollar for dollar, but for some programs, such as the interstate highway system, the congressional grant-in-aid provides 90 percent of the cost of the program. The nationwide speed limit of 55 mph was not imposed on individual drivers by an act of Congress. Instead,

categorical grants-in-aid
Funds given by Congress to states and localities, earmarked by law for specific categories such as education or crime prevention.

Congress bribed the state legislatures by threatening to withdraw the federal highway grants-in-aid if the states did not set a 55 mph speed limit. In the early 1990s, Congress began to ease up on the states, permitting them, under certain conditions, to go back to the 65 mph speed limit (or higher) without losing their highway grants.

For the most part, the categorical grants created before the 1960s simply helped the states perform their traditional functions such as education and policing.[17] In the 1960s, however, the national role expanded, and the number of categorical grants increased dramatically. For example, during the Eighty-ninth Congress (1965–1966) alone, the number of categorical grant-in-aid programs grew from 221 to 379.[18] The grants authorized during the 1960s announced national purposes much more strongly than did earlier grants. Central to that national purpose was the need to provide opportunities to the poor.

Many of the categorical grants enacted during the 1960s were *project grants,* which require state and local governments to submit proposals to federal agencies. In contrast to the older *formula grants,* which used a formula (composed of such elements as need and state and local capacities) to distribute funds, the new project grants made funding available on a competitive basis. Federal agencies would give grants to the proposals they judged to be the best. In this way, the national government acquired substantial control over which state and local governments got money, how much they got, and how they spent it.

The most important student of the history of federalism, Morton Grodzins, characterized the shift to post–New Deal cooperative federalism as a move from "layer cake federalism" to "marble cake federalism,"[19] in which intergovernmental cooperation and sharing have blurred the distinguishing line, making it difficult to say where the national government ends and the state and local governments begin (see Figure 3.2). Figure 3.3 demonstrates the financial basis of the marble cake idea. At the high point of grant-in-aid policies in the late 1970s federal aid contributed about 25–30 percent of the operating budgets of all the state and local governments in the country. The numbers in Table 3.2 present some of the more extreme examples from 1977 and the severe drop since that time.

Regulated Federalism and National Standards

Developments from the 1960s to the present have moved well beyond cooperative federalism to what might be called "regulated federalism."[20] In some areas

project grants
Grant programs in which state and local governments submit proposals to federal agencies and for which funding is provided on a competitive basis.

formula grants
Grants-in-aid in which a formula is used to determine the amount of federal funds a state or local government will receive.

[17]Kenneth T. Palmer, "The Evolution of Grant Policies," in Lawrence D. Brown, James W. Fossett, and Kenneth T Palmer, *The Changing Politics of Federal Grants,* (Washington, D.C.: Brookings Institution, 1984), p 15.

[18]Ibid., p 6.

[19]Morton Grodzins, "The Federal System," in *Goals for Americans* (Englewood Cliffs, N.J.: Prentice-Hall, 1960), p 265. In a marble cake, the white cake is distinguishable from the chocolate cake, but the two are streaked rather than in distinct layers.

[20]The concept and the best discussion of this modern phenomenon will be found in Donald F. Kettl, *The Regulation of American Federalism* (Baltimore: Johns Hopkins University Press, 1983 and 1987), especially pp. 33–41.

FIGURE 3.2

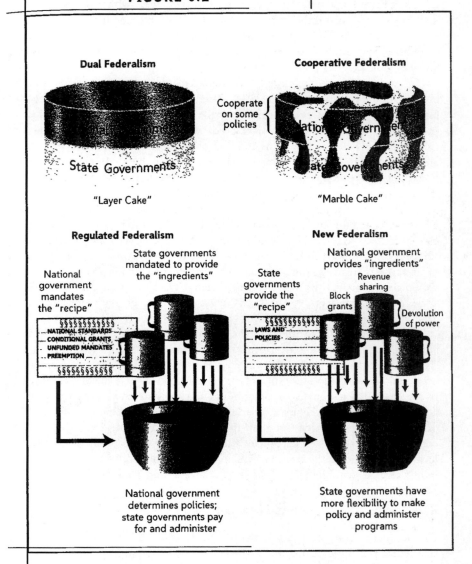

Dual Federalism

State Governments

"Layer Cake"

Cooperative Federalism

Cooperate on some policies

National Government

State Governments

"Marble Cake"

Regulated Federalism

National government mandates the "recipe"

State governments mandated to provide the "ingredients"

NATIONAL STANDARDS
CONDITIONAL GRANTS
UNFUNDED MANDATES
PREEMPTION

National government determines policies; state governments pay for and administer

New Federalism

National government provides "ingredients"

State governments provide the "recipe"

Revenue sharing

Block grants

Devolution of power

LAWS AND POLICIES

State governments have more flexibility to make policy and administer programs

Who Does What? The Changing Federal Framework **91**

60

FIGURE 3.3

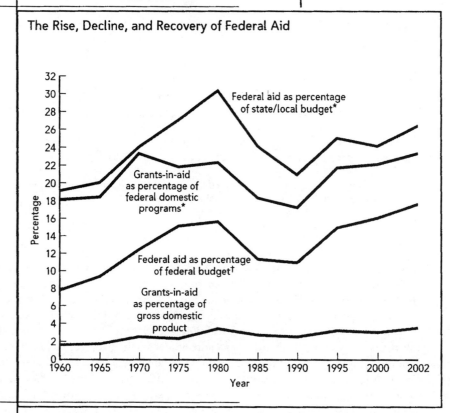

The Rise, Decline, and Recovery of Federal Aid

Federal aid as percentage of state/local budget*

Grants-in-aid as percentage of federal domestic programs*

Federal aid as percentage of federal budget†

Grants-in-aid as percentage of gross domestic product

Percentage — Year

*Federal aid as a percentage of state/local expenditures after transfers.
†Federal aid as a percentage of federal expenditures from own funds.
‡Excludes outlays for national defense, international affairs, and net interest.

SOURCE: Office of Management and Budget, *Budget of the United States Government, Fiscal Year 2004, Analytical Perspectives* (Washington, D.C.: Government Printing Office, 2003), Table 10-2, p 255.

the national government actually regulates the states by threatening to withhold grant money unless state and local governments conform to national standards. The most notable instances of this regulation are in the areas of civil rights, poverty programs, and environmental protection. This reflects a general shift in federal regulation away from the oversight and control of strictly economic activities toward "social regulation"—interventions on behalf of individual rights and liberties, environmental protection, workplace safety, and so on. In these instances, the national government provides grant-in-aid financing but sets condi-

TABLE 3.2

Federal Aid as a Percentage of General Annual Expenditure

CITY	1977	1999	CITY	1977	1999
Chicago	20	8	Houston	13	6
Cleveland	29	8	Indianapolis	21	3
Denver	14	2	Los Angeles	22	7
Detroit	31	9	San Antonio	28	2
Honolulu	30	9	Seattle	23	4

SOURCE: Department of Commerce, *Statistical Abstract of the United States, 2002* (Washington, D.C.. Government Printing Office, 2002), Tables 437 and 438.

tions the states must meet in order to keep the grants. The national government refers to these policies as "setting national standards." Important examples include the Asbestos Hazard Emergency Act of 1986, which requires school districts to inspect for asbestos hazards and to remove them from school buildings when necessary, and the Americans with Disabilities Act of 1990, which requires all state and local governments to promote access for the handicapped to all government buildings. The net effect of these national standards is that state and local policies are more uniform from coast to coast. As we noted earlier about grants-in-aid, national regulations and standards provide coordination across states and localities and solve collective action problems. However, there are a number of other programs in which the national government engages in regulated federalism by imposing national standards on the states *without providing any funding at all.* These have come to be called **unfunded mandates.** States complained that mandates took up so much of their budgets that they were not able to set their own priorities.[21]

These burdens became a major part of the rallying cry that produced the famous Republican Congress elected in 1994, with its Contract with America.

unfunded mandates Regulations or conditions for receiving grants that impose costs on state and local governments for which they are not reimbursed by the federal government.

[21]John J. DiIulio and Donald F. Kettl report that in 1980 there were thirty-six laws that could be categorized as unfunded mandates. And despite the concerted opposition of the Reagan and Bush administrations, another twenty-seven laws qualifying as unfunded mandates were adopted between 1982 and 1991. See John DiIulio, Jr , and Donald F. Kettl, *Fine Print: The Contract with America, Devolution, and the Administrative Realities of American Federalism* (Washington, D.C.: Brookings Institution, 1995), p. 41.

One of the first measures adopted by the 104th Republican Congress was an act to limit unfunded mandates—the Unfunded Mandates Reform Act (UMRA). This was considered a triumph of lobbying efforts by state and local governments, and it was "hailed as both symbol and substance of a renewed congressional commitment to federalism."[22] Under this law, any mandate with an uncompensated state and local cost estimated at greater than $50 million a year, as determined by the Congressional Budget Office (CBO), can be stopped by a point of order raised on the House or Senate floor. This was called a "stop, look and listen" requirement, forcing Congress to take positive action to own up to the mandate and its potential costs. During 1996, its first full year of operation, only eleven bills included mandates that exceeded the $50 million threshold— from a total of sixty-nine estimates of actions in which mandates were included. Examples included minimum wage increase, parity for mental health and health insurance, mandated use of Social Security numbers on driver's licenses, and extension of Federal Occupation Safety and Health to state and local employees. Most of them were modified in the House, to reduce their costs. However, as one expert put it, "The primary impact of UMRA came not from the affirmative blockage of [mandate] legislation, but rather from its effect as a deterrent to mandates in the drafting and early consideration of legislation."[23]

As indicated by the first year of its operation, the effect of UMRA will not be revolutionary. UMRA does not prevent congressional members from passing unfunded mandates; it only makes them think twice before they do. Moreover, the act exempts several areas from coverage by UMRA. And states must still enforce antidiscrimination laws and meet other requirements to receive federal assistance. But, on the other hand, UMRA does represent a serious effort to move the national/state relationship a bit further toward the state side.

New Federalism and the National-State Tug-of-War

Federalism in the United States can best be understood today as a tug-of-war between those seeking more uniform national standards and those seeking more room for variability from state to state. This is a struggle over federalism's script and scorecard—over who does what and how the various activities are structured and sequenced. Presidents Nixon and Reagan called their efforts to reverse the trend toward national standards and reestablish traditional policy making and implementation the "new federalism." They helped to craft national policies whose purpose was to return more discretion to the states. Examples of these policies include Nixon's revenue sharing and Reagan's **block grants**, which consolidated a number of categorical grants into one larger category, leaving the state (or local) government more discretion to decide how to use the money.

block grants
Federal funds given to state governments to pay for goods, services, or programs, with relatively few restrictions on how the funds may be spent.

[22]Paul Posner, "Unfunded Mandate Reform: How Is It Working?" *Rockefeller Institute Bulletin* (Albany Nelson A. Rockefeller Institute of Government, 1998): 35.
[23]Ibid , 36

Presidents Nixon and Reagan, as well as former president Bush, were sincere in wanting to return somewhat to a traditional notion of freedom of action for the states. They called it new federalism, but their concepts and their goals were really much closer to the older, traditional federalism that predated the 1930s.

In effect, President Clinton adopted the "new federalism" of Nixon and Reagan even while expanding federal grant activity: he signed the Unfunded Mandates Reform Act of 1995 as well as the Personal Responsibility and Work Opportunity Reconciliation Act of 1996, which goes further than any other act of Congress in the past sixty years to relieve the states from national mandates, funded or unfunded. This new law replaces the sixty-one-year-old program of Aid to Families with Dependent Children (AFDC) and its education, work, and training program, with block grants to states for Temporary Assistance to Needy Families (TANF). Although some national standards remain, the place of the states in the national welfare system has been virtually revolutionized through *devolution,* the strategy of delegating to the states more and more authority over a range of policies that had up until then been under national government authority, plus providing the states with a substantial portion of the cost of these programs. Since the mid-1990s, devolution has been quite consequential for the national-state tug-of-war.

By changing welfare from a combined federal-state program into a block grant to the states, Congress gave the states more responsibility for programs that serve the poor. One argument in favor of devolution is that states can act as "laboratories of democracy" by experimenting with many different approaches to find one that best meets the needs of their citizens.[24] As states have altered their welfare programs in the wake of the new law, they have indeed designed diverse approaches. For example, Minnesota has adopted an incentive-based approach that offers extra assistance to families that take low-wage jobs. Other states, such as California, have more "sticks" than "carrots" in their new welfare programs.[25]

President George W. Bush, though sometimes compared to Ronald Reagan, has not proven to be an unwavering supporter of new federalism and states' rights. On certain matters dear to his heart, Bush has been closer to the spirit of "regulated federalism." The most visible example of Bush's occasional preference for national standards is the education program known as No Child Left Behind. This program sets standards of accomplishment in reading and math that are to be applied nationally and backed by federal grants that are to be withheld if the standards are not met. The program gives the states "full freedom" to use the federal money, but states are to be held accountable for results, as measured by national standards of performance. Failure to meet the standard will be punished

devolution
A policy to remove a program from one level of government by deregulating it or passing it down to a lower level of government, such as from the national government to the state and local governments.

Collective Action Principle
States compete with one another not only for new business, but also in terms of being less attractive to welfare recipients.

Policy Principle
Devolution has had an important influence on policy outcomes, particularly welfare.

[24]The phrase "laboratories of democracy" was coined by Supreme Court Justice Louis Brandeis in his dissenting opinion in New State Ice Co. v Liebman, 285 U.S 262 (1932)

[25]For assessments of the use of welfare grants to the states for increased regulation as a condition for welfare benefits, see Frances Fox Piven, "Welfare and Work," and Dorothy Roberts, "Welfare's Ban on Poor Motherhood," in *Whose Welfare?* ed Gwendolyn Mink (Ithaca, N.Y.: Cornell University Press, 1999), pp 83–99 and 152–167.

The End of Big Government?
Federalism in the Last Quarter Century

Beginning with Roosevelt's New Deal, the federal government grew into areas tradition-ally reserved for the states or private organizations. The dominance of the federal govern-ment was once so strong that Republican president Dwight Eisenhower supported massive federal programs for building highways and expanding educational opportuni-ties. Lyndon Johnson's Great Society, begun after the watershed election of 1964, was ar-guably the apex of the twentieth century American welfare state. By the late 1960s, President Richard Nixon created the Environmental Protection Agency, instituted wage price freeze, and once proposed a minimum income for every citizen.

By the 1990s, support for new federal programs had withered away. Over the last thirty years, programs to expand the scope of the central government have stalled or been eliminated. Presidents Reagan and George H. W. Bush came to office promising to curb federal power and shrink the size and scope of the government. President Bill Clin-ton's proposal for national health insurance was an embarrassing early defeat for the ad-ministration, and eventually Clinton proposed the "end of welfare as we know it."

The principles of politics can help us understand the conditions that led to this rapid growth in federal authority as well as trace its eventual decline. During the Depression, our collective decision-making institutions—state governments and Congress—seemed unable to formulate public policies that would address the economic crisis. Institutional rules in Congress, particularly the hammerlock of seniority and the resulting control of policy making by a small group of conservative southern senators, short-circuited propos-als for a major federal response.[26]

FDR was able to get Congress to pass much of the New Deal legislation (and, by threatening the autonomy of the Supreme Court with his "court packing" plan, convince the Court not to declare it unconstitutional). By the end of World War II, federal leader-ship action in many areas of politics—areas that would have been unthinkable just a quar-ter century before—were well accepted. Thus, during the 1950s and 1960s, grants-in-aid and regulated federalism were well-accepted solutions to cooperation and coordination problems. The future of the United States, it seemed, was firmly on the path of federal dominance, with less and less policy authority residing in the states. State legislators, na-tional political leaders, and the courts went along.

Starting in the 1970s, however, support for new federal programs began to decline (in large part because many of these programs seemed to stall or decline in effectiveness). A series of presidents, beginning with Richard Nixon, tried to change our historical path. Changes in the Republican party, beginning in 1964, meant that "Rockefeller" and "Main Street" Republicans who were more positively inclined toward federal intervention were increasingly replaced in Congress by westerners and southerners who were hostile (al-though for different reasons) to federal authority. The election of Ronald Reagan (a west-erner) and the resulting conservative shift meant that strategic political actors in all three branches of government were looking for ways to reduce federal authority. Block grants, revenue sharing, devolution, and other ways of shifting power from national to state and local actors were proposed.

Still, many laws and procedures remain in place that keep policy-making authority with the federal government yet require taxation and spending by the states. Politically, this is an easy choice for strategic politicians at the federal level: they get to take credit for cutting taxes but can still promise a social safety net (paid for by the states).

There may be advantages to this newly dispersed system of authority. We may be returning to an era when state governments become the main tax collectors and service providers. This has led to some political oddities, such as conservative Republican governors in Alabama and Idaho proposing tax increases in order to maintain services, while a liberal Democratic governor in Oregon refuses to consider new revenues.

States are likely to become policy "laboratories" where innovative new policies are developed, some successful, some a failure. While the same principles of politics apply to state as well as to the federal government, this will undoubtedly make the American political system more varied and more complex.

[26]See Robert A Caro's compelling portrayal of southern dominance in the twenthieth-century Senate in *Master of the Senate: The Life and Times of Lyndon Baines Johnson* (New York: Knopf, 2002). William E Leuchtenberg, in *Franklin D. Roosevelt and the New Deal, 1932–1940* (New York· Harper & Row, 1963), argues that the political conditions of the 1920s and 1930s, particularly ineptness in Congress and in the states, required forceful and creative leadership by FDR.

by withholding federal funds. This is especially significant considering that education is the most local of all activities. On certain other matters, historical circumstance has made Bush a proponent of nationalization. Homeland security policies are the prime example. President Bush has sought billions of dollars to pull cities and states into assuming more of their own security measures. He has even supported some "unfunded mandates" on the larger and more vulnerable cities, leaving himself open to attack from such liberal Democratic senators as Charles Schumer and Hillary Clinton of New York, who are demanding a lot more federal reimbursement for federally generated local safety measures. Another circumstance that has pushed more responsibility back on the national government is the spate of recent state budget crises. Since many states are constitutionally prohibited from running budget deficits, the national government has been forced to fill in the gaps.

As these examples from the last decade show, assessments about "the right way" to divide responsibility in the federal system change over time. The case of speed limits provides another example. Speed limits have traditionally been a state and local responsibility. But in 1973, at the height of the oil shortage, Congress passed legislation to withhold federal highway funds from states that did not adopt a maximum speed limit of 55 mph. The lower speed limit, it was argued, would reduce energy consumption by cars. Although Congress had not formally taken over the authority to set speed limits, the power of its purse was so important that every state adopted the new speed limit. As the energy crisis faded, the national speed limit lost much of its support, even though it was found to have reduced the number of traffic deaths. In 1995, Congress repealed the penalties for higher speed limits, and states once again became free to set their own speed limits. Many states with large rural areas raised their maximum to 75 mph; Montana set unlimited speeds in the rural areas during daylight hours. Early research indicates that numbers of highway deaths have indeed risen in the states that increased the limits.[27] As new evidence becomes available, it will surely provide fuel for the ongoing debate about what are properly the states' responsibilities and what the federal government should do.

The Supreme Court as Referee   For much of the nineteenth century, federal power remained limited. The Tenth Amendment was used to bolster arguments about *states' rights,* which in their extreme version claimed that the states did not have to submit to national laws when they believed the national government had exceeded its authority. These arguments in favor of states' rights were voiced less often after the Civil War. But the Supreme Court continued to use the Tenth Amendment to strike down laws that it thought exceeded national power, including the Civil Rights Act passed in 1875.

In the early twentieth century, however, the Tenth Amendment appeared to lose its force. Reformers began to press for national regulations to limit the power of large corporations and to preserve the health and welfare of citizens. The Supreme Court approved of some of these laws, but it struck others down, including a law combating child labor. The Court stated that the law violated the Tenth Amendment because only states should have the power to regulate conditions of employment. By the late 1930s, however, the Supreme Court had approved such an expansion of federal power that the Tenth Amendment appeared irrelevant. In fact, in 1941, Justice Harlan Fiske Stone declared that the Tenth Amendment was simply a "truism," that it had no real meaning.[28]

Recent years have seen a revival of interest in the Tenth Amendment and important Supreme Court decisions limiting federal power. Much of the interest in the Tenth Amendment stems from conservatives who believe that a strong federal government encroaches on individual liberties. They believe such freedoms are better protected by returning more power to the states through the process of devolution. In 1996, Republican presidential candidate Bob Dole carried a copy of the Tenth Amendment in his pocket as he campaigned, pulling it out to

states' rights
The principle that states should oppose increasing authority of the national government. This view was most popular before the Civil War.

---

[27]"Motor Vehicle Fatalities in 1996 Were 12 Percent Higher on Interstates, Freeways in 12 States That Raised Speed Limits," press release of the Insurance Institute for Highway Safety, 10 October 1997.
[28]United States v. Darby Lumber Co., 312 U.S. 100 (1941).

read at rallies.[29] Around the same time, the Eleventh Amendment concept of **state sovereign immunity** was revived by the Court. This legal doctrine holds that states are immune from lawsuits by private persons or groups claiming that the state violated a statute enacted by Congress.

state sovereign immunity
Legal doctrine that holds that states cannot be sued for violating an act of Congress.

The Supreme Court's ruling in *United States v. Lopez* in 1995 fueled further interest in the Tenth Amendment. In that case, the Court, stating that Congress had exceeded its authority under the commerce clause, struck down a federal law that barred handguns near schools. This was the first time since the New Deal that the Court had limited congressional powers in this way. The Court further limited the power of the federal government over the states in a 1996 ruling based on the Eleventh Amendment that prevented Native Americans from the Seminole tribe from suing the state of Florida in federal court. A 1988 law had given Indian tribes the right to sue a state in federal court if the state did not negotiate in good faith over issues related to gambling casinos on tribal land. The Supreme Court's ruling appeared to signal a much broader limitation on national power by raising new questions about whether individuals can sue a state if it fails to uphold federal law.[30]

Another significant decision involving the relationship between the federal government and state governments was the 1997 case *Printz v. United States* (joined with *Mack v. United States*), in which the Court struck down a key provision of the Brady Bill, enacted by Congress in 1993 to regulate gun sales. Under the terms of the act, state and local law enforcement officers were required to conduct background checks on prospective gun purchasers. The Court held that the federal government cannot require states to administer or enforce federal regulatory programs. Since the states bear administrative responsibility for a variety of other federal programs, this decision could have far-reaching consequences. Finally, in another major ruling from the 1996–1997 term, in *City of Boerne v. Flores*, the Court ruled that Congress had gone too far in restricting the power of the states to enact regulations they deemed necessary for the protection of public health, safety, or welfare. These rulings signal a move toward a much more restricted federal government.

In 1999, the Court's ruling on another Eleventh Amendment case further strengthened the doctrine of state sovereign immunity, finding that "the federal system established by our Constitution preserves the sovereign status of the States. . . . The generation that designed and adopted our federal system considered immunity from private suits central to sovereign dignity."[31] In 2000 in *United States v. Morrison*,[32] the Supreme Court invalidated an important provision of the 1994 Violence against Women Act, which permitted women to bring private damage suits if their victimization was "gender-motivated." Although the

---

[29]W John Moore, "Pleading the 10th," *National Journal*, 29 July 1995, p. 1940.
[30]Seminole Indian Tribe v. Florida, 116 S. Ct. 1114 (1996).
[31]Alden v. Maine.
[32]United States v. Morrison, 529 U S. 598 (2000).

Who Does What? The Changing Federal Framework **99**

1994 act did not add any new national laws imposing liability or obligations on the states, the Supreme Court still held the act to be "an unconstitutional exercise" of Congress's power. And, although *Morrison* is a quite narrow federalism decision, when it is coupled with *United States v. Lopez* (1995)—the first modern holding against national authority to use commerce power to reach into the states—there is a definite trend toward strict scrutiny of the federal intervention aspects of all national civil rights, social, labor, and gender laws.

This puts federalism and the Court directly in the line of fire. With an aging and ailing Court, President Bush will likely have at least one Supreme Court justice appointment to make, and this will determine the future of federalism (and many other key issues) for the next quarter century. However, for an appointment to go through, the president must obtain the Senate's "advice and consent"; Senate debate over these appointments promises to be heated, since the makeup of the Supreme Court impacts the future of the federal government's authority to impose on the states national standards in many areas of social policy.[33]

There has clearly been a historical ebb and flow to the federal relationship: the national government's authority grew relative to that of the states during the middle decades of the twentieth century but moderated as the century drew to a close. For the moment, the balance seems to be tipped toward the states, although the tug-of-war between the states and national government will certainly continue. As a result of this ongoing struggle for power, federalism remains a vital part of the American system of government. States and cities may clamor (and lobby) for a larger share of the national budget, and state and local leaders have shown a willingness to cooperate with the national standards embodied in environmental protection laws and civil rights laws. But states, with the help of the Supreme Court, continue to hold on jealously to the maximum freedom of action that is embodied in the historic concept of federalism.

THE SEPARATION OF POWERS

In his discussion of the separation of powers, James Madison quotes the originator of the principle, the French political thinker Baron de Montesquieu:

> There can be no liberty where the legislative and executive powers are united in the same person . . . [or] if the power of judging be not separated from the legislative and executive powers.[34]

Using this same reasoning, many of Madison's contemporaries argued that there was not *enough* separation among the three branches, and Madison had to backtrack to insist that the principle did not require complete separation:

[33]For a superb account of the case United States v Morrison, see Linda Greenhouse, "Battle on Federalism," *New York Times*, 17 May 2000, p. 18. See also Cass Sunstein, "The Returns of States' Rights," *American Prospect*, 20 November 2000, p. 30.

[34]Clinton Rossiter, ed., *The Federalist Papers* (New York: New American Library, 1961), No. 47, p. 302

. . . unless these departments [branches] be so far connected and blended as to give to each a constitutional control over the others, the degree of separation which the maxim requires, as essential to a free government, can never in practice be duly maintained.[35]

This is the secret of how we have made the separation of powers effective: we made the principle self-enforcing by giving each branch of government the means to participate in, and partially or temporarily to obstruct, the workings of the other branches.

Checks and Balances

The means by which each branch of government interacts is known informally as *checks and balances.* The best-known examples are the presidential power to veto legislation passed by Congress; the power of Congress to override the veto by a two-thirds majority vote, to impeach the president, and (of the Senate) to approve presidential appointments; the power of the president to appoint the members of the Supreme Court and the other federal judges with Senate approval; and the power of the Supreme Court to engage in judicial review (to be discussed below). These and other examples are shown in Table 3.3. The framers sought to guarantee that the three branches would in fact use the checks and balances as weapons against each other by giving each branch a different political constituency: direct, popular election of the members of the House; indirect election of senators (until the Seventeenth Amendment, adopted in 1913); indirect election of the president (which still exists, at least formally, today); and appointment of federal judges for life. All things considered, the best characterization of the separation of powers principle in action is, as we said in Chapter 2, "separated institutions sharing power."[36]

Legislative Supremacy

Although each branch was to be given adequate means to compete with the other branches, it is also clear that within the system of separated powers the framers provided for *legislative supremacy* by making Congress the preeminent branch. Legislative supremacy made the provision of checks and balances in the other two branches all the more important.

The most important indication of the intention of legislative supremacy was made by the framers when they decided to place the provisions for national powers in Article I, the legislative article, and to treat the powers of the national government as powers of Congress. In a system based on the "rule of law," the power to make the laws is the supreme power. Section 8 provides in part that "*Congress* shall

Institution Principle
Checks and balances is a system of "separated institutions sharing power."

checks and balances
Mechanisms through which each branch of government participates in and influences the activities of the other branches. Major examples include the presidential veto power over congressional legislation, the power of the Senate to approve presidential appointments, and judicial review of congressional enactments.

legislative supremacy The preeminent position assigned to the Congress by the Constitution.

Institution Principle
The framers provided for legislative supremacy by making Congress the preeminent branch.

[35]Ibid., No. 48, p. 308.
[36]Richard E. Neustadt, *Presidential Power and the Modern Presidents: The Politics of Leadership from Roosevelt to Reagan*, rev ed. (New York: Free Press, 1990; orig. published 1960), p 33.

TABLE 3.3

Checks and Balances

	LEGISLATIVE BRANCH CAN BE CHECKED BY:	EXECUTIVE BRANCH CAN BE CHECKED BY:	JUDICIAL BRANCH CAN BE CHECKED BY:
Legislative branch can check:	NA*	Can overrule veto (two-thirds vote) Controls appropriations Controls by statute Impeachment of president Senate approval of appointments and treaties Committee oversight	Controls appropriations Can create inferior courts Can add new judges Senate approval of appointments Impeachment of judges
Executive branch can check:	Can veto legislation Can convene special session Can adjourn Congress when chambers disagree Vice president presides over Senate and votes to break ties	NA*	President appoints judges
Judicial branch can check:	Judicial review of legislation Chief justice presides over Senate during proceedings to impeach president	Judicial review over presidential actions Power to issue warrants Chief justice presides over impeachment of president	NA*

*NA = Not applicable.

have Power . . . To lay and collect Taxes . . . To borrow Money . . . To regulate Commerce . . ." [emphasis added]. The founders also provided for legislative supremacy in their decision to give Congress the sole power over appropriations and to give the House of Representatives the power to initiate all revenue bills. Madison recognized legislative supremacy as part and parcel of the separation of powers:

> . . . It is not possible to give to each department an equal power of self-defense. In republican government, the legislative authority necessarily predominates. The remedy for this inconveniency is to divide the legislature into different branches; and to render them, by different modes of election and different principles of action, as little connected with each other as the nature of their common functions and their common dependence on the society will admit.[37]

In other words, Congress was so likely to dominate the other branches that it would have to be divided against itself, into House and Senate. One could say that the Constitution provided for four branches, not three.

Although "presidential government" seemed to supplant legislative supremacy after 1937, the relative power position of the executive and legislative branches since that time has not been static. The degree of conflict between the president and Congress has varied with the rise and fall of political parties, and it has been especially tense during periods of ***divided government,*** when one party controls the White House and another controls the Congress, as has been the case almost solidly since 1969 (see Table 3.4).

The Role of the Supreme Court

The role of the judicial branch in the separation of powers has depended upon the power of judicial review (see also Chapter 8), a power not provided for in the Constitution but asserted by Chief Justice Marshall in 1803:

> If a law be in opposition to the Constitution; if both the law and the Constitution apply to a particular case, so that the Court must either decide that case conformable to the law, disregarding the Constitution, or conformable to the Constitution, disregarding the law; the Court must determine which of these conflicting rules governs the case: This is of the very essence of judicial duty.[38]

Review of the constitutionality of acts of the president or Congress is relatively rare.[39]

divided government The condition in American government wherein the presidency is controlled by one party while the opposing party controls one or both houses of Congress.

[37] *The Federalist Papers,* No. 51, p. 322.
[38] Marbury v. Madison, 1 Cranch 137 (1803).
[39] C. Herman Pritchett, *The American Constitution* (New York: McGraw-Hill, 1959), pp. 180–86.

TABLE 3.4

The Record of Divided Government

DATE	PARTY CONTROLLING: PRESIDENT	CONGRESS	GOVERNMENT: YEARS DIVIDED
1946–1948	Truman, Democratic	Republican	Divided 2
1948–1952	Truman, Democratic	Democratic	
1952–1954	Eisenhower, Republican	Republican	
1954–1960	Eisenhower, Republican	Democratic	Divided 6
1960–1964	Kennedy/Johnson, Democratic	Democratic	
1964–1968	Johnson, Democratic	Democratic	
1968–1972	Nixon, Republican	Democratic	Divided 4
1972–1976	Nixon/Ford, Republican	Democratic	Divided 4
1976–1980	Carter, Democratic	Democratic	
1980–1986	Reagan, Republican	Republican Senate Democratic House	Divided/mixed 6
1986–1988	Reagan, Republican	Democratic	Divided 2
1988–1992	Bush, Republican	Democratic	Divided 4
1992–1994	Clinton, Democratic	Democratic	
1994–2000	Clinton, Democratic	Republican	Divided 6
2000–2002	Bush, Republican	Republican House Democratic Senate	Divided/Mixed 2
2002–2004	Bush, Republican	Republican	
	TOTAL YEARS 58	TOTAL YEARS DIVIDED 36	

For example, there were no Supreme Court reviews of congressional acts in the fifty plus years between *Marbury v. Madison* (1803) and *Dred Scott* (1857). In the century or so between the Civil War and 1970, eighty-four acts of Congress were held unconstitutional (in whole or in part), but this includes long periods of complete Supreme Court deference to the Congress, punctuated by flurries of judicial review during periods of social upheaval. The most significant of these was 1935–1936, when twelve acts of Congress were invalidated, blocking virtually the entire New Deal program.[40] Then, after 1937, when the Court made its great reversals, no significant acts were voided until 1983, when the Court declared unconstitutional the legislative veto.[41] Another, in 1986, struck down the Gramm-Rudman Act mandating a balanced budget, which, the Court held, delegated too much power to the comptroller general to direct the president to reduce the budget.[42] The Supreme Court became much more activist (i.e., less deferential to Congress) after the elevation of Justice William H. Rehnquist to chief justice (1986), and "a new program of judicial activism"[43] seemed to be in place; but this could be a conservative one against Congress comparable to the liberal activism against the states during the Warren Court of the 1960s and 1970s. All of the cases in Table 3.5 altered some aspect of federalism by declaring unconstitutional all or an important portion of an act of Congress, and the end of this episode of judicial activism against Congress is not over. Between 1995 and 2002, at least twenty-six acts or parts of acts of Congress were struck down on constitutional grounds.[44]

Since the New Deal period, the Court has been far more deferential toward the president, with only four significant confrontations. One was the so-called *Steel Seizure* case of 1952, in which the Court refused to permit President Truman to use "emergency powers" to force workers back into the steel mills during the Korean War.[45] A second case was *United States v. Nixon*, in which the Court declared unconstitutional President Nixon's refusal to respond to a subpoena to make available the infamous White House tapes as evidence in a criminal prosecution. The Court argued that although *executive privilege* did protect confidentiality of communications to and from the president, this did not extend to data in presidential files or tapes varying upon criminal prosecutions.[46] During the heat of the Clinton scandal, the Supreme Court rejected the claim that the pressures and obligations of the office of president was so demanding that all litigation "but the most exceptional cases" should be deferred until his term ends.[47] Most recently, and of far greater importance, the Supreme Court

executive privilege The claim that confidential communications between a president and close advisers should not be revealed without the consent of the president.

---

[40]In response to New Deal legislation, the Supreme Court struck down eight out of ten New Deal statutes. For example, in Panama Refining Co. v. Ryan, 293 U.S. 388 (1935), the Court ruled that a section of the National Industrial Recovery Act was an invalid delegation of legislative power to the executive branch. And in Schechter Poultry Co. v. United States, 295 U.S. 495 (1935), the Court found the National Industrial Recovery Act itself to be invalid for the same reason But since 1935, the Supreme Court has rarely confronted the president or Congress on constitutional questions

[41]Immigration and Naturalization Service v. Chadha, 462 U.S. 919 (1983).

[42]Bowsher v. Synar, 478 U.S. 714 (1986).

[43]Cass R. Sunstein, "Taking Over the Courts," *New York Times*, 9 November 2002, p. A19.

[44]Ibid.

[45]Youngstown Sheet & Tube Co. v. Sawyer, 343 U.S. 579 (1952).

[46]United States v. Nixon, 418 U.S. 683 (1974).

[47]Clinton v. Jones, 117 S.Ct. 1636 (1997).

TABLE 3.5

A NEW FEDERAL SYSTEM?
The Recent Case Record

CASE	DATE	COURT HOLDING
United States v. Lopez, 514 U.S. 549	1995	Voids federal law barring handguns near schools. Beyond Congress's power to regulate commerce.
Seminole Indian Tribe v. Florida, 517 U.S. 44	1996	Voids federal law giving tribes the right to sue a state in federal court. "Sovereign immunity" requires state permission to be sued.
Printz v. United States (and *Mack v. United States*), 117 S.Ct. 2365	1997	Voids key provision of Brady Law requiring states to make background checks on gun purchases. As "unfunded mandate," it violates state sovereignty under Tenth Amendment.
City of Boerne v. Flores, 521 U.S. 507	1997	Restricts Congress's power to regulate city zoning, health and welfare policies to "remedy" rights but not expand rights, under Fourteenth Amendment.
Alden v. Maine, 119 S.Ct. 2240	1999	State also "immune" from suits by their *own* employees for overtime pay under federal Fair Labor Standards Act. (See also *Seminole* case.)
United States v. Morrison, 529 U.S. 598	2000	Extends *Seminole* case by invalidating Violence against Women Act, holding that states are immune to suits by individuals to enforce federal laws.

struck down the Line-Item Veto Act of 1996 on the grounds that it violated Article I, Section 7, which prescribed procedures for congressional enactment and presidential acceptance or veto of statutes. Any such change in the procedures of adopting laws would have to be made by amendment to the Constitution, not by legislation.[48]

ALTERING THE BALANCE OF POWER: WHAT ARE THE CONSEQUENCES?

Federalism and the separation of powers are two of the three most important constitutional principles upon which the United States' system of limited government is based (the third is the principle of individual rights). As we have seen, federalism limits the power of the national government in numerous ways. By its very existence, federalism recognizes the principle of two sovereigns, the national government and the state government (hence the term *dual federalism*). In addition, the Constitution specifically restrained the power of the national government to regulate the economy. As a result, the states were free to do most of the fundamental governing for the first century and a half of American government. This began to change during and following the New Deal, as the national government began to exert more influence over the states through grants-in-aid and mandates. In the last decade, however, we have noticed a countertrend to the growth of national power as Congress has opted to devolve some of its powers to the states. The most recent notable instance of devolution was the welfare reform plan of 1996.

But the problem that arises with devolution is that programs that were once uniform across the country (because they were the national government's responsibility) can become highly variable, with some states providing benefits not available in other states. To a point, variation can be considered one of the virtues of federalism. But there are dangers inherent in large variations and inequalities in the provision of services and benefits in a democracy. For example, since the Food and Drug Administration has been under attack in recent years, could the problem be solved by devolving its regulatory tasks to the states? Would people care if drugs would require "caution" labels in some states and not in others? Would Americans want each state to set its own air and water pollution control policies without regard to the fact that pollution flows across state boundaries? Devolution, as attractive as it may be, is not an approach that can be applied across the board without analyzing carefully the nature of the program and of the problems it is designed to solve. Even the capacity of states to handle "devolved" programs will vary. According to the Washington research organization the Brookings Institution, the level of state and local government employment varies from state to state—from a low of 400 per 10,000 residents in some states

History Principle

The legacy of cooperative federalism and national standards has raised some doubts about devolution.

---

[48]Clinton v. City of New York, 524 U.S. 417 (1998).

to a high of 700 per 10,000 in others. "Such administrative diversity is bound to mediate the course and consequences of any substantial devolution of federal responsibility; no one-size-fits-all devolution [from federal to state and local government] can work."[49]

Moreover, the temptation is ever present for federal politicians to limit state discretion in order to achieve their own policy objectives. Indeed, the "devolution revolution" promised by congressional Republicans created much more rhetoric than action. Despite the complaints of Republican governors, Congress has continued to use its power to preempt state action and impose mandates on states.

The second principle of limited government, separation of powers, is manifested in our system of checks and balances, whereby separate institutions of government share power with each other. Even though the Constitution clearly provided for legislative supremacy, checks and balances have functioned well. Some would say they have worked too well. The last fifty years have witnessed long periods of divided government, when one party has controlled the White House and the other party controlled Congress. During these periods, the level of conflict between the executive and legislative branches has been particularly divisive, resulting in what some analysts derisively call gridlock. Nevertheless, this is a genuine separation of powers, not so far removed from the intent of the framers. With the rise of political parties, Americans developed a parliamentary theory that "responsible party government" requires that the same party control both branches, including both chambers of the legislature. But that kind of parliamentary/party government is a "fusion of powers," not a separation of powers. Although it may not make for good government, having an opposition party in majority control of the legislature reinforces the separation and the competition that was built into the Constitution. We can complain at length about the inability of divided government to make decisions, and we can criticize it as stalemate or gridlock,[50] but even that is in accord with the theory of the framers of the Constitution that public policy is supposed to be difficult to make.

SUMMARY

In this chapter we have traced the development of two of the three basic principles of the U.S. Constitution—federalism and the separation of powers. Federalism involves a division between two layers of government: national and state. The separation of powers involves the division of the national government into

[49]Eliza Newlin Carney, "Power Grab," *National Journal*, 11 April 1998, p. 798.

[50]Not everybody will agree that divided government is all that less productive than government in which both branches are controlled by the same party. See David R. Mayhew, *Divided We Govern: Party Control, Lawmaking, and Investigations, 1946–1990* (New Haven: Yale University Press, 1991) For another good evaluation of divided government, see Charles O. Jones, *Separate but Equal Branches. Congress and the Presidency* (Chatham, N.J.. Chatham House, 1995).

Rationality Principle	Collective Action Principle	Institution Principle	Policy Principle	History Principle
As political institutions, federalism and the separation of powers have adapted to the purposes of various political players	States compete with one another not only for new businesses, but also in terms of being less attractive to welfare recipients	Federalism and the separation of powers are two of the most important principles on which the U.S. system of limited government is based.	Devolution has had an important influence on policy outcomes, particularly welfare.	Since the time of the founding, federalism has been shaped strongly by the Supreme Court.
	Grants-in-aid allow the national government to coordinate state and local policies around a common set of national standards	In answering "Who does what?" federalism determines the flow of government functions and, through that, the political development of the country		In 1937, the Supreme Court converted the commerce clause from a source of limitations to a source of power for the national government.
		The national-state tug-of war is an institutional feature of the federal system		The legacy of cooperative federalism and national standards has raised some doubts about devolution
		Checks and balances is a system of "separated institutions sharing power."		
		The framers provided for legislative supremacy by making Congress the preeminent branch		
		The Constitution created jurisdictional arrangements by encouraging diversity in the elected leaders occupying office and allocating the consideration of different aspects of policy to different institutional arenas.		

three branches. These principles are limitations on the powers of government; Americans made these compromises as a condition for giving their consent to be governed. And these principles became the framework within which the government operates. The persistence of local government and the reliance of the national government on grants-in-aid to coerce local governments into following national goals were used as case studies to demonstrate the continuing vitality of the federal framework. Examples were also given of the intense competition among the president, Congress, and the courts to dramatize the continuing vitality of the separation of powers.

The purpose of a constitution is to organize the makeup or the composition of the government, the *framework within which* government and politics, including actual legislation, can take place. A country does not require federalism and the separation of powers to have a real constitutional government. And the country does not have to approach individual rights in the same manner as the American Constitution. But to be a true constitutional government, a government must have a few limits so that it cannot be manipulated by people in power merely for their own convenience. This is the essence of constitutionalism—limits on power that are above the reach of everyday legislatures, executives, bureaucrats, and politicians, yet are not so far above their reach that they cannot be adapted to changing times.

FOR FURTHER READING

Bensel, Richard F. *Sectionalism and American Political Development: 1880–1980.* Madison: University of Wisconsin Press, 1984.

Bernstein, Richard B., with Jerome Agel. *Amending America—If We Love the Constitution So Much, Why Do We Keep Trying to Change It?* (Lawrence: University Press of Kansas, 1993).

Black, Charles L., Jr. *Impeachment: A Handbook.* New Haven: Yale University Press, 1974, 1998.

Caraley, Demetrios. "Dismantling the Federal Safety Net: Fictions versus Realities." *Political Science Quarterly,* 8, no. 2 (Summer 1996): 225–58.

Corwin, Edward, and J. W. Peltason. *Corwin & Peltason's Understanding the Constitution.* 13th ed. Fort Worth: Harcourt Brace, 1994.

Crovitz, L. Gordon, and Jeremy A. Rabkin, eds. *The Fettered Presidency: Legal Constraints on the Executive Branch.* Washington, D.C.: American Enterprise Institute, 1989.

Dye, Thomas R. *American Federalism: Competition among Governments.* Lexington, Mass.: Lexington Books, 1990.

Elazar, Daniel J. *American Federalism: A View from the States.* 3rd ed. New York: Harper & Row, 1984.

Ferejohn, John A., and Barry R. Weingast, eds. *The New Federalism: Can the States Be Trusted?* Stanford, Calif.: Hoover Institution Press, 1997.

Grodzins, Morton. *The American System: A New View of Government in the United States.* Chicago: Rand McNally, 1974.

Kahn, Ronald. *The Supreme Court and Constitutional Theory, 1953–1993.* Lawrence: University Kansas Press, 1994.

Kettl, Donald F. *The Regulation of American Federalism.* Baltimore: Johns Hopkins University Press, 1987.

Noonan, John T. *Narrowing the Nation's Power: The Supreme Court Sides with the States.* Berkeley: University of California Press, 2002.

Peterson, Paul E. *The Price of Federalism.* Washington, D.C.: Brookings Institution, 1995.

Smith, Rogers M. *Civic Ideals: Conflicting Visions of Citizenship in U.S. History.* New Haven: Yale University Press, 1997.

MICHAEL FOLEY AND JOHN E. OWENS

Congress and the presidency

Institutional politics in a separated system

MANCHESTER UNIVERSITY PRESS

MANCHESTER AND NEW YORK

distributed exclusively in the USA and Canada by St Martin's Press

Published by Manchester University Press
Oxford Road, Manchester M13 9NR, UK
and Room 400, 175 Fifth Avenue, New York, NY 10010, USA

Distributed exclusively in the USA and Canada
by St Martin's Press, Inc., 175 Fifth Avenue, New York,
NY 10010, USA

British Library Cataloguing-in-Publication Data
A catalogue record for this book is available from the British Library

Library of Congress Cataloging-in-Publication Data
Foley, Michael, 1948–
       Congress and the presidency: institutional politics in a
separated system / Michael Foley and John E. Owens.
          p.   cm.
       Includes index.
       ISBN 1-7190-3883-9. — ISBN 7190-3884-7 (alk. paper)
          1. Separation of powers—United States.   2. United States
Congress.   3. Presidents—United States.   4. United States—
Foreign relations.   I. Owens, John E.   II. Title.
       JK305.F64   1996
       320.473—dc20   95-21418
                                                                    CIP

ISBN   0 7190 3883 9   *hardback*
ISBN   0 7190 3884 7   *paperback*

First published 1996

00 99 98 97 96   10 9 8 7 6 5 4 3 2 1

Typeset by Carnegie Publishing, 18 Maynard Street, Preston, England
Printed in Great Britain by Redwood Books, Trowbridge

CHAPTER 2

The dynamics of institutional change in Congress

Just over a hundred years ago today, Woodrow Wilson praised the brevity of the United States Constitution. 'The fact that it attempts nothing more is its great strength', argued the future president, 'because if the Framers had gone beyond more than elementary provisions, the document's elasticity and adaptability would have been lost; and thus its ability to endure and survive.'[1] Article 1 of the Constitution granted Congress specifically enumerated powers and provided rules for electing its members and how often it should meet, but no mention was made of how the national legislature would organise itself – except that the presiding officer of the House of Representatives (the Speaker) should be elected and that the vice president (and in his absence, the president *pro tempore*) should preside over the Senate – and no mention was made of political parties or congressional committees. The Constitution's brevity allowed the Congress almost complete freedom to evolve its own organisational framework, internal rules, and behavioural norms. Brevity and silence also allowed the institution to change over time.

How and why Congress' internal organisation and status have changed over more than 200 years provides the focus for this chapter. For the Congress of the mid-1990s is very different from that envisaged in 1787; and very different from the institution which developed in the nineteenth century. Even the Congress of the 1940s or the 1970s is very different from the contemporary institution. Over more than two centuries, Congress has been transformed from an informal, non-specialised representative and legislative assembly, attempting to fulfil the republican aspirations of post-revolutionary Americans, into a complex, highly specialised, rather bureaucratic institution which acts in the late twentieth century like a complete government intervening in all policy areas and at every stage of the policy-making process. These changes were responses not only to internal congressional politics, but also to what Woodrow Wilson called 'the voices in the air which cannot be misunderstood'[2] – political, economic, and social changes which transformed the nature of problems facing constituents, and thus the public policies they were willing to support, and compelled changes in Congress' internal structure and behaviour to enable it to respond.

13

Before the constitution

Those who thought about republican government in the America of the 1770s and 1780s insisted on its representativeness, particularly that it should represent local people. When the American colonists declared independence from Britain in 1776, their major complaint was that George III's Parliament had violated a basic axiom of the 1689 Bill of Rights: that there should be no taxation without representation. As Thomas Jefferson, James Madison, and other revolutionary leaders understood it, the British system of parliamentary government established by the so-called Glorious Revolution allowed only those authorised by the people – elected representatives – to consent to taxation. Since the colonists were not permitted to elect any members of the British House of Commons three thousand miles away in Westminster, and had not authorised any to consent to taxation on their behalf, the actions of Parliament were illegitimate.

The representational imperative

When they set about creating America's first system of government under the Articles of Confederation of 1777, the leaders of the newly created United States not surprisingly drew some obvious lessons from their struggles with the undemocratic British Parliament. In the new Continental Congress, a political representative would not only be chosen by his constituents; he would also be one of them, would live among them, and in the words of John Adams 'think, feel, reason, and act like them.'[3]

Yet, it was not long before this insistence upon a locally oriented concept of representation became a major problem. Those elected as members of the Continental Congress were manifestly representatives of particular communities and states, but they were not necessarily well qualified to make laws and public policy for the new nation. Even if it was supposed that they were well qualified, would they act always in the best interests of the collectivity of American people and the new American state without losing or setting aside their local identities and their constituents' particular interests? The experiences of the Continental Congress and, even more so, the state legislatures were not comforting. If anything, these representative bodies were 'too democratic'. Their members tended to hold very parochial outlooks or were beholden to local interests which were at best partisan and at worst corrupt. By the mid-1780s, a major change in prevailing opinion had occurred. Many American leaders now saw the popular sovereignty of legislative government as the greatest threat to America's fragile democracy; as the Continental Congress acted as little more than an assembly of ambassadors of the individual states, and as representatives and the majority factions in state legislatures abused and misused powers granted them in the name of the people. Although the Articles of Confederation granted the Continental Congress important powers (but not the power to tax or legislate), almost the only way the national

14

government could act was through the states: congressional resolutions were regarded by the individual states merely as recommendations which may or may not be enforced; ratification and subsequent amendment of the Articles required the consent of all thirteen states; and members of Congress were delegates of the states paid from state funds and prohibited from serving more than three years in any six-year period. Leadership of the Continental Congress was also unstable, confused, and weak.[4] By the time the war with Britain ended in October 1781, the states had lost interest in America's now forgotten first system of government, and the Continental Congress was homeless and inert.

Congress in the new Constitution

The delegates of the individual states who met in Philadelphia in the summer of 1787 to write a new national Constitution faced the classic dilemma of democratic government: how to provide for representative government which would be responsive to the needs and demands of constituents, and yet provide government strong enough to take decisive action in promoting 'the aggregate interests of the community' while avoiding the worst excesses of 'the spirit of locality' (Madison) and 'elective despotism' (Jefferson) which had characterised representative government in the individual states.

Congress, rather than the executive, was given the primary task of resolving this dilemma. Consistent with the Whig view – that the right to govern was contingent on the people retaining the right to choose a body of people to represent them and through such a body to have a voice in the making of all laws – Madison insisted that '[i]n republican government, the legislative authority necessarily predominates'.[5] The very first sentence of the new Constitution specifically granted all legislative power to the Congress. Section 8 of Article 1 then provided Congress with formidable powers to tax, spend, and 'provide for the common defense and general welfare of the United States' – powers which affected virtually all areas of civil society. The same section also gave the national legislature substantial powers in the areas of foreign policy (to declare war, and make treaties with other countries), appointments to other branches of government (to advise and consent to presidents' nominations, and to impeach), foreign and inter-state commerce, national security (to raise and maintain armed forces), selecting the president (in case of stalemate in the electoral college, presidential disability or resignation), and proposing constitutional amendments. Members of Congress then would have a dual role in which they would be required to make laws for the collectivity of American people and the new American state, *and* represent the parochial interests of the people.

Congress' dual role was reinforced by the invention of a new national vision of popular representation which, according to Madison, should rest alongside, even above, locally oriented representation. The authority of national

15

governmental institutions would rest on a new concept of 'the American people' constituted as a separate and superior entity over and above governments and peoples of the individual states. Thus, the Constitution begins with an overtly nationalist preamble: 'We the people of the United States . . .', although 'the people' did not include most women, any native Americans, or most southern blacks. The national vision of popular sovereignty would be achieved and the excesses of locally oriented representation would be reduced through direct popular elections of the national government. All sixty-five members of the new House of Representatives would be directly elected in national elections every two years, and each legislator would represent an enormous district of about 30,000 electors apportioned to the states on the basis of their populations. It is a mute point whether such a small legislature with such large districts charged by the Constitution to originate money bills mollified the fears of ordinary electors who a few years earlier had marched under the banner 'no taxation without representation'. Following the practice of the states, the one-chamber Continental Congress was replaced by a new bicameral legislature the second chamber of which – a small Senate chosen by the state legislatures and (hopefully) composed of men with broader visions and more stable temperaments – would check the likely 'fickleness and passion' (Madison) of the directly elected House. Regardless of population size, each state would elect two senators for six-year terms, with one third of the chamber retiring every two years, thereby ensuring that the smaller states would not be constantly outvoted by their larger neighbours.

The institutional development of Congress

For any governmental organisation in a large society to be viable, for it to be able to perform the tasks it has been given – to allocate values authoritatively, make laws, resolve societal problems, settle conflicts, represent the people, and so forth – it must be institutionalised. It must develop and sustain regular and stable rules, generate normative patterns of behaviour, and establish internal structures which help the institution serve its purposes. In the case of collective institutions such as legislatures, they must develop organisational mechanisms (e.g. leadership structures, party organisations, and divisions of labour) that aggregate the actions of individual members and socialise them into the institution's internal processes, norms, and values. Applied to the United States Congress, we can say that the institution's organisational structures, rules, and norms interact with and are influenced over time by the changing needs of members and the numerous political, economic, and social forces existing within the wider society.[6] In turn, these internal arrangements and structures also influence the attitudes, expectations, and behaviour of the members, as well as the institution's collective outcomes such as legislative decisions (see Figure 2.1).

16

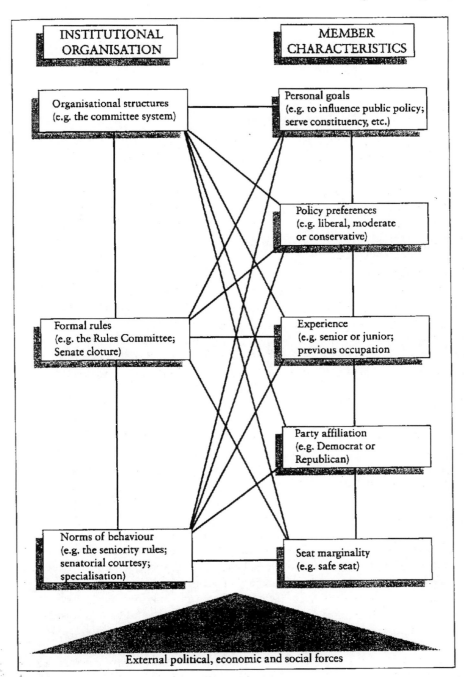

Figure 2.1 Explaining the dynamics of congressional change. *Source:* see text.

17

Four eras of institutional change

Congress' organisational history over the last two centuries may be divided into four fairly distinct institutional eras[7] – each characterised by changes in formal and informal rules, members' resources, central leadership structures and divisions of labour, and decision-making patterns; and prompted by shifting policy agendas, memberships, and varying workloads.

From the early Republic to 1860

Congress' first era – from 1787 to roughly the outbreak of the Civil War – was associated with an agrarian policy agenda and limited government. In these early days of the Republic, the Constitution and the Supreme Court ensured that state and local government performed all but a specific set of functions granted to the Congress. The federal government collected very little income and employed only a tiny percentage of the workforce. Only in times of war did decisions made in Washington impinge much on the lives of ordinary Americans who were overwhelmingly preoccupied with personal and family matters and whose society remained rural.

A Congress of amateur legislators

In an era of limited government, Congress was a leisurely, part-time legislature. House members and senators did not pursue careers in the modern sense. They attended to a small amount of undemanding constituency service and undertook less than six months' legislative work. Yet, party competition for congressional seats was intense – if only because voters and parties in many states regarded a job in Washington as too much of a good thing that ought to be shared around. When Abraham Lincoln, for example, wanted to run for re-election as a House member in 1848, he told a friend: 'If nobody else wishes to be elected, I could not refuse the people the right of sending me again.' Finding that someone else did want his job, he kept his earlier promise to serve only one term.[8] Even so, the incentives for remaining in Congress during this era were far from irresistible. Until 1800, Congress suffered an itinerant existence resident variously at Philadelphia, Princeton (where members were crammed into the college teaching room), Annapolis, Trenton, and New York (in the Federal Hall). When Congress was given a permanent home in the new capital city at Washington, it was not for another ten years that the House and Senate chambers were connected, and the quality and design of members' accommodation left much room for improvement. For many decades, the new capital was a permanent building site ridden with mosquitoes and boasting few 'respectable' white people, very little commerce, and a provincial culture.[9] Positions within Congress did not depend on length of service (seniority), so major political figures like Henry Clay and Daniel Webster drifted

18

in and out of the Congress as convenience dictated, with the result that membership of Congress was extremely unstable. The mean age of House members hovered around 43, usually more than half the membership was newly elected, and the mean term of service was just two terms (four years). In the Senate, service was more a hobby than a profession. In the space of twelve years between 1789 and 1801, as many as 94 individuals became senators, representing 32 states, and of these 33 resigned before completing their terms. Even up to the Civil War, most senators served only three to four years of their six-year terms.[10]

Either because of or in spite of the high turnover in membership, Congress did not enjoy a favourable reputation. After the entry of many western states in the early nineteenth century, the legislature developed a reputation as a vulgar, unruly, even chaotic and violent, body as James Sterling Young's splendid description shows:

> Congress at work was Hyde Park set down in the lobby of a busy hotel – hortatory outcry in milling throngs, all wearing hats as if just arrived or on the verge of departure, variously attired in the fashions of faraway places. Comings and goings were continual – to the rostrum to see the clerk, to the anterooms to meet friends, to the Speaker's chair in a sudden surge to hear the results of a vote, to the firesides for hasty caucuses and strategy-planning sessions. Some gave audiences to the speaker of the moment; some sat at their desks reading or catching up on correspondence; some stood chatting with lady friends invited on the floor; others dozed, feet propped high. Page boys weaved through the crown, 'little Mercuries' bearing messages, pitchers of water for parched throats, bundles of documents, calling out members' names, distributing mail just arrived on the stagecoach. Quills scratched, bond crackled as knuckles rapped the sand off wet ink, countless newspapers rustled. Desk drawers banged, feet shuffled in a sea of documents strewn on the floor. Bird dogs fresh from the hunt bounded in with their masters, yapping accompaniment to contenders for attention, contenders for power. Some government! 'Babeltown,' a legislator called it.[11]

The situation in the Senate was no better. During the debate on the 1850 Compromise, Senator Harry S. 'Hangman' Foote (D.MS) wielded a pistol at Missouri's Thomas Hart Benton. Only the intervention of other senators prevented bloodshed. Six years later, during the debate on the Kansas statehood bill, two South Carolina representatives entered the Senate chamber and bludgeoned Senator Charles Sumner (R.MA) as he sat at his desk.

During this first institutional era, there was really no established hierarchy among national governmental institutions. The balance of power shifted between the House and the Senate, and less often from Congress to the president (during the presidencies of Jefferson and Jackson). Within this highly fluid institutional environment, members of Congress did not develop deep loyalties to one particular

19

branch of government. Henry Clay of Kentucky, for example, entered the House at the age of 34 after having served two terms in the Senate, was elected Speaker eight months later, resigned after three years to negotiate the Treaty of Ghent on behalf of President Madison, was re-elected to the House where he was again promptly elected Speaker in 1815. He resigned in 1820, returned three years later, was again elected Speaker for another two years, and then became a senator. Even the Senate, which included the leading statesmen of the day and was the primary forum for the great anti-slavery debates before the Civil War, was 'an honorific nothing' during this era.[12]

Early institutionalisation

Spurred on by a desire to establish congressional pre-eminence in national policy-making and to affirm the new government's success,[13] Congress assumed some of the characteristics of a modern legislature right from the outset. Helped by the election of a majority of 'legislatively socialised' members like Madison who had been members of the Constitutional Convention, state legislatures, state constitutional conventions or the Continental Congress, Congress soon established a framework of formal rules and structures. The First Congress which convened in New York in 1789 successfully established procedures for developing specific policies; created a division of labour; devised mechanisms for receiving demands and producing decisions; and approved rules which guaranteed the expression of minority views and the assertion of majority rule. Thereafter, the small number of elite careerists – like Madison, Jefferson (who as vice president wrote the *Manual of Parliamentary Procedures* for the Senate), Clay, and John C. Calhoun – who wished to develop personal power bases and bolster congressional resistance to executive encroachment retained a close interest in procedural matters. Facing relatively few constituency demands, needing to spend little time in Washington, and able to participate in a genuinely deliberative body, most of the amateur politicians of the early Congresses saw little need for elaborate internal organisations and structures.

The development of standing committee systems

In the early Congresses, members were unwilling to entrust important legislative responsibilities to small subgroups of members for any significant length of time. Most House business was conducted in the Committee of the Whole, following the precedents established by the British House of Commons, colonial assemblies, and state legislatures in which many members had served. Once members agreed on general principles, a bill was then sent to a special select committee composed of specialist members who drafted legislative language. Within a few decades, however, these arrangements became unworkable. The new country's expansion westwards, the War of 1812, a larger membership (182 after 1813, 234 after 1853), and greater congressional determination to resist executive influence (especially

20

during the Washington, Jefferson, and Jackson presidencies), encouraged the House's workload to grow enormously. A more differentiated standing committee system was required which would allow legislators to focus in greater detail and on a continuing basis on such important subjects as taxation, appropriations, and inter-state commerce; and allow Congress as a governing institution to accumulate experience and expertise independent from the executive. Prompted by these pressures, the House was transformed during Clay's speakership (1811–14, 1815–21, 1823–5) from an institution which principally did its business on the floor and in select committees to one in which legislating by specialised standing committees became the norm. Between 1809 and 1825, the number of House standing committees grew from 10 to 28, and the percentage of House bills referred to standing committees grew from 47 to 93 per cent. A system of 12 standing committees was established by the Senate in 1816 with similar effects.[14]

In the ensuing decades leading up to the outbreak of the Civil War, committees were transformed from loose aggregations of *ad hoc* units appointed for specific legislative purposes into formalised systems whose members owed their appointment and advancement increasingly to party leaders and a 'sort of conditional seniority'.[15] The broader significance of this change was that independently from the president Congress embedded within its rules new divisions and specialisations of labour which significantly decentralised internal operations and gave subgroups of legislators increasingly important personal stakes in policy-making within discrete subject jurisdictions.

Weak central leadership

Having opted for internal divisions and specialisations of labour, deciding which members would be assigned to which committees became a highly charged business. In the House, the assignment of members to committees was linked inevitably with electing the Speaker whose supporters expected to receive plum committee assignments and chairs. Not surprisingly, speakership elections were often fierce and tenure of the office short (usually about three years). Although few Speakers achieved Henry Clay's stature and influence, the office was an immensely important source of power not only in the appointment of committee members and chairs but also in facilitating and guiding the development of (party) legislation, mediating parliamentary disputes, and scheduling legislation. At this time, however, the Speaker was not the majority party's floor leader in the House. This role was usually left to the chair of the Ways and Means Committee, or to assertive presidents.[16]

In the smaller more intimate Senate, centralised leadership was resisted much more strongly. The common view was expressed by Senator Daniel Webster when he declared in 1830 that the chamber was a 'Senate of equals, of men and individual honor and personal character, and of absolute independence' who knew no master and acknowledged no dictator.[17] The chair of the majority caucus performed

21

official duties at the beginning of each Congress. To the extent that effective leadership was exercised – to make committee assignments, schedule and manage important legislation on the floor, and apply party discipline – it was exercised by the chamber's intellectual leaders and leading debaters.[18]

From the Civil War to the 1910s

Congress' second institutional era – from the Civil War until the 1910s – was a period of dramatic change. As politicians opted to pursue congressional careers with much greater enthusiasm and purpose, the national legislature became fully institutionalised. Although throughout this period Congress remained a part-time legislature, meeting usually for only six months a year, its membership became professionalised, more party-dominated, and more centrally directed and its internal structure assumed more complex organisation, and new formal rules and behavioural norms.

From about 1860 until after the first decade of the new century, the United States experienced a period of remarkable economic, social, and political change. Industrialisation accelerated, inter-state commerce flourished, and the size of the country grew as more new states were admitted. The Civil War initiated the process of clarifying the Constitution's ambiguities and establishing the supremacy of the federal government. After the Civil War, the national government's economic power grew phenomenally generating in its wake powerful new democratic pressures which propelled previously unknown problems on to the national policy agenda. And, it was Congress rather than the president which responded to these new pressures and greatly enhanced its power. By the 1880s the legislature – generally under the control of the Republican Party – had become in Wilson's famous words 'the predominant and controlling force, the centre and source of all motive and of all regulative power'.[19]

The beginning of Congressional careerism

With Congress ascendant, the presidency in eclipse, federal spending more than quadrupling,[20] and the post-war reconstruction policy agenda a burgeoning responsibility, patterns of congressional recruitment changed significantly. Party leaders and citizens back home began to appreciate better the advantages of sending the same representative or senator to Washington election after election: members of Congress could perform better their representative and legislative responsibilities the longer they served, or so it was thought. Nowhere was this reasoning better appreciated than in the south after 1877 when leaders and voters saw that by returning the same (Democratic) members their states could accrue seniority more quickly and thereby greater power and influence; but other parties in regions and states dominated by one party – Republicans in the midwest and rural north-east and Democrats in urban working-class areas – also recognised

22

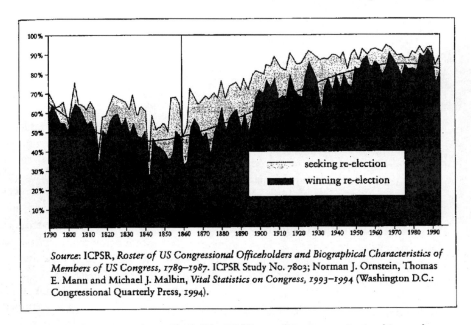

Source: ICPSR, *Roster of US Congressional Officeholders and Biographical Characteristics of Members of US Congress, 1789–1987*. ICPSR Study No. 7803; Norman J. Ornstein, Thomas E. Mann and Michael J. Malbin, *Vital Statistics on Congress, 1993–1994* (Washington D.C.: Congressional Quarterly Press, 1994).

Figure 2.2 Percentages of members of the US House of Representatives seeking and winning re-election.

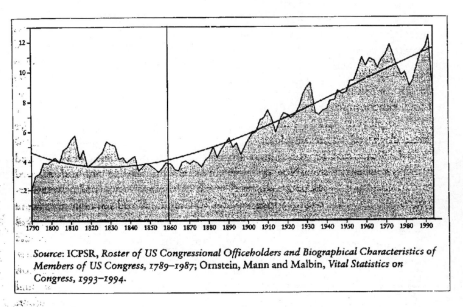

Source: ICPSR, *Roster of US Congressional Officeholders and Biographical Characteristics of Members of US Congress, 1789–1987*; Ornstein, Mann and Malbin, *Vital Statistics on Congress, 1993–1994*.

Figure 2.3 Mean years served by Members of the US House of Representatives, 1790–1994.

23

the same advantages. In consequence, the value of a congressional seat and the probability of re-election rose sharply (see Figure 2.2) and the mean length of House service increased (see Figure 2.3). So, although they still needed to be nominated by their state and district parties during this era, members increasingly opted to remain longer in Congress as life in the now magnificent capital city was much more to their liking; as the rapid expansion of Congress' workload into important areas such as the tariff, monetary policy, race, and federal patronage offered them more exciting and rewarding opportunities for power and influence; and as they came increasingly to regard their jobs in Washington as attractive full-time careers suitable for ambitious, college-educated, professionals.[21]

Nelson Polsby has observed that '[u]ntil a deliberative body has some minimum amount of work to do, the necessity for interaction among its members remains slight, and, having no purpose, coordination by means of a division of labor, rules and regulations, precedents and so on, seem unlikely to develop.'[22] The growth of congressional careerism after the Civil War stimulated legislative institutionalisation and professionalism. As career expectations soared and as a greater sense of institutional identity and loyalty developed, representatives and senators moved to adopt more complex, regular, and explicit forms of legislative organisation with clear divisions and specialisations of labour to handle better their increased numbers and workloads.

The institutionalisation of standing committees

Faced by new and complex areas of public policy and insistent that Congress rather than the president initiate policy, the new career-oriented members moved to strengthen the standing committee systems to facilitate greater subject specialisation and legislative activism. By 1913, the number of committees had risen to 61 in the House and 74 in the Senate.[23] Over this period, many committees also acquired subcommittees, were assigned more or less permanent rooms in the Capitol, employed staff (a total of 100 by 1890), and began routinely to hire full-time clerks. Greater complexity in the committees systems produced major changes in Congress' organisational structure, modes of decision-making, and internal power distribution. New divisions and specialisations of labour developed as committees and their chairs acquired much of the authority and power they enjoy today – able to act fairly independent of chambers and party control, and possessing exclusive authority to authorise, appropriate, raise revenue, and kill legislation within discrete subject jurisdictions – much to the discomfort of scholars like Wilson.[24]

Committee power was underpinned by careerism and incipient solidification of the seniority norm. As the seniority norm was strengthened congressional careerists were guaranteed automatic advancement on committees and, therefore, greater predictability in pursuing their congressional careers. Seniority became a more or less inviolable 'rule' in the Senate after 1877. In the House, it became

24

institutionalised much more gradually as formal assignment power was retained by the Speaker. By 1885, seniority was undoubtedly an important criterion for appointing the major committee chairs but there was no assumption or expectation that the chair of a committee would be reappointed to the same committee in a subsequent Congress or that members could retain their committee assignments (committee property rights) in successive Congresses.[25] Indeed, it was more likely that a member who chaired a minor committee successfully would be promoted by the Speaker to the chair of a more important one. Powerful Speakers also tended to violate seniority by naming minority as well as majority members to committees.[26]

Besides strengthening the standing committees, Congress' more career-oriented legislators also voted themselves new personal staff assistance and other resources. Individual senators were authorised to employ a single staffer (at $6 a day) in 1885; representatives were allowed to do the same in 1893 (at $100 a month). Between 1880 and 1910, House administrative spending more than doubled to $5 million, new office buildings were completed for members and their staff (in 1908 and 1909), the research facilities of the Library of Congress were expanded (1899) and augmented by a specialist Legislative Reference Service (1914), and a new Office of Legislative Counsel was created (1918) to help members draft legislation.

By the 1910s then Congress had truly discarded the part-time amateur aura of the early nineteenth century when the average member's office was under his hat and most of his time was spent on or around the House or Senate floor. Instead, the House and the Senate had adopted the trappings of a modern professional legislature which was increasingly bureaucratic with relatively small numbers of members conducting most of the floor business and the rest summoned to the floor from offices and committee rooms by electric signals.[27]

The strengthening of party leadership

Congress' second institutional era coincided with a period of party government. As the party system stabilised in the late nineteenth century around clearly defined constituency bases, producing large numbers of safe seats for each, central party leaders in the House were able to command cohesive majorities.[28] So, when legislation was especially important to the majority party House Speakers like James G. Blaine (R.ME, 1869–74), John G. Carlisle (D.KY, 1883–8), Thomas B. Reed (R.ME, 1889–90, 1895–8), and Joseph G. Cannon (D.IL, 1903–10) ignored seniority and committee property rights in their assignments and appointed favoured allies in order to assure majority party control, encourage greater policy coherence, and reduce legislative unpredictability.[29] With the House's adoption of the Reed Rules in 1890, the majority party through the Speaker (who usually chaired the Rules Committee) took a much firmer grip of the floor agenda regardless of its plurality. As a result, it was able to control the timing and content of floor bills, to prevent the minority from obstructing the majority by reducing the number for a quorum and limiting dilatory motions; and by referring all public bills to standing committees who then reported to the floor thereby allowing only nominal floor debate on amendments approved by the Rules Committee. In 1899, a separately designated position of majority floor leader was created thereby reinforcing the institutionalisation of central party leadership.

Leadership of the Senate remained as sporadic and *ad hoc* after the Civil War as before. The chair of the majority caucus remained the official leader but the position was a weak one because party unity was usually elusive. Powerful senators, who were also state party bosses – like Roscoe Conkling (R.NY), William Allison (R.IO), and Nelson Aldrich (R.RI) – exercised a sort of factionalised unofficial leadership but this was principally for organisational purposes, notably controlling committee assignments. After the mid-1880s the position of majority floor leader – the nearest equivalent to the House Speaker – became associated with the chair of the majority caucus or conference but the holder of the position was not expected to supervise and direct the majority party and often held the position only for a year. This situation changed between 1911 and 1915 as a result of Progressive insurgency when Senate Democrats merged the posts of floor leader and caucus chair to create the single office of majority leader. When Democrats won control of the presidency in 1912, they elected an ally of President Wilson, John W. Kern (D.IN), as majority leader. Kern assumed primary responsibility for directing the president's legislative programme through the Senate and assigning sympathetic committee members and chairs.[30] The introduction of new rules to expedite Senate business – such as the Anthony Rule of 1870 for speeding action on non-controversial business and the cloture rule of 1917 by which filibusters could be terminated on the vote of two-thirds of the members present – also strengthened the hand of party managers.

Emerging House–Senate differences

Notwithstanding this strengthening of party authority in both houses, organisational divergence between the House and Senate grew significantly during this era. Differences arose largely from the increasing disparity in the sizes of the two chambers and execution of their separate constitutional responsibilities. The political conflict over slavery before the Civil War had constrained the expansion of the frontier westwards. With slavery abolished, the construction of transcontinental railroads, and opening up of new markets and resources, twelve new states were admitted to the union between 1863 and 1912. As a result, the Senate grew from 72 to 96 members, while membership in the House increased from 241 to its present size of 435, reflecting a quadrupling of population. Of course, the House had always been larger than the Senate, but now the combined effects of its larger size and the requirements of party government made it imperative that the popular chamber acquire even more complex organisation, new formal rules,

26

more rigid procedures, a more elaborate committee system, and a more bureaucratic aura. The Senate meanwhile was better able retain its individualistic stately tradition with a minimum of formal rules (just 40 in 1884).

As the size and functions of the federal government grew and its proclivity for military and political intervention overseas increased, the roles of the House and the Senate in relation to one another underwent significant change. The House continued to initiate all spending and tax legislation, as the Constitution required, and became increasingly involved in tariff, monetary, and regulatory policy, but the political power and status of the Senate soared as its special constitutional responsibilities for overseeing the appointment of executive officials and for ratifying treaties became much more significant, and as the emerging mass media paid senators greater attention. By the end of the century, the Senate was successfully challenging the pre-eminence of the House; the distinctive roles of each chamber had become more clearly delineated; and bicameral policy-making had become decidedly more problematic.

From the 1910s to the early 1970s

In the wake of Progressive insurgency, the appeal of party rule as a principle of government declined after 1910. Power within Congress shifted to the decentralised and increasingly autonomous committee systems. Committee jurisdictions were formalised in House and Senate rules; seniority and committee property rights norms became entrenched (notably in the appointment of committee chairs); the number of standing committees was reduced; committee memberships became increasingly stable, expert, and distinctive; committees' legislative resources improved; and their recommendations came to be more readily accepted by colleagues on the House and Senate floors.

The revolt against central control

As membership of the House and Senate stabilised – in response to rising careerism and the fall in turnover (see Figures 2.2 and 2.3) and the probability that no new states would be admitted to the union[31] – congressional Progressives became increasingly frustrated by their respective party leaders' inability to respond to the newly emerging industrial and urban political agenda, and to accommodate their individual career ambitions.

In a dramatic series of events in the 1910s the nagging conflict between insurgent Progressives and Republican leaders of the House came to a head. The immediate cause of what became a revolt was the action taken by the autocratic Speaker 'Uncle Joe' Joseph G. Cannon (R.Il., 1903–11) to reduce the Progressives' influence. Violating fairly well established seniority and committee property rights norms, by which the chair of a committee was assigned to the majority member with the longest continuous service and which permitted members to remain on

27

committees as long as they wished, Cannon moved to punish dissident members of his party who would not submit to party discipline. Between 1907 and 1910, he removed seven incumbent committee chairs (four without giving them new committee assignments), skipped over the most senior ranking majority members to appoint favoured allies to the chairs of ten other committees, and transferred a ranking Republican member of one committee to a lowly position on another. Led by George W. Norris (R.NB) and John M. Nelson (R.WI), Republican Progressives combined with the minority Democrats in 1910 to strip Cannon of his power to appoint committee members and chairs, removed him as chair of the Rules Committee, and tripled the size of the committee by adding ten new members. When Democrats organised the House in 1911, power to assign members to committees was assumed by the party caucuses and their respective committees on committees, which in the case of House Democrats comprised Democratic members of the Ways and Means Committee.

In the Senate, a Progressive-inspired thrust also resulted in more decentralised decision-making. At the same time that Senate Democrats elected Kern as majority leader in 1913, they also gave committees greater autonomy and allowed a majority of committee members to call meetings, elect subcommittees, and appoint conferees with the House. Reinforced subsequently by the ratification of the 17th amendment to the Constitution in 1913, the effect on party government was almost immediate. President Wilson's heavy legislative programme became stalled. Over a period of a few years, the party system which had formerly linked senators downwards to a state party organisation and state legislature (which had formerly appointed them) and upwards to the party caucuses in the Senate (which ordered Senate business and dispensed jobs in the federal bureaucracy through the corrupt spoils system and senatorial courtesy) had been destroyed. Senators would henceforth build personal organisations independent of state party organisations and develop their own political records based on their own policy preferences and re-election needs. In this process, Senate party leaders lost what control they had and well disciplined party caucuses became a phenomenon of the past.[32]

The consolidation of committee government and baronial power

After the 1910s, congressional politics was transformed into committee government as power within the House and the Senate was transferred to autonomous committees which were given jurisdictions over fairly tightly defined parcels of subjects, which developed their own norms and orientations, and with which legislators' personal careers became increasingly identified and evaluated. In the previous eras, committees had conducted hearings and drafted legislation, but their activities had been controlled largely by central leaders. Now that the power of central leaders and party caucuses was curtailed, committee members – and especially chairs – moved quickly to bolster their institutional positions, establish their autonomy from central leaders (and relatively inactive party caucuses), and

28

protect themselves from the public gaze. In one of the first moves to consolidate committee power (and in anticipation of the new Budget and Accounting Act of 1921), the House moved in 1920 to reconcentrate its appropriations authority in a reconstituted Appropriations Committee with separate subcommittees exercising jurisdiction over single appropriations bills. The Senate followed in 1922. It was, however, changes in the House Rules Committee which symbolised most forcefully the new power of committees, and the problems it posed for majority rule. Under the previous conditions of centralised party government in the House established by the Reed Rules, the Speaker controlled the Rules Committee and was in a position to prevent the committee from blocking the majority party's programme. Still in full possession of its 1890 powers, the Rules Committee now enjoyed considerable autonomy under conditions of committee government, and could, if it so wished, dictate what legislation the House could approve regardless of the wishes of the majority or public opinion. In the late 1930s, majority Democrats were made painfully aware of the committee's autonomous power as conservative opposition to the New Deal grew. Conservative Democrats opposed to many New Deal programmes and the massive increase in federal and presidential power it entailed dominated this important 'gatekeeping' committee and were able to prevent a Democratic president and Democratic majorities in Congress from enacting New Deal legislation.

Committee government and chair power during this third institutional era were to a great extent founded on the seniority and committee property rights norms. In the House, these norms became almost inviolable for committee assignments in 1919;[33] much earlier, as we have explained, in the Senate. The chief beneficiaries of these norms and committee autonomy after the 1930s were conservative southern Democrats who comprised a large proportion of the party following Democratic losses in non-southern seats in the 1920s. When the Democrats took control of the House and Senate with huge majorities in 1933, it was these southerners who chaired almost all the important House committees and more than half those in the Senate – in far greater proportions than their numeric representation justified. After the 1936 elections, they used the vantage points of their committee bastions to frustrate the legislative efforts of the Roosevelt Administration and their congressional party's leaders. These confrontations signalled the emergence of an era of committee government.

In the immediate post-war period, Congress moved to consolidate committee government and reinforce the power of committee chairs or 'barons'. The Legislative Reorganisation Act of 1946 reduced the number of House standing committees from 33 to 15 and the Senate's from 48 to 19. Before 1946, major committees like the Banking and Currency Committee usually had only a clerk and a couple of stenographers even though members were expected to process legislation of huge national and international importance. Under the provisions of the 1946 Act, committees were authorised to hire up to four professional and

29

six clerical staff (except the Appropriations Committees which could appoint as many as they wished). So began a trend which by 1973 had led to House committee staff increasing more than 1,000 per cent and Senate committee staff by almost 400 per cent. With the passage of the 1946 Act and the reappearance of split-party control of Congress and the presidency in 1947 and 1953 committees entered a golden age which lasted well into the 1960s in which central party leaders were consigned to the margins directing most of their energies to brokering deals among mostly conservative committee chairs. Congressional power did not rest with Congress as a whole or in central leaders but with full standing committees and their chairs who had the power to shape legislation and deny the wishes of party majorities.

Under conditions of committee government, each committee was assigned a specific policy jurisdiction; each had the authority and the capacity to develop policy expertise independently of the executive; each had a budget to hire staff, write legislation, and conduct investigations; and each had a chair whose formal position owed nothing to his popularity, representativeness, or support from central leaders and everything to having accumulated the longest continuous period on the committee. It is no wonder, so the story goes, that when President Truman created the new Department of Defense, it was suggested that Carl Vinson (D.GA), chair of the House Armed Services Committee, would make a good Secretary of Defense. According to the story, Vinson replied: 'Shucks, I'd rather run the Pentagon from up here!'[34] In the Senate, the power of committee chairs was further enhanced by their ability to control committee assignments through the Democratic Steering Committee and by their membership of other major committees they did not chair.

Emerging problems of committee government

While committee government provided Congress as an institution with a much-needed system of specialised advice outside the tight strictures of party government, and individual members with opportunities to pursue their personal career aspirations, it posed fundamental problems for a legislature which was supposed to operate by majority rule and exercise important representative and law-making functions. First was the problem of leadership.[35] Although the Speaker in the House and the majority leader in the Senate were not exactly powerless, often they were unable to speak persuasively for their chamber and command party majorities because unlike their predecessors Reed and Cannon their party's constituency bases were divided. Even such able and prestigious leaders as Speaker Sam Rayburn (D.TX, 1940–6, 1949–52, 1955–61) and Senate majority leader Lyndon Johnson (D.TX, 1953–61) were obliged by the constraints of a divided majority party and of committee government to adopt highly personalised accommodative, brokerage leadership styles which consisted primarily of mediating conflicts between autonomous committee leaders and party factions.[36]

30

Second, there was the related problem of democratic accountability and responsibility. This was particularly acute when the Democrats were the majority. As a result of many senior non-southern Democrats losing their seats in the 1946 mid-term elections, when the Democrats regained control of Congress in 1948 it was typically southern conservatives re-elected from the one-party south who claimed committee chairs and negotiated with Democratic and Republican administrations. Because central party leaders did not have the power to discipline committee members and chairs like 'Judge' Howard Smith (D.VA), chair of the Rules Committee (1955–66) or James O. Eastland (D.MS), chair of the Senate Judiciary Committee (1956–78) – who obstructed party legislation – majority Democrats could not give those who had voted for them any reasonable assurance that campaign promises would be legislated; nor could the party be held democratically responsible for its successes and failures. Congress' democratic accountability was further weakened by the invisibility of committee activities to the American public: committee business was often conducted in secret; committees and subcommittees were numerous; and jurisdictions confusing and overlapping. By fragmenting power within Congress, committee government also made the coordination of legislative business difficult. Nowhere was this problem more apparent than in budgetary policy where three different sets of committees were involved – the relevant authorisation committees, Appropriations Committees, and the Ways and Means and Finance Committees. One consequence of the fragmented committee system was that Congress surrendered substantial responsibility for coordinating budgetary decisions to the Bureau of the Budget within the executive.[37]

What held together the fragmented committee system and perpetuated conservative power was a set of overarching norms (in the House) and folkways (in the Senate) into which new congressional recruits were socialised. New members were expected to serve a long apprenticeship; pursue their legislative responsibilities diligently; work hard on committee legislation; develop a policy specialism (especially in the House); avoid debating the broad direction of policy; maintain the prestige of their chamber; avoid self-serving acts of publicity; be courteous to seniors; and exchange favours with other members (reciprocity).[38]

From the 1970s to the present

Even as the golden age of committee government reached its apotheosis in the 1940s and 1950s, the seeds of revolt had already been sown. Congress is a representative institution as well as a law-making body. As the Progressive revolt demonstrated at the beginning of the century, representational pressures cannot long be suppressed. When Congress moved in the 1940s to streamline and modernise its committee system, it made the institution's internal structure very hierarchical. The number of members benefiting directly from committee government

31

was small, while the amount of power forfeited to committees and their chairs by rank and file members was large.

From the late 1950s on, new representational forces gained momentum, resulting in the 1970s in the most comprehensive reform of Congress' internal distribution of power since the 1910s and a much more assertive legislature. Out of this reform process emerged a new institutional era in which Congress took steps to becoming a complete government, intervening in all areas of policy (domestic and foreign), often in opposition to the president. Within Congress, power was further decentralised from full committees and their chairs to subcommittees and to individual members as the House and the Senate became much less hierarchical and more democratic, and as members came to act more for themselves rather than for their party or the president. Organisational, behavioural, and stylistic differences between the House and the Senate also narrowed as senators began increasingly to compete with their House colleagues to deliver efficient service to their increasingly attentive constituents, and the House became a fully-fledged overseer of foreign and military policy.

Membership change

The origins of the new institutional era lay in the elections of 1958 when a new generation of activist liberal northern Democrats – less willing to uphold the traditional norms of apprenticeship, restricted activism, and deference, and more determined to challenge conservative power – were elected to the 86th Congress (1959–60).[39] Immediately, they organised into the Democratic Study Group in the House, and in 1961, with a new activist Democratic administration persuaded Speaker Rayburn to reform the conservative-dominated Rules Committee. The committee was enlarged from twelve to fifteen members, allowing Rayburn to appoint two new Democrats loyal to the party's national programme. Four years later, the '21 day rule' was reintroduced to foreclose delays by the Rules Committee. The increase in liberal representation was soon reflected in the 1960s in assignments to important committees like Appropriations and even more so on authorising committees where they proceeded to initiate a basket of entitlement programmes (such as Medicare and Medicaid, and income maintenance programmes) outside the discretion of the Appropriations Committees. As congressional workloads increased (see Figure 2.4) and became more complex, and as members demanded more opportunities to demonstrate their leadership in specific policy specialisms, the number of subcommittees grew phenomenally – reaching 133 in the House and 99 in the Senate by 1967.

In the early 1970s the pace of internal congressional reform quickened. With economic stagnation deepening, a new emphasis on popular participation and environmental degradation, growing disenchantment with government and leaders (fuelled by the failures of President Johnson's Great Society, Vietnam and Watergate, and the growth of the 'imperial presidency'),[40] and the emergence of

32

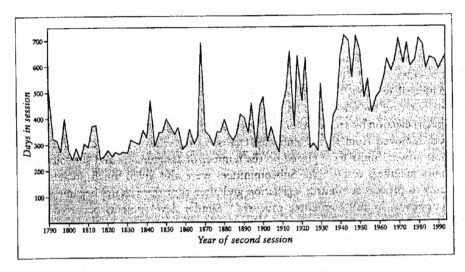

Figure 2.4 Number of days House of Representatives in session, 1789–1994.

new, more heterogeneous constituency groups, the number of members retiring voluntarily rose sharply (see the top line of Figure 2.2). In their places were elected a wave of new, younger, skilled, more ambitious and more enterprising activists schooled in the civil rights and consumer movements of the 1960s who insisted that Congress better accommodate constituents' needs, and assert its autonomy from the executive. As a result, rights and opportunities of individual committee members were enhanced, Congress' budgetary procedures were reformed, individual members' resources were further improved, the public's access to congressional deliberations was increased through electronic voting in the House and an end to secret voting in committees. Committee staffs and member resources were also expanded in the 1970s to allow members to travel more to their districts. New resource agencies such as the Congressional Budget Office and the Office of Technology Assessment were established to conduct independent policy analysis; and the budgets of the General Accounting Office and the Congressional Research Service were increased. Most significantly, as Congress' institutional capacity was expanded, Congress became more assertive in its relations with the executive – even when the president was of the same party as the majority in Congress. Symptomatic of Congress' increased assertive-ness was the passage of the War Powers Resolution in 1973, restricting the president's capacity to commit American troops abroad. In the following year, the Budget and Impoundment Control Act introduced new congressional controls over presidential budgetary decisions; and throughout the 1970s and 1980s, Congress made increasing use of the legislative veto and oversight to bring the executive to heel.

33

The challenge to committee government and chairmanship power

Besides expanding ordinary members' rights and opportunities, the reformers moved in other ways to make Congress less hierarchical, less rigid, and more democratic. After a half century of dormancy, the House Democratic Caucus was revitalised in 1969. Under new Caucus rules, seniority would no longer be the sole criterion for selecting committee chairs; in future, chairs would be subject to Caucus election by secret ballot. In 1975, as a direct result, three senior Democrats were removed from their committee chairs. In other attacks on committee and chair power, limits were placed on the number of assignments and subcommittee chairs members could hold. Subcommittees were also given much greater autonomy to process committee legislation and after 1977 their chairs became subject to approval by full committee caucuses.[41] Similar developments occurred in the Senate. In the early 1970s, secret ballots were introduced for the elections of committee chairs and in the late 1970s senators placed limits on the number of full and subcommittee chairs any one senator could hold.

Greater internal democracy/flatter authority structure

The overall effect of these changes was to flatten Congress' hierarchical power structure and limit the ability of a small number of senior members to dictate policy. Once the bastions of congressional power in the golden age, standing committees and their chairs found after the mid-1970s that their wings had been severely clipped and the seniority norm sharply devalued as they were forced to become much more beholden to their party's caucus.

In other reforms introduced in the 1970s, rank and file members demanded and received a stronger voice in the conduct of business in their chambers. House Democratic Caucus rules were revised to ensure that the preferences of party majorities prevailed. Fairly small numbers of members were permitted to call Caucus meetings. Caucus majorities were permitted to instruct majority members of the Rules Committee to grant rules allowing floor consideration of named bills; and the Speaker was authorised to ensure that Caucus opinions on particular bills were adequately represented on conference committees with the Senate. Traditional norms and folkways – apprenticeship, specialisation, reciprocity, and legislative work – which reinforced the committee and seniority systems in the previous era were undermined as much greater emphasis was placed on individualism and a new type of collegialism.

Under these new conditions, House members and senators were encouraged to participate in a much wider range of policy areas than their predecessors, to broaden their interests outside their committee assignments, to collaborate with a much wider range of colleagues, and to challenge bills reported to the floor, even by the most prestigious committees.[42] In consequence, a wider range of members in both houses were able to make their reputations and meet the demands of their constituents in a larger number of policy-making arenas – on the floor

34

of their chamber, in party committees and caucuses, in *ad hoc* groups and coalitions, in the mass media, as well as in the committee and subcommittees of which they are members. As a consequence of their increased staff and other resources, relatively junior members with good staff could acquire influence by providing their colleagues with expertise in policy areas like the budget, environment, military procurement, agriculture, and banking which became increasingly technical and even more specialised.[43] Finally, the enhancement of their official resources enabled members to adopt positions on a far wider range of issues than did their predecessors and to counter the efforts of opponents who made use of their public voting records.[44]

Strengthening central leadership structures

The curtailing of committee and chair power and the movement towards greater internal democracy served to generate important questions which had been raised at the very foundation of the Republic about Congress' capacity to represent and make laws. Fearing a legislative free-for-all, House Democrats sought to counterbalance their decentralising reforms by strengthening the powers of the Speaker and by making the holder of the office more accountable to the Democratic Caucus. In 1973, the Caucus moved to appoint the Speaker, the Majority Leader, and the Majority Whip to the Democratic Committee on Committees, thereby strengthening the party leadership's influence over committee assignments. In 1974, House Democrats created a new Democratic Steering and Policy Committee with responsibility for policy development, establishing legislative priorities, and assigning House Democrats to committees. The Speaker chaired the committee and appointed a quarter of its members. Subsequently, the Speaker was given the power to refer bills simultaneously and sequentially to several committees (multiple referral), to create *ad hoc* committees, to set time limits for committee deliberations, and to appoint and remove members of the Rules Committee. Besides increasing party control, these reforms also undercut further the power of full committees and their chairs.

As the congressional policy agenda of the 1980s and 1990s became fixated with the budget deficit, constricting opportunities for legislative individualism and policy activism, and as majority Democrats became more united ideologically, the power of central party leaders was further strengthened. In the House, Democratic Speakers 'Tip' O'Neill (D.MA, 1977–86), Jim Wright (D.TX, 1987–9), and Tom Foley (D.WA, 1989–94) exploited opportunities provided by the new congressional budget process created by the 1974, 1985, and 1990 Budget Acts to centralise budget decision-making and enhance their influence. Other unrelated legislative issues were bundled together into huge omnibus bills all or parts of which were then referred by central party leaders sequentially to one or more committees. Extensive procedural devices, such as special rules, were also used to structure members' voting choices and enhance the prospects of passage of

35

majority legislation on the floor. With Republican presidents in the White House and Democrats retaining control of Congress, O'Neill, Wright, and Foley assumed the mantle of leader of the opposition frequently appearing on television to reply to presidential messages and publicising alternative Democratic policy proposals. In 1992, Speaker Foley orchestrated removal of the chair of a House select committee. Over the same period, Senate majority leaders also increased their control of the floor timetable by restricting senators' individual privileges and by introducing weekly scheduling of business, as part of broader efforts to enhance coordination and predictability.

By 1994, then, a new consolidation and centralisation of power had occurred in the House, to a much lesser extent in the Senate. In both houses, however, congressional decision-making was much more democratic, more individualistic, and more collegial than in earlier eras. Following their resounding victories in the 1994 mid-term elections, the new House Republican majority further strengthened the power of central party leaders, albeit subject to rank and file controls and term limits.

The Republican takeover of 1994

In a bold move unprecedented since the days of Speaker Cannon, at the beginning of the 104th Congress (1995–6) the House Republican Conference – swollen by a large influx of freshmen – allowed Newt Gingrich (R.GA), the first Republican Speaker in forty years, to dictate the choice of committee chairs, in three cases passing over more senior members. House Republicans also gave Gingrich additional influence over Republican committee assignments, over the referral of bills to committees, and the administration of the House. In the style of a prime minister, Gingrich also assumed even greater responsibility than his Democratic predecessors for this party's public and media relations demanding, for example, a half-hour slot on prime-time television to address the American people. While the powers of the Speaker were further increased, the position of committees was weakened as the new Republican majority severely cut committee budgets, implemented six-year term limits for committee and subcommittee chairs, reduced committee memberships, and proposed to remove rules restrictions on floor amendments to committee bills. Three full committees and thirty-one House subcommittees were also abolished. However, even as the power of the Speaker was increased and that of committees made much more dependent on central leaders, the more open, participatory, and collegial congressional culture created in the 1970s and 1980s continues. With Gingrich's support, as many as twenty freshmen and sophomores (members with one term of service) were appointed to subcommittee chairs, and many others to prestigious committees and leadership positions. In one important area, a sharp reversal of the Democratic trend toward a more decentralised House has occurred. A number of important powers formerly held by the committee 'barons' have been reinstated. Chairs now have complete

36

control over committee budgets and subcommittee staffs, are permitted to appoint subcommittee chairs (if necessary, violating seniority), and may convene committee hearings at short notice. This will mean that at least in the short term Republican subcommittee chairs will find it much more difficult to develop autonomous fiefdoms as Democratic chairs did from the 1970s onwards. Perhaps indicative of the future should the Democrats regain control of the House was the rejection by the House Democratic Caucus in December 1994 of a move to give their leader power to select committee ranking members. While internal change in the House has been fairly dramatic, that in the more individualistic Senate has been minimal, except for substantial cuts in committee budgets.

These important changes introduced in 1994 and 1995 neatly underline a point which has always been true of Congress over the long term: that it is a

Table 2.1. Four eras of institutional change in Congress

	External Influences	Membership Characteristics	Central Leadership Organs	Divisions of Labour
ERA I – 1789–1860	Agrarian society; limited government; sectionalism; emerging party system	Amateur legislators; transient House and Senate membership; minimum resources; undemanding constituency responsibilities	Generally weak; chambers dominanted by a few elite careerists and leading debaters or occasionally by a strong president	Shift from Committee of the Whole House to standing committee systems; informal divisions and specialisations of labour
ERA II – 1860–1910s	Rapid industrialisation; pressures for increased government; sectionalism; strengthened party system; Republican domination; Progressivism	Growth of careerism; more stable membership; expanding member resources; legislative professionalisation; growing House–Senate divergences	Strong central party leadership in the House; factionalised leadership in Senate; enforcement of majority rule through formal rules	Committee systems institutionalised; growing divisions and specialisations of labour; strengthening of seniority and committee property rights
ERA III – 1910s–1970s	Advanced industrial society; mass politics; increased federal government intervention; Democratic domination after 1932	Professional career legislators; stable membership; conservative coalition; strong norms and folkways	Weak, personalised broker-style central leadership dependent on committees and presidential leadership	Institutionalisation of seniority, committee property rights and committee government; strong chairs; conservative domination
ERA IV – 1970s–now	Expansion of big government; participatory democracy; more demanding constituents; growing disenchantment with government and politicians; technocracy; mass media politics; declining party system; split-party government; deficit politics	Reform activists; individualism and collegialism; decline of traditional norms and folkways; incumbency embedded; more extensive constituency service; growing importance of expertise; increases in members' official resources	Stronger centralised leadership controls over floor and committees; greater party unity; influential party caucuses; enhanced media and party roles; centralised budgeting	Committees and chairs weakened and subjected to stronger party and floor controls; subcommittee and individual member power increased; expansion of committee resources; greater differentiation between committees

Source: see text.

37

quintessentially dynamic legislature, not only in the sense that it makes national policy, but also in the ways it responds organisationally and procedurally to the changing currents of American politics. It is not a plebiscitary conveyor of popular and transient sentiments but a deliberative body designed to filter public opinion through its internal procedures and deliver considered policy outcomes. Over this period, Congress was transformed from an unstructured representative and legislative body in the eighteenth and early nineteenth century into a highly institutionalised legislative organisation in the late twentieth century with complex structures, procedures, norms and traditions. Without ignoring crucial organisational and behavioural differences between the House and the Senate, we have placed institutional change within four eras, the chief characteristics of which are summarised in Table 2.1. The changes associated with each era have been explained as democratic responses to shifts in American politics and society over time. As the problems confronting constituents change – and therefore the policy positions and agendas that they will support – existing political alignments shift and Congress' membership changes. Over time, new members sharing common perceptions of the dominant issues of the time come to dominate the legislature. In order to promote the newly emerging policy agenda, and regardless of their partisan, ideological, and constituency differences, they find that they need to change Congress' structure and processes to make the institution respond better to their needs and the needs of those who elect them. If they succeed, a new institutional era is inaugurated.

In the next three chapters, we focus specifically on the contemporary era, to examine how Congress – America's most democratic institution – operates today. We begin by exploring the electoral connection between present-day members and their constituencies.

Notes

1 Woodrow Wilson, *Congressional Government. A Study in American Politics* (Baltimore and London: Johns Hopkins Press, 1981. Originally published 1885), p. 29.

2 *Ibid.*, p. 54.

3 Quoted in Edmund S. Morgan, *Inventing the People. The Rise of Popular Sovereignty in England and America* (New York and London: W. W. Norton, 1988), p. 241.

4 Calvin Jillson and Rick K. Wilson, *Congressional Dynamics. Structure, Coordination, and Choice in the First American Congress, 1774–1789* (Stanford, CA: Stanford University Press, 1994), esp. chapters 3–5.

5 James Madison, Alexander Hamilton, and John Jay, *The Federalist Papers* (New York and Toronto: New American Library, 1961), no. 51, p. 322.

6 James G. Marsh and Johan P. Olsen, 'The New Institutionalism: Organisational Factors in Political Life', *American Political Science Review*, 78 (1984), pp. 734–49; Nelson W. Polsby, 'The Institutionalization of the US House of Representatives', *American Political Science Review*, 62 (1968), pp. 144–68.

7 On congressional change, see Lawrence C. Dodd, 'The Cycles of Legislative Change',

38

in Herbert F. Weisberg (ed.), *Political Science: The Science of Politics* (New York: Agathon, 1986), pp. 82–104; Lawrence C. Dodd, 'A Theory of Congressional Cycles: Solving the Puzzle of Change' in Gerald C. Wright, Leroy N. Rieselbach, and Lawrence C. Dodd (eds), *Congress and Policy Change* (New York: Agathon Press, 1986), pp. 3–44.

8   Quoted in Neil MacNeil, *Forge of Democracy. The House of Representatives* (New York: David McKay, 1963), p. 124.

9   James Sterling Young, *The Washington Community, 1800–1828* (New York and London: Harcourt, Brace Jovanovich, 1966), pp. 44–5, 22–8.

10 H. Douglas Price, 'Congress and the Evolution of Legislative "Professionalism"', in Norman J. Ornstein, (ed.), *Congress in Change* (New York: Praeger, 1975), pp. 5 and 7; Nelson C. Dometrius and Lee Sigelman, 'Costs, Benefits and Careers in the US House of Representatives: A Developmental Approach', *Congress and the Presidency*, 18 (1991), pp. 55–75, 66–7; Randall B. Ripley, *Power in the Senate* (New York: St. Martin's Press, 1969), p. 43.

11 Young, *The Washington Community*, pp. 96–7. See also Alexis de Tocqueville, *Democracy in America*, vol. i (New York: Harper Collins, 1969), p. 200.

12 Price, 'Congress and the Evolution of Legislative "Professionalism"', p. 6.

13 Jack Van Der Silk, 'The Early Institutionalisation of Congress', *Congress and the Presidency*, 16 (1989), p. 2; Joel H. Silbey, '"Our Successors Will Have an Easier Task": The First Congress under the Constitution, 1789–1791', *This Constitution*, 17 (1987), p. 4; and Jillson and Wilson, *Congressional Dynamics*.

14 Gerald Gamm and Kenneth A. Shepsle, 'Emergence of Legislative Institutions: Standing Committees in the House and Senate, 1810–1825', *Legislative Studies Quarterly*, 14 (1989), p. 47; Elaine K. Swift, 'Reconstitutive Change in the US Congress: The Early Senate, 1789–1841', *Legislative Studies Quarterly*, 14 (1989), pp. 175–203; Thomas W. Skladony, 'The House Goes To Work: Select and Standing Committees in the US House of Representatives, 1789–1828', *Congress and the Presidency*, 12 (1985), pp. 165–87; Joseph Cooper, *The Origins of the Standing Committees and the Development of the Modern House* (Houston, TX: Rice University Press, 1970); and MacNeil, *Forge of Democracy*, pp. 149–50.

15 H. Douglas Price, 'Careers and Committees in the American Congress: The Problem of Structural Change', in William O. Aydelotte (ed.), *The History of Parliamentary Behavior* (Princeton, NJ: Princeton University Press, 1977), pp. 42–3.

16 Garrison Nelson, 'Leadership Position-Holding in the United States House of Representatives', *Capitol Studies*, 4 (1976), pp. 11–36; John F. Hoadley, *Origins of American Political Parties, 1789–1803*, (Lexington, KY: University Press of Kentucky, 1986), pp. 47–53; Young, *The Washington Community*, ch. 6.

17 Congressional Quarterly, *Guide to the Congress of the United States: Origins, History and Procedure* (Washington, D.C.: Congressional Quarterly, 1971), p. 83.

18 Margaret Munk, 'Origin and Development of the Party Floor Leadership in the United States Senate', *Capitol Studies*, 2 (1974), pp. 23–4; Young, *The Washington Community*, pp. 157–63.

19 Wilson, *Congressional Government*, p. 31.

20 Morris P. Fiorina, David W. Rohde, and Peter Wissel, 'Historical Change in House Turnover' in Ornstein, *Congress in Change*, p. 37.

21 Allan G. Bogue, Jerome M. Clubb, Carroll R. McKibbin, and Santa A. Traugott,

39

'Members of the House of Representatives and the Process of Modernisation, 1789–1960', *Journal of American History*, 63 (1976), pp. 275–302, p. 283.

22   Polsby, 'The Institutionalization of the US House of Representatives', p. 165.

23   George B. Galloway, *History of the House of Representatives* (New York: Thomas Crowell, 1969), p. 65.

24   Wilson, *Congressional Government*, p. 69.

25   Ripley, *Power in the Senate*, pp. 42–4; Robert W. Packwood, 'The Senate Seniority System' in Ornstein, *Congress in Change*, pp. 60–71; Nelson W. Polsby, Miriam Gallagher, and Barry R. Rundquist, 'The Growth of the Seniority System in the US House of Representatives', *American Political Science Review*, 63 (1969), table 1.

26   Lauros G. McConachie, *Congressional Committees* (New York: Thomas Crowell, 1898), pp. 159–60, 165.

27   George Rothwell Brown, *The Leadership of Congress* (Indianapolis: Bobbs-Merrill, 1922), pp. 250–1.

28   Joseph Cooper and David W. Brady, 'Institutional Context and Leadership Style: The House From Cannon to Rayburn', *American Political Science Review*, 75 (1981), p. 415.

29   James Bryce, *The American Commonwealth* (London and New York: Macmillan and Co, 1888), pp. 185–7.

30   David J. Rothman, *Politics and Power: The United States Senate 1869–1901* (Cambridge, MA: Harvard University Press, 1966), pp. 29 and 34; Munk, 'Origin and Development of the Party Floor Leadership', pp. 27–8; Joseph S. Clark, *The Senate Establishment* (New York: Hill and Wang, 1963), pp. 24–8; Ripley, *Power in the Senate*, p. 26; Congressional Quarterly, *Guide to Congress* (Washington, D.C.: Congressional Quarterly, 1982), 3rd edn, pp. 98–9.

31   In 1915, the membership of the House was frozen at 435 to avoid overcrowding.

32   Brown, *The Leadership of Congress*, pp. 195–7, 257–8, 275; Rothman, *Politics and Power*, p. 90.

33   Michael Abram and Joseph Cooper, 'The Rise of Seniority in the House of Representatives', *Polity*, 1 (1968), p. 70.

34   See Richard Bolling, *House Out Of Order* (New York: Dutton, 1965), p. 65.

35   Lawrence C. Dodd and Richard L. Schott, *Congress and the Administrative State* (New York and Chichester: Wiley, 1979), pp. 74–8.

36   Cooper and Brady, 'Institutional Context and Leadership Style', pp. 422–4; Randall B. Ripley, *Party Leaders in the House of Representatives* (Washington, D.C.: The Brookings Institution, 1967), p. 92; Rowland Evans and Robert Novak, *Lyndon B. Johnson: The Exercise of Power* (New York: New American Library, 1966); and Ralph K. Huitt, 'Democratic Party Leadership in the Senate', *American Political Science Review*, 55 (1961), pp. 333–44.

37   Allen Schick, 'The Three-Ring Budget Process: The Appropriations, Tax, and Budget Committees in Congress', in Thomas E. Mann and Norman J. Ornstein (eds), *The New Congress* (Washington, D.C.: American Enterprise Institute, 1981).

38   Donald R. Matthews, *US Senators and Their Worlds* (New York: Vintage Books, 1960); Herbert B. Asher, 'The Learning of Legislative Norms', *American Political Science Review*, 67 (1973), pp. 499–513; David W. Rohde, Norman J. Ornstein, and Robert I. Peabody, 'Political Change and Legislative Norms in the US Senate, 1957–74', in Glenn R. Parker (ed.), *Studies of Congress* (Washington, D.C.: Congressional Quarterly Press, 1985).

40

39   Michael Foley, *The New Senate. Liberal Influence on a Conservative Institution,*
     1959–1972 (New Haven and London: Yale University Press, 1980); Clark, *The Senate*
     Establishment; Lawrence C. Dodd and Bruce I. Oppenheimer, 'The House in Tran-
     sition: Change and Consolidation' and Norman J. Ornstein, Robert L. Peabody, and
     David W. Rohde, 'The Changing Senate: From the 1950s to the 1970s', both in
     Lawrence C. Dodd and Bruce I. Oppenheimer (eds), *Congress Reconsidered*, 2nd
     edn (Washington, D.C.: Congressional Quarterly Press, 1981).
40   Arthur S. Schlesinger, *The Imperial Presidency* (Boston: Houghton Mifflin, 1973).
41   See Roger H. Davidson and Walter J. Oleszek, *Congress Against Itself* (Bloomington,
     IN: Indiana University Press, 1977); Leroy N. Rieselbach, *Congressional Reform .*
     The Changing Modern Congress (Washington, D.C.: Congressional Quarterly Press,
     1994); Dodd and Oppenheimer, 'The House in Transition'; Ornstein, Peabody, and
     Rohde, 'The Changing Senate'; James L. Sundquist, *The Decline and Resurgence of*
     Congress (Washington, D.C.: The Brookings Institution, 1981).
42   Steven S. Smith, *Call To Order. Floor Politics in the House and Senate* (Washington,
     D.C.: The Brookings Institution, 1989); Steven S. Smith, 'New Patterns of Decision-
     making in Congress' in John E. Chubb and Paul E. Peterson (eds), *The New Direction*
     in American Politics (Washington, D.C.: The Brookings Institution, 1989); Burdett
     A. Loomis, 'The "Me Decade" and the Changing Context of House Leadership" in
     Frank H. Mackaman (ed.), *Understanding Congressional Leadership* (Washington,
     D.C.: Congressional Quarterly Press, 1981), pp. 157–79; cf. Edward V. Schneier,
     'Norms and Folkways in Congress: How Much Has Actually Changed?' *Congress*
     and the Presidency, 15 (1988): 117–38
43   Lawrence C. Dodd, 'The Rise of the Technocratic Congress: Congressional Reform
     in the 1970s' in Richard A. Harris and Sidney M. Milkis (eds), *Remaking American*
     Politics (Boulder and London: Westview, 1989).
44   Burdett A. Loomis, *The New American Politician: Ambition, Entrepreneurship, and*
     the Changing Face of Political Life (New York: Basic Books, 1988); Charles S. Bullock
     and Burdett A. Loomis, 'The Changing Congressional Career', in Lawrence C. Dodd
     and Bruce I. Oppenheimer (eds), *Congress Reconsidered*, 3rd edn (Washington, D.C.:
     Congressional Quarterly Press, 1985); and Herbert A. Asher, 'The Changing Status
     of the Freshman Congressman', in Ornstein, *Congress in Change.*

41

GOVERNMENT IN AMERICA

PEOPLE, POLITICS, AND POLICY

FOURTEENTH EDITION

GEORGE C. EDWARDS III

Texas A & M University

MARTIN P. WATTENBERG

University of California, Irvine

ROBERT L. LINEBERRY

University of Houston

Longman

New York   Boston   San Francisco
London   Toronto   Sydney   Tokyo   Singapore   Madrid
Mexico City   Munich   Paris   Cape Town   Hong Kong   Montreal

Editor-in-Chief: Eric Stano
Assistant Development Manager: David B. Kear
Development Editor: Terri Wise
Marketing Manager: Lindsey Prudhomme
Assistant Development Editor: Donna Garnier
Media Supplements Editor: Regina Vertiz
Production Manager: Denise Phillip
Project Coordination, Text Design, and Electronic Page Makeup: Pre-PressPMG
Cover Design Manager: John Callahan
Cover Designer: Maria Ilardi
Cover Images: Ron Sanford/Corbis and Stockbyte/Getty Images
Photo Researcher: Julie Tesser
Senior Manufacturing Buyer: Roy Pickering
Printer and Binder: Worldcolor/Dubuque
Cover Printer: Phoenix Color Corporation

For permission to use copyrighted material, grateful acknowledgment is made to the copyright holders on pp. 776-778, which are hereby made part of this copyright page.

Library of Congress Cataloging-in-Publication Data

Edwards, George C.
    Government in America : people, politics, and policy/George C. Edwards, Martin P.
    Wattenberg, Robert L. Lineberry. — 14th ed.
        p. cm.
    Includes bibliographical references and index.
    ISBN-13: 978-0-205-66289-0
    ISBN-10: 0-205-66289-7
    1. United States—Politics and government—Textbooks.   I. Wattenberg, Martin P.,
1956-   II. Lineberry, Robert L.   III. Title.
    JK276.E39 2008e
    320.473—dc22

Copyright © 2009 by Pearson Education, Inc.

Longman
is an imprint of

www.pearsonhighered.com

5 6 7 8 9 10—WCD—11 10

ISBN-13: 978-0-205-66289-0
ISBN-10:   0-205-66289-7

congressional agenda and guide legislation from its introduction to its send-off to the president for his signature. We can group committees into four types, the first of which is by far the most important.

1. **Standing committees** handle bills in different policy areas (see Table 12.3). Each house of Congress has its own standing committees; members do not belong to a committee in the other house. In the 110th Congress, the typical representative served on two committees and four subcommittees; senators averaged three committees and seven subcommittees each. Subcommittees are smaller units of a committee created out of the committee membership.
2. **Joint committees** exist in a few policy areas, such as the economy and taxation, and draw their membership from both the Senate and the House.
3. **Conference committees** are formed when the Senate and the House pass different versions of the same bill (which they typically do). Appointed by the party leadership, a conference committee consists of members of each house chosen to iron out Senate and House differences and to report back a compromise bill.
4. **Select committees** may be temporary or permanent and usually have a focused responsibility. The House and Senate each have a select committee on intelligence, for example.

standing committees
Separate subject-matter committees in each house of Congress that handle bills in different policy areas.

joint committees
Congressional committees on a few subject-matter areas with membership drawn from both houses.

conference committees
Congressional committees formed when the Senate and the House pass a particular bill in different forms. Party leadership appoints members from each house to iron out the differences and bring back a single bill.

select committees
Congressional committees appointed for a specific purpose, such as the Watergate investigation.

TABLE 12.3

Standing Committees in the Senate and in the House

SENATE COMMITTEES	HOUSE COMMITTEES
Agriculture, Nutrition, and Forestry	Agriculture
Appropriations	Appropriations
Armed Services	Armed Services
Banking, Housing, and Urban Affairs	Budget
Budget	Education and Labor
Commerce, Science, and Transportation	Energy and Commerce
Energy and Natural Resources	Financial Services
Environment and Public Works	Foreign Affairs
Finance	Homeland Security
Foreign Relations	House Administration
Health, Education, Labor, and Pensions	Judiciary
Homeland Security and Governmental Affairs	Natural Resources
Judiciary	Oversight and Government Reform
Rules and Administration	Rules
Small Business and Entrepreneurship	Science and Technology
Veterans' Affairs	Small Business
	Standards of Official Conduct
	Transportation and Infrastructure
	Veterans' Affairs
	Ways and Means

YOU ARE THE **Policymaker**

The Debate over Original Intentions

The most contentious issue involving the courts is the role of judicial discretion. According to Christopher Wolfe, "The Constitution itself nowhere specifies a particular set of rules by which it is to be interpreted. Where does one go, then, in order to discover the proper way to interpret the Constitution?"

Some have argued for a jurisprudence of **original intent** (sometimes referred to as *strict constructionism*). This view holds that judges and justices should attempt to determine the intent of the Framers of the Constitution regarding a particular matter and decide cases in line with that intent. Such a view is popular with conservatives.

Advocates of strict constructionism view it as a means of constraining the exercise of judicial discretion, which they see as the foundation of the liberal decisions, especially on matters of civil liberties, civil rights, and defendants' rights (discussed in Chapters 4 and 5).

They also see following original intent as the only basis of interpretation consistent with democracy. Judges, they argue, should not dress up constitutional interpretations with *their* views on "contemporary needs," "today's conditions," or "what is right." It is the job of legislators, not judges, to make such judgments.

Other jurists, such as former Justice William Brennan, disagree. They maintain that what appears to be deference to the intentions of the Framers is simply a cover for making conservative decisions. Opponents of original intent assert that the Constitution is subject to multiple meanings by thoughtful people in different ages. Judges will differ in time and place about what they think the Constitution means. Thus, basing decisions on original intent is not likely to have much effect on judicial discretion.

In addition, Brennan and his supporters contend that the Constitution is not like a paint-by-numbers kit. Trying to reconstruct or guess the Framers' intentions is very difficult. Recent key cases before the Supreme Court have concerned issues such as school busing, abortions, the Internet, and wiretapping that the Framers could not have imagined; there were no public schools or buses, no contraceptives or modern abortion techniques, and certainly no computers or electronic surveillance equipment or telephones in 1787.

The Founders embraced general principles, not specific solutions when they wrote the Constitution. They frequently lacked discrete, discoverable intent. Moreover, there is often no record of their intentions, nor is it clear whose intentions should count—those of the writers of the Constitution, those of the more than 1,600 members who attended the ratifying conventions, or those of the voters who sent them there. This problem grows more complex when you consider the amendments to the Constitution, which involve thousands of additional "Framers."

Historian Jack N. Rakove points out that there is little historical evidence that the Framers believed their intentions should guide later interpretations of the Constitution. In fact, there is some evidence for believing that Madison—the key delegate—left the Constitutional Convention bitterly disappointed with the results. What if Madison had one set of intentions but—like anyone working in a committee—got a different set of results?

The lines are drawn. On one side is the argument that any deviation from following the original intentions of the Constitution's Framers is a deviation from principle, leaving unelected judges to impose their views on the American people. If judges do not follow original intentions, then on what do they base their decisions?

On the other side are those who believe that it is often impossible to discern the views of the Framers and that there is no good reason to be constrained by the views of the eighteenth century, which reflect a more limited conception of constitutional rights. In order to cope with current needs, they argue, it is necessary to adapt the principles in the Constitution to the demands of each era.

The choice here is at the very heart of the judicial process. If you were a justice sitting on the Supreme Court and were asked to interpret the meaning of the Constitution, what would *you* do?

Sources: Christopher Wolfe, *The Rise of Modern Judicial Review* (New York: Basic Books, 1986); Raoul Berger, *Government by Judiciary: The Transformation of the Fourteenth Amendment* (Cambridge, MA: Harvard University Press, 1977); Traciel V. Reid, "A Critique of Interpretivism and Its Claimed Influence upon Judicial Decision Making," *American Politics Quarterly* 16 (July 1988): 329–56; Jack N. Rakove, ed., *Interpreting the Constitution* (Boston: Northeastern University Press, 1990); Arthur S. Miller, "In Defense of Judicial Activism," in *Supreme Court Activism and Restraint*, ed. Stephen C. Halpern and Charles M. Lamb (Lexington, MA: D.C. Heath, 1982); Stephen Breyer, *Active Liberty: Interpreting Our Democratic Constitution* (New York: Knopf, 2005); Antonin Scalia, *A Matter of Interpretation: Federal Courts and the Law* (Princeton, NJ: Princeton University Press, 1998).

original intent
A view that the Constitution should be interpreted according to the original intent of the Framers. Many conservatives support this view.

1984 the Reagan administration went before the Supreme Court and argued *against* school busing in a case in Norfolk, Virginia.

THE COURTS AND THE POLICY AGENDA

Even though American courts and judges work largely alone and in isolation from daily contact with other political institutions, they play a key role in shaping the policy agenda. Ultimately, their decisions affect us all (see "Young People and Politics: The Supreme Court Is Closer Than You Think"). Like all policymakers, the courts are choice takers. Confronted with controversial policies, they make controversial decisions that leave some people winners and others losers. The courts have made policy about slavery and segregation, corporate power and capital punishment, and dozens of other controversial matters.

A HISTORICAL REVIEW

Until the Civil War, the dominant questions before the Court concerned the strength and legitimacy of the federal government and slavery. These issues of nation building were resolved in favor of the supremacy of the national government. From the Civil War until 1937, questions of the relationship between the federal

YOUNG PEOPLE AND POLITICS

The Supreme Court Is Closer Than You Think

The Supreme Court of the United States may seem remote and not especially relevant to a college student. Yet a surprising number of its most important decisions have been brought by young adults seeking protection for their civil rights and liberties. For example, we saw in Chapter 5 that in *Rostker v. Goldberg* (1981) several young men filed a suit claiming that the Military Selective Service Act's requirement that only males register for the draft was unconstitutional. Although the Court held that the requirement was constitutional, draft registration was suspended temporarily during the suit.

Students were the center of *Board of Regents of University of Wisconsin System v. Southworth* (2000), in which the Court upheld the University of Wisconsin's requirement of a fee to fund speakers on campus—even if the speakers advocated views that offended some students. The right of the police to search newspaper files was fought over the actions of a campus newspaper in *Zurcher v. Stanford Daily* (1978). In 1992, the Supreme Court ruled that legislatures and universities may not single out racial, religious, or sexual insults or threats for prosecution as "hate speech" or "bias crimes" (*R.A.V. v. St. Paul*). From Gregory Johnson's burning an American flag at the 1984 Republican National Convention to protest nuclear arms buildup (which the Court protected in *Texas v. Johnson* [1989]) to burning a draft card (which the Court did not protect in *United States v. O'Brien*

[1968]), young adults have also been pioneers in the area of symbolic speech.

Issues of religious freedom have also prominently featured college students. In *Widmar v. Vincent* (1981), the Court decided that public universities that permit student groups to use their facilities must allow student religious groups on campus to use the facilities for religious worship. In 1995, the Court held that the University of Virginia was constitutionally required to subsidize a student religious magazine on the same basis as other student publications (*Rosenberger v. University of Virginia*). However, in 2004 the Court held that the state of Washington was within its rights when it excluded students pursuing a devotional theology degree from its general scholarship program (*Locke v. Davey*).

Thus, the Supreme Court has a long history of dealing with issues of importance to young adults. Often it is young adults themselves who initiate the cases—and who take them all the way to the nation's highest court.

QUESTIONS FOR DISCUSSION

1. Why do you think cases involving young people tend to involve civil liberties issues?

2. What other issues of particular importance to young people should the Supreme Court decide?

John Marshall, chief justice from 1801 to 1835, established the Supreme Court's power of judicial review in the 1803 case *Marbury v. Madison*. In their ruling on the case, Marshall and his associates declared that the Court has the power to determine the constitutionality of congressional actions.

TIMELINE

Chief Justices of the
Supreme Court

Marbury v. Madison
The 1803 case in which Chief Justice John Marshall and his associates first asserted the right of the Supreme Court to determine the meaning of the U.S. Constitution. The decision established the Court's power of judicial review over acts of Congress, in this case the Judiciary Act of 1789.

government and the economy predominated. During this period, the Court restricted the power of the federal government to regulate the economy. From 1938 to the present, the paramount issues before the Court have concerned personal liberty and social and political equality. In this era, the Court has enlarged the scope of personal freedom and civil rights and has removed many of the constitutional restraints on the regulation of the economy.

Few justices played a more important role in making the Court a significant national agenda setter than John Marshall, chief justice from 1801 to 1835. His successors have continued not only to respond to the political agenda but also to shape discussion and debate about it.

John Marshall and the Growth of Judicial Review

Scarcely was the government housed in its new capital when Federalists and Democratic-Republicans clashed over the courts. In the election of 1800, Democratic-Republican Thomas Jefferson beat Federalist incumbent John Adams. Determined to leave at least the judiciary in trusted hands, Adams tried to fill it with Federalists. He is alleged to have stayed at his desk until 9:00 P.M. signing commissions on his last night in the White House (March 3, 1801).

In the midst of this flurry, Adams appointed William Marbury to the minor post of justice of the peace in the District of Columbia. In the rush of last-minute business, however, Secretary of State John Marshall failed to deliver commissions to Marbury and 16 others. He left the commissions to be delivered by the incoming secretary of state, James Madison.

Madison and Jefferson were furious at Adams's actions and refused to deliver the commissions. Marbury and three others in the same situation sued Madison, asking the Supreme Court to order Madison to give them their commissions. They took their case directly to the Supreme Court under the Judiciary Act of 1789, which gave the Court original jurisdiction in such matters.

The new chief justice was none other than Adams's former secretary of state and arch-Federalist John Marshall, himself one of the "midnight appointments" (he took his seat on the Court barely three weeks before Adams's term ended). Marshall and his Federalist colleagues were in a tight spot. Threats of impeachment came from Jeffersonians fearful that the Court would vote for Marbury. Moreover, if the Court ordered Madison to deliver the commissions, he was likely to ignore the order, putting the nation's highest court at risk over a minor issue. Marshall had no means of compelling Madison to act.

The Court could also deny Marbury's claim. Taking that option, however, would concede the issue to the Jeffersonians and give the appearance of retreat in the face of opposition, thereby reducing the power of the Court.

Marshall devised a shrewd solution to the case of **Marbury v. Madison**. In February 1803, he delivered the unanimous opinion of the Court. First, Marshall and his colleagues argued that Madison was wrong to withhold Marbury's commission. The Court also found, however, that the Judiciary Act of 1789, under which Marbury had brought suit, contradicted the plain words of the Constitution about the Court's original jurisdiction. Thus, Marshall dismissed Marbury's claim, saying that the Court, according to the Constitution, had no power to require that the commission be delivered.

Conceding a small battle over Marbury's commission (he did not get it), Marshall won a much larger war, asserting for the courts the power to determine what is and what is not constitutional. As Marshall wrote, "An act of the legislature repugnant to the Constitution is void," and "it is emphatically the province and duty of the judicial department to say what the law is." The chief justice established the power of **judicial review**, the power of the courts to hold acts of Congress and, by implication, the executive in violation of the Constitution.

Marbury v. Madison was part of a skirmish between the Federalists on the Court and the Democratic-Republican–controlled Congress. Partly to rein in the Supreme Court, for example, the Jeffersonian Congress in 1801 abolished the lower federal appeals courts and made the Supreme Court judges return to the unpleasant task of "riding circuit"—serving as lower-court judges around the country. This was an act of studied harassment of the Court by its enemies.

After *Marbury*, angry members of Congress, together with other Jeffersonians, claimed that Marshall was a "usurper of power," setting himself above Congress and the president. This view, however, was unfair. State courts, before and after the Constitution, had declared acts of their legislatures unconstitutional. In the *Federalist Papers*, Alexander Hamilton had expressly assumed the power of the federal courts to review legislation, and the federal courts had actually done so. *Marbury* was not even the first case to strike down an act of Congress; a lower federal court had done so in 1792, and the Supreme Court itself had approved a law after a constitutional review in 1796. Marshall was neither inventing nor imagining his right to review laws for their constitutionality.

The case also illustrates that the courts must be politically astute in exercising their power over the other branches. By in effect reducing its *own* power—the authority to hear cases such as Marbury's under its original jurisdiction—the Court was able to assert the right of judicial review in a fashion that the other branches could not easily rebuke.

More than any other power of the courts, judicial review has embroiled them in policy controversy. Before the Civil War, the Supreme Court, headed by Chief Justice Roger Taney, held the Missouri Compromise unconstitutional because it restricted slavery in the territories. The decision was one of many steps along the road to the Civil War. After the Civil War, the Court was again active, this time using judicial review to strike down dozens of state and federal laws curbing the growing might of business corporations.

The "Nine Old Men"   Never was the Court so controversial as during the New Deal. At President Roosevelt's urging, Congress passed dozens of laws designed to end the Depression. However, conservatives (most nominated by Republican presidents), who viewed federal intervention in the economy as unconstitutional and tantamount to socialism, dominated the Court.

The Supreme Court began to dismantle New Deal policies one by one. The National Industrial Recovery Act was one of a string of anti-Depression measures. Although it was never particularly popular, the Court sealed its doom in *Schechter Poultry Corporation v. United States* (1935), declaring the act unconstitutional because it regulated purely local business that did not affect interstate commerce.

Incensed, Roosevelt in 1937 proposed what critics called a "court-packing plan." Noting that the average age of the Court was over 70, Roosevelt railed against those "nine old men." The Constitution gave the justices lifetime jobs (see "America in Perspective: The Tenure of Supreme Court Judges"), but

judicial review
The power of the courts to determine whether acts of Congress and, by implication, the executive are in accord with the U.S. Constitution. Judicial review was established by John Marshall and his associates in *Marbury v. Madison*.

AMERICA IN PERSPECTIVE

The Tenure of Supreme Court Judges

The U.S. Supreme Court plays a crucial role in American government, and federal judges, including Supreme Court justices, have tenure for life. As a result, the average age of U.S. justices is high, and there are typically many justices who are over 75 years old. Life tenure also means that there are fewer changes of justices than there would be in a system with shorter terms.

Interestingly, *every* other established democracy provides for some limits on the tenure of judges on its highest constitutional court. Here are some examples:

Country	Term for Judges on Highest Constitutional Court
France	9-year non-renewable term
Italy	9-year non-renewable term
Portugal	9-year non-renewable term
Spain	9-year non-renewable term
Germany	12-year term, must retire at 68
Japan	10-year term, must retire at 70; voters vote to renew justices every 10 years
India	serve under good behavior up to age 65
Australia	serve under good behavior up to age 70
Canada	serve under good behavior up to age 75

DISCUSSION QUESTIONS:

▶ If a constitutional convention were reconvened today, would we still opt for life tenure?

▶ Do you agree with Alexander Hamilton's argument in Federalist #78 that life tenure was an excellent means of securing "a steady, upright, and impartial administration of the laws"?

Source: Steven G. Calabresi and James Lindgren, "Term Limits for the Supreme Court: Life Tenure Reconsidered," *Harvard Journal of Law and Public Policy* 29 (Summer 2006), pp. 819–822.

Congress can determine the number of justices. Thus, FDR proposed that Congress expand the size of the Court, a move that would have allowed him to appoint additional justices sympathetic to the New Deal. Congress objected and never passed the plan. It became irrelevant, however, when two justices, Chief Justice Charles Evans Hughes and Associate Justice Owen Roberts, began switching their votes in favor of New Deal legislation. (One wit called it the "switch in time that saved nine.") Shortly thereafter, Associate Justice William Van Devanter retired, and Roosevelt got to make the first of his many appointments to the Court.

The Warren Court Few eras of the Supreme Court have been as active in shaping public policy as that of the Warren Court (1953–1969), presided over by Chief Justice Earl Warren. Scarcely had President Eisenhower appointed Warren when the Court faced the issue of school segregation. In 1954, it held that laws requiring segregation of the public schools were unconstitutional. Later it expanded the rights of criminal defendants, extending the right to counsel and protections against unreasonable search and seizure and self-incrimination (see Chapter 4). It ordered states to reapportion both their legislatures and their congressional districts according to the principle of one person, one vote, and it prohibited organized prayer in public schools. So active was the Warren Court that right-wing groups, fearing that it was remaking the country, posted billboards all over the United States urging Congress to "Impeach Earl Warren."[33]

The Burger Court Warren's retirement in 1969 gave President Richard Nixon his hoped-for opportunity to appoint a "strict constructionist"—that is, one who interprets the Constitution narrowly—as chief justice. He chose Minnesotan Warren E. Burger, then a conservative judge on the District of Columbia Court of Appeals. As Nixon hoped, the Burger Court turned out to be more conservative than the liberal Warren Court. It narrowed defendants' rights, though it did not overturn the fundamental contours of the *Miranda* decision. The conservative Burger Court, however, also wrote the abortion decision in *Roe v. Wade*, required school busing in certain cases to eliminate historic segregation, and upheld affirmative action programs in the *Weber* case (see Chapter 5). One of the most notable decisions of the Burger Court weighed against Burger's appointer, Richard Nixon. At the height of the Watergate scandal (see Chapter 13), the Supreme Court was called on to decide whether Nixon had to turn his White House tapes over to the courts. It unanimously ordered him to do so in *United States v. Nixon* (1974), thus hastening the president's resignation.

United States v. Nixon
The 1974 case in which the Supreme Court unanimously held that the doctrine of executive privilege was implicit in the Constitution but could not be extended to protect documents relevant to criminal prosecutions.

The Rehnquist Court By the late 1990s, the conservative nominees of Republican presidents, led by Chief Justice William Rehnquist, composed a clear Supreme Court majority. Like the Burger Court, it was conservative, and like both the Warren and the Burger Courts, it was neither deferential to Congress nor reluctant to enter the political fray. The Court's decision in *Bush v. Gore* (2000) that decided the 2000 presidential election certainly represents a high point of judicial activism.

However one evaluates the Court's direction, in most cases the Rehnquist Court did not create a revolution in constitutional law. Instead, as discussed in Chapters 4 and 5, it limited rather than reversed rights established by liberal decisions such as those regarding defendants' rights and abortion. Although its protection of the First Amendment rights of free speech and free press remained robust, the Court no longer saw itself as the special protector of individual liberties and civil rights for minorities. In the area of federalism, however, the Court blazed new paths in constraining the federal government's power over the states, as we saw in Chapter 3.

The Supreme Court frequently makes controversial decisions regarding important matters of politics and public policy. Critics often argue that unelected judges are making policy decisions that should be made by elected officials. Here, demonstrators express their opinions about the Supreme Court's abortion decisions.

UNDERSTANDING THE COURTS

Powerful courts are unusual; few nations have them. The power of American judges raises questions about the compatibility of unelected courts with a democracy and about the appropriate role for the judiciary in policymaking.

THE COURTS AND DEMOCRACY

Announcing his retirement in 1981, Justice Potter Stewart made a few remarks to the handful of reporters present. Embedded in his brief statement was this observation: "It seems to me that there's nothing more antithetical to the idea of what a good judge should be than to think it has something to do with representative democracy." He meant that judges should not be subject to the whims of popular majorities. In a nation that insists so strongly that it is democratic, where do the courts fit in?

In some ways, the courts are not a very democratic institution. Federal judges are not elected and are almost impossible to remove. Indeed, their social backgrounds probably make the courts the most elite-dominated policymaking institution. If democracy requires that key policymakers always be elected or be continually responsible to those who are, then the courts diverge sharply from the requirements of democratic government.

As you saw in Chapter 2, the Constitution's framers wanted it that way. Chief Justice Rehnquist, a judicial conservative, put the case as follows: "A mere change in public opinion since the adoption of the Constitution, unaccompanied by a constitutional amendment, should not change the meaning of the Constitution. A merely temporary majoritarian groundswell should not abrogate some individual liberty protected by the Constitution."[34]

The courts are not entirely independent of popular preferences, however. Turn-of-the-century Chicago humorist Finley Peter Dunne had his Irish saloonkeeper character "Mr. Dooley" quip that "th' Supreme Court follows th' iliction returns." Many years later, political scientists have found that the Court usually reflects popular majorities.[35] Even when the Court seems out of step with other policymakers, it eventually swings around to join the policy consensus,[36] as it did in the New Deal. A study of the period from 1937 to 1980 found that the Court was clearly out of line with public opinion only on the issue of prayers in public schools.[37]

Interest groups often use the judicial system to pursue their policy goals, forcing the courts to rule on important social issues. Some Hispanic parents, for example, have successfully sued local school districts to compel them to offer bilingual education.

Despite the fact that the Supreme Court sits in a "marble palace," it is not as insulated from the normal forms of politics as one might think. The two sides in the abortion debate flooded the Court with mail, targeted it with advertisements and protests, and bombarded it with 78 *amicus curiae* briefs in the *Webster v. Reproductive Health Services* (1989) case. Members of the Supreme Court are unlikely to cave in to interest group pressures, but they are aware of the public's concern about issues, and this awareness becomes part of their consciousness as they decide cases. Political scientists have found that the Court is more likely to hear cases for which interest groups have filed *amicus curiae* briefs.[38]

Courts can also promote pluralism. When groups go to court, they use litigation to achieve their policy objectives.[39] Both civil rights groups and environmentalists, for example, have blazed a path to show how interest groups can effectively use the courts to achieve their policy goals. Thurgood Marshall, the legal wizard of the NAACP's litigation strategy, not only won most of his cases but also won for himself a seat on the Supreme Court. Almost every major policy decision these days ends up in court. Chances are good that some judge can be found who will rule in an interest group's favor. On the other hand, agencies and businesses commonly find themselves ordered by different courts to do opposite things. The habit of always turning to the courts as a last resort can add to policy delay, deadlock, and inconsistency.

WHAT COURTS SHOULD DO: THE SCOPE OF JUDICIAL POWER

The courts, Alexander Hamilton wrote in *The Federalist Papers*, "will be least in capacity to annoy or injure" the people and their liberties.[40] Throughout American history, critics of judicial power have disagreed. They see the courts as too powerful for their own—or the nation's—good. Yesterday's critics focused on John Marshall's "usurpations" of power, on the proslavery decision in *Dred Scott*, or on the efforts of the "nine old men" to kill off Franklin D. Roosevelt's New Deal legislation. Today's critics are never short of arguments to show that courts go too far in making policy.[41]

Courts make policy on both large and small issues. In the past few decades, courts have made policies on major issues involving school busing, abortion, affirmative action, nuclear power, legislative redistricting, bilingual education, prison conditions, counting votes in the 2000 presidential election, and many other key issues.[42]

There are strong disagreements about the appropriateness of allowing the courts to have a policymaking role. Many scholars and judges favor a policy of **judicial restraint**, in which judges adhere closely to precedent and play minimal policymaking roles, leaving policy decisions strictly to the legislatures. These observers stress that the federal courts, composed of unelected judges, are the least democratic branch of government and question the qualifications of judges for making policy decisions and balancing interests. Advocates of judicial restraint believe that decisions such as those on abortion and prayer in public schools go well beyond the "referee" role they say is appropriate for courts in a democracy.

On the other side are proponents of **judicial activism**, in which judges make bolder policy decisions, even charting new constitutional ground with a particular decision. Advocates of judicial activism emphasize that the courts may alleviate pressing needs—especially needs of those who are politically or economically weak—left unmet by the majoritarian political process.

It is important not to confuse judicial activism or restraint with liberalism or conservatism. In Table 16.5, you can see the varying levels of the Supreme Court's use of judicial review to void laws passed by Congress in different eras. In the early years of the New Deal, judicial activists were conservatives. During the tenure of Earl Warren as chief justice (1953–1969), activists made liberal decisions. The Courts under Chief Justices Warren Burger (1969–1986) and William Rehnquist (1986–2005), composed of mostly conservative nominees of Republican presidents, marked the most active use of judicial review in the nation's history. In the latter period, conservative justices were the most likely to vote to void congressional legislation.[43]

The problem remains of reconciling the American democratic heritage with an active policymaking role for the judiciary. The federal courts have developed a doctrine of **political questions** as a means to avoid deciding some cases, principally those that involve conflicts between the president and Congress. The courts have shown no willingness, for example, to settle disputes regarding the War Powers Resolution (see Chapter 13).

Similarly, judges typically attempt, whenever possible, to avoid deciding a case on the basis of the Constitution, preferring less contentious "technical" grounds. They also employ issues of jurisdiction, mootness (whether a case presents a real controversy in which a judicial decision can have a practical effect), standing, ripeness (whether the issues of a case are clear enough and evolved enough to serve as the basis of a decision), and other conditions to avoid adjudication of some politically charged cases. The Supreme Court refused to decide, for example, whether it was legal to carry out the war in Vietnam without an explicit declaration of war from Congress.

Comparing Judiciaries

judicial restraint
A judicial philosophy in which judges play minimal policymaking roles, leaving that duty strictly to the legislatures.

judicial activism
A judicial philosophy in which judges make bold policy decisions, even charting new constitutional ground. Advocates of this approach emphasize that the courts can correct pressing needs, especially those unmet by the majoritarian political process.

political questions
A doctrine developed by the federal courts and used as a means to avoid deciding some cases, principally those involving conflicts between the president and Congress.

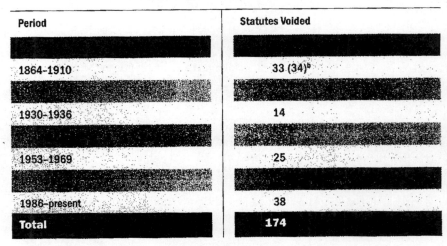

TABLE 16.5

Supreme Court Rulings in Which Federal Statutes Have Been Found Unconstitutional[a]

Period	Statutes Voided
1864–1910	33 (34)[b]
1930–1936	14
1953–1969	25
1986–present	38
Total	**174**

[a]In whole or in part.

[b]An 1883 decision in the *Civil Rights Cases* consolidated five different cases into one opinion declaring one act of Congress void. In 1895, *Pollock v. Farmers Loan and Trust Co.* was heard twice, with the same result both times.

Source: Henry J. Abraham, *The Judicial Process: An Introductory Analysis of the Courts of the United States, England, and France*, 7th ed. (Oxford: Oxford University Press, 1998), 309. Used by permission of Oxford University Press, Inc. Updated by the authors.

As you saw in the discussion of *Marbury v. Madison*, from the earliest days of the Republic, federal judges have been politically astute in their efforts to maintain the legitimacy of the judiciary and to conserve their resources. (Remember that judges are typically recruited from political backgrounds.) They have tried not to take on too many politically controversial issues at one time. They have also been much more likely to find state and local laws unconstitutional (about 1,100) than federal laws (fewer than 200, as shown in Table 16.4).

Another factor that increases the acceptability of activist courts is the ability to overturn their decisions. First, the president and the Senate determine who sits on the federal bench. Second, Congress, with or without the president's urging, can begin the process of amending the Constitution to overcome a constitutional decision of the Supreme Court. Although this process does not occur rapidly, it is a safety valve. The Eleventh Amendment in 1795 reversed the decision in *Chisolm v. Georgia*, which permitted an individual to sue a state in federal court; the Fourteenth Amendment in 1868 reversed the decision in *Scott v. Sandford*, which held African Americans not to be citizens of the United States; the Sixteenth Amendment in 1913 reversed the decision in *Pollock v. Farmer's Loan and Trust Co.*, which prohibited a federal income tax; and the Twenty-sixth Amendment in 1971 reversed part of *Oregon v. Mitchell*, which voided a congressional act according 18- to 20-year-olds the right to vote in state elections.

Even more drastic options are available as well. Just before leaving office in 1801, the Federalists created a tier of circuit courts and populated them with Federalist judges; the Jeffersonian Democrats took over the reins of power and promptly abolished the entire level of courts. In 1869, the Radical Republicans in Congress altered the appellate jurisdiction of the Supreme Court to prevent it from hearing a case (*Ex parte McCardle*) that concerned the Reconstruction Acts. This kind of alteration is rare, but it occurred recently. The George W. Bush administration selected the naval base at Guantánamo as the site for a detention camp for terrorism suspects in the expectation that its actions would not be subject to review by federal courts. In June 2004, however, the Supreme Court ruled that the naval base fell within the jurisdiction of U.S. law and that the habeas corpus statute that allows prisoners to challenge their detentions was applicable. In 2005 and again in 2006, Congress stripped federal courts from hearing habeas corpus petitions from the detainees.

Finally, if the issue is one of **statutory construction**, in which a court interprets an act of Congress, then the legislature routinely passes legislation that clarifies existing laws and, in effect, overturns the courts.[44] In 1984, for example, the Supreme Court ruled in *Grove City College v. Bell* that when an institution receives federal aid, only the program or activity that actually gets the aid, not the entire institution, is covered by four federal civil rights laws. In 1988, Congress passed a law specifying that the entire institution is affected. Congress may also pass laws with detailed language to constrain judicial decisionmaking.[45] The description of the judiciary as the "ultimate arbiter of the Constitution" is hyperbolic; all the branches of government help define and shape the Constitution.

> **statutory construction**
> The judicial interpretation of an act of Congress. In some cases where statutory construction is an issue, Congress passes new legislation to clarify existing laws.

SUMMARY

The American judicial system is complex. Sitting at the pinnacle of the judicial system is the Supreme Court, but it is possible to exaggerate its importance. Most judicial policymaking and enforcement of laws take place in the state courts and the lower federal courts.

Throughout American political history, courts have shaped public policy with regard to the economy, liberty, equality, and, most recently, ecology. In the economic arena, until the time of Franklin D. Roosevelt, courts traditionally favored corporations, especially when government tried to regulate them. Since the New Deal, however, the courts have been more tolerant of government regulation of business, shifting much of their policymaking attention to issues of liberty and equality. From *Dred Scott* to *Plessy* to *Brown*, the Supreme Court moved from a role of reinforcing discriminatory policy toward racial minorities to a role of shaping new policies for protecting civil rights. Most recently, environmental groups have used the courts to achieve their policy goals.

A critical view of the courts claims that they are too powerful for the nation's own good and are rather ineffective policymakers besides. Throughout American history, however, judges have been important agenda setters in the political system. Many of the most important political questions make their way into the courts at one time or another. The judiciary is an alternative point of access for those seeking to obtain public policy decisions to their liking, especially those who are not in the majority.

Once in court, litigants face judges whose discretion in decision making is typically limited by precedent. Nevertheless, on questions that raise novel issues (as do many of the most important questions that reach the Supreme Court), the law is less firmly established. Here there is more leeway and judges become more purely political players, balancing different interests and linked to the rest of the political system by their own policy preferences and the politics of their selection.

The unelected and powerful federal courts raise important issues of democracy and the scope of judicial power. Yet court decisions are typically consistent with public opinion, and judges and justices have often used their power to promote democracy. Reconciling the American democratic heritage with an active policy-making role for the judiciary remains a matter of debate. The courts have been sensitive to the issue of their power and often avoid the most controversial issues, at least for a time. It has also been easier for opponents of court decisions to accept judicial power because it is possible to overturn judicial decisions.

THE
NEW FACE
OF
STATE
AND
LOCAL
GOVERNMENT

POLITICS IN ACTION:
SUBNATIONAL GOVERNMENTS AND HOMELAND SECURITY

Following the terrorist attacks of September 11, 2001, the national government passed laws that created new categories of crime for terrorist acts and increased the power and authority of national law enforcement and intelligence agencies. At the same time, state governments adopted similar laws, consolidated bureaucratic agencies charged with law enforcement and emergency response, and took new steps in attempting to slow the flood of undocumented immigrants. For example, by November 2002, 13 states had adopted laws that provided for the death penalty in cases of murder committed in the furtherance of a terrorist act. New Jersey even adopted a law that carries penalties for recruiting members of a terrorist organization. By 2008, a number of states, including New Mexico, had adopted laws allowing illegal immigrants to obtain a drivers license. In part these laws have been an attempt to document people who cross the border illegally.

Traditionally, state and local governments have been responsible for most criminal justice policy and maintaining the civil order for situations contained within state borders. However, the national government response to September 11 reflects a pattern of growing national involvement in criminal justice policy. The states have been reluctant to forfeit their policymaking role or their role in prosecuting criminals. This competition has led some to suggest that states should maintain

661

their traditional dominant role in criminal justice policy, but in issues involving national security and defense, state and local governments should defer to the national government, or confusion will abound.[1] Such an example occurred in 2002 as Maryland and Virginia argued with the national government over who would be the first to prosecute the accused in the Washington, D.C.–area sniper case, with Virginia arguing it should go first and make use of its new antiterrorism law that carried the death penalty.

The debate over government jurisdiction in criminal justice policy is important for several reasons. First, maintaining the civil order is a fundamental role for any government. Without civil order, commerce cannot occur and democratic practices, such as elections, cannot take place. Second, the ultimate power of the government comes from its ability to take away the rights and liberties of individuals. Our fear of this power has led us to place limits on the government and to traditionally keep this power close at hand—with state and local governments.

Does increasing national involvement in criminal justice policy, from drug crimes to carjacking to terrorism, threaten our liberties more than traditional state and local government involvement in this area? On the other hand, are state governments threatening the security of our homeland by adopting their own policies and refusing to participate in national intelligence-sharing programs? If we assume that local and state officials are closer to citizens, do we lose some accountability over officials if the states defer to the national government? Clearly there are no simple answers, but the questions reflect the tensions within our federalist system between levels of government and the difficulty of establishing distinct policy jurisdictions.

subnational governments
Another way of referring to state and local governments. Through a process of reform, modernization, and changing intergovernmental relations since the 1960s, subnational governments have assumed new responsibilities and importance.

State and local governments, or **subnational governments**, touch our lives every day. They pick up our garbage; educate us; keep us safe from criminals; protect our critical infrastructure systems, such as the water supply; and perform a myriad of other vital services. Odds are that you are attending a state or city university right now. You will drive home on locally maintained streets (and may perhaps be issued a speeding ticket from a local official). Subnational governments regulate a wide range of business activities, from generating electric power to cutting hair. The state government is also the single largest employer in every state; in aggregate, local governments employ even more people than do the states. So, as a consumer of government services, as a regulated businessperson, and/or as an employee, subnational governments are intimately involved in our lives.

However, not long ago, some political observers predicted that state governments would cease to exist in the near future.[2] The states seemed to some like archaic accidents of history rather than meaningful political entities. For example, how could one possibly equate Wyoming, with fewer than a half million people and fewer than 5 people per square mile, to California with over 34 million people and 217 people per square mile? What do Hawaii and Alaska have in common with Rhode Island and Louisiana as political entities? Some critics in the 1950s and 1960s thought, "Not much." Further, a generation ago, state governments were ridiculed as being "horse and buggy" institutions in an era of space travel.[3] Their institutions were weak, outdated, resource poor, and were simply not up to the task of running a modern government. The states were also seen by social liberals as obstacles to addressing the grievances of racial and ethnic minorities and urban dwellers—witness Governor George Wallace's stand against the racial integration of Alabama schools (Chapter 3). The national government was seen as the driver of progressive policymaking, and the states were encouraged to step aside or get replaced.

But as Mark Twain said about his mistaken obituary, these reports of the death of the states were greatly exaggerated. Through a process of reform, modernization,

MyState | How Have States Responded to Illegal Immigration?

Estimates suggest that more than 11 million people illegally reside in the United States, and that illegal immigration has been on the increase since the 1980s. However, the national government has not adopted any significant policies to address illegal immigration since the late 1980s. As Congress failed to act on this issue in 2006 and 2007, states began to adopt new policies to address local problems stemming from illegal immigration. Some of these policies have tried to address problems faced by the children of illegal immigrants. For example, by early 2008 six states had adopted policies to provide health insurance to the children of illegal immigrants. Other states have tried to discourage illegal immigrants in their states by adopting new policies to require employers to verify employee work status. In sum, during 2007 the 50 states considered over 1,562 bills related to immigration, nearly three times the number of immigration bills considered in 2006. At least 240 of these bills were adopted

The map at right classifies states based on the type of illegal immigra-tion policy adopted in 2007. Many of the uncolored states adopted other legislation related to illegal immigration, but not addressing the issues here.

QUESTIONS FOR DISCUSSION

- What immigration legislation has your state considered? What legislation has it adopted?

- What problems does immigration pose in your state?

- How does your state benefit from immigration?

■ Allow driver's license for illegal immigrants
  Allow in-state tuition for the children of illegal immigrants
■ Employer verification laws
■ Health insurance for the children of illegal immigrants

Source: State of the States, 2008, March 8, 2008, *http://www.stateline.org/live/publications/pdf-request.*

and changing intergovernmental relations since the 1960s, subnational governments have become more vital to our democratic system than ever. They have assumed new and costly responsibilities in areas such as social welfare, education, health, economic development, and criminal justice. States and localities have also gained importance as national policymakers have confronted budgetary limits and policymakers have recognized the virtues of grass-roots democracy—of giving decision-making power to governments closer to the people.

In this chapter, we discuss subnational government with an eye toward two important characteristics: *revitalization* and *diversity*. Since the early 1960s, the states have become revitalized in their institutions, their personnel, and their role in the federal system.[4] State legislatures, governors' offices, courts, and even bureaucracies have undergone dramatic changes that have allowed them to move forward as strong and active players in the U.S. policymaking process. The peo-ple involved in governing the states and localities are more representative of their constituents than was previously the case, and they tend to be better educated and more professionalized and have greater policy expertise. With the weight of the philosophical argument about where policymaking power should lie in the

The long, straight, and empty freeways of Montana allowed policymakers there to set a speed limit that would be unthinkable on the crowded highways of New Jersey.

federal system swinging toward the states for the past four decades (Chapter 3), the national government has provided states and localities with increasing control over many policy areas.

The second characteristic important to understanding subnational government in the United States is diversity. As anyone who has ever traveled outside their hometown knows, government, policy, and political behavior differ from place to place. For example, in California citizens can propose and pass laws through the ballot box; in Delaware they can't. On the freeways of New Jersey, you may legally drive no faster than 65 miles per hour, whereas until recently in Montana, the only limit was your own judgment and the power of your car's engine. In South Dakota, almost twice the proportion of eligible voters cast votes as in Louisiana during any given election. To understand this diversity among the states is to understand the politics and history of the United States better. Why do these differences exist and what effects do they have?

STATE CONSTITUTIONS

Each state is governed by a separate and unique constitution that spells out the basic rules of that state's political game. Every state elects a governor as its chief executive officer, and most states have a legislature with two chambers like the Congress (except for Nebraska, which only has a senate). However, the states endow their governors with different powers and organize and elect their legislatures differently. Each state's constitution was written under unique historical conditions and with a unique set of philosophical principles in mind. Each is unique in its length and provisions. Some are modern documents; others were written over 100 years ago. The differences among these documents also reflect the diversity—social, economic, geographic, historic, and political—of the states.[5]

State constitutions are subordinate to the U.S. Constitution and the laws of the United States, but they take precedence over state law. State constitutions share many features in common with the U.S. Constitution. Both provide for separation of powers; the creation of executive, judicial, and legislative branches; and means of taxation and finance, and all include a bill of rights. Figure 21.1 shows how the Texas state constitution arranges the state's governmental structure.

The key difference between the national and state constitutions is that the state documents often provide far more detail about specific policies. The Oklahoma constitution, for example, requires that "stock feeding" be taught in public schools, and the South Dakota constitution authorizes a twine and cordage plant at its state penitentiary.[6] This level of specificity leads to constitutions that are long and sometimes confusing. Whereas the U.S. Constitution is a brief document of 8,700 words, state constitutions can be as long as Alabama's 220,000-word tome. In contrast, a few states try to stick to the point as closely as the national constitution does—Vermont's constitution, adopted in 1793, is a model of brevity with only 6,880 words.

FIGURE 21.1

Government Under the Texas State Constitution

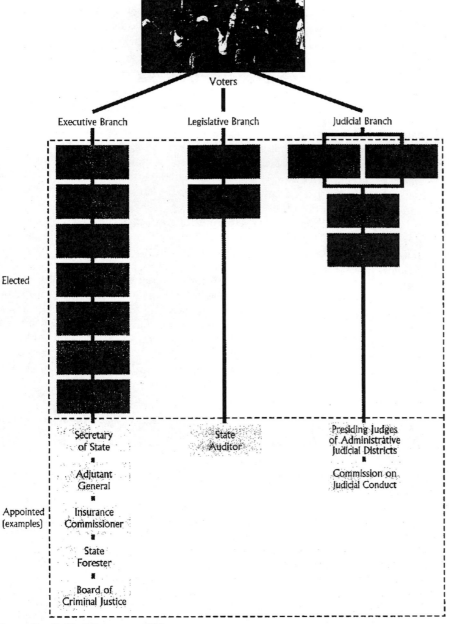

Source: Council of State Governments, 2008.

Why do some states try to embed specific policy into what is supposed to be a document detailing fundamental principles and government organization? It has long been argued that powerful interest groups have encouraged lengthy constitutions in order to protect their interests. It is far more difficult to amend a state constitution than to change a law, so activists try to include policy statements in the constitution in order to guard against their future repeal. In Southern states, where

131

most constitutions were rewritten after the Civil War, state constitutions tend to be longer and more particularistic. Even so, some argue that longer constitutions help limit government interference with Americans' valued individualism.[7]

AMENDING STATE CONSTITUTIONS

Periodically, a state considers changes to the basic rules of its political game. Most avoid the politically difficult process of writing an entirely new constitution. Massachusetts, for example, is governed by a constitution written in 1780. Mississippi, Nebraska, New York, and Utah are among 29 states that have nineteenth-century constitutions. Although a few states have attempted to write entirely new constitutions since World War II (the most recent successful attempt being Georgia in 1983), most states have adapted their governing documents to the late twentieth century by the "cut and paste" method of constitutional amendment.

The most common way that state constitutions are amended is through a two-step process by which the legislature "proposes" an amendment (usually by passing a resolution to this effect by a vote of two-thirds of the legislature and in 12 states doing so in two consecutive sessions) and a majority vote in the next general election "ratifies" it. Although this process is difficult, it is used every election year, typically for taxation and public debt issues. Indeed, California has amended its constitution 493 times since 1879. And across all states between 1898 and 1998, 827 direct (from voters) and indirect (through legislature) initiatives for constitutional amendments were proposed, and voters approved 343 (42 percent) measures.[8] Although rarely used, state constitutions can also be amended through a constitutional convention; Massachusetts used a convention most recently when legislators attempted to ban same-sex marriage in 2004.

You Are Attempting to Revise the California Constitution

STATE ELECTIONS

Most top-level state policymakers are elected to office. To an even greater extent than national officials, state officials must achieve office through the ballot box and respond to the voters' preferences if they wish to remain there. At the national level, voters can elect only one member of the executive branch (the president), while they can elect no one in the judicial branch. However, at the state level, voters usually have far more power to determine who governs them. For example, in California voters select eight statewide executive officers (including the governor, treasurer, and even the insurance commissioner) as well as many judges down to the trial court level.[9] Further, in some states voters are authorized to make law directly through the ballot box by using the direct democracy mechanisms we will discuss shortly.

Historically, state elections have been decided by the general political mood of the country or state, with those running for office having little ability to influence their own electoral fortunes. Voters cared little and knew less about state legislative or even gubernatorial races. But as the states have become more important and as their institutions have become more effective and respected in the past generation, average voters and political activists are more attentive to state elections. As a result, state officials look more like their constituents, in terms of partisanship, ideology, and demographics.

GUBERNATORIAL ELECTIONS

Gubernatorial races have increasingly become focused on individual candidates rather than party affiliations. Political scientists call this the "presidentialization" of gubernatorial elections since they have come to resemble the personality-focused modern campaigns for the White House. This has occurred because of the increasing importance of television (and subsequently money) to gubernatorial campaigns and the decoupling of gubernatorial races from presidential races and state political party organizations.[10]

Historically, most governors were elected during presidential years, either because their term of office was only two years or because their four-year term coincided with that of the presidential term. But since the 1960s, most states have adopted a four-year gubernatorial term and shifted that term so that elections are held during nonpresidential election years. Today, only 11 states hold their gubernatorial elections at the same time as presidential elections.[11]

The change means that the gubernatorial race is the "top of the ticket" in most states, which makes it more likely that voters will pay attention. Races are therefore more likely to be decided on what voters think about the candidates than on any coattail effect from the presidential race. This means that candidates for governor can no longer expect to garner much help from a popular presidential candidate for their party, nor can they assume any candidate's campaign suffers from an unpopular presidential candidate topping the ticket. Political scientists refer to the pattern of running on your own as a "candidate-centered campaign."[12]

In order to run on their own, gubernatorial candidates have taken to television advertising in a big way, just as presidential candidates have, and largely for the same reasons. There are simply too many people in a state for a candidate to meet them all face-to-face. Gubernatorial candidates hire nationally known advertising agencies to develop slick ad campaigns. These campaigns are not cheap. The use of television is one of the main reasons why the costs of gubernatorial campaigns have skyrocketed. For elections between 1977 and 1980, the total cost of gubernatorial elections was $524 million (adjusted for 2006 dollars). That cost increased by 107 percent, to $1,084 million, for elections between 2003 and 2006. Although the largest states have some of the most expensive elections, if we adjust for the cost per general election vote, we find that the 2002 to 2006 election costs were the most in New Hampshire at $47.16 per vote and much less in a larger state like Virginia at $24.03 per vote. However, collectively the elections in California and Texas are the most expensive, with the average costs of the last five races in California at $114 million and in Texas at $59 million through the 2006 election, and the California gubernatorial recall election at nearly $204 million.[13]

Most of this money has to be raised by the candidates themselves. At one time, state political party organizations had a strong hand in funding these campaigns and in selecting the party nominees for the general election. Those days are long gone in most states. With the advent of the direct primary for nominating party candidates, a person who wants to become governor must organize and fund a major campaign in the primary. And by the time a candidate wins the primary, he or she has built a solid campaign organization and has little need for the party's help in the general election.

One result of the personalization of gubernatorial elections has been that parties have a harder time predicting their success. Because voters now become familiar with gubernatorial candidates during campaigns, they more frequently vote based on their attitude toward the candidates rather than resorting to party loyalty. This can lead to ticket splitting and divided government, as citizens vote for less well-known state legislative candidates strictly based on their party affiliation.[14] We see the results of this when states whose voters are predominantly of one party elect governors of the other party. For example, in 2002, Virginia voters elected Democrat Mark R. Warner to the governorship, even though registered Republican voters outnumber registered Democrats and Republicans maintained majorities in the 2004 to 2006 state legislative session. At the extreme, this has led to four Independent governors being elected in recent years. Two of these—Lowell Weicker of Connecticut and Walter Hickel of

Alaska—were politicians formerly associated with a major party who challenged their parties' candidates in the general election due to intraparty squabbles. But the two governors serving in 2002—Angus King of Maine (Independent) and Jesse Ventura of Minnesota (Reform Party)—were truly independent of the Democratic and Republican parties and owed their election completely to the efforts of their personal campaign organizations. However, both of these governors left office in 2003, leaving no Independents in governorships.

STATE LEGISLATIVE ELECTIONS

Of all state- and national-level officials, state legislators face the smallest constituencies, ranging from fewer than 3,000 people in a New Hampshire House of Representatives district to almost 800,000 people in a California Senate district, but with an average size of about 140,000 for state senate districts and 50,000 for state house districts.[15] By comparison, governors (600,000 to 57 million constituents) and members of the U.S. House of Representatives (average 646,952 constituents) need to respond to considerably more constituents.

Throughout much of the twentieth century, state legislatures were horribly malapportioned, giving greater representation to rural areas than their population warranted. One hundred years ago, most state legislators represented rural areas because that was where people lived. However, by the early 1960s the population had become overwhelmingly urban. Since the legislative district boundaries had rarely changed, state legislatures continued to be dominated by rural politicians. The main reason for the underrepresentation of urban areas was that districts were often constructed on the basis of the boundaries of some local government, such as a county, regardless of how many people lived there. This meant that in many states, rural counties with a few thousand residents and urban counties with hundreds of thousands of residents all had the same representation in the state legislature.

In 1962, after decades of avoiding the issue, the U.S. Supreme Court ruled that the districts of the lower chamber of state legislatures must be based on the number of people living in them. This landmark decision in *Baker v. Carr* established the principle of "one person, one vote" in drawing up state house districts. Two years later, the Court ruled in *Reynolds v. Sims* that state senates must also be apportioned in this fashion.

Demonstrators stand on the steps of San Francisco City Hall on the first full day of legal same-sex marriage in San Francisco, California, June 17, 2008.

These cases dramatically changed the face of state legislatures. Gone was the rural dominance of these chambers. New representatives arrived from the central cities and suburbs. Urban and metropolitan area problems became the focus of state legislatures.

Periodic redrawing of legislative districts is required as population shifts. This is now done following every decennial census, further changing the composition of state legislatures. The late twentieth-century migration of citizens to the suburbs has resulted in new voting power for suburban metropolitan interests and a decline in the power of central cities in state capitals.

Ironically, although state legislators have smaller districts than any other state or national elected officials, they are the least well known by voters. This is largely due to the historic lack of media coverage given to state legislatures and the lack of campaign resources of candidates for the office. The result is that races for state legislature, at least in general elections, have been decided on the basis of forces beyond candidates' control—party identification of district voters and the parties' candidates in the race for governor and president.[16]

But with the recent shifting of more policy responsibilities to the states and increases in state legislative salaries (discussed shortly) making the office both more important and attractive, campaigns for the state legislature have started to become more candidate-centered, although not nearly to the extent that gubernatorial campaigns have. This "congressionalization" of state legislative races is encouraged by increased resources (mainly staff and time) for incumbent legislators to retain their seats, and increases in the activities of political action committees (PACs) at the state level willing to fund expensive campaigns.[17] Campaign costs skyrocketed for state legislative campaigns beginning in the 1980s and continue to be high today, with candidates in large states such as California and Illinois finding it necessary to raise at least $200,000; highly competitive races might cost over $2 million. Although it is still possible to run a less closely contested campaign in a less populous state for only several thousand dollars, this is no longer the norm.[18]

The need to raise and spend more money on these campaigns favors incumbent legislators. Incumbents can use the resources and prestige of office both to enhance their visibility with their constituents and to attract campaign contributions from PACs and others interested in garnering favor in the legislature. State legislative leaders also help incumbents through their own PACs and party funds in order to enhance their personal influence as leaders and the prospects of their party retaining or regaining control of their chamber.[19]

Partisan Competition, Legislative Turnover, and Term Limits   The 2006–2007 elections continued the 30-year trend in state legislatures of increasing party competition, closer partisan splits, and changing party control (see Table 21.1). Although much of this change has occurred as a result of Republican gains in the South (for example, the South Carolina statehouse now has a majority of Republicans, as do both chambers of the Florida state legislature), even Northern states have been experiencing increasingly close legislative party divisions. Following the 2006–2007 elections Democrats hold 54 percent of all seats in state legislatures, stemming what had been a steady downward trend since the Watergate scandal buoyed the party's fortunes in the mid-1970s.[20]

Although some state legislative chambers have very lopsided partisan splits (for example, in the Idaho state senate Republicans hold 80 percent of the seats, and in the Massachusetts state senate Democrats hold 87 percent), some legislatures are closely divided. In fifteen legislative chambers, there are three or fewer seats separating the parties. The Oklahoma senate is an extreme case, with exactly 24 Republicans and 24 Democrats. And finally, following the 2006–2007 elections, 13 chambers changed majority party control or are now split. This change is consistent with a 20-year trend that indicates a remarkable period of increasing party competition in the state legislatures. However, even as competition has increased in some states, such as Maine, it has declined in others, such as Illinois. And the percentage of contested legislative seats varies widely across the states with some states seeing a large increase in contested seats (Missouri) while others have seen significant declines (Pennsylvania) from the 1970s to 2000s.[21]

Divided government exists when a single party does not control both chambers of the state legislature and the governor's office. With divided government, it is usually much more difficult for coherent policy action to take place because the parties that control the different components of state government have conflicting policy and electoral goals.

Increased switching of party control and party competition has inevitably led to more divided control of state government than in the past, when party affiliation of voters within states was more stable and electorates more homogeneous.[22] After the 2006–2007 elections, 24 states had divided government. In contrast, in 1946 only seven states had divided government. Increased party competition, divided government, and majority party switching in state legislatures has tended to increase legislative partisanship and polarize legislative deliberations, thereby making compromise harder to come by. Further, this sort of swinging from party to party can lead to a lack of policy continuity in a state. On the other hand, high levels of party competition tend to make elected officials more attentive and responsive to voters.[23]

Aside from partisan change, there is the question of turnover in state legislatures. Turnover levels—the rate that state legislators are replaced from election to election—give us an understanding both of how much experience and expertise state legislators have relative to other political actors in the states and how closely they are "connected" to their constituencies and the normal life of a state citizen.

Recent history has shown that in any 10-year period, about 75 percent of state senate and 77 percent of state house legislative seats are turned over.[24] Thus, significant change in the people holding state legislative office is the norm. In 2000, Pennsylvania and Missouri had the lowest average annual percent turnover in their Senates (less than 10 percent). Oregon and Colorado had the highest annual turnover rates, both in their upper chambers, at 48 and 35 percent, respectively.[25] Across all states, the current average annual turnover rate in any election year is about 26 percent in lower chambers and 23 percent in upper chambers.[26]

In recent years, voters in many states have attempted to increase turnover rates by legally restricting the number of terms a member may serve. Increasingly, voters appear to support the argument that professional, career-oriented legislators become so entrenched and difficult to unseat that they lose touch with their constituents and instead pander to special interests. Since 1990, 21 states have adopted term limits for state legislators, almost exclusively through direct democracy mechanisms (discussed shortly). However, four states have seen their term limits overturned in court, or in the case of Idaho and Utah, by the state legislature, leaving only 15 term-limit laws intact.[27] The number of terms permitted varies from state to state. For example, California limits its assembly (its lower house) members to six years and its senators to eight years in office.[28] In the 2002 elections, term-limited states had turnover rates in lower chambers that were 13 percentage points higher than non–term-limited states and almost 9 percentage points higher in upper chambers. In some states the effects of term limits is quite dramatic. For example, 41 percent of Nebraska legislators were term limited out of office in 2006.[29]

THE CHANGING FACE OF STATE ELECTED OFFICIALS

In November 1996, Washington state voters chose Gary Locke, the son of Chinese immigrants, as their governor. Locke became the first Asian American ever to be elected governor of one of the 48 contiguous states. Seven years before, Virginia voters made Douglas Wilder the first elected African American governor. These two governors are exceptions to the rule that governors are White, married men who are often lawyers, and state voters are increasingly electing a wider variety of people to state offices.

Women have made strong inroads into the governors' offices (see Figure 21.2). Before 1974, only a few women had ever been governors, and those were elected because they were married to a former governor who could not run again. But in 1974, Ella Grasso was elected to the governor's office of Connecticut in her own right. Dixie Lee Ray followed her in 1976 in Washington. Since 1925, 29 women have served as governors in states as varied as Delaware, Oregon, Kansas, and

FIGURE 21.2

Female Representation in State Government

Percentage of females in the state legislature in 2008.

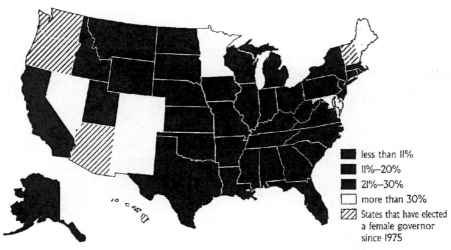

■	less than 11%
■	11%–20%
■	21%–30%
□	more than 30%
▨	States that have elected a female governor since 1975

Source: Center for American Women and Politics, "Facts and Findings," *http://www.cawp.rutgers.edu/Facts.html#leg, March 5, 2008.*

In 1998, women were elected to all five statewide executive offices in Arizona—governor, secretary of state, treasurer, superintendent of public instruction, and attorney general. The so-called Fab Five were sworn into office by another powerful Arizona female—U.S. Supreme Court Justice Sandra Day O'Connor.

Kentucky, representing both the Democratic and Republican parties. At least two prominent female governors—Ann Richards of Texas and Christine Whitman of New Jersey—were mentioned as potential presidential candidates in 2000. In 2006, 36 states held gubernatorial elections, and in 9 of these states women ran for the office. In 2008, there were 8 female state governors and 10 Lieutenant Governors serving in the United States. Being female or a person of color is no longer an insurmountable hurdle to being elected to a state's highest office.

State legislatures too have been looking more and more like the diverse population of the United States.[30] In 2008, 23.6 percent of all state legislators were women, a tremendous increase over 1969, when only about 4 percent of state legislators were women.[31] Women are also taking more leadership roles in state legislatures. In 2007, there were 59 women in legislative leadership positions, serving in positions such as senate or house majority leader. However, state legislatures do vary widely in the percentage of female legislators, from almost 38 percent in Vermont to less than 9 percent in South Carolina during the 2008 legislative session. In 2007, there were 608 state legislators of African American descent—8 percent, a figure that has also been mostly increasing for 30 years. Asians and Hispanics have also been increasing in their state legislative representation, primarily in Florida and the Western states. Indeed, 3 percent of state legislators were Hispanic in 2007.[32]

The less-than-representative percentage of women and ethnic minorities in state elected positions (although at a historic high) shows the slowness with which progress is made in this area, due at least in part to informal qualifications for higher-level offices that can include experience at lower-level offices. Women and minorities are making the inroads today in the state and local offices that may well lead to them being elected more frequently to national positions in the future. For example, the sharp jump in the representation of women in the U.S. Senate and statewide elective office in the 1990s was encouraged by increases in women being elected to state legislative positions in the 1970s and 1980s.

GOVERNORS AND THE EXECUTIVE BRANCH

During his first several months as governor of California in 2003 and 2004, Arnold Schwarzenegger traveled to Israel, Japan, and China to promote investment in California industries, such as biotechnology, and to promote trade between those countries and his state. Schwarzenegger also appeared in television commercials aired oversees that promoted California. Such actions are becoming increasingly common for governors who are interested in creating more economic growth, even though they have no legal capacity to sign formal trade agreements with foreign nations. Governor Kathleen Sebelius of Kansas and former governor of Minnesota Jesse Ventura made similar trips to foreign countries, including Cuba.

The actions of these governors highlight the modern role of the governor. Not only is the governor the chief executive officer of a state, with the responsibility to execute the laws passed by the legislature, but he or she is also the best-known state public official, to whom the public looks for leadership, assurance, conflict resolution, and policy initiatives. If administering public policy is the governor's main constitutional responsibility, then promoting his or her vision of what public policy ought to be is the modern governor's primary responsibility to the public.

THE JOB OF GOVERNOR

Like presidents, governors are expected to wear many hats—sometimes fulfilling constitutionally assigned duties, sometimes performing political tasks. But the powers of governors are not always commensurate with citizens' expectations. State constitutions often hamstring a governor, dividing executive power among many different administrative actors and agencies. But a generation of modernization and reform has resulted in enhanced powers for governors by reducing the number of independently elected officials and independent boards and commissions in the state executive branch, as well as by enhancing governors' other formal powers.[33] These reforms have established clearer lines of authority and enhanced the governor's appointment, reorganization, and budgetary powers. Most states have also raised their governors' salaries and increased the number of years a governor can serve. Nevertheless, the limited formal powers of governors make it very difficult for them to fulfill their responsibilities to the state without resorting to more "informal powers," such as the use of the media and a public relations staff.

How powerful are the nation's governors? Political scientist Thad Beyle has devoted considerable attention to this subject. On the basis of an analysis of gubernatorial powers outlined in state constitutions and statutes and in the strength of their

You Are a Governor

party in their states' legislatures, he has rated each of the states' governor's institutional powers. Figure 21.3 displays this rating, based on the governor's ability to stay in office, make major appointments, prepare the state budget, veto legislation, and direct political parties. Seven states' governors—those in Hawaii, Maryland, New Jersey, New York, Ohio, Pennsylvania, and Utah—have very strong powers. Another 18 governors enjoy strong executive powers. Ten states accord their governors moderate powers. The remaining 15 states, including states as diverse as Massachusetts, California, and Nevada, give only weak powers to their governors.[34]

Two of a governor's most important formal powers for controlling state government are the veto and the executive budget. The governor's veto is similar to that of the president—a governor can refuse to sign a bill passed by the state legislature, blocking it from becoming law. But in most states, the governor's veto power is far more potent than the president's. First, gubernatorial vetoes have been very difficult for state legislatures to override historically, and this remains true today.[35] Although state legislatures have become more aggressive in overriding vetoes in recent years, still less than 10 percent of gubernatorial vetoes are overridden.

Further, 42 state governors have the **line-item veto**, which allows them to veto only certain parts of a bill while allowing the rest of the bill to pass into law. This keeps the legislature from being able to hold a bill hostage, forcing the governor to sign a popular bill even though it contains a provision that the governor thinks is unwise. This is especially useful on appropriations bills, allowing the governor to trim pork barrel spending as he or she sees fit. In Wisconsin, the governor is even allowed to veto individual words and letters from a bill, sometimes changing its basic meaning. In 1987, newly elected Governor Tommy Thompson used this power over 350 times on the budget passed by the Democratic state legislature.[36] With this power, a governor with a sizable minority in the legislature to support him or her can force or cajole the legislature into passing much of his or her agenda. The governor also has the power to initiate the state budget process in almost all states. This allows the governor to set the agenda for what is by far the most important bill(s) of the state legislative session. The budget details how state tax dollars

line-item veto
The power possessed by 42 state governors to veto only certain parts of a bill while allowing the rest of it to pass into law.

FIGURE 21.3

Institutional Powers of the Governors

Very strong
Strong
Moderate
Weak

Source: Adapted from Thad Beyle and Margaret Ferguson, "Governors and the Executive Branch," in *Politics in the American States*, 9th ed., ed. Virginia Gray and Russell L. Hanson (Washington, DC: Congressional Quarterly Press, 2008), 192-228.

are going to be spent—it is where state public policy "puts up or shuts up." Although the legislature may amend and must pass the governor's proposal as it does any other bill, the limited staff and session time of most state legislatures, especially compared to that available to the governor, makes the massive budget sent by the governor difficult to change substantially. Further, since the governor has the ability to veto—and sometimes item veto—the budget passed by the legislature, he or she also has the last word in the process. This provides a governor the ability to gain help for his or her policy goals from both state legislators and bureaucrats interested in furthering their own policy goals through state spending.

To enhance their influence, governors supplement their formal institutional powers with more "personal powers."[37] A governor's real power depends on the way he or she uses character, leadership style, and persuasive abilities in conjunction with the formal prerogatives of the office. Building public support is an increasingly important part of the policymaking process. This is true as a means for influencing legislative decision making in all states but also applies to influencing citizen behavior directly in states with direct democracy mechanisms. For example, in 2004 California Governor Schwarzenegger expended most of his informal powers in a failed attempt to generate public support for ballot propositions concerning government finances rather than trying to influence legislators.

Illinios Governor Rob Blagojevich speaks to the media after surveying tornado damage April 21, 2004 in Utica, Illinois. Utica, located about 90 miles southwest of Chicago, is home to about 1,000 people and has sustained significant tornado damage leaving eight people dead.

Not surprisingly, public relations and media experts have become a key part of many governors' staffs. Although press coverage of state politics is intermittent at best, focusing on only the most salient controversies and such predictable events as the governor's State of the State Address, a savvy governor can create media events and opportunities that enhance his or her popularity and political clout. Whether it is Governor Arnold Schwarzenegger visiting the prime minister of Israel or New York Governor George Pataki visiting Ground Zero of the World Trade Center, the media image of a caring, active, busy governor can be parlayed into political clout with the legislature and executive agencies. Likewise, governors are subjected to media frenzies over failures in the bureaucracies they oversee. For example, as Florida Governor Jeb Bush pursued what seemed to be an easy reelection in 2002, the media and Democrats attacked Bush over the unexplained disappearance of a four-year-old girl in the state's foster care system and the system's reputation for being the worst in the country.

After languishing for most of the twentieth century as a political backwater office where political hacks, business leaders, and others went to cap off their careers before retiring to the country club, today's governors are politically savvy and active and have strong policy agendas.[38] Modern governors are likely to highly educated, experienced, and capable of managing the diverse problems of a state. In addition to being better educated than their predecessors, recent governors have often had previous experience as a statewide elected official or held a national position.

Today's governors increasingly have the tools and skills to control state government and guide the state in the policy directions they think are best. Demonstrating

As the state's legal counsel, the attorney general watches out for the state's legal interests. New York Attorney General Eliot Spitzer fought against corporate corruption and greed, even going so far as to sue the former director of the famed New York Stock Exchange.

lieutenant governor

Often the second-highest executive official in state government who is elected with the governor as a ticket in some states and is elected separately in others. She or he may have legislative and executive branch responsibilities.

the esteem in which the modern governorship is held is the fact that in the last quarter of the twentieth century, the U.S. president has been a former governor in all but five years. In each presidential race in this period, at least one of the major party nominees was a sitting or former governor.

OTHER EXECUTIVE OFFICERS

Unlike the U.S. president, most governors must work with an array of independently elected executive branch officials in conducting the affairs of state government. At various times, these officials may assist or oppose the governor. Voters in 43 states choose a **lieutenant governor**. The governor and lieutenant governor are elected as a team in 24 states. In states where the governor and lieutenant governor are chosen independently, it is possible for the two top state executives to be political rivals or even members of different political parties. This can result in some real battles between them. For example, in 1990 when then-Governor (and Democrat) Michael Dukakis of Massachusetts left the state on an international trade mission, Republican Lieutenant Governor Evelyn Murphy initiated major cuts in public employment in an attempt to jump-start her floundering campaign for governor. Perhaps in anticipation of such antics, when Republican Steve Windom became lieutenant governor of Alabama, the Democrat-dominated state legislature and Democratic governor promptly stripped the office of almost all its powers.[40] Most lieutenant governors have few formal duties aside from presiding over the state senate and being in the succession path for governor.

Other major executive positions elected in some states include the following:

- Attorney general—The state's legal counsel and prosecutor (elected in 43 states)
- Treasurer—The manager of the state's bank accounts (elected in 38 states)
- Secretary of state—In charge of elections and record-keeping (elected in 36 states)
- Auditor—Financial comptroller for the state (elected in 25 states)

Other officials elected in fewer states include education secretary and commissioners for land, labor, mines, agriculture, and utilities, among others.[41]

So many independent executives, commissions, and boards work within state governments that many politicians and scholars have called for major state government reorganization to allow governors more control and to increase efficiency generally. Every state has undertaken some kind of reorganization of the executive branch in the past 30 years. However, research shows that the expected benefits of reorganized state governments are not always achieved. Such reorganization only sometimes increases accountability and seldom results in cost saving and efficiency—benefits often promised by its proponents.[42] Although state residents may value smaller governments, they enjoy having electoral control over the leaders of state executive branches.

STATE LEGISLATURES

State legislatures are often easy targets for criticism. Their work is not well understood, and the institution does not typically receive the public attention that the governor's office or national institutions do. Further, up until a generation ago, state legislatures and legislators had a history of poor performance that still haunts them. At that time, they were "malapportioned, unrepresentative, dominated by their governors and/or special interests, and unable and unwilling to deal with the pressing issues of the day."[43]

But between 1965 and 1985, many state legislatures underwent a metamorphosis into more full-time, professional bodies—several like state-level congresses. According to political scientist Alan Rosenthal, "They increased the time they spent on their tasks; they established or increased their professional staffs; and they streamlined their procedures, enlarged their facilities, invigorated their processes, attended to their ethics, disclosed their finances, and reduced their conflicts of interest."[44] As a result, state legislatures are far more active, informed, representative, and democratic today than they were 40 years ago.

State legislatures serve the same basic function in the states as Congress does in the national government, and they do it with the same basic mechanisms. State legislatures make almost all the basic laws of the state by approving identical bills in each of their two-chambered bodies (except in Nebraska's unicameral legislature). They appropriate the money that is needed for a state government to function. They oversee the activities of the executive branch through confirming gubernatorial appointments, controlling the budgets of the agencies, and investigating complaints and concerns of citizens and the press. State legislators themselves attend closely to the needs of their constituents, whether through voting on bills in line with their constituents' interests or chasing down problems a citizen has with a bureaucratic agency.

Members of the state legislature are at the front line of interaction between citizens and government. Because most state legislatures meet for only a limited number of months each year and because state capitals are typically closer to their districts than Washington, D.C., is to the districts of most congresspersons, state legislators usually live among the people they represent. They are closely involved with their constituents not only at election time but also throughout the year. They coach basketball and run restaurants, they teach school and preach at local churches, and they are local attorneys and bankers. In short, the state legislature in almost all states comes closest to the sort of citizen-directed government envisioned by Thomas Jefferson over 200 years ago.

The reforms of the past generation designed to improve the efficiency and effectiveness of state legislatures are collectively called *legislative professionalism.*[45] That is, these are reforms designed "to enhance the capacity of the legislature to perform its role in the policymaking process with an expertise, seriousness, and effort comparable to that of other actors in the process."[46] Changes have been primarily in three areas. First, legislative sessions have been lengthened to give legislators more time to deal with the increasingly complex problems of the states. Before 1965, most state legislatures only met for several weeks each year, and many would only meet every other year. In 2008, 44 state legislatures had annual sessions, usually meeting for between three and five months, with a few (such as in Michigan, Massachusetts, and Wisconsin) meeting year-round.

The second legislative professionalism reform was to increase legislators' salaries so they could devote more of their time to considering the states' business and less to their "regular" job. The idea was also that if service in the state legislature paid a living wage, legislators would have fewer conflicts of interest and a wider variety of people would be willing to serve. For instance, the only people who could afford to serve in the West Virginia state legislature in 1960 for a salary of $1,500 were those with either an outside source of income or who were independently wealthy. In 2008, the roughly $73,613 a Pennsylvania state representative earned could allow him or her to focus full-time on legislative duties.

The third major professionalism reform was the increase in the staff available to help legislators in their duties. Even since 1979 (after many of the big professionalism changes had already occurred), permanent state legislative staff has increased over 60 percent.[47] By increasing their session length, salary, and staff, state legislatures have dramatically increased their ability to have an impact on the state policymaking process.

Not all the effects of this drive toward legislative professionalism are seen as good, and not all states have professionalized their legislatures to the same level. Some argue that professionalism leads to an overemphasis on reelection, inflated campaign costs, and lack of leadership in the lawmaking process.[48] Legislative professionalism threatens the existence of the "citizen legislature," in which people leave their job for a couple of months each year to serve the state and inject some "common sense" into government. The recent spate of state term limits laws indicates the esteem in which many Americans hold this sort of nonprofessional state legislature. There is also some evidence that increased professionalism does not enhance even some of the aspects of the process that proponents argued it would, such as increasing membership diversity in state legislatures.[49]

Explaining Differences in State Laws

It is also important to note that not all state legislatures are in any sense full-time, professional bodies. Members of the New Hampshire House of Representatives earn $200 for a two-year term, which consists of only one 30-day period of service in each year. These are clearly not professional legislators. On the other hand, across the border in Massachusetts, state legislators earn over $58,000 and meet virtually the entire year. Figure 21.4 shows which states have professionalized legislatures, which still have citizen legislatures, and which have legislatures that are hybrids, having some characteristics of both. Those states that have developed professional legislatures tend to be those with large and heterogeneous populations that both need and can afford them, although there is a regional effect that may have to do with political preferences for a professional government.[50]

Although this selective process makes it difficult to assess the independent effects of legislative professionalism, there is some evidence that more professionalism leads to more liberal welfare policy and perhaps more divided government in the states.[51]

FIGURE 21.4

Legislative Professionalism

Professional legislatures

Hybrid

Citizen legislatures

Source: Adapted from Keith E. Hamm and Gary F. Moncrief, "Legislative Politics in the States," in *Politics in the American States*, 9th ed., ed. Virginia Gray and Russell L. Hanson (Washington, DC: Congressional Quarterly Press, 2008), 154–91.

We may now be seeing the beginning of a "deprofessionalizing" trend in some states, as some hearken back to the Jeffersonian ideal of the citizen legislature. Term limits laws are the most obvious manifestation of this, but recent laws in California limiting legislative staffing and in Colorado limiting the powers of the legislative leadership may also signal that the legislative professionalism movement is cyclical.[52]

STATE COURT SYSTEMS

The organization of the states' courts reflects two major influences: (1) the model of organization set by the national courts and (2) the judicial preferences of each state's citizens as manifested in state constitutions and statutes. State courts are far more involved in administering justice than is the national judiciary. Indeed, 98 percent of all litigation in the United States is settled in state courts. Recent data show that state courts have 52 times the number of criminal cases and 27 times more civil cases than national courts with only 24 times as many judges.[53] In addition, state court workloads have been increasing in both criminal and civil cases, forcing states to experiment with alternatives to trial courts like mediation, arbitration, and plea bargaining, among others. The volume of cases heard by state courts is significant, but courts are also policymaking bodies. Particularly when the highest court in the state rules on a case, judges are doing more than just interpreting the law; they are often making policy in the same fashion as the U.S. Supreme Court.[54]

Since World War II, many state court systems have undergone reforms designed to modernize and rationalize their procedures and structure, much like the reforms undergone in the states' governors' offices and legislatures. These include reforms both of organizational structure and judicial selection.

STATE COURT ORGANIZATION

State court systems often developed as a hodgepodge of individual courts set up at odd times and for odd reasons at the subnational level. Many states have low-level courts, such as justices of the peace or magistrate courts, whose presiding officials may not even be lawyers. Many states developed a variety of specialized courts to deal with specific judicial matters involving traffic, family, or taxes. These systems, which included courts that were completely independent of any higher authority, often led to confusion, duplication of effort, and unfair treatment of cases and people.

Comparing Judicial Systems

In the past generation, efforts have been made to consolidate and coordinate many state courts systems so that they parallel the federal system, discussed in Chapter 16. First, specialized courts have been consolidated and subsumed into trial courts with more general jurisdiction. These courts are usually established for county-sized areas and are the setting for most trials. They are known by a variety of labels—district courts, circuit courts, superior courts, and (in the case of New York) supreme courts. Judges assigned to these trial courts often work in only one county and specialize in criminal, juvenile, or civil litigation. A single judge presides over each case, and citizens may be called on to serve as jurors and members of grand jury panels.

Many states have also moved toward coordinating their court systems through their court of last resort, usually called the state supreme court. Under a coordinated system, the state supreme court not only serves as the court of final appeal for all cases in the state court system but also has the responsibility for administering and regulating the justice system in the state. This usually involves appointing a chief court administrator to handle the day-to-day budgeting, operations, and organization of all the courts in the state, and establishing boards to oversee and deal with complaints against lawyers and judges in the states.

A major innovation adopted by most states in the past 30 years is an *intermediate court of appeal*. Like national appeals courts, states organize these courts on a regional basis and with judges working together in panels of three or more, with a majority deciding each case. No witnesses are called before appellate courts, and juries are not used. Instead, judges read briefs and hear arguments prepared by lawyers that address whether the law was appropriately applied at the trial court level and whether due process of law was followed. The job of judges at this level is not to determine the facts of a case but to interpret the laws and the state or national constitution as they apply to the case.

The organizational purpose of an intermediate court of appeal is to reduce the pressure on the state supreme court of the many "routine" appeals of trial court decisions (see Figure 21.5). These are appeals that have few implications for state policy or procedure; they are appeals that primarily impact only the case at hand. An intermediate appeals court frees up the state supreme court to consider only those cases with statewide policy importance. Twelve states, all with small populations, do not have intermediate courts of appeal,[55] so the appellate work in these states falls solely to the supreme court, reducing its ability to concentrate on making policy through judicial interpretation.

FIGURE 21.5

Prototypical Modern State Court System

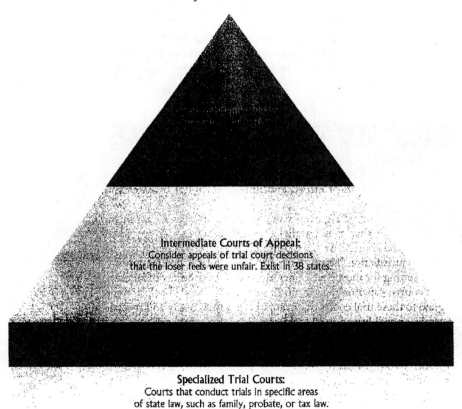

Intermediate Courts of Appeal:
Consider appeals of trial court decisions that the loser feels were unfair. Exist in 38 states.

Specialized Trial Courts:
Courts that conduct trials in specific areas of state law, such as family, probate, or tax law.

SELECTING JUDGES

In contrast to national judges, all of whom are appointed by the president for life, judges rise to the bench in the states in a variety of ways (see Table 21.2). These judicial selection mechanisms are each relics of values that were manifested in a series of reform movements over the past 200 years.

At the founding of the country, almost all state judges were appointed, as in the federal system, either by the governor or the state legislature, and 13 states still use this method of judicial selection for some or all their judges. With the Jacksonian democratic impulse of the early to mid-nineteenth century, states began to select their judges by partisan ballot, just as other state officials were selected. Currently, 11 states select some or all of their judges this way. In the Progressive Era (1890–1920), reformers argued that to be administered fairly, justice should be nonpartisan because a judge elected on a party platform might be more biased in his or her decisions. Persuaded by this argument, many states changed their judicial selection mechanism to that of nonpartisan election, where candidates ran against one another but without a party label. Nineteen states still use nonpartisan elections to select some or all their judges. But electing judges remains both common and controversial.[56]

The most recent wave of judicial selection reforms since World War II has been 17 states adopting a hybrid system of appointment and election known as the **Merit Plan**. In this system, the governor appoints the state's judges from a list of persons recommended by the state bar or a committee of jurists and other officials. Each appointed judge then serves a short "trial run" term, usually one year, in which citizens may assess the judge's performance. After this, an election is held in which voters are asked whether the judge should be retained in office—they simply vote yes or no, not for one candidate or another. If voters approve retention by a majority vote (Illinois requires 60 percent), then the judge continues in office for a lengthy term (usually 6 to 12 years), after which another retention election is held if the judge wishes to continue serving. Few judges lose in this type of retention election, which raises the question of whether the Merit Plan's democratic component truly enhances responsiveness to citizens. Indeed, recent research suggests there is little difference between the various selection plans and election outcomes as well as the political responsiveness of judges.[57]

Merit Plan
Method for selecting state judges in which governors appoint persons based on the recommendations of a committee. After serving a short term, the judge then often faces a retention election.

TABLE 21.2

State Judicial Selection Mechanisms

APPOINTMENT	ELECTION	MERIT PLAN
By Governor:		AK, AZ, CA, CO, FL, IA, KS, MD, MO, NE, OK, SD, UT, WY
By Legislature: CT, HI, RI, SC, VA	**Nonpartisan:** AZ, CA, FL, GA, ID, KS, KY, LA, MI, MN, MT, NV, NM, ND, OH, OK, OR, SD, WA	

Note: States may appear more than once, since some states select different types of judges through different mechanisms. Minor local judges, such as justices of the peace, are not considered in this table.

Source: Council of State Governments, *The Book of the States, 2003 Edition* (Washington, DC: Council of State Governments, 2004), 235.

DIRECT DEMOCRACY

direct democracy

Government controlled directly by citizens. In some U.S. states, procedures such as the initiative, the referendum, and the recall give voters a direct impact on policymaking and the political process by means of the voting booth and can therefore be considered forms of direct democracy.

initiative

A process permitted in some states whereby voters may place proposed changes to state law on the ballot if sufficient signatures are obtained on petitions calling for such a vote.

? Why It Matters

Direct Democracy

Direct democracy has a special appeal to Americans, who believe in government by the people. But what if all laws passed by a state legislature had to be approved by the voters? We might adopt many policies that infringe on the rights of numerical minorities. We would also have to vote more often and spend more time voting. Extensive voting demands might decrease citizen participation and lead to ill-informed policy choices. At the same time, citizens would likely view government actions as more legitimate.

A method of policymaking that is unique in the United States to subnational governments is **direct democracy**. Three procedures—the initiative, the referendum, and the recall—provide voters with ways they can directly impact policymaking and the political process through the voting booth. One or more of these procedures is available in all but one state (Alabama); the referendum for ratifying constitutional amendments is especially common. The more proactive of these are less widely available—the initiative (24 states) and recall (17 states) (see Table 21.3). These procedures were developed in the Progressive Era largely in the Western and Midwestern states as a way to bring more power to the people by cutting out the middle persons in the policymaking system—political parties, politicians, and interest groups.

The **initiative** is the purest form of direct democracy. Although its details vary from state to state, the basic procedure is as follows. First, a citizen decides that he or she wants to see a law passed. The specific language of that proposal is then registered with a state official (typically the secretary of state), and permission to circulate a petition is given. The advocates of the proposal then try to get a specified number of eligible voters (typically 5 to 10 percent of those voting in the previous election) to sign a petition saying they would like to see the proposal on the ballot. When the appropriate number of signatures has been verified, the proposal is placed on the next general election ballot for an approve/disapprove vote. If a majority of voters approve it, the proposal becomes law. Between 1904 and 2006, at least 2,155 initiatives have been placed on state ballots, and only 41 percent have passed. But both the average number and passage rate of initiatives has increased in the past 15 years.[58]

The initiative allows for the adoption of policy that might otherwise be ignored or opposed by policymakers in the state legislature and governor's offices. The best example of this is the state legislative term-limits movement of the 1990s. Since this policy would directly and negatively affect some state legislators, it is easy to see why such a policy would be difficult to pass through the state legislature. Of the 21 states that have passed such limits, only Louisiana does not have the initiative. Perhaps just as telling, of the 24 states that have the initiative in some form, only four (Alaska, Illinois, Mississippi, and North Dakota) have not passed term limits. Other sorts of ideas become state law through this process that might not otherwise do so, for good or ill. These include everything from a series of property tax limitations in many states in the 1970s and 1980s to recent initiatives allowing marijuana

TABLE 21.3

Direct Democracy Mechanisms

INITIATIVE[a]	LEGISLATIVE REFERENDUM[b]	RECALL
AK, AZ, AR, CA, CO, FL, ID, IL, ME, MA, MI, MS, MO, MT, NE, NV, ND, OH, OK, OR, SD, UT, WA, WY	AZ, AR, CA, DE, ID, IL, KY, ME, MD, MA, MI, MO, MT, NE, NV, NM, ND, OH, OK, OR, SD, UT, WA	AK, AZ, CA, GA, ID, KS, LA, MI, MN, MT, NV, NM, ND, OR, SD, WA, WI

[a] These states have at least one of the several forms of initiative.
[b] All states except Alabama allow or require a referendum for state constitutional amendments. The states listed in this column also allow referenda on the passage of legislative issues that are not constitutional amendments.

Source: Council of State Governments, *The Book of the States, 2003 Edition* (Washington, DC: Council of State Governments, 2004), 281-87.

to be used for medical purposes in California and seven other states. Some research even suggests that legislatures in states with the initiative may pass laws more in line with citizen preferences when the threat of citizen action through the initiative is present,[59] but other research disputes this finding.[60]

Perhaps not surprisingly there is considerable debate over the wisdom of making state law through citizen-initiated proposals. Constitutional amendments and legislation passed through initiative are often poorly drafted and may contain ambiguous or contradictory provisions. As a result, initiatives often create new problems, leading to lawsuits and court interpretation and, often, action by the legislature.

It is also unclear to what extent the initiative process empowers citizens or merely gives new tools to well-financed interest groups. In larger states, special interests can pay professional firms to gather the required number of signatures. Monied interests also have the advantage in mounting expensive television advertising campaigns. These ads can present voters with a biased or incomplete set of facts on an issue they would otherwise know little about. For example, in the 1998 California initiative campaign to legalize Indian tribal casinos, the gambling industry spent more than $71 million on *both sides* of the issue, with advertisements that were often confusing to citizens.[61] In initiative and referendum campaigns, complex public policy questions too often are reduced to simplistic sloganeering. As Ann O' M. Bowman and Richard C. Kearney argue,

> Seldom are issues so simple that a yes-or-no ballot question can adequately reflect appropriate options and alternatives. A legislative setting, in contrast, fosters the negotiation and compromise that produce workable solutions. Legislatures are deliberative bodies, not instant problem solvers.[62]

A hybrid of legislative and direct democratic policymaking is the **referendum**. Unlike the initiative, which is proposed by a citizen or group, the referendum begins life as a legislative resolution. Typically, the state legislature deliberates on and passes the proposal in both chambers in identical form, as required for any bill to become law, but then instead of sending the bill to the governor for his or her approval, the proposal is presented to the voters in a general election. If a majority of voters approve it, it becomes law; otherwise, it does not. In all states (except Alabama), this procedure is required for amendments to the state constitution, and in many subnational governments referenda are required for bond issues (government debt), tax changes, and other fiscal matters.

The **recall** is different than the initiative or referendum because it is about elected officials rather than public policy. In essence, the recall allows voters to call a special election for a specific official in an attempt to throw him or her out of office before the end of his or her term. The process involves gathering signatures on a petition of voters in the jurisdiction of the official being recalled, much like an initiative. Once enough signatures are gathered, a special election is held, usually within three months of official confirmation of the valid number of signatures, in which the official being recalled runs against any forthcoming challenger(s), if he or she desires to do so.

TIMELINE

Initiatives and Referendums

referendum
A state-level method of direct legislation that gives voters a chance to approve or disapprove legislation or a constitutional amendment proposed by the state legislature.

recall
A procedure that allows voters to call a special election for a specific official in an attempt to throw him or her out of office before the end of term. Recalls are permitted in only 17 states, seldom used because of their cost and disruptiveness, and rarely successful.

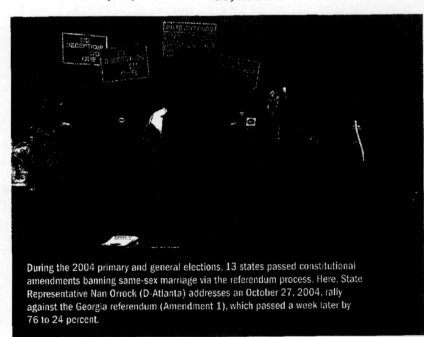

During the 2004 primary and general elections, 13 states passed constitutional amendments banning same-sex marriage via the referendum process. Here, State Representative Nan Orrock (D-Atlanta) addresses an October 27, 2004, rally against the Georgia referendum (Amendment 1), which passed a week later by 76 to 24 percent.

Needless to say, this is a drastic action and it is infrequently undertaken successfully. It is disruptive of the routine political process and very costly for the jurisdiction having to hold the special election. Because of this, only 17 states allow for the recall, and these states make it difficult to undertake, with the required number of signatures being much higher than that required to place an initiative on the ballot. Historically, those who have been recalled have been accused of a serious breach of propriety, morals, or ethics and often are local officials or judges serving long terms. For example, in 1982 a district judge in Madison, Wisconsin, made the highly publicized and inflammatory statement that he thought a very young victim in a sexual assault case appeared promiscuous; the judge was recalled and removed from office.[63] However, in recent years, some state and local officials have been recalled for more policy-oriented reasons, such as for supporting tax increases in Michigan, a stadium sales tax in Wisconsin, and gun control in California. Most dramatically, California Governor Gray Davis was recalled in 2003 after voters came to believe that he had failed to solve the state's energy and fiscal crisis. California voters elected action-movie star Arnold Schwarzenegger. This was the first successful recall of a governor since North Dakota voters recalled Governor Lynn Frazier in 1921.

STATE AND LOCAL GOVERNMENT RELATIONS

In Chapter 3, you read about the concept of federalism and how the nation's Founders tried to strike a balance between the powers of the central government and those of the states. This state–federal *intergovernmental relationship* has evolved in the past 200 years through statutes passed by Congress, constitutional amendments and their interpretation by the U.S. Supreme Court, civil war, and tradition. The relationship between the states and the national government is both contentious and one of the defining characteristics of government in the United States.

The intergovernmental relationship between the states and their inferior governments—local governments—is no less important in defining how our government works. But this relationship is far less ambiguous and involves no balance and little interpretation.

The basic relationship is that local governments are totally subservient to the state government. According to **Dillon's Rule** (after Iowa Judge John Dillon, who expressed this idea in an 1868 court decision), local governments have only those powers that are explicitly given to them by the states. Dillon argued definitively that local governments were "creatures of the state" and that the state legislature gave local governments the "breath of life without which they cannot exist."[64] This means that local governments have very little discretion over which policies they pursue or how they pursue them. In fact, the states have been known to take away policymaking and administrative power from local governments completely, as when the state of Missouri recently took over a school district that state officials felt was being run improperly. An extreme case of state usurpation of local power took place in 1997 when the Massachusetts state legislature actually *abolished* Middlesex County because of mismanagement and corruption.[65]

The basis of this shocking imbalance of power is the U.S. Constitution. Although the Constitution discusses at length the role of the states and the relationship between the states and the central government, local governments are never explicitly mentioned. The establishment and supervision of local government has been interpreted to be one of the "reserve powers" for the states, under the

Dillon's Rule

The idea that local governments have only those powers that are explicitly given them by the states. This means that local governments have very little discretion over what policies they pursue or how they pursue them. It was named for Iowa Judge John Dillon, who expressed this idea in an 1868 court decision.

Why It Matters

State Boundaries

State boundaries typically result from historical accidents rather than efforts to define regions that have similar interests and needs. For example, the people of the Florida panhandle probably have more in common with those of southern Alabama and Georgia than those of south Florida. But what if the states were reconstructed so as to make them more homogeneous and therefore more different from one another? How do you think this would affect state policy? For example, would state policies also be more dissimilar? Would citizens be happier with the policies in their state?

Tenth Amendment of the Bill of Rights. The idea is that states have certain responsibilities and policy goals they must fulfill, but sometimes the best way to do this is through local units of government they establish. For example, the states have the responsibility to educate children, but all states (except Hawaii) have opted to establish regional school districts to do this for the states.

Although local governments have no constitutional sovereignty, local government officials are certainly not powerless in their efforts to control their own destiny. But the power of local government arises from informal political clout rather than formal powers. First, many people feel more strongly connected to their local governments than to the state. After all, it is the local government officials they see most frequently—the police officer responding to an emergency call, the teacher in the school educating their child, or the city council member helping to get the potholes filled in the street. State officials understand the sympathy (and political clout) these officials have among citizens, so they do not try to rile them without good reason. Further, local government officials of all stripes form interest groups to lobby state officials. In all states, organizations of local officials, such as the Wisconsin League of Municipalities or the Texas Association of Counties, are among the most powerful interest groups in the state capitol.[66]

Many cities have also managed to get state legislatures to grant them a degree of autonomy through a **local charter**. A charter is an organizational statement and grant of authority from the state to a local government, much like a state or national constitution. States sometimes allow cities to write their own charters and to change them without permission from the state legislature, within limits. Today, this practice of **home rule** is widely used to organize and modernize city government.

LOCAL GOVERNMENTS

The U.S. Bureau of the Census counts not only people but also governments. Its latest count revealed an astonishing 89,476 American local governments (see Table 21.4). In addition to being a citizen of the United States and of a state, the average citizen also resides within the jurisdiction of perhaps 10 to 20 local governments. The state of Illinois holds the current record for the largest number of local governments: 6,994 at the latest count. The six-county Chicago metropolitan area alone has more than 1,200 governments.

local charter
An organizational statement and grant of authority from the state to a local government, much like a state or national constitution. States sometimes allow municipalities to write their own charters and to change them without permission of the state legislature, within limits. See also home rule.

home rule
The practice by which municipalities are permitted by the states to write their own charters and change them without permission of the state legislature, within limits. Today this practice is widely used to organize and modernize municipal government. See also local charter.

TABLE 21.4

Local Governments in the United States

TYPE OF GOVERNMENT	1962	2007	% CHANGE, 1962–2007
All local governments	91,186	89,476	−1.1%
Single-purpose governments			
School district	34,678	13,051	−66.4%
Special district	18,323	37,381	+49.0%

Source: U.S. Bureau of the Census, "Local Governments and Public School Systems by Type and State: 2007," March 7, 2008, http://www.census.gov/govs/www/cog2007.html.

The sheer number of governments in the United States is, however, as much a burden as a boon to democracy. Citizens are governed by a complex maze of local governments—some with broad powers, others performing very specialized services. This plethora of local governments creates voter overload and ignorance, thereby defeating the democratic purpose of citizen control.

TYPES OF LOCAL GOVERNMENT

Local governments can be classified into five types based on their legal purpose and the scope of their responsibilities: counties, townships, municipalities, school districts, and special districts.

Counties   The largest geographic unit of government at the local level is the *county* government, although they are called "parishes" in Louisiana and "boroughs" in Alaska. Texas has the most counties with 254, while Delaware and Hawaii have only three. Los Angeles County serves the most people—over 9.5 million residents— whereas Loving County, Texas, serves only 67 residents.

The 3,033 county governments are administrative arms of state government. Typically, counties are responsible for keeping records of births, deaths, and marriages; establishing a system of justice and law enforcement; maintaining roads and bridges; collecting taxes; conducting voter registration and elections; and providing for public welfare and education. Rural residents more often rely on county governments for services because they have fewer local governments to turn to than city dwellers.

County governments usually consist of an elected *county commission*, the legislative body that makes policy, and a collection of "row officers," including sheriffs, prosecutors, county clerks, and assessors, who run county services. Some urban counties, such as Milwaukee County, St. Louis County, and Wayne (Detroit) County, now elect a county executive (like a mayor or governor). In some counties, such as Dade (Miami) County and Sacramento County, the county commission appoints a county administrator to take responsibility for the administration of county policies.

Townships   *Township* governments are found in only 20 states, including Maine, Michigan, New Hampshire, New York, Vermont, and Wisconsin. Most of the 16,519 township governments have limited powers and primarily just assist with county services in rural areas; however, some, such as those in New England, function much like city governments. Voters typically elect a township board, a supervisor, and perhaps a very small number of other executives. Township officers oversee public highways and local law enforcement, keep records of vital statistics and tax collections, and administer elections. However, most lack the power to pass local ordinances since they serve as administrative extensions of state and county governments.

Municipalities   Cities are more formally referred to as municipal governments or *municipalities*, and they supply most local programs and services for 19,492 communities in the United States. Municipalities typically provide police and fire protection, street maintenance, solid waste collection, water and sewer works, park and recreation services, and public planning. Some larger cities also run public hospitals and health programs, administer public welfare services, operate public transit and utilities, manage housing and urban development programs, and even run universities. Citizen satisfaction with the delivery of such services varies greatly. Originally, many municipalities in the United States were run with a special form of direct democracy—the **town meeting**. Under this system, all voting-age adults in a community gathered once a year to make public policy such as passing new local laws,

town meeting
A special form of direct democracy under which all voting-age adults in a community gather once a year to make public policy. Now used only in a few villages in upper New England.

151

YOUNG PEOPLE AND POLITICS
Public Service Through Elective Office

Many young Americans are concerned about particular issues and government policy, and some are inspired to mobilize other young adults to register to vote, attend city council meetings, and sign petitions. However, even though issues such as public spending on education, economic development, and the drinking age have a direct impact on youth, few young people are motivated enough about these issues to run for public office. And because of age restrictions, most national and statewide offices are closed to young adults. However, in most states there are no age requirements for state and local legislative positions, and some young adults successfully run for these offices.

In Kansas, 20-year-old Tanner Fortney ran for the Spring Hill city council in 2001 after becoming interested in public policy through his high school debate team and, later, through an internship with Congressman Dennis Moore (D-Kans.) and through his political science classes at the University of Kansas. Fortney survived the primary election for the city council but lost the general election by 75 votes. After the election, Fortney did not wallow in defeat. Instead, he gained an appointment to the Spring Hill planning commission and immersed himself in the details of zoning and infrastructure.

Fortney's vigor impressed the town's mayor, and when a city council member resigned in October 2001, Mayor Mark Squire appointed Fortney to the council. The appointment made Fortney the council's youngest member ever. Fortney focused his attention on development and economic growth issues, trying to make sure the town balanced residential and commercial development. Fortney's hard work, zeal, and fresh perspective helped to revitalize city government in the sleepy suburb of 3,000 near Kansas City. Voters appreciated Fortney's efforts and reelected him in April 2003 for a four-year term.

Fortney says that he will likely continue in public service, perhaps running for the county commission. In the meantime, he will serve on the council, complete law school, and perhaps dream of serving in the state legislature. Fortney's example clearly demonstrates that young people can become involved and make a difference.

QUESTIONS FOR DISCUSSION

- What are the minimum age limits for running for local and state offices in your state? Do you think they are too low or too high?

- Would you ever consider running for local or state office? Why or why not? Would a specific issue or desire for a policy change encourage you to run? Explain.

- If you did run for office at a young age, what steps would you take to encourage more young people to become involved in politics?

approving a town budget, and electing a small number of local residents to serve as town officials. But as cities became too large for the town meeting style of governance, three modern forms of municipal government developed.

Mayor–Council Government. In a typical mayor–council government (Figure 21.6), local residents elect a mayor and a city council. In "strong mayor" cities, such as New York City, the city council makes public policy, and the mayor and city bureaucrats who report to the mayor are responsible for policy implementation. Strong mayors may also veto actions of the city council. In "weak mayor" cities, most power is vested in the city council, which directs the activities of the city bureaucracy. The mayor serves as the presiding officer for city council meetings and as the ceremonial head of city government. Most mayor–council cities have this weak mayor form of governance because most of the numerous small cities of 10,000 or fewer residents use this system. San Diego is one major city that uses the weak mayor form of government.

Council-Manager Government. In this form of municipal government, voters elect a city council and sometimes a mayor who often acts as both presiding officer and voting member of the council (see Figure 21.7). The council is responsible for setting policy for the city. The implementation and administration of the council's actions are placed in the hands of an appointed **city manager**, who is expected to carry out policy with the aid of city bureaucracy. More than one-third of cities use this form of government, including such major cities as Dallas, Kansas City, and Phoenix.

city manager
An official appointed by the city council who is responsible for implementing and administering the council's actions. More than one-third of U.S. cities use the council-manager form of government.

FIGURE 21.6

Mayor–Council Government

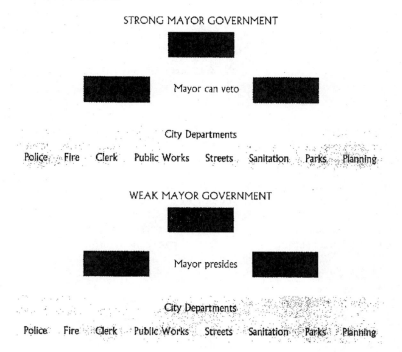

Commission Government. In commission government, voters elect a panel of city commissioners, each of whom serves as both legislator and executive. These officials make public policy just as city council members do in the other two forms of government. However, each member is also elected as a commissioner of a functional area of city government (for example, public safety), and bureaucrats report to a single commissioner. Among the few cities that still use a commission government are Vicksburg, Mississippi, and St. Petersburg, Florida.[67]

Most city council members and many mayors are elected in nonpartisan elections. Traditionally, city council members represented a district or ward of the city—a practice that permitted ward-based machine party bosses to control elections and to try to create public policies that were good for individual wards rather than for the city as a whole. Reformers advocated at-large city elections, with all members of the city council chosen by voters throughout the city. These at-large representatives could not create public policies to benefit only their own neighborhoods because they would have to answer to all the city's voters. A majority of cities use at-large elections today.

A consequence of at-large elections is that they make it more difficult for minority group members to be elected to the city council. This is because African American and other ethnic minorities in U.S. cities have tended to live in more or less homogeneous neighborhoods. Therefore, although they may be a minority of the entire city's population (and so fail to generate a majority in at-large elections), they may be a majority in smaller sections of the city, and so could elect candidates to pursue their interests in district-based electoral systems. Cities that employ district elections may have a greater degree of representational equity for African Americans and Hispanics on city councils than cities that use at-large elections.[68]

FIGURE 21.7

Council–Manager Government

Mayor is member
Mayor presides

appoints

City Departments

Police   Fire   Clerk   Public Works   Streets   Sanitation   Parks   Planning

School Districts   The nation's 13,051 *school districts* are responsible for educating children. Although some cities, counties, townships, and one state (Hawaii) operate dependent public school systems (a total of 1,510), school districts are run as independent local governments. Consolidation of small, often rural, districts into larger ones is the major reason for a 66 percent drop in the number of school districts during the past 45 years.

In an independent school district, voters within a geographically defined area are responsible for their own public education system, including electing a board of education, selecting administrators and teachers, building and operating schools, designing and running education programs, and raising the revenues to meet a locally adopted school budget. Because the states are ultimately responsible for public education, state governments adopt general standards for education, mandate certain school programs, and provide a system of state financial assistance to public schools. But within the guidelines of state policy and the parameters of state funding, locally elected school boards and their appointed administrators deliver education services to the nation's children.

School districts have become the focus for many emotionally charged issues at the local level. Prayer in public schools, sex education, equity in school funding, English as a second-language classes, charter schools, gay and lesbian student groups, and lingering racial discrimination are just a few of the more explosive issues surrounding schools in the 2000s. For example, although the Supreme Court declared that states have a responsibility to eliminate discrimination in education in such important decisions as *Brown v. Board of Education* (1954) and *Swann v. Charlotte-Mecklenberg County Schools* (1971) (see Chapter 5), inequities in the public school systems persist, with racial minorities still encountering poorly funded public education in many instances. In fact, political scientists have discovered an extensive pattern of second-generation discrimination—a shortage of minority teachers "which leads to negative outcome for minority students."[69] Furthermore, in 2007 the Supreme Court ruled that public schools cannot use race as a criteria when assigning children to schools. The ruling overturned policies that attempted to create racial diversity across and within schools (*Parents Involved in Community Schools v. Seattle School Dist. No. 1*). How this ruling may influence efforts to prevent racial segregation in the long term is not clear.

This inequity is coupled with a financial crisis in many public school systems. States have widely divergent school aid policies—some states are good providers to their neediest local schools, whereas others leave the financing responsibility largely to local districts. Local revenue sources are disproportionately based on the local property tax—a policy choice that results in wealthier districts having an abundance of resources, while poorer districts have inadequate revenues for their schoolchildren.[70] Schools around the country continue to struggle with providing quality education with limited resources.

Special Districts The fastest-growing form of local government in the United States is the *special district*. The last official U.S. Census Bureau count showed 37,381 of these independent, limited-purpose governments. Generally, special districts provide only a single service, such as flood control, waste disposal, fire protection, public libraries, or public parks. There is no standard model of special district government organization—the types of organizational arrangements are almost as plentiful as the number of districts. Some districts have elected policymaking boards; a governor or mayor appoints others. Special districts are highly flexible units of local government because their boundary lines can be drawn across the usual municipal, county, and township borders. By providing services on a larger scale, they help localities realize certain economies and efficiencies.

However, important questions about democracy are inherent in the growth of special districts. Special districts are, to a great extent, invisible governments; the local press rarely covers their operations, and there is little direct public participation in their decision making. Most citizens do not even know who serves on these district boards or when the boards meet. As a result, the public has great difficulty holding special districts accountable.

FRAGMENTATION, COOPERATION, AND COMPETITION

Each governing body in a fragmented metropolis tends to look at problems from its own narrow perspective. As a result, local bodies fail to cooperate with one another and plan effectively for the region's future needs. For example, the development of an effective mass transit system is often hindered when not all communities are willing to share in financing a new metropolitan bus network or light rail system, or a narrowly focused special district devoted to maintaining the region's road network may not be willing to divert its funds to help finance new rail construction.

Traditionally, regional cooperation on specific policy areas has been undertaken through the use of special districts. For example, local water and sewer needs transcend municipality borders. To address this issue, special sewer and water districts have been set up in most metropolitan areas to coordinate the delivery of this service.

But there are limits to the number of special districts that can be established efficiently and the level of coordination these districts can achieve. What can be done to coordinate a variety of public services in a metropolitan area? A few areas have developed super-locals, institutional arrangements that act almost as general purpose governments for an entire region. Seattle, Miami, and Minneapolis–St. Paul each have a metropolitan council that serves such a function. For example, the Minneapolis–St. Paul Metropolitan Council operates the region's bus service, provides sewer and water services, operates a regional housing and development authority, and funds and plans regional parks and trails, all activities that cut across traditional local governments' physical and policy area boundaries.

But examples of institutionalized regional coordination are the exception rather than the rule. For the most part, the prospects for promoting regional cooperation to correct the inequalities and coordination problems that result from metropolitan fragmentation have been dim. Generally speaking, the United States lacks the strong tradition of regional planning evident in Europe (see "America in Perspective: Urban

? Why It Matters
Local Services
The multitude of local governments with independent authority can make the delivery of public services in a metropolitan area inefficient, contentious, and just plain confusing. If all government services in a metropolitan area were taken over by a single government entity, such as the county, then these services might be provided more effectively and at a lower cost. And inequities in services between wealthy neighborhoods and poor neighborhoods might be resolved. However, such consolidation would allow fewer access points to government, perhaps making it less democratic.

AMERICA IN PERSPECTIVE

Urban Planning in the European Union and the United States

The nations of the European Union play a much stronger role in guiding urban development than does the United States. Europe's strong planning has helped to preserve cities, control the pace of development, protect agricultural land and the environment, and minimize urban sprawl to a degree that is hardly imaginable in the United States. Typically, these urban planning actions are initiated by regional agencies that get their authority from the central government.

In Great Britain, planners prevented the overgrowth of London by encircling the city with a "green belt"—a designated area in which the countryside would be preserved and no new development permitted. The growth of the region's population was absorbed in planned "new towns" that were built some distance from the central city. The result was a mixture of city and countryside in a metropolitan area and the avoidance of American-style urban sprawl.

Faced with the prospect of excessive growth in Paris, France's national agency for development steered new industries into the suburbs and more distant cities. Still the lure of Paris proved attractive. In response, central government and regional planners built two new towns of high-rise office buildings, convention centers, and hotels in different spots just outside the city's borders. These towns became the main office centers of the metropolitan Paris area. High-rise residential new towns were built in a ring around Paris to absorb the area's rapidly growing population. These new commercial and residential centers were connected to the old city by a new commuter rail system.

The Netherlands has also relied on strong government planning and controls over land use to prevent the country's limited supply of land from being eaten up by rapid urbanization. Dutch planners saved valuable agricultural land and recreational space in a "green heart" in the midst of the metropolitan Amsterdam–The Hague-Rotterdam Randstad ("Ring City") area, one of the most densely populated areas in the world. Riding a train through the area today, you can easily see exactly where the city ends and the land designated for agricultural purposes begins. The planning boundaries are extremely clear and well guarded.

European planners now confront new problems. With the globalization of their economies, cities in Europe find that they are increasingly competing with one another for new business. As a result, spatial planning considerations are sometimes sacrificed in order to give a corporation a site it desires. Citizens' demands for individual homes of their own have also led to pressures for continued suburban development, sometimes compromising the integrity of regional land-use plans. Rush-hour traffic jams have become increasingly common in major European metropolises.

Despite these new problems, European nations have been able to ward off the ills of uncontrolled growth. In the United States, by contrast, the private sector and the free market—not government—play the dominant role in deciding where growth will occur. Compared to Europe, regional planning in the United States is essentially toothless.

Sources: Peter Hall, *Urban and Regional Planning*, 4th ed. (Independence, KY: Routledge, 2002); H. V. Savitch, *Post-Industrial Cities: Politics and Planning in New York, Paris, and London* (Princeton, NJ: Princeton University Press, 1988); Hans Thor Andersen and Ronald Van Kempen, *Governing European Cities: Social Fragmentation, Social Exclusion and Urban Governance* (London: Ashgate, 2000).

Planning in the European Union and the United States"). In large part, this reflects the strong localism inherent in American democracy. Americans prefer living in small, autonomous communities. In the United States, there is a tradition (or perhaps a myth) of people being able to "vote with their feet," that is, of people moving to the place where the government's policies best reflect their values.[71] This exacerbates the problem of regional coordination because local governments in different parts of the same metropolitan area will sometimes offer very different services to their citizens. This often manifests itself as a conflict between city dwellers and suburbanites.

A good (if disturbing) example of this is seen in the conflict over the racial integration of the Milwaukee public schools. When its schools were ordered to desegregate in the 1970s and 1980s, many White families moved out of the school district into neighboring suburban districts. In a classic case of "White flight," White student enrollment in the Milwaukee Public Schools dropped rapidly. In response, the federal court that issued the original desegregation order then expanded its order to include other school districts within Milwaukee County, thus attempting to force a regional coordination for educational policy by judicial fiat and with the backing of the national government. But again, many White families voted with their feet and left the county entirely, making the attempt at coordination a failure.

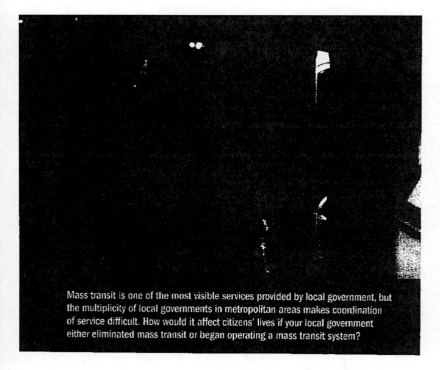

Mass transit is one of the most visible services provided by local government, but the multiplicity of local governments in metropolitan areas makes coordination of service difficult. How would it affect citizens' lives if your local government either eliminated mass transit or began operating a mass transit system?

Other typical conflicts between the preferences and needs of suburbanites and city dwellers involve taxes, roads, and central city services. Many people move to the suburbs because property taxes are lower and land is cheaper. The denser population of an urban area causes a higher need for most local government services and therefore a higher tax burden. Regional coordination often looks to suburbanites to subsidize the taxes of the urban dwellers they left behind. Because suburbanites live more spread out and often far away from their jobs, they need plenty of good roads and highways on which to commute. Meanwhile, urban dwellers would rather that more transportation money be spent on mass transit, which is economical for dense populations. Urban dwellers also complain that suburbanites drive into the central city each workday, using city services like roads, police, water, and so forth, and then take themselves and their tax dollars back to the suburbs at night. These examples offer the barest outline of the differences in preferences and viewpoints of people in different areas of a metropolis. It is easy to understand why coordination and cooperation are hard to come by.

Local governments are also engaged in serious competition for economic development. That is, they try to expand their tax base through commercial and residential development. Some analysts believe that cities are quite limited in their ability to control economic change within their borders, but local officials often believe that development policies are a community's lifeblood.[72] A business owner can simply threaten to leave a community or locate facilities in another town if he or she is unhappy with local policies. Thus, business owners and corporate officials have great leverage to extract concessions from local officials because no local government wants to face the loss of jobs or tax base. As a result, cities compete with one another for desirable business facilities by offering tax reductions, promises of subsidized infrastructure development, and other services demanded by business.

However, local governments can cooperate with one another when they find it in their mutual interest to do so. Central cities and suburbs are often willing, for instance, to share the costs of a new sewage disposal facility. They may also cooperate in ventures to attract a major new employer to the area, or to keep one, as in the case of the massive efforts by local governments in the Chicago metropolitan area to construct a new baseball stadium to keep the White Sox from leaving town in the late 1980s. Sometimes two or more governments may cooperate informally to share equipment and services. In many areas of the country, a **council of governments** (frequently referred to as a COG) exists wherein officials from various localities meet to discuss mutual problems and plan joint, cooperative action. These COGs are often formally very weak, underfunded, poorly staffed, and lacking in any real legislative or taxing power.

You Are a Restaurant Owner

council of governments
Councils in many areas of the country where officials from various localities meet to discuss mutual problems and plan joint, cooperative action.

STATE AND LOCAL FINANCE POLICY

When a state or local government approves its budget for the next year, the basic policy objectives of the government have also been approved. These objectives are contained in the taxing and spending plans that make up the budget. Lofty speeches

FIGURE 21.8

State Government Revenues and Expenditures

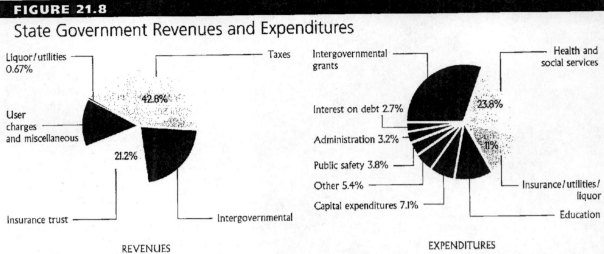

Source: U.S. Bureau of the Census, "State and Local Government Finances, 2004–05," March 7, 2008, *http://www.census.gov/govs/www/estimate05.html.*

can be made and bills passed into law, but without some significant and specific budgetary commitment, a policy will usually have little impact on citizens' lives. Taxpayers increasingly demand more accountability and efficiency from their subnational governments, forcing officials to squeeze services and programs out of limited revenue dollars. Figure 21.8 shows how state governments get their money and how they spend it.

State government revenues are derived from a variety of sources. States receive the largest share of revenue, 42.8 percent, from taxes. States' major sources of tax revenue are sales taxes, income taxes, and motor vehicle and fuel taxes. The second-largest source of state revenue is intergovernmental revenue (21.7 percent)—almost all as grants from the national government. The third major revenue source is state insurance programs (21.2 percent). Charges and fees for services such as state hospitals, college courses, and state parks have become an increasingly important source of revenue for states in the past 20 years (13.5 percent, along with miscellaneous revenue).

Changes in their constitutions over the past 40 years have given states wider access to income and sales taxes and other sources of revenue. Today, 45 states levy a general sales tax; Alaska, Delaware, Montana, New Hampshire, and Oregon are the only holdouts. Only seven states—Alaska, Florida, Nevada, South Dakota, Texas, Washington, and Wyoming—do not have a personal income tax, and New Hampshire and Tennessee have only a limited form of income tax. The modernization of state revenue structures gives the states new money to finance the public programs demanded by citizens.

How do states spend their money? Most of the states' money—about 50 percent—goes to operate state programs (in public safety, education, health and social services, and so on), construct state buildings, and provide direct assistance to individuals. Another 30 percent is allocated as aid to local governments. Since so much of the money that states spend is given to local governments (and since so much of the local governments' revenue comes from the states), the states have even more leverage over the locals than is given to them by Dillon's Rule.

Local government finances can be confusing because of the fragmentation of local governments and the varied ways in which states support and constrain their local authorities. This situation is primarily due to the different ways in which states and their local governments have sorted out the assignment of policy responsibilities

You Are the Mayor and Need to Get a Town Budget Passed

The Fruits of **Devolution**

In the 1980s, President Reagan's revolution of devolving more power and responsibility to the states was well under way. However, few observers foresaw just how important state and local politics and policymaking was becoming.

Throughout the 1990s, state experiments with education, health care, and social welfare policy provided the foundation for national policy change in the late 1990s and 2000s. Meanwhile, governors were increasingly in the national spotlight as potential presidential candidates and possible appointees to executive branch positions. Consider that from 1992 to 2004, voters preferred presidential candidates who were former governors rather than their Washington insider opponents.

Likewise, besides the Iraq War and the war on terrorism, the most prominent national issues have arisen from ongoing debates in the states. From illegal immigration, to abortion, to religion in schools, to same-sex marriage, it has been the actions of state legislatures, state courts, and direct democracy proposals placed on state ballots that have shaped national debate. Meanwhile, state governments have continued to play a primary role in implementing national regulations, including environmental protection, at the same time they have pursued more stringent regulations than those outlined by the national government.

Finally, states have also provided the basis for a gambling revolution in America. Since the 1980s, state governments around the country have increasingly expanded legal gambling in the form of lotteries, tribal casinos, and privately managed casinos. Indeed, there are few areas left in the country where citizens cannot at least buy lottery tickets, and revenues from gambling have given many states new pots of money for spending on basic services, including education. The figure shows that in the state of Indiana, gambling revenues for the state increased from $165.3 million in 1994 to $775 million in 2003. The majority of this revenue goes to the state's Build Indiana Fund, which was created to keep local property taxes down by paying for capital projects in communities across the state.

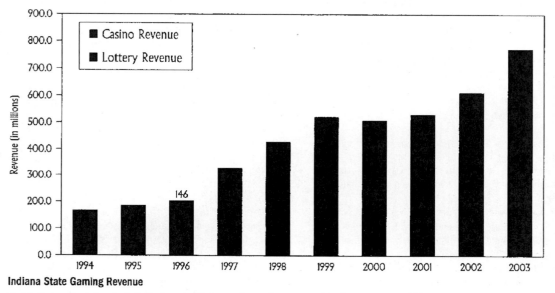

Indiana State Gaming Revenue

Source: Comparative Lottery Analysis: The Impact of Casinos on Lottery Revenues and Total Gaming Revenues, 2004, www.umassd.edu/cfpa/docs/casinolottery.pdf.

among local governments. Figure 21.9 offers a snapshot of local government finances—combining county, city, township, school, and special district budgets—across the United States. Local governments receive their revenues from three main sources: taxes, user charges, and intergovernmental aid. Intergovernmental aid (primarily from the states) and "own source" taxes are now about equal in their contribution to local government revenue, again showing the great dependence of local governments on their states. Local taxes are mainly property taxes, but sales and income taxes also contribute to the revenue of some local governments. Charges on the users of certain services, such as libraries and recreation facilities,

Local Government Revenues and Expenditures

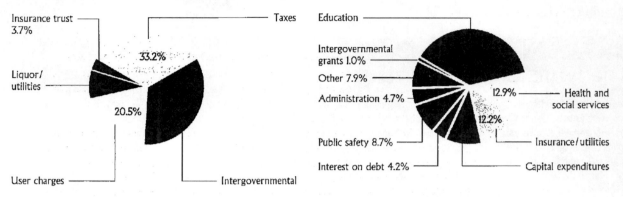

REVENUES   EXPENDITURES

Source: U.S. Bureau of the Census, "State and Local Government Finances, 2004–05," March 7, 2008, *http://www.census.gov/govs/www/estimate05.html.*

YOU ARE THE **Policymaker**

Should Your State Take a Chance on Gambling?

No one likes taxes, but government services have to be paid for somehow. In the 1980s through 2000s, many states tried to earn money for state programs "painlessly" through legalized gambling. Thirty years ago, only Nevada allowed most forms of gambling; in some states children couldn't even enter a sweepstakes on the back of a cereal box. Today, many states not only allow a variety of types of gambling but even sponsor and earn money from such activities. Various states run lotteries and allow casino and riverboat gambling, horse and dog racing, slot machines, video lottery, bingo, and other forms of what proponents call "gaming."

Suppose you are a state legislator faced with the question of legalizing gambling in your state in order to earn extra revenue without raising taxes. To what extent are you willing to accept the negative aspects of gambling in order to gain its monetary rewards?

States earn money from gambling in two main ways. First, states may run a gambling operation outright. State lotteries are the best example. States skim off as much as 50 percent of the receipts from lottery tickets, offering most of the rest as prize money. Second, states may earn money from gambling by taxing bets and winnings heavily, as is commonly done with casino and racetrack gambling.

This sort of revenue is a very attractive alternative to direct taxation as a way to help states fund public services. First, it is seen as a voluntary source of revenue rather than mandatory taxation. Some characterize it as a tax on stupidity. Second, some forms of gambling are argued to encourage economic development in a local area, thereby being a positive good aside from a

source of revenue. The prosperity that some Native American tribes have gained through opening casinos (allowed by the national government since 1988) is evidence in favor of this position. Third, there are those who view gambling as a harmless recreational activity that the state has no business banning anyway—why not make a little money on it?

Even though dozens of states have legalized and earned money from a wide variety of forms of gambling in the past 20 years, not all states have done so, and not all people are convinced that it is good public policy. One argument against legalized gambling is that it is a regressive form of taxation because the people who gamble the highest proportions of their incomes are those who are relatively poor. There has been increasing concern about compulsive gambling, a psychological disorder akin to alcoholism that drives people to gamble incessantly. Like alcoholism, compulsive gambling can lead to financial ruin and the destruction of families. There are also those who argue that gambling is simply immoral and that legalizing and especially encouraging it (as in state lottery TV commercials) leads people to pursue false hope and a destructive lifestyle. Finally, there is some debate as to just how much money a state can actually earn from gambling, now that it has become so common in the United States.

As a state legislator, you must weigh the benefits of "painless" gambling revenue against the arguments of those who oppose it. Should your state legalize gambling? If so, what form should it adopt? Should it run a lottery? Should it allow casinos and tax them? What difference does it make if neighboring states do or do not have legalized gambling? What would *you* do?

provide another 21 percent of local government revenue. They receive 8 percent of their revenue from the operation of municipally owned utilities and liquor sales.

Local governments allocate their monies to a range of services, but the main areas are public education (38 percent), health and social services (13 percent), and public safety (9 percent). These are services that citizens need on a regular basis and expect local governments to provide.

The difference between state and local expenditures reflects the distribution of public services between these levels of government that has developed over the course of the history of the United States. Local government is expected to provide two of the most important and broadly used services of all government in the United States—education and public safety (police and fire protection). State governments, on the other hand, are mainly in charge of making sure that the poorest of the state's citizens have their basic physical needs met. Further, the state is charged with gathering the state's resources and distributing them where they are most needed via intergovernmental grants. While local governments are busy providing direct citizen service, the state governments can take a broader view to enhance equity in public service.

UNDERSTANDING STATE AND LOCAL GOVERNMENTS

A full understanding of the complexity of subnational government cannot be gleaned from a single textbook chapter, but you should remember a few important points about these 89,476 governments.

DEMOCRACY AT THE SUBNATIONAL LEVEL

The very existence of so many governments to handle complex as well as ordinary—but needed—services, testifies to the health of our democracy. States have been willing to decentralize their governing arrangements to permit the creation of local governments to address citizens' policy demands. Today, local voters choose their own representatives to serve on county commissions, city councils, school boards, and some special district boards. As small legislatures elected from among the community's residents, these governing bodies are usually the policymaking institutions closest and most open to all citizens. In many ways, local governments encourage individual participation in government and promote the value of individualism at the local level.

The states also operate in an open policymaking environment. Many of the most important of state officials are elected to office, far more than in the national government. Direct primaries permit voters to select nominees for state offices. The recall even allows voters to oust an official from office before his or her term is over in about one-third of the states. The initiative and the referendum permit voters in many states to make policy or amend their state constitutions directly. In most states, voters have a far more direct role in selecting judges than is the case in the national court system. And by the 1990s, subnational elections were putting officials into office who are far more representative of the U.S. population demographically than is the case in the national government today or subnational governments in previous years.

Even so, subnational politics may not be as democratic as this initial assessment would seem to indicate. Politics at the state level is poorly covered by the media and, as a result, is relatively invisible to the public. Voters can hardly hold elected

161

officials accountable if they know little about what is going on in the state capital. Even at the local level, there is little press coverage of anything other than the results of city council meetings or a mayor's actions—and that doesn't even happen regularly in smaller communities or in suburbs that lack their own daily newspaper.

When, as is often the case, only 30 to 35 percent of voters participate in statewide elections and fewer than 20 percent turn out for local elections, there are real concerns about the health of our grass-roots governments. In one effort to boost citizen participation, states have begun experimenting with vote-by-mail elections. Instead of having to show up on a specific day to cast a ballot, citizens in Oregon were able to mail in their ballots in 1996, and in 1998 Oregon voters passed an initiative making vote-by-mail the only way to vote for every election. Further, in a small number of cities, including Birmingham, Dayton, Portland, and St. Paul, vigorous programs of neighborhood democracy have been developed where citizen participation in public affairs goes far beyond voting. In these cities, neighborhood boards are given control over meaningful policy decisions and program resources, and their actions are not merely advisory. These cities also reward municipal officials who listen to the views of these neighborhood bodies. The experience in these and other cities shows that citizens will devote the considerable time necessary to participate in public affairs if they are convinced that participation is meaningful and that city officials are not just manipulating them.[73]

Competition between subnational governments for economic development also raises significant questions about democracy. As a result of this competition, state and local governments have subsidized business growth and economic development, often at the cost of slighting redistribution services and human resource needs. Business interests have substantial leverage in state and city affairs as a result of their ability to threaten to leave or locate facilities in another jurisdiction. The increasing importance of money in subnational elections has only added to the influence that special interests exert in state and local affairs.

Comparing State and Local Governments

The workings of democracy are often difficult to see in the judicial branch of government. Because most citizens do not attend trials and only lawyers and judges are directly involved in the appeals process, the proceedings of the judiciary are seldom visible to the public until a significant case or decision is announced. This judicial process is not subject to quite the same scrutiny as the legislative and executive functions of state governments. Even though most state and local judges and justices must face the voters to gain or retain their positions, the lack of information that voters have about the judicial process makes the level of true democracy in this process suspect. Citizens will have to take more interest in the crucial role of courts in our democracy in order for courts to assume the same political importance in states as the other branches of government.

THE SCOPE OF SUBNATIONAL GOVERNMENT

Growth in subnational government employment has proceeded at a pace exceeding that of the national government for most of the past 100 years, as we learned in Chapter 15. Most of this growth has been driven by citizen demand for more government services. Although most American voters want their elected representatives to control the size of government, voters also want government to provide them with more and better programs.

Has the reform and professionalization of subnational government in the past generation made any difference for taxpayers? In most cases, it has not resulted in smaller government. By its very nature, legislative professionalism costs tax dollars and leads to a legislature that is more permanent and continuous. School district consolidation has occurred, reducing the overall number of districts by 66 percent in the past 45 years. This declining number of school districts comes at a time of growing demand for more special district governments, which have increased by over 49 percent in four decades.

Most state governments have experimented with *sunset legislation*, which involves periodically reviewing agencies to control the growth of government and eliminate unneeded programs. States have also empowered their legislatures to review executive branch regulations and rules to ensure that citizens or businesses are not overregulated by government. These practices help limit the scope of governments.

But as citizen demand in the late twentieth century led to growth and development in the areas of technology, communications, and public health and safety, subnational governments have had to grow, not diminish. More police, more health care providers, more computer technicians, and more social welfare caseworkers have been needed to meet the expanding range of problems that confront people daily. Although some local governments are barely able to fulfill their basic responsibilities for public safety and maintenance of the local infrastructure, other cities and counties have become much more competent at managing local affairs. Indeed, recent research suggests that local governments often lead their states and the nation in devising innovative ways to deliver public services.[74]

In sum, with the greater responsibilities thrust on them by the national government and the demands of their citizens, subnational governments have responded by enhancing their capacity to provide services to their citizens. In the past 40 years, the enhanced capacity of democratically elected officials in the states, especially state legislators and governors, and the greater use of direct democracy mechanisms has led to stronger and more effective subnational governments that are also more extensive and expensive.

SUMMARY

Our nation's 50 states and its tens of thousands of local governments are responsible for most public policies with which we are most familiar: education, fire protection, police protection, highway maintenance, public welfare, public health, and trash collection. The states are a diverse group, but each has a government that makes, enforces, and interprets laws for its citizens. The structure for state governments is specified in state constitutions—some very long, others quite short. Citizens may modify these state constitutions when necessary to keep pace with changing demands of government.

State legislatures include elected representatives who make laws, appropriate money, oversee the executive branch, perform casework, and help manage conflict across the state. Legislators are increasingly diverse demographically, but most tend to be from a somewhat higher socioeconomic position than the majority of the people they represent. Significant turnover takes place in state legislatures, and voters in some states have ensured that this will continue by enacting term limits for their public officials.

The governors of our states are elected to administer public policy and to attend to citizen needs. Once in office, a governor directs a complex set of state government institutions and programs, conducts state affairs with other governors and the president, initiates much of the legislation state legislatures will adopt, and helps manage conflict. Governors must often work with a number of other elected executive officials to produce public policy.

The state court systems are similar in organization to national courts. Most states have trial courts, intermediate courts of appeal, and a court of last resort; all have jurisdiction over both civil and criminal cases. Judges may attain office through appointment, election, or a hybrid of both known as the Merit Plan. The actions of state judges, especially those serving on the court of last resort, can affect policy significantly.

Local governments in the United States—counties, municipalities, townships, school districts, and special districts—were established by the states to decide on and administer policy in limited geographic and policy areas. Most cities are run by city councils with either a mayor or a city manager directing the day-to-day affairs of city bureaucracies. Counties and townships help states perform many local functions, such as record keeping and the administration of justice. School districts run public schools, and special districts provide limited services for multiple communities. The existence of nearly 88,000 local governments indicates that democracy truly thrives at the local level in the United States.

Politics of Power

A Critical Introduction to American Government

SEVENTH EDITION

MULTIPLE CHOICE

1. What percent of the U.S.'s total income is earned by the richest 20 percent of the country's households?
   A. approximately 20 percent
   B. approximately 30 percent
   C. approximately 40 percent
   D. more than 50 percent
   E. more than 80 percent

   ANS: D   DIF: Moderate   REF: Page 3
   TOP: Introduction   MSC: Remembering

2. What percent of the U.S.'s total income is earned by the poorest 20 percent of U.S. households?
   A. approximately 3 percent
   B. approximately 9 percent
   C. approximately 15 percent
   D. approximately 20 percent
   E. approximately 50 percent

   ANS: A   DIF: Difficult   REF: Page 3
   TOP: Introduction   MSC: Remembering

3. Since 1980, the gap between rich and poor in the United States has
   A. decreased a lot.
   B. decreased a little.
   C. stayed about the same.
   D. increased.
   E. been so difficult to measure that there's no way of knowing whether the gap has decreased, increased, or remained the same.

   ANS: D   DIF: Moderate   REF: Page 3
   TOP: Introduction   MSC: Applying

4. Compared to the gap between high and low *incomes* in the United States, the *wealth* gap is
   A. much smaller.
   B. slightly smaller.
   C. about the same.
   D. greater.
   E. so difficult to measure that it's impossible to make such comparisons.

   ANS: D   DIF: Easy   REF: Page 3
   TOP: Introduction   MSC: Applying

5. In 2011, the top 1 percent of income earners in the United States owned about _____ of the nation's wealth.
   A. 5 percent
   B. 25 percent
   C. 40 percent
   D. 60 percent
   E. 80 percent

   ANS: C   DIF: Moderate   REF: Page 3
   TOP: Introduction   MSC: Remembering

6. Compared with other economically developed countries, the gap between rich and poor in the United States is
   A. greater.
   B. about the same.
   C. slightly less.
   D. much less.
   E. so difficult to measure that it's impossible to make such comparisons.

   ANS: A   DIF: Easy   REF: Page 4
   TOP: Introduction   MSC: Applying

7. According to the text, the lopsided distribution of income and wealth is or was a central concern of

   _____.
   A. the Tea Party movement
   B. the Occupy Wall Street movement
   C. the Business Roundtable
   D. the Federalists
   E. the abolitionist movement

   ANS: B   DIF: Easy   REF: Page 4
   TOP: Introduction   MSC: Remembering

8. According to the text, the most powerful predictor of an individual's health and mortality is that individual's

   _____.
   A. genetics
   B. exposure to carcinogens
   C. smoking
   D. social class position
   E. race

   ANS: D   DIF: Moderate   REF: Page 4
   TOP: Introduction   MSC: Remembering

9. As a result of the election of Barack Obama, the country's first black president, people of color now
   A. earn as much as whites.
   B. live as long as whites.
   C. are less victimized by street crime than whites are.
   D. are as well educated as whites are.
   E. experience similar conditions as before; the income and wealth of people of color has not significantly improved since the election of Barack Obama.

   ANS: E   DIF: Moderate   REF: Page 5
   TOP: Introduction   MSC: Applying

10. According to the text, the *Titanic* offers a powerful metaphor for U.S. society and politics for all of the following reasons *except*
    A. like the *Titanic*, the U.S. political system is doomed to fail.
    B. U.S. businesses' concerns with profits resemble the similar concerns of the *Titanic*'s owners.
    C. the *Titanic* was the world's most powerful ship, and the United States is the world's most powerful nation.
    D. there was great economic inequality among the *Titanic*'s passengers, and there is great economic inequality in the United States.
    E. the *Titanic*'s first-class passengers were treated much better than those in steerage, and the U.S. rich have much more of the good things in life than poor people have.

    ANS: A   DIF: Moderate   REF: Page 6
    TOP: Constitutional Democracy: The Founding
    MSC: Applying

11. All of the following statements about the Bill of Rights are true *except*
    A. it constitutes the first ten amendments of the Constitution.
    B. it prohibits Congress from designating any religion as an official one.
    C. it prohibits courts from requiring people to testify against themselves.
    D. it guarantees all adults over the age of twenty-one the right to vote.
    E. it reserves to the people or the states any powers not explicitly assigned to the federal government.

    ANS: D   DIF: Moderate   REF: Pages 6–7
    TOP: Constitutional Democracy: The Founding
    MSC: Applying

12. The Declaration of Independence
    A. was signed in 1787.
    B. was written to compensate for the weaknesses of the Articles of Confederation.
    C. states that all human beings have certain unalienable rights.
    D. is just another name for what is usually called the Constitution.
    E. affirmed Great Britain's right to rule the thirteen colonies.

    ANS: C   DIF: Easy   REF: Page 8
    TOP: Constitutional Democracy: The Founding
    MSC: Understanding

13. The Articles of Confederation
    A. allowed each state to retain its sovereignty and independence.
    B. were signed in 1787.
    C. provided for an extremely strong and powerful national government.
    D. gave the president much more power than it gave Congress.
    E. is just another name for what is usually called the Constitution.

    ANS: A   DIF: Easy   REF: Page 8
    TOP: Constitutional Democracy: The Founding
    MSC: Understanding

14. Under the Articles of Confederation, the federal government had the exclusive power to
    A. coin money.
    B. levy taxes.
    C. raise a militia.
    D. make rules regarding international trade.
    E. negotiate treaties with other nations.

    ANS: E   DIF: Moderate   REF: Page 8
    TOP: Constitutional Democracy: The Founding
    MSC: Understanding

15. The national government is characterized by a system of checks and balances that includes all of the following *except*
    A. the capacity to govern is shared by the executive, legislative, and judicial branches.
    B. the president can veto congressional legislation.
    C. the Senate must approve key presidential appointments.
    D. the president can remove Supreme Court justices whose decisions are unconstitutional.
    E. the Supreme Court can review laws passed by Congress and signed by the president.

    ANS: D   DIF: Moderate   REF: Page 9
    TOP: Constitutional Democracy: The Founding
    MSC: Applying

16. Federalism is a political system in which
    A. national power is limited by the reservation of certain powers to the states.
    B. the Constitution guarantees citizens certain basic political liberties.
    C. there are checks and balances among the legislative, executive, and judicial branches of government.
    D. state constitutions trump the national constitution if there is a conflict between the two.
    E. the Constitution outlines the powers of state and local governments.

    ANS: A   DIF: Moderate   REF: Page 9
    TOP: Constitutional Democracy: The Founding
    MSC: Understanding

17. According to the Constitution as it was originally ratified
    A. members of the House of Representatives would be elected by the people every six years.
    B. senators would be chosen by the state legislatures.
    C. the president has the power to declare war.
    D. Congress is prohibited from regulating interstate commerce.
    E. justices of the Supreme Court are elected by the House of Representatives and the Senate.

    ANS: B   DIF: Difficult   REF: Page 10
    TOP: Constitutional Democracy: The Founding
    MSC: Applying

18. The Great Compromise refers to the Constitutional Convention debate concerning
    A. ratification of the Constitution.
    B. representation in Congress.
    C. the division of power between the federal government and the states.
    D. the election of the president.
    E. the number of justices on the U.S. Supreme Court.

    ANS: B   DIF: Moderate   REF: Page 10
    TOP: Constitutional Democracy: The Founding
    MSC: Understanding

19. The number of representatives from each state elected to the House of Representatives is based on
    A. the state's population.
    B. the geographic size of the state.
    C. the year the state is admitted to the union (older states have greater representation).
    D. the amount of federal tax revenue generated in that state.
    E. equal representation of each state.

    ANS: A   DIF: Easy   REF: Page 10
    TOP: Constitutional Democracy: The Founding
    MSC: Remembering

20. All House of Representatives members are
    A. chosen by direct election every 2 years.
    B. selected by state legislatures every 2 years.
    C. chosen by direct election every 6 years.
    D. selected by state legislatures every 6 years.
    E. chosen by direct election every 4 years.

    ANS: A   DIF: Moderate   REF: Page 10
    TOP: Constitutional Democracy: The Founding
    MSC: Understanding

21. The Constitution dealt with slavery by
    A. making slaves citizens.
    B. counting every five slaves as three persons for apportioning seats in the House of Representatives.
    C. prohibiting Congress from ever passing laws abolishing the importation of slaves.
    D. declaring that a slave would be free forever if she or he escaped to a state that prohibited slavery.
    E. outlawing slavery in the North, but not in the South.

    ANS: B   DIF: Easy   REF: Page 11
    TOP: Constitutional Democracy: The Founding
    MSC: Applying

22. The number of a state's electors in the Electoral College is determined by
    A. the state's population.
    B. the number of members the state elects to the House of Representatives.
    C. the sum of the state's members in the House of Representatives and the U.S. Senate.
    D. the number of the state's U.S. Senators.
    E. electoral laws established by Congress.

    ANS: C   DIF: Moderate   REF: Page 11
    TOP: Constitutional Democracy: The Founding
    MSC: Understanding

23. _____ is the idea that the ultimate and supreme source of political authority lies not with rulers but with the people, the citizens of a republic.
    A. The market
    B. The Bill of Rights
    C. The separation of powers
    D. Popular sovereignty
    E. Federalism

    ANS: D   DIF: Moderate   REF: Page 14
    TOP: Constitutional Democracy: The Founding
    MSC: Understanding

24. According to the text, the United States's capitalist market system
    A. is inherently not democratic.
    B. is inherently democratic.
    C. may or may not be democratic depending on who is president.
    D. may or may not be democratic depending on which party controls Congress.
    E. may or may not be democratic depending on whether the government officials adhere to the Constitution's basic principles.

    ANS: A   DIF: Easy   REF: Page 15
    TOP: Standards of Democracy   MSC: Applying

25. According to the text, large corporations have dispro-portionate political power mainly because
    A. almost all of their top executives are white men.
    B. the Constitution prohibits government from regulating business too heavily.
    C. the well-being of everyone as measured by jobs and income depends on the investment decisions and the profits of private firms.
    D. most politicians are susceptible to bribes.
    E. most government leaders were once CEOs of large corporations.

    ANS: C   DIF: Moderate   REF: Page 15
    TOP: Standards of Democracy   MSC: Applying

26. When political scientists talk about the "privileged position of business," they mainly mean that
    A. business executives are greedy.
    B. top corporate executives get away with more illegal activity than most other people.
    C. top corporate executives are admitted to elite private clubs that exclude blue-collar workers.
    D. top corporate executives get paid much more than factory workers.
    E. business leaders have an advantage in influencing public policy debates.

    ANS: E   DIF: Moderate   REF: Page 15
    TOP: Standards of Democracy   MSC: Applying

27. An economic system based on the private ownership of property in which profit is pursued through the invest-ment of capital and the employment of labor is called

    _____.
    A. the market.
    B. the corporate complex.
    C. capitalism.
    D. republicanism.
    E. democracy.

    ANS: C   DIF: Moderate   REF: Page 15
    TOP: Standards of Democracy   MSC: Understanding

28. The close relationship between business and govern-ment is referred to as a
    A. market economy.
    B. constitutional democracy.
    C. system of checks and balances.
    D. corporate complex.
    E. superpower.

    ANS: D   DIF: Moderate   REF: Pages 15–16
    TOP: Standards of Democracy   MSC: Understanding

29. According to the text, the principle of majority rule
    A. is of no relevance in a representative democracy.
    B. is applied in the United States to virtually every important issue.
    C. is applied in the United States only to a confined range of issues.
    D. is the principle upon which the Declaration of Inde-pendence is based.
    E. is the principle upon which the Constitution is based.

    ANS: C   DIF: Moderate   REF: Page 16
    TOP: Standards of Democracy   MSC: Applying

30. According to the text, it is important to consider sub-stantive as well as procedural democracy. If a political scientist were studying the extent to which there is sub-stantive democracy in a political system, she or he would most likely be concerned with
    A. what the Constitution said.
    B. whether the political system had a bill of rights.
    C. how much federalism existed.
    D. what the laws said about how members of the legislature are elected.
    E. how economic inequality affected the operation of the political system.

    ANS: E   DIF: Difficult   REF: Page 16
    TOP: Standards of Democracy   MSC: Applying

31. Substantive democracy refers to
    A. whether all citizens have equitable chances to influence and control the making of decisions that affect them.
    B. the existence of democratic procedures such as the right to vote.
    C. the existence of democratic institutions such as a legislative branch elected by the people.
    D. the existence of a Bill of Rights.
    E. the right to run for public office regardless of one's race, gender, ethnicity, religion, or sexual orientation.

ANS: A   DIF: Moderate   REF: Page 18
TOP: Standards of Democracy   MSC: Applying

32. In discussing criteria for assessing how well a representative democracy is working, the text says all of the following *except*
    A. it's important to consider whether representatives are aware of constituents' interests.
    B. it's important to consider whether representatives are responsive to constituents' interests.
    C. it's important to consider whether representatives are effective in acting on behalf of constituents.
    D. it's important to consider whether the representatives live in the same neighborhood as their constituents.
    E. it's important to consider how inequality of resources affects the operation of the representative democracy.

    ANS: D   DIF: Moderate   REF: Pages 19–20
    TOP: Standards of Democracy   MSC: Applying

33. The United States contains about _____ percent of the world's population, but accounts for about _____ percent of the world's gross domestic product (GDP).
    A. 5 . . . 13
    B. 5 . . . 23
    C. 5 . . . 33
    D. 15 . . . 33
    E. 15 . . . 53

    ANS: B   DIF: Moderate   REF: Page 21
    TOP: Political Change   MSC: Remembering

34. A country's combined military and economic strength that results in it having a dominant position in the world is called a _____.
    A. democracy
    B. corporate complex
    C. superpower
    D. *Titanic*
    E. New World Order

    ANS: C   DIF: Easy   REF: Page 21
    TOP: Political Change   MSC: Understanding

35. Regarding military spending, the United States spends _____.
    A. about the same as the second-biggest military spending nation, China
    B. slightly more than the second-biggest military spending nation, China
    C. about the same as the next five highest military spending nations combined
    D. more than the next fifteen highest military spending nations combined
    E. more than all other nations combined

ANS: D   DIF: Moderate   REF: Page 21
TOP: Political Change   MSC: Applying

36. According to the text
    A. the world is no more interconnected now than it was a century ago.
    B. it is only in the twentieth century that U.S. politics have been shaped by war and trade.
    C. despite increased global interconnectedness, domestic and international affairs remain largely separate from one another.
    D. as a result of the attacks of 9/11, the United States is no longer the world's lone superpower.
    E. global interdependence increases U.S. power and vulnerability at one and the same time.

    ANS: E   DIF: Moderate   REF: Page 22
    TOP: Political Change   MSC: Applying

37. According to the text
    A. contrary to popular belief, politics is less polarized now than it was fifty years ago.
    B. U.S. politics is more divided by income and social class than it is by race.
    C. throughout the twentieth century, the vast majority of southern whites voted Republican.
    D. in the past half-century, differences *within* the Democratic and Republican parties have gotten *larger* at the same time as differences *between* the two parties have become *smaller*.
    E. in the past half-century, differences *within* the Democratic and Republican parties have gotten *smaller* at the same time as differences *between* the two parties have become *larger*.

    ANS: E   DIF: Moderate   REF: Page 23
    TOP: Political Change   MSC: Applying

38. In the contemporary United States
    A. the vast majority of Evangelical Protestants vote Republican, as do the vast majority of Catholics and other Protestants.
    B. the vast majority of Protestants vote Democratic.
    C. the vast majority of Catholics vote Republican.
    D. the vast majority of Jews vote Republican.
    E. roughly half of Catholics vote Democratic and roughly half vote Republican.

    ANS: E   DIF: Moderate   REF: Page 23
    TOP: Political Change   MSC: Remembering

39. According to the text, the Reagan Revolution
    A. resulted in conservatives setting the main terms of the public debate.
    B. pushed conservative ideas further outside of the political mainstream than they had ever been.
    C. led the Democratic Party to champion the virtues of big government more strongly than ever.
    D. was a myth manufactured by political pundits.
    E. was successful at dismantling the welfare state.

    ANS: A   DIF: Moderate   REF: Page 25
    TOP: Political Change   MSC: Applying

40. According to the text, the recession and global economic crisis of 2008
    A. reaffirmed the dangers of too much government regulation of the market.
    B. called into question the ideology and practice of less-regulated capitalism.
    C. shows that the world is less interconnected than is generally believed.
    D. was predicted a decade earlier by Federal Reserve Chair Alan Greenspan.
    E. is conclusive proof of the validity of Ronald Reagan's ideas.

    ANS: B   DIF: Moderate   REF: Page 25
    TOP: Political Change   MSC: Applying

ESSAY

1. Summarize the ways in which, according to the text, the tale of the *Titanic* is a powerful metaphor for key features of U.S. society and politics today. In what ways, however, does the *Titanic* metaphor break down?

   ANS: Answers will vary.   DIF: Moderate
   REF: Pages 1–6   TOP: Introduction
   MSC: Analyzing/Creating

2. Compare and contrast the power of the federal government under the Articles of Confederation and the U.S. Constitution.

   ANS: Answers will vary.   DIF: Moderate
   REF: Pages 8–9   TOP: Constitutional Democracy: The Founding   MSC: Analyzing

3. In what ways is formal political power in the United States distributed and checked? What is the role of federalism and the system of "checks and balances"?

   ANS: Answers will vary.   DIF: Moderate
   REF: Pages 9–12   TOP: Constitutional Democracy: The Founding   MSC: Analyzing

4. Why do leaders in the marketplace have disproportionate political power? What is the privileged position of business? What in the operation of the U.S. political economy gives business this privileged position?

   ANS: Answers will vary.   DIF: Moderate
   REF: Pages 15–18   TOP: Standards of Democracy
   MSC: Analyzing

5. Why, according to the text, is the U.S. capitalist market system inherently undemocratic?

   ANS: Answers will vary.   DIF: Moderate
   REF: Pages 15–20   TOP: Standards of Democracy
   MSC: Analyzing/Evaluating

6. Summarize the standards presented in the text for assessing the extent to which a political system is democratic.

   ANS: Answers will vary.   DIF: Difficult
   REF: Pages 16–20   TOP: Standards of Democracy
   MSC: Analyzing/Evaluating

7. What is the evidence presented in the text in support of the assertion that the United States has become more democratic over the course of its history?

   ANS: Answers will vary.   DIF: Moderate
   REF: Pages 18–20   TOP: Standards of Democracy
   MSC: Analyzing

8. What are the differences between procedural and substantive democracy? Are both necessary for a well-functioning democracy? Explain your answer.

   ANS: Answers will vary.   DIF: Difficult
   REF: Pages 18–20   TOP: Standards of Democracy
   MSC: Analyzing/Evaluating

9. According to the text, the United States is the lone superpower in a world that is more interconnected and more unpredictable. What are the arguments and evidence that the book presents in support of these assertions: (1) the United States is the lone superpower, (2) the world is more interconnected, and (3) the world is more unpredictable?

   ANS: Answers will vary.   DIF: Difficult
   REF: Pages 21–22   TOP: Political Change
   MSC: Analyzing/Creating

10. Evaluate the authors' claim that "greater global interdependence increases American power and vulnerability."

    ANS: Answers will vary.   DIF: Moderate
    REF: Pages 21–22   TOP: Political Change
    MSC: Evaluating

MULTIPLE CHOICE

1. According to the text, what accounts for capitalism's dynamism and innovation?
   A. technological change
   B. fulfilling society's needs
   C. competitive drive for profits
   D. the diversity of businesses
   E. government regulation of business practices

   ANS: C   DIF: Moderate   REF: Page 32
   TOP: Introduction   MSC: Applying

2. In the text, the "Monopoly" game metaphor refers to
   A. the virtues of a self-regulating market economy.
   B. the need for the state to set rules governing the market.
   C. the idea that greed leads to success in the market.
   D. the idea that the rules made by the state make the market unfair and inefficient.
   E. the assertion that market relations are completely voluntary.

   ANS: B   DIF: Moderate   REF: Page 32
   TOP: Introduction   MSC: Applying

3. According to the text, capitalism is usually defined as a system in which
   A. everyone has the opportunity to succeed.
   B. everyone has the opportunity to start a business.
   C. capital is privately owned and controlled.
   D. capital is controlled and owned by the government.
   E. there is a free market.

   ANS: C   DIF: Easy   REF: Page 33
   TOP: Introduction   MSC: Understanding

4. The following are all elements of capitalism *except*
   A. the private ownership of the means of production.
   B. wage labor.
   C. without a buyer for their labor, workers have no means of supporting themselves.
   D. peasants are tied to a lord's domain.
   E. production for the market.

   ANS: D   DIF: Moderate   REF: Page 33
   TOP: Introduction   MSC: Understanding

5. The text makes all of the following claims *except*
   A. capitalism's dynamism is also the source of its instability.
   B. the alteration of boom and bust is a universal characteristic of capitalism.
   C. capitalism is uniquely qualified to promote efficiency and production.
   D. capitalism is an inherently undemocratic form of production.
   E. of all possible economic systems, capitalism is the least dynamic.

   ANS: E   DIF: Moderate   REF: Pages 33–34
   TOP: The Dilemmas of Markets   MSC: Applying

6. According to the text
   A. what's good for major U.S. corporations always turns out to be good for the public.
   B. capitalism does *not* require a constant expansion of commodity production.
   C. capitalism does require a constant expansion of commodity production, but this expansion has no adverse affects.
   D. capitalism does require a constant expansion of commodity production, and this expansion frequently collides with the fact that the world has finite resources.
   E. of all possible economic systems, capitalism is the most environmentally friendly.

   ANS: D   DIF: Moderate   REF: Page 34
   TOP: The Dilemmas of Markets   MSC: Applying

7. The costs that firms create but taxpayers and individuals end up liable for are called _____.
   A. externalities
   B. investments
   C. public goods
   D. business cycles
   E. subsidies

   ANS: A   DIF: Moderate   REF: Page 34
   TOP: The Dilemmas of Markets
   MSC: Understanding

8. According to the text, the principal cause of the housing crisis in the first decade of the twenty-first century was
   A. too much government regulation.
   B. a severe drop in the stock market.
   C. the government's refusal to bail out Lehman Brothers.
   D. mortgage lenders peddling risky mortgages.
   E. President George W. Bush's firing of the chair of the Federal Reserve.

   ANS: D   DIF: Easy   REF: Page 34
   TOP: The Dilemmas of Markets   MSC: Applying

9. Of the following, which is the best example of an externality?
   A. a decision made by a U.S. company to move its operations overseas
   B. a decision by a company to fire undocumented workers
   C. the pollution that results from a firm's manufacturing process but for which the firm doesn't have to pay
   D. the share of a firm's profits that are donated to charities
   E. the share of a firm's profits that are paid out as dividends to stock holders

   ANS: C   DIF: Moderate   REF: Pages 34–35
   TOP: The Dilemmas of Markets   MSC: Applying

10. When critics charge that the bailout package sponsored by President Obama is one in which "losses are socialized and profits privatized," they mainly mean
   A. the U.S. economy has become a socialist economy in which the government gets all the profits from economic activity.
   B. taxpayers end up paying for corporate losses, but corporations keep the profits.
   C. corporate profits eventually go to the government, but losses are borne by the corporations.
   D. there is too much government regulation of business.
   E. there is not enough government regulation of business.

   ANS: B   DIF: Difficult   REF: Pages 34–35
   TOP: The Dilemmas of Markets   MSC: Applying

11. According to the text, government regulation
   A. invariably undermines capitalism.
   B. is essential to the operation and survival of capitalism.
   C. is contradictory to the principles upon which a democracy is supposed to operate.
   D. was the main cause of the economic downturn that began in 2008.
   E. may have been essential to U.S. capitalism in the nineteenth century but is no longer necessary.

   ANS: B   DIF: Moderate   REF: Pages 35–36
   TOP: The Dilemmas of Markets   MSC: Applying

12. The term private government refers to
   A. corporations' charitable donations in national emergencies.
   B. a corporation's political campaign contributions.
   C. a system where a private organization, such as a business firm, exercises power over its members and others.
   D. a set of institutions that exercises binding legitimate authority within a territory.
   E. the close relationship between lobbyists, members of Congress, and officials in the federal bureaucracy.

   ANS: C   DIF: Moderate   REF: Page 36
   TOP: The Dilemmas of Markets
   MSC: Understanding

13. Because they own and control the means of production, the prerogative of capitalists includes all of the following *except*
   A. the decision whether to invest.
   B. the decision where to invest.
   C. the decision what to invest in.
   D. the decision to discriminate on the basis of race or gender in hiring a workforce.
   E. the decision over how production is organized.

   ANS: D   DIF: Moderate   REF: Page 36
   TOP: The Dilemmas of Markets   MSC: Applying

14. According to the text, corporations have all of the following powers *except*
   A. the ability to choose how production is organized.
   B. the ability to choose where to invest.
   C. the ability to choose what to invest in.
   D. the ability to choose whether to invest at all.
   E. the ability to set their tax rates.

   ANS: E   DIF: Easy   REF: Page 39
   TOP: The Dilemmas of Markets   MSC: Applying

15. Compared with workers who do the same kind of work but who do *not* belong to labor unions, the wages of union members are approximately
   A. 30 percent lower.
   B. 10 percent lower.
   C. the same.
   D. 10 percent higher.
   E. 30 percent higher.

   ANS: E   DIF: Moderate   REF: Page 42
   TOP: The Dilemmas of Markets
   MSC: Understanding

16. According to the text, elected officials are under enormous pressure to offer inducements to business primarily because
    A. wealthy business executives provide almost 90 percent of all campaign contributions.
    B. the country's economic well-being heavily depends on decisions made by businesses.
    C. high-priced corporate lawyers allow corporate CEOs to break the law without getting caught.
    D. the vast majority of elected officials previously served as corporate CEOs.
    E. most elected officials are corrupt.

    ANS: B   DIF: Moderate   REF: Page 43
    TOP: The Structural Advantage of Business
    MSC: Applying

17. In response to the financial crisis that began during his presidency, George W. Bush
    A. fired the secretary of the Treasury.
    B. fired the chair of the Federal Reserve.
    C. sponsored a $700 billion financial bailout package.
    D. called for tax increases of almost $1 trillion to stop the federal debt from increasing.
    E. signed legislation that created approximately 3 million temporary jobs for low-income citizens.

    ANS: C   DIF: Easy   REF: Page 43
    TOP: The Structural Advantage of Business
    MSC: Understanding

18. Which of the following is a reason why, according to the text, business interests are sometimes thwarted in politics?
    A. The Constitution establishes a system of checks and balances.
    B. Companies have conflicting political interests.
    C. Contrary to popular belief, there is no tension between democracy and capitalism.
    D. Most CEOs know they can't get away with trying to buy the votes of members of Congress.
    E. Most CEOs are basically honest people.

    ANS: B   DIF: Easy   REF: Page 44
    TOP: The Structural Advantage of Business
    MSC: Applying

19. The main component of the structural bias of business in the political system is
    A. political campaign contributions made by businesses.
    B. business control over the means of production.
    C. the power of business lobbyists.
    D. the weakening of labor unions.
    E. the dismantling of the welfare state.

    ANS: B   DIF: Difficult   REF: Page 44
    TOP: The Structural Advantage of Business
    MSC: Understanding

20. Which of the following is a *second* reason why, according to the text, business interests are sometimes thwarted in politics?
    A. The U.S. political system is a federal one.
    B. The Bill of Rights guarantees all adult citizens the right to vote.
    C. The political clout of labor unions is much greater in the United States than elsewhere.
    D. The public is much more informed about politics than it was a century ago.
    E. Democratic procedures require policy makers to respond to many interests, not just those of business.

    ANS: E   DIF: Moderate   REF: Page 45
    TOP: The Structural Advantage of Business
    MSC: Applying

21. An economy dominated by large firms that produce for national and international markets and are able to dictate prices to suppliers and retailers, as well as wages to their workers, is called _____.
    A. monopoly capitalism
    B. corporate capitalism
    C. competitive capitalism
    D. democratic socialism
    E. cartel capitalism

    ANS: B   DIF: Moderate   REF: Page 47
    TOP: The Corporate and Competitive Sectors of the Economy   MSC: Understanding

22. The competitive sector of the economy refers to
    A. the ten largest U.S. firms.
    B. the companies listed in the Forbes 500.
    C. the competition between the U.S. economy and the economies of other countries.
    D. the firms that operate in many different countries.
    E. small businesses and firms.

    ANS: E   DIF: Moderate   REF: Page 47
    TOP: The Corporate and Competitive Sectors of the Economy   MSC: Understanding

23. According to the text, the growing concentration of economic power
    A. makes capitalism more efficient than it has ever been.
    B. makes it easier for citizens to hold corporations accountable for their illegal behavior.
    C. facilitates economic equality.
    D. is the main reason for the increase in racism in the United States.
    E. threatens democracy.

    ANS: E   DIF: Moderate   REF: Page 50
    TOP: The Corporate and Competitive Sectors of the Economy   MSC: Applying

24. According to the text
    A. the notion of shareholder democracy is misleading.
    B. the gap between the pay of CEOs and the pay of average workers has decreased in recent years.
    C. business executives are the most poorly organized group in U.S. society.
    D. as a result of affirmative action, the majority of corporate CEOs are now either women or people of color.
    E. the vast majority of Americans own at least some stock in the form of being shareholders themselves or indirectly through mutual funds or retirement plans.

    ANS: A   DIF: Moderate   REF: Pages 50–51
    TOP: Who Owns America's Private Government?
    MSC: Applying

25. Approximately what percent of all income that is earned in the United States is earned by the top quintile (top 20 percent) of households?
    A. 10 percent
    B. 20 percent
    C. 30 percent
    D. 40 percent
    E. 50 percent

    ANS: E   DIF: Moderate   REF: Page 51
    TOP: Who Owns America's Private Government?
    MSC: Remembering

26. Approximately what percent of all stock that is owned in the United States is owned by the wealthiest 10 percent of the population?
    A. 10 percent
    B. 30 percent
    C. 50 percent
    D. 80 percent
    E. 100 percent

    ANS: D   DIF: Difficult   REF: Page 51
    TOP: Who Owns America's Private Government?
    MSC: Remembering

27. Of all current Fortune 500 CEOs
    A. 50 percent are female.
    B. 40 percent are white males.
    C. 20 percent are African American or Latino.
    D. 30 percent are white females.
    E. 90 percent are white males.

    ANS: E   DIF: Moderate   REF: Page 52
    TOP: Who Owns America's Private Government?
    MSC: Remembering

28. All of the following are sources of capitalist class cohesion *except*
    A. the existence of interlocking boards of directors.
    B. membership in exclusive social clubs.
    C. attendance at public colleges and universities.
    D. membership in peak business associations such as the Business Roundtable.
    E. membership in other business associations such as the U.S. Chamber of Commerce.

    ANS: C   DIF: Moderate   REF: Page 53
    TOP: Capitalist Class Cohesion   MSC: Applying

29. When political scientists and economists say that the U.S. economy has been "financialized" over the past generation, they most nearly mean that
    A. ATMs are in greater use than ever before.
    B. more citizens are using banks than ever before.
    C. more than 90 percent of the U.S. population now owns stock in a large corporation.
    D. fewer people than ever before are paying for things in cash.
    E. the business of moving money around has increased in importance compared with the manufacture and production of goods.

    ANS: E   DIF: Moderate   REF: Pages 54–55
    TOP: The Changing Structure of Employment
    MSC: Applying

30. In the year 2000, three-quarters of U.S. workers were employed in
    A. manufacturing jobs.
    B. white-collar and service sector jobs.
    C. agriculture.
    D. union jobs.
    E. public sector jobs.

    ANS: B   DIF: Moderate   REF: Page 55
    TOP: The Changing Structure of Employment
    MSC: Remembering

31. Compared with the percentage of workers who are in unions in other industrialized countries, the percentage of U.S. workers who are in unions is
    A. lower.
    B. about the same.
    C. slightly higher.
    D. much higher.
    E. so difficult to measure that such comparisons are impossible to make.

    ANS: A   DIF: Moderate   REF: Page 58
    TOP: The Changing Structure of Employment
    MSC: Remembering

32. Comparing class mobility in the U.S. and in other Western countries, the data indicate that
    A. class mobility is higher in the United States than in all other Western countries.
    B. class mobility is lower in the United States than in all other Western countries.
    C. the United States is in the middle regarding class mobility compared to other Western countries.
    D. the United States fluctuates between high and low levels of class mobility depending on which party is in power.
    E. class mobility cannot be measured.

    ANS: C   DIF: Moderate   REF: Page 57
    TOP: American Corporate Capitalism
    MSC: Remembering

33. Compared with most democratic capitalist countries, the amount of government regulation in the United States is
    A. much greater.
    B. slightly greater.
    C. about the same.
    D. less.
    E. so difficult to measure that it's impossible to make comparisons with other countries.

    ANS: D   DIF: Moderate   REF: Page 57
    TOP: American Corporate Capitalism
    MSC: Understanding

34. Approximately what percentage of the U.S. labor force are members of a labor union?
    A. 2 percent
    B. 12 percent
    C. 22 percent
    D. 32 percent
    E. 42 percent

    ANS: B   DIF: Moderate   REF: Page 58
    TOP: American Corporate Capitalism
    MSC: Remembering

35. Compared with other rich capitalist democracies, the gap between rich and poor in the United States is
    A. much less.
    B. slightly less.
    C. about the same.
    D. greater.
    E. so difficult to measure that comparisons are impossible.

    ANS: D   DIF: Difficult   REF: Page 60
    TOP: American Corporate Capitalism
    MSC: Remembering

36. According to the text, capitalism distributes money and wealth _____, and it distributes economic power _____.
    A. equally . . . . . unequally
    B. equally . . . . equally
    C. unequally . . . . unequally
    D. unequally . . . . equally
    E. in ways that defy rational explanation . . . . in ways that also defy rational explanation

    ANS: C   DIF: Easy   REF: Page 62
    TOP: Conclusion   MSC: Understanding

ESSAY

1. Explain and evaluate the authors' statement that "market systems have their benefits, but they also have their dark side."

   ANS: Answers will vary.   DIF: Moderate
   REF: Pages 33–37   TOP: The Dilemmas of Markets
   MSC: Evaluating/Creating

2. Summarize with examples how, according to the text, the same factor that accounts for the dynamism of capitalism also produces collisions with public interests.

   ANS: Answers will vary.   DIF: Moderate
   REF: Pages 33–37   TOP: The Dilemmas of Markets
   MSC: Analyzing

3. The authors make the claim that "the workplace is an authoritarian political system in which employers rule." Summarize the reasons why the authors make this claim.

   ANS: Answers will vary.   DIF: Moderate
   REF: Pages 35–36   TOP: The Dilemmas of Markets
   MSC: Evaluating

4. Summarize the reasons why, according to the text, capitalism can be considered a form of private government.

   ANS: Answers will vary.   DIF: Moderate
   REF: Pages 36–38   TOP: The Dilemmas of Markets
   MSC: Analyzing

5. The authors make the claim that the decisions made by business firms are "preeminently political." What evidence do the authors use to support their claim? Do you agree or disagree with the authors' claim? Explain your answer.

   ANS: Answers will vary.   DIF: Difficult
   REF: Page 42   TOP: The Structural Advantage of Business   MSC: Evaluating/Creating

MULTIPLE CHOICE

1. A federal system is one in which
   A. the states retain full sovereignty.
   B. authority is divided between national and state governments.
   C. the president is elected by an Electoral College.
   D. power is shared among the executive, legislative, and judicial branches of the government.
   E. all government officials are elected by the people.

   ANS: B   DIF: Easy   REF: Page 185   TOP: Political Institutions   MSC: Understanding

2. Which of the amendments to the Constitution indicates that powers not delegated to the national government nor prohibited to the states are reserved to the states or the people?
   A. First
   B. Third
   C. Fifth
   D. Eighth
   E. Tenth

   ANS: E   DIF: Moderate   REF: Page 185
   TOP: Political Institutions   MSC: Applying

3. According to the text, today considerable power has gravitated to the federal government, but for much of U.S. history, the bulk of government power
   A. was also exercised by the national government.
   B. was exercised by local governments such as those of cities and towns.
   C. was exercised by state governments.
   D. was exercised by the Supreme Court.
   E. was exercised by small businesses.

   ANS: C   DIF: Easy   REF: Page 185
   TOP: Political Institutions   MSC: Applying

4. According to the text, the U.S. Constitution divides political power
   A. vertically but not horizontally.
   B. horizontally but not vertically.
   C. neither horizontally nor vertically.
   D. both horizontally and vertically.
   E. horizontally, vertically, and circularly.

   ANS: D   DIF: Moderate   REF: Page 186
   TOP: Political Institutions   MSC: Understanding

5. In the realm of foreign policy, the Constitution sets up a structure of government in which
   A. the Congress and the president share power.
   B. the Congress, the president, and the United States's twenty largest cities share power.
   C. only the Congress has power.
   D. only the president has power.
   E. only ambassadors and the military's top generals have power.

   ANS: A   DIF: Moderate   REF: Page 186
   TOP: Political Institutions   MSC: Understanding

6. According to the text
   A. the balance of power among the three branches of the national government has remained constant throughout U.S. history.
   B. the Congress, led by the Speaker of the House and Senate majority leader, is now the preeminent branch.
   C. the executive, directed by the president, is now the preeminent branch.
   D. the Supreme Court, directed by the chief justice, is now the preeminent branch.
   E. the federal bureaucracy is now the preeminent institution.

   ANS: C   DIF: Moderate   REF: Page 186
   TOP: Political Institutions   MSC: Applying

7. The text says the U.S. system of political power incorporates all of the following elements *except*
   A. a system of separation of powers.
   B. a system of shared powers.
   C. a system of checks and balances.
   D. a system where the executive and legislative branches are fused.
   E. a system of federalism.

   ANS: D   DIF: Moderate   REF: Page 187
   TOP: Political Institutions   MSC: Understanding

8. According to the text, the Constitution sets up a governmental structure that
   A. makes it very difficult for government to bring about major changes in policy.
   B. has no effect one way or the other on how easy it is for government to make major policy changes.
   C. makes it very easy for government to bring about major changes in policy.
   D. makes it very easy for the government to respond to the slightest changes in public opinion.
   E. was the very opposite of what the Founders hoped it would be.

   ANS: A   DIF: Moderate   REF: Page 187
   TOP: Political Institutions   MSC: Applying

9. According to the text, the Founders
   A. all secretly wanted the United States to be a monarchy.
   B. wanted to make it easy for government to respond to the wishes of the majority of citizens.
   C. were not concerned with protecting property rights.
   D. feared that democracy could endanger the rights of property owners.
   E. were following the examples of dozens of other countries in trying to establish government in which political authority would be in the hands of the people, not a king.

   ANS: D   DIF: Moderate   REF: Page 188
   TOP: Political Institutions   MSC: Applying

10. According to the Constitution, in order for a candidate to be elected president, the candidate
    A. must receive a majority of the popular vote.
    B. must receive a majority of the popular vote *and* a majority of votes in the Electoral College.
    C. must receive a majority of votes in the Electoral College *and* a majority of votes in the Senate.
    D. must receive two-thirds of the votes in the Electoral College.
    E. must receive a majority of votes in the Electoral College.

    ANS: E   DIF: Moderate   REF: Page 190
    TOP: Introduction   MSC: Remembering

11. According to the text
    A. the Electoral College tends to over-represent large states.
    B. the Electoral College tends to over-represent medium-size states.
    C. the Electoral College tends to over-represent small states.
    D. the size of the states that are better represented in the Electoral College depends on whether the president is a Republican or Democrat.
    E. the Electoral College represents all states equally.

    ANS: C   DIF: Easy   REF: Pages 190–1
    TOP: Introduction   MSC: Applying

12. According to the Constitution, the number of Electoral College votes assigned to each state is determined by
    A. the state's population.
    B. the number of members that state has in the House of Representatives.
    C. the number of counties in the state.
    D. by adding together the number of members the state has in the House of Representatives plus its two senators.
    E. the number of active political parties in the state.

    ANS: D   DIF: Moderate   REF: Pages 190–1
    TOP: Introduction   MSC: Remembering

13. According to the text, at the Constitutional Convention, the Founders rejected a suggestion that the president be directly elected by the people because
    A. most wanted the presidency to be weaker than it was under the Articles of Confederation.
    B. doing so would make the president responsive to the democratic spirit they wanted to tame.
    C. like James Wilson, most wanted the president to be chosen by Congress.
    D. like Alexander Hamilton, most wanted the president to serve a life term.
    E. most wanted the president to be chosen by the Supreme Court.

    ANS: B   DIF: Moderate   REF: Page 191
    TOP: Introduction   MSC: Applying

14. In presidential elections, the *unit rule* most commonly refers to the fact that
    A. the unit of government that chooses the president is the Electoral College.
    B. each member of the Electoral College has only one vote.
    C. each member of the House of Representatives has only one vote.
    D. the House of Representatives is the unit of government that elects the president if no majority is reached in the Electoral College.
    E. the candidate who gets more popular votes in a state than any other candidate gets all of that state's Electoral College votes.

    ANS: E   DIF: Easy   REF: Page 191
    TOP: Introduction   MSC: Understanding

15. Currently, the unit rule in presidential elections is used
    A. in all states because the Constitution requires that it be used.
    B. in all states even though the Constitution doesn't require that it be used.
    C. in the vast majority of states.
    D. in about half the states.
    E. in only a few states.

    ANS: C   DIF: Difficult   REF: Page 191
    TOP: Introduction   MSC: Remembering

16. The power of the president to reject a bill passed by Congress is called a(n)
    A. pardon.
    B. veto.
    C. presidential privilege.
    D. discretionary power.
    E. executive order.

    ANS: B   DIF: Moderate   REF: Page 192
    TOP: The Historical Presidency   MSC: Remembering

17. According to the text, all of the following have contributed to the growth of presidential power in the twentieth century *except* that
    A. corporations outgrew the narrow boundaries of the states.
    B. the federal government became responsible for managing the economy.
    C. the federal government took on new social responsibilities.
    D. the United States became a global power.
    E. the Twenty-second Amendment to the Constitution was ratified.

    ANS: E   DIF: Moderate   REF: Pages 192–3
    TOP: The Historical Presidency   MSC: Applying

18. According to the text, all of the following are key presidential roles *except*
    A. conducting foreign policy.
    B. supervising the federal bureaucracy.
    C. directing the economy.
    D. managing conflict.
    E. voting in the U.S. Congress.

    ANS: E   DIF: Moderate   REF: Page 193
    TOP: The Historical Presidency   MSC: Applying

19. Of the following, which is an independent regulatory commission?
    A. the Office of Management and Budget
    B. the National Security Council
    C. the Federal Reserve Board
    D. the Department of State
    E. the Bureau of the Census

    ANS: C   DIF: Difficult   REF: Page 193
    TOP: The Historical Presidency   MSC: Remembering

20. In discussing the consequences of the president being the commander in chief of the armed forces, the text says all of the following *except*
    A. the Constitution gives Congress, not the president, the power to declare war.
    B. the Founders intended the president's power as commander in chief to be confined to the limited occasions when hostilities begin.
    C. President Reagan ordered the invasion of Grenada without seeking Congressional authorization.
    D. President Lincoln was unique among U.S. presidents in that he never undertook military action without first obtaining Congressional approval.
    E. President Polk provoked war with Mexico in 1846 by sending U.S. troops into disputed land between Texas and Mexico.

    ANS: D   DIF: Moderate   REF: Page 194
    TOP: Roles of the President   MSC: Applying

21. The U.S. Constitution makes the _____ commander in chief of the military.
    A. highest-ranking U.S. Army General
    B. Secretary of Defense
    C. President
    D. Joint Chiefs of Staff
    E. highest-ranking U.S. Navy Officer

    ANS: C   DIF: Easy   REF: Page 194
    TOP: Roles of the President   MSC: Remembering

22. The U.S. Constitution grants the power to declare war to
    A. the people.
    B. Congress.
    C. the Secretary of Defense.
    D. the House of Representatives.
    E. the President.

    ANS: B   DIF: Easy   REF: Page 194
    TOP: Roles of the President   MSC: Remembering

23. According to the Constitution, the president has all of the following powers *except*
    A. she or he is commander in chief of the armed forces.
    B. she or he can veto legislation.
    C. she or he can appoint government officials.
    D. she or he can make treaties.
    E. she or he can declare war.

    ANS: E   DIF: Difficult   REF: Page 194
    TOP: Roles of the President   MSC: Applying

24. According to the text, contemporary presidents exercise power for all of the following purposes *except*
    A. making capitalism work at home.
    B. maintaining political stability.
    C. defending the United States at home.
    D. defending the United States abroad.
    E. promoting moral values.

    ANS: E   DIF: Easy   REF: Page 194–202
    TOP: Roles of the President   MSC: Applying

25. Which presidential role is illustrated by the presidential authority to negotiate treaties, appoint ambassadors, and receive ambassadors from foreign countries?
    A. commander in chief
    B. chief diplomat
    C. manager of the bureaucracy
    D. head of government
    E. party leader

    ANS: B   DIF: Moderate   REF: Page 195
    TOP: Roles of the President   MSC: Applying

26. The set of key executive institutions that are close advisers to the president on major policy areas, including the budget, social and economic issues, intelligence, and security is the _____.
    A. Executive Office of the President
    B. Cabinet
    C. Independent Regulatory Commission
    D. military-industrial complex
    E. Conference Committee

    ANS: A   DIF: Moderate   REF: Page 196
    TOP: Roles of the President   MSC: Remembering

27. According to the text, the executive branch of government consists of a series of concentric circles surrounding the president. The circle which is the closest to the president is
    A. the president's cabinet.
    B. the Executive Office of the President.
    C. the independent agencies.
    D. the Office of Presidential Appointees.
    E. the White House Office of Presidential Advisors.

    ANS: B   DIF: Difficult   REF: Pages 196–7
    TOP: Roles of the President   MSC: Applying

28. The National Labor Relations Board, the Federal Trade Commission, and the Federal Reserve Board are all examples of
    A. the Cabinet.
    B. Congressional Committees.
    C. Special Presidential Committees.
    D. Independent Regulatory Commissions.
    E. Executive Departments.

    ANS: D   DIF: Moderate   REF: Page 197
    TOP: Roles of the President   MSC: Applying

29. The _____ is a group of key administrative officials appointed by the president to direct major departments of government.
    A. Executive Office of the President
    B. Cabinet
    C. Independent Regulatory Commission
    D. Conference Committee
    E. Chiefs of Staff

    ANS: B   DIF: Moderate   REF: Pages 197–8
    TOP: Roles of the President   MSC: Applying

30. According to the text, the most powerful vice president ever is/was
    A. Joseph Biden
    B. Richard Cheney
    C. Al Gore
    D. Dan Quayle
    E. George H.W. Bush

    ANS: B   DIF: Moderate   REF: Page 198
    TOP: Roles of the President   MSC: Remembering

31. In discussing what it terms "the Imperial Presidency," the text identifies all of the following as sources of presidential power *except*
    A. the president's unlimited access to the media.
    B. the Fourteenth Amendment to the Constitution.
    C. the president's power to manage the federal bureaucracy.
    D. the president's ability to raise money and make appearances for other candidates for public office.
    E. Article II of the Constitution.

    ANS: B   DIF: Moderate   REF: Page 205
    TOP: The Imperial President   MSC: Understanding

32. The president's powers are enumerated in _____ of the U.S. Constitution.
    A. the Bill of Rights
    B. Article I
    C. Article II
    D. the Preamble
    E. the Amendments

    ANS: C   DIF: Moderate   REF: Page 205
    TOP: The Imperial President   MSC: Remembering

33. Unlike the situation in parliamentary regimes, the president is
    A. head of state and head of government.
    B. neither the head of state nor the head of government.
    C. the head of state but not the head of government.
    D. the head of government but not the head of state.
    E. there is no difference between being the head of state and being the head of government in a parliamentary regime.

    ANS: A   DIF: Moderate   REF: Page 206
    TOP: The Imperial President   MSC: Remembering

34. The official who directs the day-to-day work of government is called
    A. the head of state.
    B. the head of government.
    C. a U.S. Senator.
    D. a member of the U.S. House of Representatives.
    E. Supreme Court Justice.

    ANS: B   DIF: Easy   REF: Page 206
    TOP: The Imperial President   MSC: Remembering

35. In the United States, the president serves as
    A. the head of state only.
    B. the head of government only.
    C. both the head of state and the head of government.
    D. head of state, while the vice president serves as head of government.
    E. head of government, while the vice president serves as head of state.

    ANS: C   DIF: Moderate   REF: Page 206
    TOP: The Imperial President   MSC: Understanding

36. The text points out that for years after the 9/11 attacks, seven out of ten U.S. citizens believed that Iraqi leader Saddam Hussein was linked to the attacks despite there being no credible evidence of this connection. The book makes this point primarily to support its claim that
    A. U.S. citizens know less about foreign affairs than do citizens in other countries.
    B. the media is filled with lies, half-truths, and meaningless propaganda.
    C. the George W. Bush administration lied to the public more than any other administration.
    D. the president has an unparalleled advantage in defining political reality for most U.S. citizens.
    E. Hussein's U.S. supporters failed to make effective arguments on his behalf.

    ANS: D   DIF: Moderate   REF: Page 207
    TOP: The Imperial President   MSC: Applying

37. In discussing the sources of presidential power, the text says presidents can make skillful use of patronage. Of the following, which is the best example of patronage?
    A. modifying proposed legislation in ways that benefit particular members of Congress
    B. nominating federal judges
    C. delivering speeches in carefully selected locations
    D. refusing to meet with particular members of Congress
    E. raising money for particular candidates

    ANS: B   DIF: Difficult   REF: Page 207
    TOP: The Imperial President   MSC: Understanding

38. A(n) _____ is a binding directive issued by the president, within areas in which the president has constitutional authority, to members of the executive branch and private citizens or groups.
    A. veto
    B. makeup
    C. discharge petition
    D. pardon
    E. executive order

    ANS: E   DIF: Moderate   REF: Page 207
    TOP: The Imperial President   MSC: Understanding

39. According to the text, which president has claimed the right of the president to order—without judicial review—targeted killings not only of foreigners but of American citizens regarded as security threats?
    A. Ronald Reagan
    B. George H.W. Bush
    C. Bill Clinton
    D. George W. Bush
    E. Barack Obama

    ANS: E   DIF: Moderate   REF: Page 208
    TOP: The Imperial President   MSC: Remembering

40. According to the text, all of the following have served to weaken presidential power in the past half-century *except*
    A. the decrease in the number of interest groups.
    B. President Johnson's lying about the progress of the Vietnam War.
    C. President Nixon's attempted cover-up of the Watergate burglary.
    D. the end of the golden age of capitalism.
    E. the increase in divided government.

    ANS: A   DIF: Moderate   REF: Page 210
    TOP: The Imperiled President   MSC: Applying

ESSAY

1. What does the text mean when it says that the Constitution fragments government authority in two ways?

   ANS: Answers will vary.   DIF: Moderate
   REF: Page 186   TOP: Political Institutions
   MSC: Analyzing

2. Explain why, according to the text, "the design of government in the Constitution . . . has highly conservative implications."

   ANS: Answers will vary.   DIF: Moderate
   REF: Pages 187–8   TOP: Political Institutions
   MSC: Analyzing

3. Explain why, according to the text, the Founders designed the U.S. government as they did.

   ANS: Answers will vary.   DIF: Moderate
   REF: Pages 187–8   TOP: Political Institutions
   MSC: Analyzing

4. Summarize the reasons for the existence of the Electoral College, the Constitutional provisions and the political practices governing its operation, and the consequences of these provisions and practices.

   ANS: Answers will vary.   DIF: Difficult
   REF: Pages 190–1   TOP: Introduction
   MSC: Analyzing

MULTIPLE CHOICE

1. Article I, Section 8 of the Constitution states that Congress shall have all of the following powers *except* the power to
   A. declare war.
   B. collect taxes.
   C. make treaties. –
   D. borrow money.
   E. establish post offices.

   ANS: C   DIF: Moderate   REF: Page 219
   TOP: Introduction   MSC: Applying

2. John Locke was
   A. a political philosopher who said the executive branch was the supreme power in any government.
   B. a political philosopher who said the legislature was the supreme power in any government. –
   C. a political philosopher who said the judiciary was the supreme power in any government.
   D. the author of Article I, Section 8 of the Constitution.
   E. the first Speaker of the House of Representatives.

   ANS: B   DIF: Easy   REF: Page 219
   TOP: Introduction   MSC: Applying

3. Which institution of the federal government has the power to impeach a public official?
   A. U.S. Supreme Court
   B. House of Representatives –
   C. U.S. Senate
   D. the President
   E. the Attorney General

   ANS: B   DIF: Easy   REF: Page 219
   TOP: Introduction   MSC: Remembering

4. The trial of impeachment takes place in

   _____.

   A. U.S. Supreme Court
   B. Federal District Court
   C. the House of Representatives –
   D. the U.S. Senate –
   E. the Office of the Executive

   ANS: D   DIF: Easy   REF: Page 219
   TOP: Introduction   MSC: Remembering

5. The approval of presidential appointments and foreign treaties requires
   A. approval and confirmation by the House of Representatives.
   B. approval and confirmation by the U.S. Senate.
   C. approval and confirmation by the states.
   D. approval and confirmation by the U.S. Supreme Court.
   E. no approval or confirmation is necessary by other branches of government.

   ANS: B   DIF: Moderate   REF: Page 219
   TOP: Introduction   MSC: Remembering

6. According to the text, the most open and accessible branch of government is the
   A. presidency.
   B. Supreme Court.
   C. Federal Reserve.
   D. Congress. –
   E. Federal Elections Commission.

   ANS: D   DIF: Easy   REF: Page 221
   TOP: Introduction   MSC: Applying

7. According to the text
   A. the Founders expected members of Congress to represent a national constituency.
   B. the Founders had no expectations about what kind of constituency members of Congress would represent.
   C. all members of Congress represent a national constituency.
   D. no members of Congress represent a national constituency.
   E. the Founders expected members of Congress to represent a local constituency. –

   ANS: E   DIF: Moderate   REF: Page 221
   TOP: Introduction   MSC: Applying

8. According to the text, the public often lacks respect for Congress mainly because
   A. members of Congress are seen as spending too much time arguing with one another.
   B. Congress is seen as focusing too much on foreign policy at the expense of domestic issues.
   C. Congress is seen as failing to follow the agenda set for it by the president.
   D. the House of Representatives is seen as having more influence than the Senate.
   E. special interests are seen as having more influence than the people. –

   ANS: E   DIF: Moderate   REF: Page 221
   TOP: Introduction   MSC: Applying

9. According to the text:
    A. Senators are generally more centrist than House members because they are older.
    B. Senators are generally more centrist than House members because they represent broader constituencies.
    C. House members are more centrist because they stand for election more frequently.
    D. House members are more centrist because they have longer careers than senators.
    E. Senators are more extreme because they are older and in general have more money than House members.

    ANS: B   DIF: Moderate   REF: Page 222
    TOP: Introduction   MSC: Applying

10. Senators serve _____ –year terms, and each state has _____ senator(s).
    A. two . . . one
    B. four . . . one
    C. four . . . two
    D. six . . . two
    E. eight . . . two

    ANS: D   DIF: Easy   REF: Page 222
    TOP: Introduction   MSC: Remembering

11. Members of the House of Representatives serve _____–year terms, and the House currently has _____ members.
    A. 2 . . . 235
    B. 2 . . . 335
    C. 2 . . . 435
    D. 4 . . . 335
    E. 4 . . . 435

    ANS: C   DIF: Easy   REF: Page 222
    TOP: Introduction   MSC: Remembering

12. What constituency does a Senator represent?
    A. congressional district within a state
    B. county
    C. state
    D. city
    E. the United States as a whole

    ANS: C   DIF: Easy   REF: Page 222
    TOP: Introduction   MSC: Understanding

13. What constituency does a member of the House of Representatives represent?
    A. congressional district within a state
    B. county
    C. state
    D. city
    E. the United States as a whole

    ANS: A   DIF: Easy   REF: Page 222
    TOP: Introduction   MSC: Understanding

14. The House of Representatives is composed of _____ members.
    A. 50
    B. 100
    C. 270
    D. 435
    E. 535

    ANS: D   DIF: Easy   REF: Page 222
    TOP: Introduction   MSC: Remembering

15. According to the text, the Founders
    A. were not worried about an excess of democracy.
    B. were worried about an excess of democracy but thought nothing could be done to prevent it.
    C. viewed the House as providing more protection against excess of democracy than would the Senate.
    D. viewed the Senate as providing more protection against excess of democracy than would the House.
    E. viewed the House and the Senate as providing equal protection against excess of democracy.

    ANS: D   DIF: Difficult   REF: Page 223
    TOP: The Origin of Two Legislative Chambers
    MSC: Applying

16. The Constitution as initially ratified said that senators would be _____, and members of the House of Representatives would be _____ .
    A. elected by the people . . . elected by the people
    B. elected by the people . . . appointed by the state legislatures
    C. elected by the people . . . appointed by the president and the state legislatures working together
    D. appointed by the state legislatures . . . elected by the people
    E. appointed by the state legislatures . . . appointed by the state legislatures

    ANS: D   DIF: Easy   REF: Page 223
    TOP: The Origin of Two Legislative Chambers
    MSC: Remembering

17. Employed in the U.S. Senate, a(n) _____ is a technique to stop the progress of a piece of legislation by continuing debate and thus not permitting a vote.
    A. filibuster
    B. cloture
    C. discharge petition
    D. committee system
    E. reconciliation

    ANS: A   DIF: Moderate   REF: Pages 224–5
    TOP: The Origin of Two Legislative Chambers
    MSC: Understanding

18. According to the text
    A. voters in large states are more represented in the Senate than are voters in small states.
    B. voters in small states are more represented in the Senate than are voters in the large states.
    C. voters in small and large states are equally represented in the Senate.
    D. racial and ethnic minorities are the ones who most benefit from whatever malapportionment exists in the Senate.
    E. voters in small and large states are equally represented in the House of Representatives.

    ANS: B   DIF: Moderate   REF: Page 225
    TOP: The Origin of Two Legislative Chambers
    MSC: Applying

19. The Seventeenth Amendment to the U.S. Constitution
    A. dealt with the election of senators.
    B. dealt with the election of members of the House of Representatives.
    C. changed the constitutional authority of the Speaker of the House.
    D. legalized filibusters.
    E. made the Senate less malapportioned than the House.

    ANS: A   DIF: Moderate   REF: Page 226
    TOP: Congress: Past and Present
    MSC: Remembering

20. When political scientists use the term *divided government*, they are referring mainly to
    A. the inability of Republicans and Democrats to agree with one another.
    B. the fact that the president is not a member of Congress.
    C. situations in which the divisions *within* the parties are as large as the differences *between* them.
    D. situations in which one party controls the House and the other party controls the Senate.
    E. situations in which one party controls the presidency and the other party controls one or both houses of Congress.

    ANS: E   DIF: Moderate   REF: Page 227
    TOP: Congress: Past and Present   MSC: Applying

21. According to the text, earmarks are
    A. all money appropriated by Congress.
    B. the practice of inserting authorizations for a specific project in a bill.
    C. the practice of inserting signing statements into a bill.
    D. the practice of specifying that a bill won't be subject to a filibuster.
    E. the practice of letting lobbyists write provisions of important legislation.

    ANS: B   DIF: Moderate   REF: Page 231
    TOP: Congressional Careers and the Electoral Connection   MSC: Understanding

22. The incentive to get reelected powerfully shapes the preferences and decisions of legislators. This incentive is often referred to as the _____.
    A. policy position
    B. constituents
    C. electoral connection
    D. political action committee
    E. earmark

    ANS: C   DIF: Moderate   REF: Page 231
    TOP: Congressional Careers and the Electoral Connection   MSC: Understanding

23. The campaign money that a congressional candidate raises
    A. comes exclusively from donors within the candidate's district.
    B. comes exclusively from donors outside the candidate's district.
    C. comes from donors inside and outside the candidate's district.
    D. comes exclusively from government funds earmarked for congressional elections.
    E. always comes exclusively from their own private wealth.

    ANS: C   DIF: Moderate   REF: Pages 232–4
    TOP: Congressional Careers and the Electoral Connection   MSC: Applying

24. In the 2008 Congressional elections, the candidate who raised the most money won _____ of the time.
    A. approximately 50 percent
    B. approximately 60 percent
    C. approximately 70 percent
    D. approximately 80 percent
    E. approximately 90 percent

    ANS: E   DIF: Moderate   REF: Page 233
    TOP: Congressional Careers and the Electoral Connection   MSC: Remembering

25. Who/what is an incumbent?
    A. a person running for political office
    B. a person that currently holds a political office –
    C. the most senior member in the House of Representatives
    D. the most junior member in the House of Representatives
    E. the president of the Senate

    ANS: B   DIF: Easy   REF: Page 233
    TOP: Congressional Careers and the Electoral Connection   MSC: Understanding

26. Incumbents generally enjoy an advantage in elections for all of the following reasons *except*
    A. they have experience at their jobs.
    B. seniority makes them more likely to influence legislation that advantage their constituents.
    C. generally incumbents have a fund-raising advantage.
    D. they run as political outsiders. –
    E. they have mailing privileges that others do not.

    ANS: D   DIF: Difficult   REF: Page 235
    TOP: Congressional Careers and the Electoral Connection   MSC: Applying

27. Generally, Senate races are more competitive than House of Representatives races for all of the following reasons *except*
    A. Senate incumbents face more experienced challengers.
    B. Senate incumbents face better-financed challengers.
    C. statewide constituencies are large enough that one party does not dominate them.
    D. the two-year term of office for Senators does not allow them sufficient time to raise enough campaign money to discourage challengers. –
    E. Senate incumbents tend to ride the president's electoral "coattails" much more effectively than incumbents in the House of Representatives.

    ANS: D   DIF: Difficult   REF: Page 236
    TOP: Congressional Careers and the Electoral Connection   MSC: Applying

28. The text cites Senator Jay Rockefeller of West Virginia to illustrate its point that
    A. senators' reelection depends heavily on their taking consistent ideological stands.
    B. money determines who wins almost all senatorial elections.
    C. there are some Republican members of Congress who are leading advocates of social programs for the poor.
    D. there are some wealthy members of Congress who lose elections no matter how much money they spend.
    E. there are some wealthy members of Congress who are leading advocates of social programs for the poor. –

    ANS: E   DIF: Moderate   REF: Page 237
    TOP: Members of Congress   MSC: Applying

29. Although the text notes that some legislators do a good job of representing constituents whose demographic characteristics are different from those of the legislators, the book states that the social background of legislators is important because
    A. the Constitution says it is.
    B. it's necessary to remedy the sexism of the Declaration of Independence's statement that all men are created equal.
    C. some men may be able to represent women effectively (or vice versa), but racial divisions in this country are so deep that it's impossible for most whites to represent blacks effectively (or vice versa).
    D. legislators bring assumptions to their work based on their life experiences, and variations in life experience are likely to affect legislators' sensitivity to and awareness of certain issues. –
    E. it is impossible for a legislator to represent constituents who do not share his or her religion.

    ANS: D   DIF: Moderate   REF: Page 237
    TOP: Members of Congress   MSC: Applying

30. As of 2013, African Americans comprised approximately 12 percent of the electorate, occupied approximately _____ percent of the seats in the House, and occupied approximately _____ percent of the seats in the Senate.
    A. 12 . . . 5
    B. 12 . . . 1
    C. 9 . . . 1
    D. 12 . . . 12
    E. 1 . . . 1

    ANS: C   DIF: Difficult   REF: Page 237
    TOP: Members of Congress   MSC: Remembering

185

31. All of the following statements are true about Congress *except*
    A. Congress is the most democratic institution in the federal government.
    B. Congress is less male and less white than it used to be.
    C. a large number of members are from working-class occupations.
    D. Congress contains a much higher proportion of whites than the population as a whole.
    E. Congress contains a much higher proportion of males than the population as a whole.

    ANS: C   DIF: Moderate   REF: Page 237
    TOP: Members of Congress   MSC: Applying

32. As of 2013, women accounted for approximately 52 percent of the electorate, occupied approximately _____ percent of the seats in the House, and occupied approximately _____ percent of the seats in the Senate.
    A. 52 . . . 52
    B. 48 . . . 48
    C. 38 . . . 38
    D. 28 . . . 28
    E. 18 . . . 20

    ANS: E   DIF: Difficult   REF: Page 238
    TOP: Members of Congress   MSC: Remembering

33. The text quotes a study by political scientist Larry Bartels comparing the preferences of constituents who are wealthy, middle class, and poor with the voting of senators on government spending, abortion, civil rights, and the minimum wage. The study found that
    A. senators were equally responsive to the wealthy, the middle class, and the poor.
    B. senators were more responsive to the opinions of the middle class than to those of the wealthy or the poor.
    C. senators were more responsive to the opinions of the wealthy than to those of the middle class, and weren't at all responsive to the poor.
    D. senators were most responsive to the poor.
    E. senators weren't responsive to the rich, the middle class, or the poor.

    ANS: C   DIF: Moderate   REF: Page 239
    TOP: Members of Congress   MSC: Applying

34. In the House of Representatives over the past fifty years, the number of Republicans from the South has _____, and the number of Republicans from the Northeast has _____.
    A. increased . . . increased
    B. increased . . . decreased
    C. decreased . . . increased
    D. decreased . . . decreased
    E. stayed approximately the same . . . stayed approximately the same

    ANS: B   DIF: Moderate   REF: Pages 240–1
    TOP: Realignment and Polarization
    MSC: Remembering

35. Which of the following statements about political polarization is true?
    A. Political differences within parties have increased.
    B. Political differences between the parties have decreased.
    C. The average Democrat has become more conservative on social issues and more liberal on economic issues.
    D. The average Republican has become more conservative on both social and economic issues.
    E. The average Republican has become more conservative on social issues but more liberal on economic issues.

    ANS: D   DIF: Difficult   REF: Page 241
    TOP: Realignment and Polarization   MSC: Applying

36. A supermajority of _____ votes is needed to end a filibuster in the U.S. Senate.
    A. 50
    B. 51
    C. 60
    D. 75
    E. 100

    ANS: C   DIF: Moderate   REF: Page 245
    TOP: The Legislative Process   MSC: Remembering

37. All of the following statements regarding congressional committees are true *except*
    A. committees are legislative gatekeepers.
    B. the Speaker of the House is a member of all of the House of Representatives' committees.
    C. committees perform the bulk of the legislative work in Congress.
    D. more than 90 percent of all bills submitted to Congress do not make it out of committee.
    E. conference committees are composed of members of the House and the Senate that meet to reconcile differences in a bill passed by the two chambers.

    ANS: B   DIF: Moderate   REF: Page 245
    TOP: The Legislative Process   MSC: Applying

38. Congress may override a presidential veto
_____.
A. never. Presidential vetoes are final
B. by majority vote in the U.S. Senate
C. by a two-thirds vote in the House of Representatives
D. by majority vote in both Houses of Congress
E. by a two-thirds vote in both Houses of Congress

ANS: E   DIF: Moderate   REF: Page 246
TOP: The Legislative Process   MSC: Remembering

39. In discussing the operation of Congress, the text quotes a statement by John F. Kennedy that says
A. it's much easier to defeat a bill in Congress than to pass one.
B. it's much easier to pass a bill in Congress than to defeat one.
C. it's about as easy to defeat a bill in Congress as it is to pass one.
D. conference committees are unnecessary.
E. conference committees should undertake more responsibility for overseeing the federal bureaucracy.

ANS: A   DIF: Moderate   REF: Pages 246–7
TOP: The Legislative Process   MSC: Applying

40. Congress' responsibility to monitor, supervise, and review how the executive agencies of the federal government conduct their affairs is called _____.
A. casework
B. the electoral connection
C. confirmation
D. oversight
E. earmark

ANS: D   DIF: Moderate   REF: Page 249
TOP: The Legislative Process   MSC: Understanding

41. According to the text, between the years 1998–2012, labor unions spent $528 million on lobbying. In the same period, the finance, insurance, and real estate sectors alone spent _____ on lobbying.
A. $300 million
B. $492 million
C. $1 billion
D. $3.6 billion
E. $5.2 billion

ANS: E   DIF: Moderate   REF: Page 250
TOP: Seeking Influence   MSC: Remembering

ESSAY

1. Describe at least six powers given to Congress by the Constitution.

ANS: Answers will vary.   DIF: Moderate
REF: Page 219   TOP: Introduction   MSC: Analyzing

2. Summarize the role the Founders envisaged for the Senate, and the Constitutional provisions aimed at allowing the Senate to fulfill this role.

ANS: Answers will vary.   DIF: Moderate
REF: Page 219   TOP: Introduction   MSC: Analyzing

3. Explain why, according to the text, the presidency and Congress are often attuned to different voices.

ANS: Answers will vary.   DIF: Moderate
REF: Page 221   TOP: Introduction   MSC: Analyzing

4. What is "the electoral connection" and what is its relation to congressional careers?

ANS: Answers will vary.   DIF: Moderate
REF: Pages 231–2   TOP: Congressional Careers and the Electoral Connection   MSC: Analyzing

5. Summarize the consequences of the high cost of running for election to Congress in the United States.

ANS: Answers will vary.   DIF: Moderate
REF: Pages 232–3   TOP: Congressional Careers and the Electoral Connection   MSC: Analyzing

6. Summarize the reasons why, according to the text, the social backgrounds of members of Congress are important, and indicate some of the important disparities between the demographic characteristics of members of Congress and members of the electorate.

ANS: Answers will vary.   DIF: Moderate
REF: Page 237   TOP: Members of Congress
MSC: Analyzing

7. Summarize the past half-century's changes in patterns of partisanship in the South and Northeast and what the consequences of these changes have been.

ANS: Answers will vary.   DIF: Difficult
REF: Pages 240–1   TOP: Realignment and Polarization
MSC: Analyzing

8. What are the main steps in the legislative process by which a bill becomes a law? Why did that process lead John F. Kennedy to say that it's much harder to pass a bill than to defeat one?

ANS: Answers will vary.   DIF: Moderate
REF: Pages 243–7   TOP: The Legislative Process
MSC: Analyzing

MULTIPLE CHOICE

1. In 2011, the Affordable Care Act, popularly known as Obamacare, was upheld in a _____ decision by the U.S. Supreme Court.
   A. 9–0
   B. 8–1
   C. 7–2
   D. 6–3
   E. 5–4

   ANS: E   DIF: Moderate   REF: Page 257
   TOP: Introduction   MSC: Remembering

2. What was the Constitutional reasoning that the Supreme Court used to uphold the Affordable Care Act?
   A. Congress's power to tax
   B. Congress's power to regulate commerce
   C. the federal government's responsibility to provide for the general welfare
   D. the president's power to execute the laws of Congress
   E. the police power of state governments

   ANS: A   DIF: Difficult   REF: Page 257
   TOP: Introduction   MSC: Applying

3. When political scientists say that the courts have the power of judicial review, they mainly mean that the courts
   A. have the power to review movies distributed in the United States to see whether they are impermissibly pornographic.
   B. have the power to review all elections in the United States to see whether there has been cheating.
   C. have the power to overturn any federal laws but not state laws that conflict with the Constitution.
   D. have the power to overturn any federal or state law that conflicts with the Constitution.
   E. have the power to rule that parts of the Constitution are unconstitutional.

   ANS: D   DIF: Easy   REF: Page 258
   TOP: Introduction   MSC: Applying

4. The final interpreter of the U.S. Constitution is

   _____.
   A. the president
   B. the people
   C. Congress
   D. the U.S. Supreme Court
   E. the states

   ANS: D   DIF: Easy   REF: Page 258
   TOP: Introduction   MSC: Understanding

5. The term of office for a federal justice is

   _____.
   A. 2 years
   B. 4 years
   C. 6 years
   D. 10 years
   E. a life term

   ANS: E   DIF: Easy   REF: Page 258
   TOP: Introduction   MSC: Remembering

6. The text cites President Andrew Jackson's comment on a Supreme Court decision mainly to illustrate the book's point that
   A. it is very difficult to remove federal judges from office.
   B. there are many limitations on the power of the courts.
   C. the courts are the most powerful branch of government because they have the power of judicial review.
   D. federal judges have extraordinary independence.
   E. federal judges' salaries cannot be reduced.

   ANS: B   DIF: Moderate   REF: Page 259
   TOP: Introduction   MSC: Applying

7. The text makes all of the following claims *except*
   A. formal, legal equality is compromised in a society with racial, gender, and class inequalities.
   B. as opposed to what Chief Justice John Roberts has said, courts don't merely apply the rules; they decide what the rules are.
   C. judges do not have policy goals and should never be influenced by public opinion.
   D. it's hard to pin down whether the law is a progressive or conservative force.
   E. many people on death row are there because they're poor and can't afford to hire good lawyers.

   ANS: C   DIF: Moderate   REF: Page 260
   TOP: Introduction   MSC: Applying

8. When political scientists say that the United States has a dual court system, they most often mean that
   A. the Senate must confirm all appointees to the Supreme Court.
   B. the House of Representatives must confirm all appointees to the Supreme Court.
   C. the federal judiciary has both district and appeals courts.
   D. state and federal systems of justice exist side by side.
   E. not all judges take a strict constructionist approach to the Constitution.

   ANS: D   DIF: Easy   REF: Page 261
   TOP: A Dual Court System   MSC: Understanding

9. How many federal district courts are there?
A. 1
B. 50
C. 94
D. 435
E. 535

ANS: C   DIF: Difficult   REF: Page 261
TOP: A Dual Court System   MSC: Remembering

10. How many federal courts of appeals are there?
A. 5
B. 12
C. 25
D. 32
E. 50

ANS: B   DIF: Difficult   REF: Page 261
TOP: A Dual Court System   MSC: Remembering

11. How are federal judges chosen?
A. elected directly by the people
B. appointed by the American Bar Association
C. nominated by state governors and selected by the President
D. nominated by the President and confirmed by the U.S. Senate
E. nominated by the President and confirmed by the House of Representatives

ANS: D   DIF: Moderate   REF: Page 262
TOP: A Dual Court System   MSC: Remembering

12. According to the text, the appointment of judges is hard to reconcile with democratic theory because
A. Congress cannot lower their salaries.
B. Judges have the power of judicial review.
C. Judges serve as umpires in courts of law.
D. Judges selected by appointment are not accountable to voters.
E. Judges can be removed by referendum.

ANS: D   DIF: Moderate   REF: Page 262
TOP: A Dual Court System   MSC: Applying

13. The election of judges may be problematic for a democracy because
A. the President has no role in choosing judges.
B. as the cost of campaigning increases, judges may be tempted to rule in favor of those who contribute to their campaigns.
C. the House of Representatives has not reviewed the judges' credentials.
D. private financing of judicial elections is illegal.
E. elected judges have less experience in the legal profession than appointed judges.

ANS: B   DIF: Moderate   REF: Page 262
TOP: A Dual Court System   MSC: Applying

14. _____ was the Supreme Court decision that outlawed state-sanctioned segregation in public schools.
A. *Dred Scott v. Sandford*
B. *Plessy v. Ferguson*
C. *Brown v. Board of Education*
D. *Engel v. Vitale*
E. *McCulloch v. Maryland*

ANS: C   DIF: Easy   REF: Page 264
TOP: The Federal Court System   MSC: Remembering

15. Ten years after the *Brown* decision, what percentage of Southern black children were in non-segregated schools?
A. 1 percent
B. 25 percent
C. 50 percent
D. 75 percent
E. Nearly 100 percent

ANS: A   DIF: Moderate   REF: Page 264
TOP: The Federal Court System   MSC: Remembering

16. On average, the U.S. Supreme Court usually hears _____ cases per year.
A. about 50
B. less than 100
C. about 200
D. about 1,000
E. more than 1,000

ANS: B   DIF: Easy   REF: Page 264
TOP: The Federal Court System   MSC: Remembering

17. A decision by the federal appeals court for the Fifth Circuit is binding
A. only in the Fifth Circuit.
B. only in the Fourth, Fifth, and Sixth Circuits.
C. only in the Fifth Circuit and in Washington, D.C.
D. in all circuits unless the Supreme Court overturns the decision.
E. nowhere until the Supreme Court issues a ruling affirming the Fifth Circuit's decision.

ANS: A   DIF: Moderate   REF: Pages 264–5
TOP: The Federal Court System
MSC: Understanding

18. According to the text, why do federal courts tend to lag behind other political institutions and act as a drag on political change?
A. because there are only nine Supreme Court Justices
B. because federal court judges tend to be elderly
C. because the federal courts lack democratic legitimacy
D. because federal judges enjoy a lifetime tenure
E. because the federal courts have always been a conservative institution

ANS: D   DIF: Moderate   REF: Page 267
TOP: The Federal Court System   MSC: Applying

19. In the areas of civil liberties and civil rights, President George W. Bush's judicial appointees have been
    A. the most liberal on record.
    B. the most conservative on record.
    C. the most progressive on record.
    D. balanced liberal and conservative.
    E. the most socialist on record.

    ANS: B   DIF: Moderate   REF: Page 267
    TOP: The Federal Court System   MSC: Applying

20. Which statement about the U.S. Supreme Court is true?
    A. It is required by the Constitution to hear any case that it is asked to hear.
    B. It agrees to hear approximately half the cases that it is asked to hear.
    C. It is required by the Constitution to have nine justices.
    D. It has never had an African American justice.
    E. Justices on the U.S. Supreme Court serve life terms of office.

    ANS: E   DIF: Difficult   REF: Page 267
    TOP: The Federal Court System   MSC: Applying

21. The rule of four refers to
    A. the minimum number of Supreme Court justices needed to choose cases.
    B. the minimum number of Supreme Court justices needed to decide a case.
    C. the number of justices on the U.S. Supreme Court.
    D. the number of justices presiding over an impeachment.
    E. the number of conservative justices on the Roberts Court.

    ANS: A   DIF: Moderate   REF: Page 269
    TOP: The Supreme Court   MSC: Understanding

22. The first African American on the U.S. Supreme Court is/was
    A. Dred Scott.
    B. Earl Warren.
    C. Thurgood Marshall.
    D. Clarence Thomas.
    E. William Brandeis.

    ANS: C   DIF: Moderate   REF: Page 271
    TOP: The Supreme Court   MSC: Remembering

23. The first woman appointed to the U.S. Supreme Court is/was
    A. Sandra Day O'Connor.
    B. Ruth Bader Ginsburg.
    C. Sonia Sotomayor.
    D. Elena Kagan.
    E. Nancy Pelosi.

    ANS: A   DIF: Moderate   REF: Page 271
    TOP: The Supreme Court   MSC: Remembering

24. The first Hispanic appointed to the U.S. Supreme Court is/was
    A. Samuel Alito.
    B. Antonin Scalia.
    C. Sonia Sotomayor.
    D. Alberto Gonzales.
    E. Ken Salazar.

    ANS: C   DIF: Moderate   REF: Page 271
    TOP: The Supreme Court   MSC: Remembering

25. According to the text, which factor is most important in selecting federal court judges?
    A. racial diversity
    B. regional diversity
    C. religious diversity
    D. gender diversity
    E. ideology

    ANS: E   DIF: Moderate   REF: Page 272
    TOP: The Supreme Court   MSC: Understanding

26. The case of *Marbury v. Madison*
    A. established the precedent that the Supreme Court could declare laws unconstitutional.
    B. dealt with the scope of national power as opposed to state power.
    C. established that blacks could not be considered property under the law.
    D. established that states could not pass laws abridging free speech.
    E. involved the phrase, "a switch in time saved nine."

    ANS: A   DIF: Moderate   REF: Page 273
    TOP: Judicial Activism and Restraint   MSC: Applying

27. The case of *McCulloch v. Maryland*
    A. established the precedent that the Supreme Court could declare laws unconstitutional.
    B. dealt with the scope of national power as opposed to state power.
    C. established that blacks could not be considered property under the law.
    D. established that states could not pass laws abridging free speech.
    E. involved the phrase, "a switch in time saved nine."

    ANS: B   DIF: Moderate   REF: Page 274
    TOP: The Supreme Court in History   MSC: Applying

28. Following Reconstruction, the Fourteenth Amendment, according to the text
    A. did an excellent job of protecting both corporate interests and black civil rights.
    B. did nothing to protect either corporate interests or black civil rights.
    C. served to protect black civil rights more than corporate interests.
    D. served to protect corporate interests more than black civil rights. =
    E. allowed the Supreme Court to overrule its earlier decision in *Marbury v. Madison.*

    ANS: D   DIF: Moderate   REF: Page 275
    TOP: The Supreme Court in History   MSC: Applying

29. The "switch in time that saved nine" refers primarily to
    A. a Congressional vote that led to the approval of much of FDR's New Deal legislation.
    B. the *Dred Scott* decision.
    C. a change in the way the Supreme Court voted on FDR's New Deal legislation. =
    D. a change in the way the Supreme Court voted on free speech cases.
    E. a change in the way the Supreme Court voted to end racial discrimination.

    ANS: C   DIF: Moderate   REF: Page 276
    TOP: The Supreme Court in History   MSC: Applying

30. When *Brown v. Board of Education* was decided, the chief justice was
    A. William Brennan.
    B. Earl Warren.
    C. William Rehnquist.
    D. Thurgood Marshall.
    E. David Souter.

    ANS: B   DIF: Moderate   REF: Page 277
    TOP: The Modern Court: From Warren to Roberts
    MSC: Remembering

31. Which of the following issues is *not* associated with the Warren Court's "rights revolution"?
    A. one person, one vote
    B. school desegregation
    C. the right to be represented by a lawyer
    D. election fraud
    E. freedom of speech

    ANS: D   DIF: Moderate   REF: Page 278
    TOP: The Modern Court: From Warren to Roberts
    MSC: Remembering

32. *Baker v. Carr* and *Reynolds v. Sims* were Supreme Court cases
    A. that dealt primarily with school desegregation.
    B. that dealt primarily with the rights of people charged with crimes.
    C. that dealt with voting rights.
    D. that overturned the rule of four.
    E. that led to the Constitutional Revolution of 1937.

    ANS: C   DIF: Moderate   REF: Page 278
    TOP: The Modern Court: From Warren to Roberts
    MSC: Applying

33. *Swann v. Charlotte-Mecklenburg* is best known as the case in which the Supreme Court unanimously ruled
    A. that state elections must adhere to the principle of one person, one vote.
    B. that judges must adhere to the philosophy of judicial restraint.
    C. that people who are arrested must be read their rights.
    D. that any person charged with a capital crime must be provided with a competent attorney.
    E. that busing could be used to achieve school desegregation. =

    ANS: E   DIF: Moderate   REF: Page 280
    TOP: The Modern Court: From Warren to Roberts
    MSC: Applying

34. The case of *Roe v. Wade* dealt with
    A. the right of a criminal defendant to be represented by an attorney.
    B. school busing to achieve racial desegregation.
    C. a woman's right to an abortion.
    D. one person, one vote.
    E. affirmative action.

    ANS: C   DIF: Easy   REF: Page 280
    TOP: The Modern Court: From Warren to Roberts
    MSC: Remembering

35. According to the text, the greatest difference between the U.S. judicial system and that of other nations is
    A. the existence of judicial review in the United States.
    B. the way judges in the United States are chosen.
    C. the large number of women in the United States who are judges.
    D. the small number of people of color in the United States who are judges.
    E. the vast prison complex in the United States and the harsh nature of punishment in the United States.

    ANS: E   DIF: Moderate   REF: Page 289
    TOP: The Courts in Comparative Perspective:
        Incarceration Nation   MSC: Applying

MULTIPLE CHOICE

1. The largest part of the welfare state consists of
   A. social insurance programs.
   B. federal aid to education.
   C. Medicaid.
   D. food stamps.
   E. Temporary Assistance to Needy Families (TANF).

   ANS: A   DIF: Easy   REF: Page 325
   TOP: Introduction   MSC: Remembering

2. The program that offers health insurance to the elderly is called _____.
   A. Medicare
   B. Medicaid
   C. Temporary Assistance to Needy Families
   D. Social Security
   E. the Affordable Health Care Act

   ANS: A   DIF: Moderate   REF: Page 325
   TOP: Introduction   MSC: Remembering

3. Government social policy programs that are funded by premiums paid by people in the labor market to support the benefits given to participants are called _____.
   A. social insurance programs
   B. public assistance programs
   C. private insurance programs
   D. unemployment insurance programs
   E. the Temporary Assistance to Needy Families program

   ANS: A   DIF: Moderate   REF: Pages 325–6
   TOP: Introduction   MSC: Understanding

4. Most social insurance programs benefit
   A. unemployed people.
   B. unmarried women with more than one child.
   C. African Americans.
   D. the working middle class.
   E. insurance companies.

   ANS: D   DIF: Moderate   REF: Page 326
   TOP: Introduction   MSC: Applying

5. Which statement is true regarding public assistance programs?
   A. They are no different from social insurance programs.
   B. They include TANF.
   C. They are not means tested.
   D. They provide benefits that are identical throughout the United States.
   E. They are rarely eroded by inflation.

   ANS: B   DIF: Moderate   REF: Page 326
   TOP: Introduction   MSC: Applying

6. When the text says that Social Security benefits are indexed, it means that these benefits
   A. are generally distributed in alphabetical order.
   B. are distributed to older beneficiaries before younger beneficiaries.
   C. depend on the state in which the beneficiary resides.
   D. are adjusted to take account of the age of the beneficiary.
   E. are adjusted to take account of the rate of inflation.

   ANS: E   DIF: Moderate   REF: Page 326
   TOP: Introduction   MSC: Applying

7. Government protection of citizens' economic and social well-being through instruments of social insurance and transfers to the needs broadly refers to
   A. the welfare state.
   B. public assistance programs.
   C. charity contributions.
   D. Social Security.
   E. economic regulation.

   ANS: A   DIF: Moderate   REF: Page 326
   TOP: Introduction   MSC: Understanding

8. Welfare state programs that transfer funds to needy persons and families to help them secure a decent standard of living and become more self-sufficient are called _____.
   A. social insurance programs
   B. public assistance programs
   C. Social Security programs
   D. charity programs
   E. private insurance programs

   ANS: B   DIF: Easy   REF: Page 326
   TOP: Introduction   MSC: Applying

9. Means-tested programs are programs that are available to
   A. all citizens in the labor force.
   B. all citizens regardless of labor force participation.
   C. citizens whose income or wealth is below a level set by law.
   D. citizens whose income or wealth is above a level set by law.
   E. only to citizens above the age of 65.

   ANS: C   DIF: Moderate   REF: Page 326
   TOP: Introduction   MSC: Understanding

10. The program that offers health insurance to the needy is called _____.
    A. Medicare
    B. Medicaid ―
    C. Temporary Assistance to Needy Families
    D. Aid to Families with Dependent Children
    E. the Affordable Health Care Act

    ANS: B   DIF: Moderate   REF: Page 326
    TOP: Introduction   MSC: Remembering

11. When the text discusses the private or hidden welfare state, it is referring primarily to
    A. TANF benefits obtained through fraud.
    B. Social Security benefits obtained through fraud.
    C. pensions, health insurance, and other benefits provided by employers. ―
    D. the underground economy in which people are paid in cash and don't pay any taxes.
    E. the benefits received by undocumented immigrants.

    ANS: C   DIF: Easy   REF: Page 327
    TOP: Introduction   MSC: Applying

12. When the text says that "the private welfare state is really not so private," this mainly means that
    A. the data on these issues is readily available to the public.
    B. the U.S. government collects taxes on the benefits paid through the private welfare state.
    C. the government subsidizes the private welfare state through the tax code. ―
    D. beneficiaries of the private welfare state are U.S. citizens.
    E. Congress determines the level and duration of all benefits paid by the private welfare state.

    ANS: C   DIF: Moderate   REF: Page 327
    TOP: Introduction   MSC: Understanding

13. The private welfare state is _____ government programs in terms of who benefits and how much they benefit.
    A. much less inequitable than
    B. slightly less inequitable than
    C. equally inequitable as
    D. more inequitable than ―
    E. more equitable than

    ANS: D   DIF: Moderate   REF: Page 328
    TOP: Introduction   MSC: Remembering

14. Compared with people in most other industrial societies, people in the United States enjoy _____ social rights.
    A. less generous and fewer ―
    B. equally generous and about the same number of
    C. slightly more generous and a slightly greater number of
    D. much more generous
    E. a much greater number of

    ANS: A   DIF: Easy   REF: Page 328
    TOP: Introduction   MSC: Understanding

15. In 2010, _____ Americans lacked health insurance.
    A. no
    B. nearly 1 million
    C. nearly 10 million
    D. nearly 50 million ―
    E. nearly 100 million

    ANS: D   DIF: Moderate   REF: Page 328
    TOP: Introduction   MSC: Remembering

16. The social insurance program passed in 1935 that offers income in old age and protection against disability and unemployment is called _____.
    A. unemployment compensation
    B. workers' compensation
    C. Social Security ―
    D. public assistance
    E. Medicaid

    ANS: C   DIF: Moderate   REF: Page 329
    TOP: The Historical Welfare State
    MSC: Understanding

17. The Social Security Act was passed in
    A. 1925.
    B. 1935. ―
    C. 1945.
    D. 1955.
    E. 1965.

    ANS: B   DIF: Easy   REF: Page 329
    TOP: The Historical Welfare State
    MSC: Remembering

18. Prior to the passage of the Social Security Act, the early U.S. welfare state differed from that in most western European countries in that
    A. the United States did not extend social protection to any segment of the population.
    B. most western European countries targeted their early welfare state programs to mothers.
    C. most western European countries targeted their early welfare programs to veterans.
    D. the United States extended social protection to mothers but to no other segment of the population.
    E. the United States extended social protection to mothers and veteran soldiers. —

    ANS: E   DIF: Moderate   REF: Page 330
    TOP: The Historical Welfare State   MSC: Applying

19. In support of its claim that mothers' pensions are an example of how roles based on gender and race can be inscribed in social policy, the text points out that
    A. mothers' pensions benefited African American women, especially those who had been slaves or whose mothers had been slaves.
    B. only women who proved they were unable to find a job were eligible for mothers' pensions.
    C. to receive mothers' pensions, women had to conform to traditional gender roles, and black women were denied pensions in many places. —
    D. the legislation authorizing these pensions was written by white men.
    E. the bureaucrats administering these pensions were white men.

    ANS: C   DIF: Moderate   REF: Pages 330–1
    TOP: The Historical Welfare State   MSC: Applying

20. In discussing social programs instituted during the New Deal, the text says all of the following *except*
    A. the federal government set the benefit levels for all of these programs. —
    B. when the threat of civil disorder arose, the federal government expanded work relief programs.
    C. when the threat of disorder decreased, federally funded jobs diminished.
    D. social reform was part of the administration's strategy to keep the market economy functioning.
    E. many benefit levels were generally set quite low.

    ANS: A   DIF: Difficult   REF: Page 332
    TOP: The New Deal and Beyond   MSC: Applying

21. The 40-hour work week and the first national minimum wage were established by _____.
    A. voluntary agreement among businesses
    B. the *Lochner* U.S. Supreme Court decision
    C. President Harry Truman's executive order
    D. the Fair Labor Standards Act of 1938 —
    E. the Social Security Act of 1935

    ANS: D   DIF: Moderate   REF: Page 334
    TOP: The New Deal and Beyond
    MSC: Remembering

22. The gains in health insurance and employer-funded pensions gained by unions for workers in large corporations
    A. failed to keep pace with similar gains for workers who worked for smaller companies.
    B. made workers for these large companies even more dependent on government social programs.
    C. allowed President Truman's Fair Deal to achieve all of its goals.
    D. greatly boosted the political unity between workers in large and small companies.
    E. lowered pressure from corporate sector workers to increase government social programs. —

    ANS: E   DIF: Moderate   REF: Page 335
    TOP: The New Deal and Beyond   MSC: Applying

23. Michael Harrington was
    A. President Truman's Secretary of Health, Education, and Welfare.
    B. an author whose book drew national attention to poverty.
    C. the author of the GI Bill.
    D. the author of the Fair Labor Standards Act.
    E. the union leader during whose tenure unionized workers obtained the best health insurance in the United States.

    ANS: B   DIF: Easy   REF: Page 336
    TOP: The New Poverty   MSC: Remembering

24. Between 1967 and 2007, the poverty rate for the elderly _____, and the poverty rate for children _____.
    A. declined . . . stayed roughly the same —
    B. stayed roughly the same . . . stayed roughly the same
    C. increased . . . stayed roughly the same
    D. increased . . . increased
    E. increased . . . declined

    ANS: A   DIF: Difficult   REF: Page 338
    TOP: The New Poverty   MSC: Understanding

25. In constant (1996) dollars, the value of the minimum wage was highest in
    A. 1968
    B. 1978
    C. 1988
    D. 1998
    E. 2008

    ANS: A   DIF: Difficult   REF: Page 339
    TOP: The Great Society Program
    MSC: Remembering

26. The Great Society was initiated by President
    A. Truman.
    B. Eisenhower.
    C. Kennedy.
    D. Johnson.
    E. Nixon.

    ANS: D   DIF: Easy   REF: Page 340
    TOP: The Great Society Program
    MSC: Remembering

27. Which of the following was *not* part of the Great Society's War on Poverty?
    A. Medicare
    B. Head Start and Upward Bound
    C. Medicaid
    D. national health insurance
    E. Job Corps

    ANS: D   DIF: Difficult   REF: Page 340
    TOP: The Great Society Program
    MSC: Remembering

28. The text attributes the political downfall of President Johnson's Great Society initiative to all of the following *except*
    A. divisions between private sector and public sector workers.
    B. divisions between men and women.
    C. the division of workers covered by social insurance programs versus poor people receiving public assistance.
    D. the resentment of some whites over the racial focus of the Great Society.
    E. the Vietnam War.

    ANS: B   DIF: Moderate   REF: Pages 340–1
    TOP: The Great Society Program   MSC: Applying

29. According to the text, the War on Poverty
    A. was so flawed in design that there was no way it could have succeeded.
    B. was designed well but failed because it was poorly implemented.
    C. reduced the number of people in poverty.
    D. increased the political unity between people receiving public assistance and those covered by social insurance.
    E. was a program that almost all conservatives had to admit was a success.

    ANS: C   DIF: Moderate   REF: Page 341
    TOP: The Great Society Program   MSC: Applying

30. According to the text, President Clinton's social policy was shaped by
    A. his unswerving commitment to the programs of the Great Society and of the New Deal.
    B. the need to reduce the federal deficit and a conservative definition of the welfare problem.
    C. the need to gain the support of black and Latino voters.
    D. the Democratic Party's hope to regain the support of white voters in the South.
    E. the need for the Democratic Party to gain the support of women voters.

    ANS: B   DIF: Easy   REF: Page 343
    TOP: From Reagan to Clinton   MSC: Applying

31. Which Democratic president worked with Republicans to create the Temporary Assistance to Needy Families program and to "end welfare as we know it"?
    A. Franklin Delano Roosevelt
    B. John F. Kennedy
    C. Lyndon Baines Johnson
    D. Jimmy Carter
    E. Bill Clinton

    ANS: E   DIF: Easy   REF: Pages 343–4
    TOP: From Reagan to Clinton   MSC: Remembering

32. The welfare reform implemented during Clinton's administration
    A. eliminated the program known as TANF.
    B. was an entitlement program.
    C. requires the federal government to give all aid directly to eligible citizens.
    D. channels welfare funds through state governments and the amount of these funds automatically increases when the welfare rolls increase.
    E. channels welfare funds through state governments and sets a two-year time limit for recipients.

    ANS: E   DIF: Moderate   REF: Page 344
    TOP: From Reagan to Clinton   MSC: Applying

33. The Elementary and Secondary Education Act, which provided significant federal aid to K–12 education for the first time, was first passed in
    A. 1955.
    B. 1965.
    C. 1975.
    D. 1985.
    E. 1995.

    ANS: B   DIF: Easy   REF: Page 345
    TOP: From Bush to Obama   MSC: Remembering

34. Elementary and high school education in the United States is mostly financed by _____.
    A. the federal government
    B. state governments
    C. local governments
    D. local school boards
    E. tuition paid by individuals

    ANS: C   DIF: Moderate   REF: Page 345
    TOP: From Bush to Obama   MSC: Understanding

35. All of the following about No Child Left Behind are true *except*
    A. it was passed during the administration of President George W. Bush.
    B. one of its main aims was to decrease the achievement gap between advantaged and disadvantaged students.
    C. it had very little support from Democrats.
    D. many states consider it an unfunded mandate.
    E. many critics charge that the federal government has failed to fund it adequately.

    ANS: C   DIF: Moderate   REF: Page 346
    TOP: From Bush to Obama   MSC: Applying

36. As of 2006, compared with other industrialized democracies, the United States spent _____ percent of its GDP on health.
    A. a larger
    B. about the same
    C. a slightly lower
    D. a much lower
    E. an equal

    ANS: A   DIF: Easy   REF: Pages 347, 349
    TOP: From Bush to Obama   MSC: Remembering

37. According to the text, the primary purpose of the health reform that passed in 2010 was to
    A. help President Obama get reelected by strengthening the electoral coalition that brought the Democrats to power in 2008.
    B. resolve the tension between democracy and capitalism.
    C. facilitate a government takeover of almost one-sixth of the U.S. economy.
    D. reduce the number of people in the United States who were outside the system of health insurance.
    E. decrease federal expenditures for TANF, food stamps, and other forms of public assistance.

    ANS: D   DIF: Easy   REF: Page 348
    TOP: From Bush to Obama   MSC: Understanding

38. The health reform passed in 2010 says that beginning in 2014
    A. the federal government will pay 50 percent of the cost of an abortion for women who receive Medicaid.
    B. the federal government will pay 100 percent of the cost of an abortion for women who receive Medicaid.
    C. employers with more than fifty workers will have to provide affordable insurance or pay a penalty.
    D. all people in the U.S. will have an opportunity to enroll in a public option, that is, insurance provided by the government that competes effectively with plans offered by insurance companies.
    E. 25 percent of the patients of dermatologists, surgeons, neurologists, and other specialists must be either Medicare or Medicaid recipients.

    ANS: C   DIF: Easy   REF: Pages 348–9
    TOP: From Bush to Obama   MSC: Remembering

39. Over the subsequent ten years, the health reform that became law in 2010 is estimated by the Congressional Budget to
    A. increase the federal deficit by $138 billion.
    B. decrease the federal deficit by $138 billion.
    C. increase the federal deficit by a trillion dollars.
    D. decrease the federal deficit by a trillion dollars.
    E. have no effect on the federal deficit.

    ANS: B   DIF: Moderate   REF: Page 349
    TOP: From Bush to Obama   MSC: Understanding

40. Within months of its passage, health reform resulted in all of the following *except*
    A. a temporary high-risk insurance pool was created for people who have medical problems and have been rejected by insurers.
    B. insurers were no longer able to place lifetime limits on coverage.
    C. provisions were phased in prohibiting insurance companies from denying coverage because of a person's medical condition or prior illness.
    D. children were able to stay on their parents' policies until they reached the age of twenty-six.
    E. the federal government began paying 50 percent of the cost of an abortion for women who receive Medicaid.

    ANS: E   DIF: Easy   REF: Page 350
    TOP: From Bush to Obama   MSC: Applying

41. According to the text, business has generally opposed extending the welfare state because
    A. business wants to extend the private welfare state instead.
    B. the welfare state benefits are too limited.
    C. the welfare state operates according to market principles.
    D. the welfare state reduces the power that employers exercise over employees.
    E. the welfare state violates the egalitarian logic of capitalism.

    ANS: D   DIF: Difficult   REF: Page 351
    TOP: Conclusion   MSC: Understanding

42. According to the text, the U.S. welfare state is *conservative* because
    A. it corrects the basic structural inequalities of corporate capitalism.
    B. it stabilizes the corporate capitalist system.
    C. it offers a more egalitarian alternative to the marketplace.
    D. generally, working-class and poor people support it.
    E. its costs and benefits are equally shared.

    ANS: B   DIF: Difficult   REF: Pages 351–2
    TOP: Conclusion   MSC: Understanding

43. According to the text
    A. the U.S. welfare state doesn't face any significant financial problems, and its future is certain.
    B. the public welfare state is under pressure, but the private welfare state isn't.
    C. both the public and private welfare states are under pressure.
    D. the private welfare state is under pressure, but the public welfare state isn't.
    E. the 2010 health reform will have so big an effect on both the private and public welfare states that it's impossible at this point to say anything about the pressures and strains on either the public or private welfare states.

    ANS: C   DIF: Moderate   REF: Page 352
    TOP: Conclusion   MSC: Applying

44. In discussing the effects of the United States's many welfare programs on class, regional, generational, and racial inequalities, the text says that taken together
    A. these programs don't have any effect on such inequalities.
    B. these programs are so complex that it's impossible to discern how they affect such inequalities.
    C. these programs always serve to ease such inequalities.
    D. these programs always serve to exacerbate such inequalities.
    E. these programs sometimes ease such inequalities and sometimes exacerbate them.

    ANS: E   DIF: Easy   REF: Pages 352–3
    TOP: Conclusion   MSC: Applying

45. In the first decade of the twenty-first century, approximately _____ percent of people in the United States were living in poverty at some point.
    A. 10
    B. 20
    C. 30
    D. 40
    E. 50

    ANS: D   DIF: Easy   REF: Page 353
    TOP: Conclusion   MSC: Remembering

ESSAY

1. Summarize the difference between social insurance programs and public assistance programs. Give two examples of each.

   ANS: Answers will vary.   DIF: Moderate
   REF: Page 326   TOP: Introduction   MSC: Analyzing

MULTIPLE CHOICE

1. The United States has approximately _____ percent of the world's population, and accounts for approximately _____ percent of the world's wealth.
   A. 5 . . . 5
   B. 5 . . . 33
   C. 5 . . . 50
   D. 10 . . . 20
   E. 10 . . . 40

   ANS: B   DIF: Easy   REF: Page 356
   TOP: Introduction   MSC: Remembering

2. In 2012, the U.S. military budget was _____.
   A. $100 million
   B. $500 million
   C. $100 billion
   D. $500 billion
   E. $700 billion

   ANS: E   DIF: Easy   REF: Page 356
   TOP: Introduction   MSC: Remembering

3. In 2010, U.S. government expenditures for social and economic development in poor regions of the world were approximately _____ the U.S. military budget.
   A. 4 percent of
   B. 10 percent of
   C. half of
   D. equal to
   E. twice as much as

   ANS: A   DIF: Moderate   REF: Page 357
   TOP: Introduction   MSC: Remembering

4. According to the text, U.S. hegemony in the half-century after World War II
   A. was based on global acceptance of the principles stated in the Declaration of Independence.
   B. consisted of "hard power" but not "soft power."
   C. consisted of "soft power" but not "hard power."
   D. consisted of both "hard power" and "soft power."
   E. involved neither "hard power" nor "soft power."

   ANS: D   DIF: Moderate   REF: Page 358
   TOP: Introduction   MSC: Applying

5. The making of foreign policy
   A. is concentrated within the executive branch.
   B. is concentrated within the Congress.
   C. frequently involves the House of Representatives but never the Senate.
   D. frequently involves the Senate but never the House of Representatives.
   E. takes place without any input from transnational corporations (TNCs).

   ANS: A   DIF: Easy   REF: Pages 358–9
   TOP: Making Foreign Policy   MSC: Applying

6. For the most part, U.S. foreign policy is formulated and implemented by _____.
   A. transnational corporations
   B. the U.S. Senate
   C. the U.S. House of Representatives
   D. the President
   E. the voting public

   ANS: D   DIF: Moderate   REF: Pages 358–9
   TOP: Making Foreign Policy   MSC: Understanding

7. In developing foreign policy, presidents must consider all of the following *except*
   A. pressure of foreign governments.
   B. preferences of allies.
   C. domestic partisan and political issues.
   D. his or her own ideological preferences.
   E. including a large number of public and private actors in the decision-making process.

   ANS: E   DIF: Moderate   REF: Pages 358–9
   TOP: Making Foreign Policy   MSC: Applying

8. The role of Congress in the realm of foreign policy includes all of the following *except*
   A. authority to appropriate funds for the Department of Defense.
   B. authority to legislation relating to foreign affairs.
   C. authority to summon military and civilian leaders to testify before congressional committees.
   D. Senate authority to approve treaties.
   E. Senate authority to appoint military officers.

   ANS: E   DIF: Difficult   REF: Page 359
   TOP: Making Foreign Policy   MSC: Applying

9. Firms with significant foreign operations are called _____.
   A. horizontal businesses
   B. vertical businesses
   C. transnational corporations
   D. constellation corporations
   E. multi-government organizations

   ANS: C   DIF: Moderate   REF: Page 359
   TOP: Making Foreign Policy   MSC: Understanding

10. In his presidential farewell address, George Washington
    A. urged the United States to avoid entangling alliances.
    B. encouraged the United States to seek as many alliances as possible to keep Great Britain from trying to regain control of its former colonies.
    C. said the United States should reaffirm its commitment to the Monroe Doctrine.
    D. said the United States should renounce its commitment to the Monroe Doctrine.
    E. emphasized the numerous geographic disadvantages facing the United States.

    ANS: A   DIF: Easy   REF: Page 359
    TOP: American Foreign Policy Before World War II
    MSC: Remembering

11. The Monroe Doctrine dealt primarily with the United States, Europe, and
    A. Africa.
    B. Asia.
    C. Latin America.
    D. the Mediterranean.
    E. the increased Russian colonization of Alaska.

    ANS: C   DIF: Easy   REF: Page 360
    TOP: American Foreign Policy Before World War II
    MSC: Remembering

12. According to the text, during the settlement of North America, Europeans slaughtered approximately _____ Native Americans.
    A. 3,000
    B. 30,000
    C. 300,000
    D. 3 million
    E. 30 million

    ANS: D   DIF: Difficult   REF: Page 360
    TOP: American Foreign Policy Before World War II
    MSC: Remembering

13. _____ is the doctrine that U.S. interests are best served by minimizing U.S. involvement in international affairs.
    A. Multilateralism
    B. Unilateralism
    C. Isolationism
    D. Internationalism
    E. The Monroe Doctrine

    ANS: C   DIF: Moderate   REF: Pages 360–1
    TOP: American Foreign Policy Before World War II
    MSC: Remembering

14. In the aftermath of the Spanish-American War, the United States
    A. retreated to a policy of isolationism.
    B. renounced the policy of gunboat diplomacy.
    C. acquired Venezuela as a colony.
    D. made a colony of Puerto Rico and imposed a protectorate on Cuba.
    E. was forced to acknowledge the legitimacy of ongoing Spanish rule over Puerto Rico and Cuba.

    ANS: D   DIF: Easy   REF: Page 361
    TOP: American Foreign Policy Before World War II
    MSC: Applying

15. According to the text, between 1801 and 1904, the United States engaged in _____ military actions in Latin America.
    A. 1
    B. 11
    C. 101
    D. 1,001
    E. 1,000,001

    ANS: C   DIF: Moderate   REF: Page 361
    TOP: American Foreign Policy Before World War II
    MSC: Remembering

16. All of the following are cited in the text as reasons for the expansion of the U.S. foreign policy agenda in the wake of World War II *except*
    A. the weakened international economic position the United States found itself in at the end of the war.
    B. the decline of the major European capitalist powers.
    C. the growth of nationalism in newly independent countries in Asia and Africa.
    D. the challenge posed by the Soviet Union.
    E. the risk of a resumption of prewar economic depression.

    ANS: A   DIF: Moderate   REF: Page 361
    TOP: American Foreign Policy Before World War II
    MSC: Applying

17. According to the text, during the Cold War
    A. the Soviet Union had a sphere of influence, but the United States did not.
    B. neither the United States nor the Soviet Union had a sphere of influence.
    C. the United States sponsored the Warsaw Pact, and the Soviet Union organized the North Atlantic Treaty Organization.
    D. there was never any real threat of a nuclear war.
    E. nuclear war almost resulted from the Cuban Missile Crisis.

    ANS: E   DIF: Easy   REF: Page 362
    TOP: American Foreign Policy After World War II
    MSC: Applying

18. _____ is the organization created during the Cold War by most democratic states in Western Europe and North America pledging a common military response if any one of them was attacked.
    A. The United Nations
    B. The Warsaw Pact
    C. The North Atlantic Treaty Organization (NATO)
    D. NAFTA
    E. The WTO

    ANS: C   DIF: Moderate   REF: Page 362
    TOP: American Foreign Policy After World War II
    MSC: Understanding

19. The Cold War occurred in the years
    A. leading up to World War I.
    B. immediately after World War I.
    C. leading up to World War II.
    D. after World War II.
    E. following the breakup of the Soviet Union.

    ANS: D   DIF: Easy   REF: Pages 362–3
    TOP: American Foreign Policy After World War II
    MSC: Remembering

20. In its discussion of the Cold War, the text uses the term "proxy war" in reference to
    A. the armed conflicts between U.S. client states and insurgent movements backed by the Soviet Union.
    B. the bitter diplomatic negotiations between the Soviet Union and the United States.
    C. the intense controversies among U.S. citizens over the merits of U.S. foreign policy.
    D. the frequent nuclear confrontations between the Soviet Union and the United States.
    E. the military skirmishes in Europe between the U.S. and Soviet troops that never developed into all-out war.

    ANS: A   DIF: Moderate   REF: Page 363
    TOP: American Foreign Policy After World War II
    MSC: Understanding

21. According to the text, in addition to the Cold War, another immensely significant aspect of the half-century after World War II was
    A. the global expansion of U.S. military, economic, political, and cultural influence.
    B. a sharp decline in U.S. military, economic, political, and cultural influence.
    C. the overwhelming superiority of "soft power" over "hard power" in foreign affairs.
    D. the emergence of the Soviet Union as the world's single most powerful country.
    E. the emergence of the European Union as the world's dominant economic region.

    ANS: A   DIF: Moderate   REF: Page 363
    TOP: American Foreign Policy After World War II
    MSC: Applying

22. The Cold War refers to the period of hostile relations just short of open war that prevailed between the United States and _____ from 1947 to the late 1980s.
    A. Afghanistan
    B. Iraq
    C. France
    D. Russia
    E. The Soviet Union

    ANS: E   DIF: Easy   REF: Page 363
    TOP: American Foreign Policy After World War II
    MSC: Remembering

23. Which president warned against "unwarranted influence . . . by the military-industrial complex"?
    A. Franklin Delano Roosevelt
    B. Dwight D. Eisenhower
    C. John F. Kennedy
    D. Ronald Reagan
    E. Bill Clinton

    ANS: B   DIF: Moderate   REF: Page 363
    TOP: American Foreign Policy After World War II
    MSC: Remembering

24. The Marshall Plan
    A. was a restatement of the Monroe Doctrine.
    B. was the failed plan for a military victory in Vietnam.
    C. was primarily about U.S. aid to countries in Asia and Africa in the years after World War II.
    D. involved aid to Europe in the years after World War II.
    E. laid the basis for the formation of the United Nations.

    ANS: D   DIF: Easy   REF: Page 364
    TOP: American Foreign Policy After World War II
    MSC: Remembering

25. According to the text, in the years after World War II, income from foreign investments
    A. virtually disappeared.
    B. became an important factor in U.S. global hegemony.
    C. was outlawed by the UN Charter.
    D. served primarily to finance public health and education in the developing world.
    E. was of no importance to transnational corporations (TNCs).

    ANS: B   DIF: Easy   REF: Page 364
    TOP: American Foreign Policy After World War II
    MSC: Applying

26. According to the text, in the years after World War II, the United States
    A. ignored the developing countries of Asia, Africa, and Latin America.
    B. publicly renounced the Monroe Doctrine.
    C. expanded the scope of the Monroe Doctrine to include developing regions in Asia and Africa.
    D. passed legislation requiring transnational corporations (TNCs) to subscribe to the principles of the Monroe Doctrine.
    E. refused to allow TNCs to invest in the developing countries of Asia, Africa, and Latin America.

    ANS: C   DIF: Easy   REF: Page 365
    TOP: American Foreign Policy After World War II
    MSC: Understanding

27. In the years after World War II, a principal goal of U.S. foreign policy was to
    A. encourage Middle Eastern countries to take control of their vast petroleum resources.
    B. support France's efforts to maintain control of its large share of the Middle East's oil.
    C. support the Soviet Union's efforts to increase its influence in the Middle East.
    D. establish U.S. government ownership of the Middle East's petroleum reserves.
    E. help U.S. oil companies gain control of the Middle East's petroleum reserves.

    ANS: E   DIF: Moderate   REF: Page 365
    TOP: American Foreign Policy After World War II
    MSC: Applying

28. The United States produces approximately _____ percent of the world's oil, and accounts for approximately _____ percent of the world's oil consumption.
    A. 1 . . . 10
    B. 5 . . . 5
    C. 5 . . . 25
    D. 5 . . . 50
    E. 10 . . . 75

    ANS: C   DIF: Moderate   REF: Page 365
    TOP: American Foreign Policy After World War II
    MSC: Remembering

29. According to the text, the common thread among the UN, IMF, GATT, WTO, and OECD is
    A. they were created to promote world peace.
    B. they were created to promote democracy.
    C. they were created to regulate the world's political and economic order.
    D. they were created to protect the financial interests of the United States.
    E. they were organized to give equal voice to all countries.

    ANS: C   DIF: Moderate   REF: Page 367
    TOP: American Foreign Policy After World War II
    MSC: Understanding

30. According to the text, transnational corporations (TNCs)
    A. are those corporations with significant foreign operations.
    B. are exclusively headquartered in the United States.
    C. play much less of a role in contemporary economic affairs than is generally believed.
    D. experienced their most dramatic growth in the decade following World War II.
    E. are prohibited by a provision of the UN Charter that is never enforced.

    ANS: A   DIF: Moderate   REF: Page 369
    TOP: A New Era of Globalization?   MSC: Applying

31. All of the following statements about transnational corporations (TNCs) are true *except*
    A. as a result of the operations of TNCs, U.S. consumers frequently benefit from low prices that are subsidized by the social costs absorbed by citizens in much poorer countries.
    B. to locate themselves near consumers who buy their products, TNCs direct most investment to affluent countries north of the equator.
    C. TNCs often benefit from lax labor laws in poor countries.
    D. TNCs often benefit from poor countries' weak enforcement of environmental regulations.
    E. there is no significant foreign-based TNC investment in the United States.

    ANS: E   DIF: Easy   REF: Page 369
    TOP: A New Era of Globalization?   MSC: Applying

32. "Skeptics" differ from "globalists" in that the skeptics
    A. stress the political causes of what is usually called globalization.
    B. stress the technological causes of what is usually called globalization.
    C. deny there has been an increase in any key global economic flows.
    D. include all labor unions among their ranks.
    E. include all large corporations among their ranks.

    ANS: A   DIF: Difficult   REF: Pages 369–70
    TOP: A New Era of Globalization?
    MSC: Understanding

33. _____ was a term that designated a multidimensional American strategy—using diplomacy, economic power, and military means—to limit the influence and potential for expansion of the Soviet Union.
    A. Détente
    B. Isolationism
    C. Multilateralism
    D. Containment
    E. The Bush Doctrine

    ANS: D   DIF: Moderate   REF: Page 370
    TOP: The Military Establishment
    MSC: Understanding

34. Which of the following is included on the text's list of countries that possess nuclear weapons?
    A. Israel
    B. Iraq
    C. Cuba
    D. Egypt
    E. Canada

    ANS: A   DIF: Moderate   REF: Page 371
    TOP: The Military Establishment
    MSC: Remembering

35. According to the text, the principal mission of the U.S. military and foreign policy defense establishment is to
    A. generate profits for military contractors.
    B. expand human rights around the world.
    C. oppose Islamic fundamentalism.
    D. maintain a stable, integrated world order under U.S. dominance.
    E. address the U.S. trade and budgetary deficits.

    ANS: D   DIF: Moderate   REF: Page 371
    TOP: The Military Establishment   MSC: Applying

36. As evidence of the dramatic increase in unilateralism that occurred during the presidency of George W. Bush, the text cites all of the following *except*
    A. the invasion of Grenada without a Declaration of War by Congress.
    B. opposition to the Kyoto Protocol on global warming.
    C. rejection of the jurisdiction of the International Criminal Court.
    D. rejection of previously negotiated limits on antiballistic missile development.
    E. the shelving of a previously signed nuclear test ban treaty.

    ANS: A   DIF: Moderate   REF: Page 375
    TOP: The Shift to Unilateralism   MSC: Applying

37. The foreign policy approach that asserted the right of the United States to launch a preemptive military attack if the president decided that an opponent was planning an attack is called _____.
    A. Gunboat diplomacy
    B. the Monroe Doctrine
    C. the Truman Doctrine
    D. the Bush Doctrine
    E. the Obama Doctrine

    ANS: D   DIF: Moderate   REF: Page 376
    TOP: The Shift to Unilateralism   MSC: Applying

38. In the aftermath of the U.S. invasion of Iraq
    A. the United Nations found definitive proof that Iraq had weapons of mass destruction (WMDs).
    B. the United States produced conclusive evidence that Iraq had WMDs.
    C. no WMDs were found, but there was definitive proof that Iraq was actively producing them.
    D. no WMDs were found, nor was there any evidence of an active program to build them.
    E. the United States said it would destroy all of its WMDs since Iraq was no longer a threat.

    ANS: D   DIF: Easy   REF: Page 377
    TOP: The Shift to Unilateralism
    MSC: Understanding

39. In discussing the expansion of the government's internal security apparatus during the George W. Bush administration, the text makes all of the following claims *except*
    A. the Patriot Act's definition of terrorism was extremely vague and broad.
    B. Pentagon lawyers unanimously supported President Bush's order about how to deal with unlawful combatants.
    C. Attorney General Alberto Gonzales said that the Geneva Convention's strict limitations on questioning enemy prisoners were obsolete.
    D. the United States violated many international agreements that it had ratified.
    E. 2004 saw the start of a pushback against the Bush administration's handling of prisoners and detainees.

    ANS: B   DIF: Difficult   REF: Page 377
    TOP: The Shift to Unilateralism   MSC: Applying

40. Abu Ghraib is the name of the
    A. Iraqi leader who succeeded Saddam Hussein.
    B. prison in which Iraqi prisoners were abused.
    C. city that was the location of the most important battle of the Iraqi War.
    D. first al-Qaeda operative illegally tortured by the CIA.
    E. city in which U.S. missiles aimed at al-Qaeda leaders also killed many civilians.

    ANS: B   DIF: Moderate   REF: Page 378
    TOP: The Shift to Unilateralism   MSC: Remembering

41. The term *extraordinary rendition* refers to
    A. the ways that presidents mislead the public about foreign policy.
    B. the highly destructive roadside bombs used by insurgents in Iraq and Afghanistan.
    C. drone missiles and other high-tech weapons used to combat al-Qaeda.
    D. the dedication and religious zeal of suicide bombers in Iraq and Afghanistan.
    E. handing prisoners over to authoritarian regimes, where they are subjected to torture.

    ANS: E   DIF: Difficult   REF: Page 378
    TOP: The Shift to Unilateralism
    MSC: Understanding

42. According to the text, the polices of the Obama administration have been similar to those of the George W. Bush administration in all of the following areas *except*
    A. using the doctrine of state secrets to oppose lawsuits challenging alleged torture.
    B. continuing to issue wiretaps without warrants for U.S. citizens suspected of links to terrorism.
    C. pursuing plans to build a missile-defense system in Poland and the Czech Republic.
    D. defending the policy of extraordinary rendition.
    E. practicing preventive detention.

    ANS: C   DIF: Moderate   REF: Page 379
    TOP: Obama's Foreign Policy: Continuity or Change?
    MSC: Applying

43. Who was the president that put an end to the practice of preventive detention, which involves imprisoning detainees without access to lawyers, judicial review, or trial?
    A. John F. Kennedy
    B. Ronald Reagan
    C. George W. Bush
    D. Barack Obama
    E. None. The policy has not ended.

    ANS: E   DIF: Moderate   REF: Page 379
    TOP: Obama's Foreign Policy: Continuity or Change?
    MSC: Remembering

44. According to the text, in ordering a sizable troop buildup in Afghanistan, President Obama
    A. went beyond President George W. Bush in seeking a military solution.
    B. chose a policy that relied less on a military solution than did Bush administration policy.
    C. acknowledged that a U.S. defeat in Iraq was inevitable.
    D. chose a policy extremely likely to increase U.S. security.
    E. chose a policy extremely likely to produce a democratic and stable Afghanistan.

    ANS: A   DIF: Easy   REF: Page 381
    TOP: Obama's Foreign Policy: Continuity or Change?
    MSC: Applying

45. In 2011, the United States intervened militarily in _____ to depose Muammar al-Gaddafi.
    A. Afghanistan
    B. Pakistan
    C. Syria
    D. Libya
    E. Egypt

    ANS: D   DIF: Moderate   REF: Page 382
    TOP: Obama's Foreign Policy: Continuity or Change?
    MSC: Remembering

APPENDIX

THE DECLARATION OF INDEPENDENCE*

In Congress, July 4, 1776

The Unanimous Declaration of the Thirteen United States of America

When in the Course of human events it becomes necessary for one people to dissolve the political bands which have connected them with another, and to assume among the powers of the earth, the separate and equal station to which the Laws of Nature and of Nature's God entitle them, a decent respect to the opinions of mankind requires that they should declare the causes which impel them to the separation.

We hold these truths to be self-evident, that all men are created equal, that they are endowed by their Creator with certain unalienable Rights, that among these are Life, Liberty and the pursuit of Happiness.— That to secure these rights, Governments are instituted among Men, deriving their just powers from the consent of the governed,—That whenever any Form of Government becomes destructive of these ends, it is the Right of the People to alter or to abolish it, and to institute new Government, laying its foundation on such principles and organizing its powers in such form, as to them shall seem most likely to effect their Safety and Happiness. Prudence, indeed, will dictate that Governments long established should not be changed for light and transient causes; and accordingly all experience hath shewn that mankind are more disposed to suffer, while evils are sufferable, than to right themselves by abolishing the forms to which they are accustomed. But when a long train of abuses and usurpations, pursuing invariably the same Object evinces a design to reduce them under absolute Despotism, it is their right, it is their duty, to throw off such Government, and to provide new Guards for their future security.

Such has been the patient sufferance of these Colonies; and such is now the necessity which constrains them to alter their former Systems of Government. The history of the present King of Great Britain is a history of repeated injuries and usurpations, all having in direct object the establishment of an absolute Tyranny over these States. To prove this, let Facts be submitted to a candid world.

He has refused his Assent to Laws, the most wholesome and necessary for the public good.

He has forbidden his Governors to pass Laws of immediate and pressing importance, unless suspended in their operation till his Assent should be obtained; and when so suspended, he has utterly neglected to attend to them.

He has refused to pass other Laws for the accommodation of large districts of people, unless those people would relinquish the right of Representation in the Legislature, a right inestimable to them and formidable to tyrants only.

He has called together legislative bodies at places unusual, uncomfortable, and distant from the depository of their Public Records, for the sole purpose of fatiguing them into compliance with his measures.

He has dissolved Representative Houses repeatedly, for opposing with manly firmness his invasions on the rights of the people.

He has refused for a long time, after such dissolutions, to cause others to be elected; whereby the

---

*This text retains the spelling, capitalization, and punctuation of the original.

Legislative Powers, incapable of Annihilation, have returned to the People at large for their exercise; the State remaining in the mean time exposed to all the dangers of invasion from without, and convulsions within.

He has endeavored to prevent the population of these States; for that purpose obstructing the Laws for Naturalization of Foreigners; refusing to pass others to encourage their migration hither, and raising the conditions of new Appropriations of Lands.

He has obstructed the Administration of Justice, by refusing his Assent to Laws for establishing Judiciary powers.

He has made Judges dependent on his Will alone, for the tenure of their offices, and the amount and payment of their salaries.

He has erected a multitude of New Offices, and sent hither swarms of Officers to harass our people, and eat out their substance.

He has kept among us, in times of peace, Standing Armies without the Consent of our legislatures.

He has affected to render the Military independent of and superior to the Civil power.

He has combined with others to subject us to a jurisdiction foreign to our constitution, and unacknowledged by our laws; giving his Assent to their Acts of pretended Legislation:

For quartering large bodies of armed troops among us:

For protecting them, by a mock Trial, from punishment for any Murders which they should commit on the Inhabitants of these States:

For cutting off our Trade with all parts of the world:

For imposing Taxes on us without our Consent:

For depriving us in many cases, of the benefits of Trial by Jury:

For transporting us beyond Seas to be tried for pretended offences:

For abolishing the free System of English Laws in a neighboring Province, establishing therein an Arbitrary government, and enlarging its Boundaries so as to render it at once an example and fit instrument for introducing the same absolute rule into these Colonies:

For taking away our Charters, abolishing our most valuable Laws, and altering fundamentally the Forms of our Governments:

For suspending our own Legislatures, and declaring themselves invested with power to legislate for us in all cases whatsoever.

He has abdicated Government here, by declaring us out of his Protection and waging War against us.

He has plundered our seas, ravaged our Coasts, burnt our towns, and destroyed the lives of our people.

He is at this time transporting large Armies of foreign Mercenaries to compleat the works of death, desolation and tyranny, already begun with circumstances of Cruelty & perfidy scarcely paralleled in the most barbarous ages, and totally unworthy the Head of a civilized nation.

He has constrained our fellow Citizens taken Captive on the high Seas to bear Arms against their Country, to become the executioners of their friends and Brethren, or to fall themselves by their Hands.

He has excited domestic insurrections amongst us, and has endeavored to bring on the inhabitants of our frontiers, the merciless Indian Savages, whose known rule of warfare, is an undistinguished destruction of all ages, sexes and conditions.

In every stage of these Oppressions We have Petitioned for Redress in the most humble terms: Our repeated Petitions have been answered only by repeated injury. A Prince, whose character is thus marked by every act which may define a Tyrant, is unfit to be the ruler of a free people.

Nor have We been wanting in attention to our British brethren. We have warned them from time to time of attempts by their legislature to extend an unwarrantable jurisdiction over us. We have reminded them of the circumstances of our emigration and settlement here. We have appealed to their native justice and magnanimity, and we have conjured them by the ties of our common kindred to disavow these usurpations, which would inevitably interrupt our connections and correspondence. They too have been deaf to the voice of justice and consanguinity. We must, therefore, acquiesce in the necessity, which denounces our Separation, and hold them, as we hold the rest of mankind, Enemies in War, in Peace Friends.

We, therefore, the Representatives of the United States of America, in General Congress, Assembled, appealing to the Supreme Judge of the world for the rectitude of our intentions, do, in the Name, and by Authority of the good People of these Colonies, solemnly publish and declare, That these United Colonies are, and of Right ought to be Free and Independent States; that they are Absolved from all Allegiance to the British Crown, and that all political connection between them and the State of Great Britain, is and ought to be totally dissolved; and that as Free and Independent States, they have full Power to levy War, conclude Peace, contract Alliances, establish Commerce, and to do all other Acts and Things which Independent States may of right do. And for the support of this Declaration, with a firm reliance on the protection of divine Providence, we mutually pledge to each other our Lives, our Fortunes and our sacred Honor.

John Hancock

NEW HAMPSHIRE
Josiah Bartlett,
Wm. Whipple,
Matthew Thornton.

MASSACHUSETTS BAY
Saml. Adams,
John Adams,
Robt. Treat Paine,
Elbridge Gerry.

RHODE ISLAND
Step. Hopkins,
William Ellery.

CONNECTICUT
Roger Sherman,
Samuel Huntington,
Wm. Williams,
Oliver Wolcott.

NEW YORK
Wm. Floyd,
Phil. Livingston,
Frans. Lewis,
Lewis Morris.

NEW JERSEY
Richd. Stockton,
Jno. Witherspoon,
Fras. Hopkinson,
John Hart,
Abra. Clark.

PENNSYLVANIA
Robt. Morris,
Benjamin Rush,
Benjamin Franklin,
John Morton,
Geo. Clymer,
Jas. Smith,
Geo. Taylor,
James Wilson,
Geo. Ross.

DELAWARE
Caesar Rodney,
Geo. Read,
Tho. M'kean.

MARYLAND
Samuel Chase,
Wm. Paca,
Thos. Stone,
Charles Caroll of
Carrollton.

VIRGINIA
George Wythe,
Richard Henry Lee,
Th. Jefferson,
Benjamin Harrison,
Thos. Nelson, jr.,
Francis Lightfoot Lee,
Carter Braxton.

NORTH CAROLINA
Wm. Hooper,
Joseph Hewes,
John Penn.

SOUTH CAROLINA
Edward Rutledge,
Thos. Heyward, Junr.,
Thomas Lynch, jnr.,
Arthur Middleton.

GEORGIA
Button Gwinnett,
Lyman Hall,
Geo. Walton.

THE FEDERALIST NO. 10

James Madison

November 22, 1787

To the People of the State of New York.

Among the numerous advantages promised by a well constructed Union, none deserves to be more accurately developed than its tendency to break and control the violence of faction. The friend of popular governments, never finds himself so much alarmed for their character and fate, as when he contemplates their propensity to this dangerous vice. He will not fail therefore to set a due value on any plan which, without violating the principles to which he is attached, provides a proper cure for it. The instability, injustice and confusion introduced into the public councils, have in truth been the mortal diseases under which popular governments have every where perished; as they continue to be the favorite and fruitful topics from which the adversaries to liberty derive their most specious declamations. The valuable improvements made by the American Constitutions on the popular models, both ancient and modern, cannot certainly be too much admired; but it would be an unwarrantable partiality, to contend that they have as effectually obviated the danger on this side as was wished and expected. Complaints are every where heard from our most considerate and virtuous citizens, equally the friends of public and private faith, and of public and personal liberty; that our governments are too unstable; that the public good is disregarded in the conflicts of rival parties; and that measures are too often decided, not according to the rules of justice, and the rights of the minor party; but by the superior force of an interested and over-bearing majority. However anxiously we may wish that these complaints had no foundation, the evidence of known facts will not permit us to deny that they are in some degree true. It will be found indeed, on a candid review of our situation, that some of the distresses under which we labor, have been erroneously charged on the operation of our governments; but it will be found, at the same time, that other causes will not alone account for many of our heaviest misfortunes; and particularly, for that prevailing and increasing distrust of public engagements, and alarm for private rights, which are echoed from one end of the continent to the other. These must be chiefly, if not wholly, effects of the unsteadiness and injustice, with which a factious spirit has tainted our public administrations.

By a faction I understand a number of citizens, whether amounting to a majority or minority of the whole, who are united and actuated by some common impulse of passion, or of interest, adverse to the rights of other citizens, or to the permanent and aggregate interests of the community.

There are two methods of curing the mischiefs of faction: the one, by removing its causes; the other, by controlling its effects.

There are again two methods of removing the causes of faction: the one by destroying the liberty which is essential to its existence; the other, by giving to every citizen the same opinions, the same passions, and the same interests.

It could never be more truly said than of the first remedy, that it is worse than the disease. Liberty is to faction, what air is to fire, an aliment without which it instantly expires. But it could not be a less folly to abolish liberty, which is essential to political life, because it nourishes faction, than it would be to wish the annihilation of air, which is essential to animal life, because it imparts to fire its destructive agency.

The second expedient is as impracticable, as the first would be unwise. As long as the reason of man continues fallible, and he is at liberty to exercise it, different opinions will be formed. As long as the connection subsists between his reason and his self-love, his opinions and his passions will have a reciprocal influence on each other; and the former will be objects to which the latter will attach themselves. The diversity in the faculties of men from which the rights of property originate, is not less an insuperable obstacle to a uniformity of interests. The protection of these faculties is the first object of Government. From the protection of different and unequal faculties of acquiring property, the possession of different degrees and kinds of property immediately results: and from the influence of these on the sentiments and views of the respective proprietors, ensues a division of the society into different interests and parties.

The latent causes of faction are thus sown in the nature of man; and we see them every where brought into different degrees of activity, according to the different circumstances of civil society. A zeal for different opinions concerning religion, concerning Government and many other points, as well of speculation as of practice; an attachment to different leaders ambitiously contending for pre-eminence and power; or to persons of other descriptions whose fortunes have been interesting to the human passions, have in turn divided mankind into parties, inflamed them with mutual animosity, and rendered them much more disposed to vex and oppress each other, than to co-operate for their common good. So strong is this propensity of mankind to fall into mutual animosities, that where no substantial occasion presents itself, the most frivolous and fanciful distinctions have been sufficient to kindle their unfriendly passions, and excite their most violent conflicts. But the most common and durable source of factions, has been the various and unequal distribution of property. Those who hold, and those who are without property, have ever formed distinct interests in society. Those who are creditors, and those who are debtors, fall under a like discrimination. A landed interest, a manufacturing interest, a mercantile interest, a monied interest, with many lesser interests, grow up of necessity in civilized nations, and divide them into different classes, actuated by different sentiments and views. The regulation of these various and interfering interests forms the principal task of modern Legislation, and involves the spirit of party and faction in the necessary and ordinary operations of Government.

No man is allowed to be a judge in his own cause; because his interest would certainly bias his judgment, and, not improbably, corrupt his integrity. With equal, nay with greater reason, a body of men, are unfit to be both judges and parties, at the same time; yet, what are many of the most important acts of legislation, but so many judicial determinations, not indeed concerning the rights of single persons, but concerning the rights of large bodies of citizens, and what are the different classes of legislators, but advocates and parties to the causes which they determine? Is a law proposed concerning private debts? It is a question to which the creditors are parties on one side, and the debtors on the other. Justice ought to hold the balance between them. Yet the parties are and must be themselves the judges; and the most numerous party, or, in other words, the most powerful faction must be expected to prevail. Shall domestic manufactures be encouraged, and in what degree, by restrictions on foreign manufactures? are questions which would be differently decided by the landed and the manufacturing classes; and probably by neither, with a sole regard to justice and the public good. The apportionment of taxes on the various descriptions of property, is an act which seems to require the most exact impartiality; yet, there is perhaps no legislative act in which greater opportunity and temptation are given to a predominant party, to trample on the rules of justice. Every shilling with which they over-burden the inferior number, is a shilling saved to their own pockets.

It is in vain to say, that enlightened statesmen will be able to adjust these clashing interests, and render them all subservient to the public good. Enlightened statesmen will not always be at the helm: Nor, in many cases, can such an adjustment be made at all, without taking into view indirect and remote considerations, which will rarely prevail over the immediate interest which one party may find in disregarding the rights of another, or the good of the whole.

The inference to which we are brought, is, that the causes of faction cannot be removed; and that relief is only to be sought in the means of controlling its effects.

If a faction consists of less than a majority, relief is supplied by the republican principle, which enables the majority to defeat its sinister views by regular vote: It may clog the administration, it may convulse the society; but it will be unable to execute and mask its violence under the forms of the Constitution. When a majority is included in a faction, the form of popular government on the other hand enables it to sacrifice to its ruling passion or interest, both the public good and the rights of other citizens. To secure the public good, and private rights, against the danger of such a faction, and at the same time to preserve the spirit and the form of popular government, is then the great object to which our enquiries are directed: Let me add that it is the great desideratum, by which alone this form of government can be rescued from the opprobrium under which it has so long labored, and be recommended to the esteem and adoption of mankind.

By what means is this object attainable? Evidently by one of two only. Either the existence of the same passion or interest in a majority at the same time, must be prevented; or the majority, having such co-existent passion or interest, must be rendered, by their number and local situation, unable to concert and carry into effect schemes of oppression. If the impulse and the opportunity be suffered to coincide, we well know that neither moral nor religious motives can be relied on as an adequate control. They are not found to be such on the injustice and violence of individuals, and lose their efficacy in proportion to the number combined together; that is, in proportion as their efficacy becomes needful.

From this view of the subject, it may be concluded, that a pure Democracy, by which I mean, a Society, consisting of a small number of citizens, who assemble and administer the Government in person, can admit of no cure for the mischiefs of faction. A common passion or interest will, in almost every case, be felt by a majority of the whole; a communication and concert results from the form of Government itself; and there is nothing to check the inducements to sacrifice the weaker party, or an obnoxious individual. Hence it is, that such Democracies have ever been spectacles of turbulence and contention; have ever been found incompatible with personal security, or the rights of property; and have in general been as short in their lives, as they have been violent in their deaths. Theoretic politicians, who have patronized this species of Government, have erroneously supposed, that by reducing mankind to a perfect equality in their political rights, they would, at the same time, be perfectly equalized and assimilated in their possessions, their opinions, and their passions.

A republic, by which I mean a government in which the scheme of representation takes place, opens a different prospect, and promises the cure for which we are seeking. Let us examine the points in which it varies from pure democracy, and we shall comprehend both the nature of the cure and the efficacy which it must derive from the union.

The two great points of difference, between a democracy and a republic, are, first, the delegation of the government, in the latter, to a small number of citizens, elected by the rest; secondly, the greater number of citizens, and greater sphere of country, over which the latter may be extended.

The effect of the first difference is, on the one hand, to refine and enlarge the public views, by passing them through the medium of a chosen body of citizens, whose wisdom may best discern the true interest of their country, and whose patriotism and love of justice, will be least likely to sacrifice it to temporary or partial considerations. Under such a regulation, it may well happen, that the public voice, pronounced by the representatives of the people, will be more consonant to the public good, than if pronounced by the people themselves, convened for the purpose. On the other hand the effect may be inverted. Men of factious tempers, of local prejudices, or of sinister designs, may by intrigue, by corruption, or by other means, first obtain the suffrages, and then betray the interest of the people. The question resulting is, whether small or extensive republics are most favorable to the election of proper guardians of the public weal, and it is clearly decided in favor of the latter by two obvious considerations.

In the first place, it is to be remarked that, however small the republic may be, the representatives must be raised to a certain number, in order to guard against the cabals of a few; and that however large it may be, they must be limited to a certain number, in order to guard against the confusion of a multitude. Hence, the number of representatives in the two cases not being in proportion to that of the constituents, and being proportionally greatest in the small republic, it follows, that if the proportion of fit characters be not less in the large than in the small republic, the former will present a greater option, and consequently a greater probability of a fit choice.

In the next place, as each Representative will be chosen by a greater number of citizens in the large than in the small Republic, it will be more difficult for unworthy candidates to practise with success the vicious arts, by which elections are too often carried; and the suffrages of the people being more free, will be more likely to center on men who possess the most attractive merit, and the most diffusive and established characters.

It must be confessed, that in this, as in most other cases, there is a mean, on both sides of which inconveniences will be found to lie. By enlarging too much the number of electors, you render the representative too little acquainted with all their local circumstances and lesser interests; as by reducing it too much, you render him unduly attached to these, and too little fit to comprehend and pursue great and national objects. The Federal Constitution forms a happy combination in this respect; the great and aggregate interests being referred to the national, the local and particular, to the state legislatures.

The other point of difference is, the greater number of citizens and extent of territory which may be brought within the compass of Republican, than of Democratic Government; and it is this circumstance principally which renders factious combinations less to be dreaded in the former, than in the latter. The smaller the society, the fewer probably will be the distinct parties and interests composing it; the fewer the distinct parties and interests, the more frequently will a majority be found of the same party; and the smaller the number of individuals composing a majority, and the smaller the compass within which they are placed, the more easily will they concert and execute their plans of oppression. Extend the sphere, and you take in a greater variety of parties and interests; you make it less probable that a majority of the whole will have a common motive to invade the rights of other citizens; or if such a common motive exists, it will be more difficult for all who feel it to discover their own strength, and to act in unison with each other. Besides other impediments, it may be remarked, that where there is a consciousness of unjust or dishonorable purposes, communication is always checked by distrust, in proportion to the number whose concurrence is necessary.

Hence it clearly appears, that the same advantage, which a Republic has over a Democracy, in controlling the effects of faction, is enjoyed by a large over a small Republic—is enjoyed by the Union over the States composing it. Does this advantage consist in the substitution of Representatives, whose enlightened views and virtuous sentiments render them superior to local prejudices, and to schemes of injustice? It will not be denied, that the Representation of the Union will be most likely to possess these requisite endowments. Does it consist in the greater security afforded by a greater variety of parties, against the event of any one party being able to outnumber and oppress the rest? In an equal degree does the increased variety of parties, comprised within the Union, increase this security? Does it, in fine, consist in the greater obstacles opposed to the concert and accomplishment of the secret wishes of an unjust and interested majority? Here, again, the extent of the Union gives it the most palpable advantage.

The influence of factious leaders may kindle a flame within their particular States, but will be unable to spread a general conflagration through the other States: a religious sect may degenerate into a political faction in a part of the Confederacy but the variety of sects dispersed over the entire face of it, must secure the national Councils against any danger from that source: a rage for paper money, for an abolition of debts, for an equal division of property, or for any other improper or wicked project, will be less apt to pervade the whole body of the Union, than a particular member of it; in the same proportion as such a malady is more likely to taint a particular county or district, than an entire State.

In the extent and proper structure of the Union, therefore, we behold a Republican remedy for the diseases most incident to Republican Government. And according to the degree of pleasure and pride, we feel in being Republicans, ought to be our zeal in cherishing the spirit, and supporting the character of Federalists.

PUBLIUS

THE FEDERALIST NO. 51

James Madison

February 6, 1788

To the People of the State of New York.

To what expedient then shall we finally resort for maintaining in practice the necessary partition of power among the several departments, as laid down in the constitution? The only answer that can be given is, that as all these exterior provisions are found to be inadequate, the defect must be supplied, by so contriving the interior structure of the government, as that its several constituent parts may, by their mutual relations, be the means of keeping each other in their proper places. Without presuming to undertake a full development of this important idea, I will hazard a few general observations, which may perhaps place it in a clearer light, and enable us to form a more correct judgment of the principles and structure of the government planned by the convention.

In order to lay a due foundation for that separate and distinct exercise of the different powers of government, which to a certain extent, is admitted on all hands to be essential to the preservation of liberty, it is evident that each department should have a will of its own; and consequently should be so constituted, that the members of each should have as little agency as possible in the appointment of the members of the others. Were this principle rigorously adhered to, it would require that all the appointments for the supreme executive, legislative, and judiciary magistracies, should be drawn from the same fountain of authority, the people, through channels, having no communication whatever with one another. Perhaps such a plan of constructing the several departments would be less difficult in practice than it may in contemplation appear. Some difficulties however, and some additional expense, would attend the execution of it. Some deviations therefore from the principle must be admitted. In the constitution of the judiciary department in particular, it might be inexpedient to insist rigorously on the principle; first, because peculiar qualifications being essential in the members, the primary consideration ought to be to select that mode of choice, which best secures these qualifications; secondly, because the permanent tenure by which the appointments are held in that department, must soon destroy all sense of dependence on the authority conferring them.

It is equally evident that the members of each department should be as little dependent as possible on those of the others, for the emoluments annexed to their offices. Were the executive magistrate, or the judges, not independent of the legislature in this particular, their independence in every other would be merely nominal.

But the great security against a gradual concentration of the several powers in the same department, consists in giving to those who administer each department, the necessary constitutional means, and personal motives, to resist encroachments of the others. The provision for defense must in this, as in all other cases, be made commensurate to the danger of attack. Ambition must be made to counteract ambition. The interest of the man must be connected with the constitutional right of the place. It may be a reflection on human nature, that such devices should be necessary to control the abuses of government. But what is government itself but the greatest of all reflections on human nature? If men were angels, no government would be necessary. If angels were to govern men, neither external nor internal controls on government would be necessary. In framing a government which is to be administered by men over men, the great difficulty lies in this: You must first enable the government to control the governed; and in the next place, oblige it to control itself. A dependence on the people is no doubt the primary control on the government; but experience has taught mankind the necessity of auxiliary precautions.

This policy of supplying by opposite and rival interests, the defect of better motives, might be traced through the whole system of human affairs, private as well as public. We see it particularly displayed in all the subordinate distributions of power; where the constant aim is to divide and arrange the several offices in such a manner as that each may be a check on the other; that the private interest of every individual, may be a sentinel over the public rights. These inventions of prudence cannot be less requisite in the distribution of the supreme powers of the state.

But it is not possible to give to each department an equal power of self defense. In republican government

the legislative authority, necessarily, predominates. The remedy for this inconveniency is, to divide the legislature into different branches; and to render them by different modes of election, and different principles of action, as little connected with each other, as the nature of their common functions, and their common dependence on the society, will admit. It may even be necessary to guard against dangerous encroachments by still further precautions. As the weight of the legislative authority requires that it should be thus divided, the weakness of the executive may require, on the other hand, that it should be fortified. An absolute negative, on the legislature, appears at first view to be the natural defense with which the executive magistrate should be armed. But perhaps it would be neither altogether safe, nor alone sufficient. On ordinary occasions, it might not be exerted with the requisite firmness; and on extraordinary occasions, it might be perfidiously abused. May not this defect of an absolute negative be supplied, by some qualified connection between this weaker department, and the weaker branch of the stronger department, by which the latter may be led to support the constitutional rights of the former, without being too much detached from the rights of its own department?

If the principles on which these observations are founded be just, as I persuade myself they are, and they be applied as a criterion, to the several state constitutions, and to the federal constitution, it will be found, that if the latter does not perfectly correspond with them, the former are infinitely less able to bear such a test.

There are moreover two considerations particularly applicable to the federal system of America, which place that system in a very interesting point of view.

First. In a single republic, all the power surrendered by the people, is submitted to the administration of a single government; and usurpations are guarded against by a division of the government into distinct and separate departments. In the compound republic of America, the power surrendered by the people, is first divided between two distinct governments, and then the portion allotted to each, subdivided among distinct and separate departments. Hence a double security arises to the rights of the people. The different governments will control each other; at the same time that each will be controlled by itself.

Second. It is of great importance in a republic, not only to guard the society against the oppression of its rulers; but to guard one part of the society against the injustice of the other part. Different interests necessarily exist in different classes of citizens. If a majority be united by a common interest, the rights of the minority will be insecure. There are but two methods of providing against this evil: The one by creating a will in the community independent of the majority, that is, of the society itself, the other by comprehending in the society so many separate descriptions of citizens, as will render an unjust combination of a majority of the whole, very improbable, if not impracticable. The first method prevails in all governments possessing an hereditary or self appointed authority. This at best is but a precarious security; because a power independent of the society may as well espouse the unjust views of the major, as the rightful interests, of the minor party, and may possibly be turned against both parties. The second method will be exemplified in the federal republic of the United States. While all authority in it will be derived from and dependent on the society, the society itself will be broken into so many parts, interests and classes of citizens, that the rights of individuals or of the minority, will be in little danger from interested combinations of the majority. In a free government, the security for civil rights must be the same as for religious rights. It consists in the one case in the multiplicity of interests, and in the other, in the multiplicity of sects. The degree of security in both cases will depend on the number of interests and sects; and this may be presumed to depend on the extent of country and number of people comprehended under the same government. This view of the subject must particularly recommend a proper federal system to all the sincere and considerate friends of republican government: Since it shows that in exact proportion as the territory of the union may be formed into more circumscribed confederacies or states, oppressive combinations of a majority will be facilitated, the best security under the republican form, for the rights of every class of citizens, will be diminished; and consequently, the stability and independence of some member of the government, the only other security, must be proportionally increased. Justice is the end of government. It is the end of civil society. It ever has been, and ever will be pursued, until it be obtained, or until liberty be lost in the pursuit. In a society under the forms of which the stronger faction can readily unite and oppress the weaker, anarchy may as truly be said to reign, as in a state of nature where the weaker individual is not secured against the violence of the stronger: And as in the latter state even the stronger individuals are prompted by the uncertainty of their condition, to submit to a government which may protect the weak as well as themselves: So in the former state, will the more powerful factions or parties be gradually induced by a like motive, to wish for a government which will protect all parties, the weaker as well as the more powerful. It can be little doubted, that if the state of Rhode Island was separated from the confederacy, and left to itself, the insecurity of rights under the popular form of government within such narrow limits, would be displayed by such reiterated oppressions of factious majorities, that some power altogether independent of the people would soon be called for by the voice of the very factions whose misrule had proved the necessity of it. In the extended republic of the United States, and among the great variety of interests, parties and sects which it embraces, a coalition of a majority of the whole society could seldom take place on any other principles than those of justice and the general good; and there being thus less danger to a minor from the will of the major party, there must be less pretext also, to provide for the security of the former, by introducing into the government a will not dependent on the latter; or in other words, a will independent of the society itself. It is no less certain than it is important, notwithstanding the contrary opinions which have been entertained, that the larger the society, provided it lie within a practicable sphere, the more duly capable it will be of self government. And happily for the *republican cause*, the practicable sphere may be carried to a very great extent, by a judicious modification and mixture of the *federal principle*.

PUBLIUS

THE CONSTITUTION OF THE UNITED STATES OF AMERICA*

(Preamble)

We the People of the United States, in Order to form a more perfect Union, establish Justice, insure domestic Tranquility, provide for the common defence, promote the general Welfare, and secure the Blessings of Liberty to ourselves and our Posterity, do ordain and establish this Constitution for the United States of America.

ARTICLE I.

(The Legislature)

Section 1. All legislative Powers herein granted shall be vested in a Congress of the United States, which shall consist of a Senate and House of Representatives.

*This text retains the spelling, capitalization, and punctuation of the original. Brackets indicate passages that have been altered by amendments.

Section 2. The House of Representatives shall be composed of Members chosen every second Year by the People of the several States, and the Electors in each State shall have the Qualifications requisite for Electors of the most numerous Branch of the State Legislature.

No person shall be a Representative who shall not have attained to the Age of twenty five Years, and been seven Years a Citizen of the United States, and who shall not, when elected, be an Inhabitant of that State in which he shall be chosen.

Representatives and direct [Taxes][1] shall be apportioned among the several States which may be included within this Union, according to their respective Numbers [which shall be determined by adding to the whole Number of free Persons, including those bound to Service for a Term of Years, and excluding Indians not taxed, three fifths of all other Persons].[2] The actual Enumeration shall be made within three Years after the first Meeting of the Congress of the United States, and within every subsequent Term of ten Years, in such Manner as they shall by Law direct. The Number of Representatives shall not exceed one for every thirty Thousand, but each State shall have at Least one Representative; and until such enumeration shall be made, the State of New Hampshire shall be entitled to chuse three, Massachusetts eight, Rhode-Island and Providence Plantations one, Connecticut five, New-York six, New Jersey four, Pennsylvania eight, Delaware one, Maryland six, Virginia ten, North Carolina five, South Carolina five, and Georgia three.

When vacancies happen in the Representation from any State, the Executive Authority thereof shall issue Writs of Election to fill such Vacancies.

The House of Representatives shall chuse their speaker and other Officers; and shall have the sole Power of Impeachment.

Section 3. The Senate of the United States shall be composed of two Senators from each State [chosen by the Legislature thereof],[3] for six Years; and each Senator shall have one Vote.

Immediately after they shall be assembled in Consequence of the first Election, they shall be divided as equally as may be into three Classes. The Seats of the Senators of the first Class shall be vacated at the Expiration of the second year, of the second Class at the Expiration of the fourth Year, and of the third Class at the Expiration of the sixth Year, so that one third may be chosen every second Year [and if Vacancies happen

by Resignation, or otherwise, during the Recess of the Legislature of any State, the Executive thereof may make temporary Appointments until the next Meeting of the Legislature, which shall then fill such Vacancies].[4]

No Person shall be a Senator who shall not have attained to the Age of thirty Years, and been nine Years a Citizen of the United States, and who shall not, when elected, be an Inhabitant of that State for which he shall be chosen.

The Vice President of the United States shall be President of the Senate, but shall have no Vote, unless they be equally divided.

The Senate shall chuse their other Officers, and also a President pro tempore, in the Absence of the Vice President, or when he shall exercise the Office of President of the United States.

The Senate shall have the sole Power to try all Impeachments. When sitting for that Purpose, they shall be on Oath or Affirmation. When the President of the United States is tried, the Chief Justice shall preside: And no Person shall be convicted without the Concurrence of two thirds of the Members present.

Judgment in Cases of Impeachment shall not extend further than to removal from Office, and disqualification to hold and enjoy any Office of honor, Trust or Profit under the United States; but the Party convicted shall nevertheless be liable and subject to Indictment, Trial, Judgment and Punishment, according to Law.

Section 4. The Times, Places and Manner of holding Elections for Senators and Representatives, shall be prescribed in each State by the Legislature thereof; but the Congress may at any time by Law make or alter such Regulations, except as to the Places of chusing Senators.

[The Congress shall assemble at least once in every Year, and such Meeting shall be on the first Monday in December, unless they shall by Law appoint a different Day.][5]

Section 5. Each House shall be the Judge of the Elections, Returns and Qualifications of its own Members, and a Majority of each shall constitute a Quorum to do Business; but a smaller Number may adjourn from day to day, and may be authorized to compel the Attendance of absent Members, in such Manner, and under such Penalties as each House may provide.

[1]See Amendment XVI.
[2]See Amendment XIV.
[3]See Amendment XVII.

[4]See Amendment XVII.
[5]See Amendment XX.

Each House may determine the Rules of its Proceedings, punish its Members for disorderly Behaviour, and, with the Concurrence of two thirds, expel a Member.

Each House shall keep a Journal of its Proceedings, and from time to time publish the same, excepting such Parts as may in their judgment require Secrecy; and the Yeas and Nays of the Members of either House on any question shall, at the Desire of one fifth of those present, be entered on the Journal.

Neither House, during the Session of Congress, shall, without the Consent of the other, adjourn for more than three days, nor to any other Place than that in which the two Houses shall be sitting.

Section 6. The Senators and Representatives shall receive a Compensation for their Services, to be ascertained by Law, and paid out of the Treasury of the United States. They shall in all Cases, except Treason, Felony and Breach of the Peace, be privileged from Arrest during their Attendance at the Session of their respective Houses, and in going to and returning from the same; and for any Speech or Debate in either House, they shall not be questioned in any other Place.

No Senator or Representative shall, during the Time for which he was elected, be appointed to any civil Office under the Authority of the United States, which shall have been created, or the Emoluments whereof shall have been encreased during such time; and no Person holding any Office under the United States, shall be a Member of either House during his Continuance in Office.

Section 7. All Bills for raising Revenue shall originate in the House of Representatives; but the Senate may propose or concur with Amendments as on other Bills.

Every Bill which shall have passed the House of Representatives and the Senate, shall, before it becomes a Law, be presented to the President of the United States; If he approves he shall sign it, but if not he shall return it, with his Objections to that House in which it shall have originated, who shall enter the Objections at large on their Journal, and proceed to reconsider it. If after such Reconsideration two thirds of that House shall agree to pass the Bill, it shall be sent, together with the Objections, to the other House, by which it shall likewise be reconsidered, and if approved by two thirds of that House, it shall become a Law. But in all such Cases the Votes of both Houses shall be determined by yeas and Nays, and the Names of the Persons voting for and against the Bill shall be entered on the Journal of each House respectively. If any Bill shall not be returned by the President within ten Days (Sundays excepted) after it shall have been presented to him, the Same shall be a Law, in like Manner as if he had signed it, unless the Congress by their Adjournment prevent its Return, in which Case it shall not be a Law.

Every Order, Resolution, or Vote to which the Concurrence of the Senate and House of Representatives may be necessary (except on a question of Adjournment) shall be presented to the President of the United States; and before the Same shall take Effect, shall be approved by him, or being disapproved by him, shall be repassed by two thirds of the Senate and House of Representatives, according to the Rules and Limitations prescribed in the Case of a Bill.

Section 8. The Congress shall have Power To lay and collect Taxes, Duties, Imposts and Excises, to pay the Debts and provide for the common Defence and general Welfare of the United States; but all Duties, Imposts and Excises shall be uniform throughout the United States;

To borrow Money on the credit of the United States;

To regulate Commerce with foreign Nations, and among the several States, and with the Indian Tribes;

To establish a uniform Rule of Naturalization, and uniform Laws on the subject of Bankruptcies throughout the United States;

To coin Money, regulate the Value thereof, and of foreign Coin, and fix the Standard of Weights and Measures;

To provide for the Punishment of counterfeiting the Securities and current Coin of the United States;

To establish Post Offices and post Roads;

To promote the Progress of Science and useful Arts, by securing for limited Times to Authors and Inventors the exclusive Right to their respective Writings and Discoveries;

To constitute Tribunals inferior to the supreme Court;

To define and punish Piracies and Felonies committed on the high Seas, and Offences against the Law of Nations;

To declare War, grant Letters of Marque and Reprisal, and make Rules concerning Captures on Land and Water;

To raise and support Armies, but no Appropriation of Money to that Use shall be for a longer Term than two Years;

To provide and maintain a Navy;

To make Rules for the Government and Regulation of the land and naval Forces;

To provide for calling forth the Militia to execute the Laws of the Union, suppress Insurrections and repel Invasions;

To provide for organizing, arming, and disciplining, the Militia, and for governing such Part of them as may be employed in the Service of the United States, reserving to the States respectively, the Appointment of the Officers, and the Authority of training the Militia according to the discipline prescribed by Congress;

To exercise exclusive Legislation in all Cases whatsoever, over such District (not exceeding ten Miles square) as may, by Cession of particular States, and the Acceptance of Congress, become the Seat of the Government of the United States, and to exercise like Authority over all Places purchased by the Consent of the Legislature of the State in which the Same shall be, for the Erection of Forts, Magazines, Arsenals, dock-Yards, and other needful Buildings;—And

To make all Laws which shall be necessary and proper for carrying into Execution the foregoing Powers, and all other Powers vested by this Constitution in the Government of the United States, or in any Department or Officer thereof.

Section 9. The Migration or Importation of such Persons as any of the States now existing shall think proper to admit, shall not be prohibited by the Congress prior to the Year one thousand eight hundred and eight, but a Tax or duty may be imposed on such Importation, not exceeding ten dollars for each Person.

The Privilege of the Writ of Habeas Corpus shall not be suspended, unless when in Cases of Rebellion or Invasion the public Safety may require it.

No Bill of Attainder or ex post facto Law shall be passed.

[No Capitation, or other direct, Tax shall be laid, unless in Proportion to the Census or Enumeration herein before directed to be taken.][6]

No Tax or Duty shall be laid on Articles exported from any State.

No Preference shall be given by any Regulation of Commerce or Revenue to the Ports of one State over those of another; nor shall Vessels bound to, or from, one State, be obliged to enter, clear, or pay Duties in another.

No Money shall be drawn from the Treasury, but in Consequence of Appropriations made by Law; and a regular Statement and Account of the Receipts and Expenditures of all public Money shall be published from time to time.

No Title of Nobility shall be granted by the United States: And no Person holding any Office of Profit or Trust under them, shall, without the Consent of the Congress, accept of any present, Emolument, Office, or Title, of any kind whatever, from any King, Prince, or foreign State.

[6]See Amendment XVI.

Section 10. No State shall enter into any Treaty, Alliance, or Confederation; grant Letters of Marque and Reprisal; coin Money; emit Bills of Credit; make any Thing but gold and silver Coin a Tender in Payment of Debts; pass any Bill of Attainder, ex post facto Law, or Law impairing the Obligation of Contracts, or grant any Title of Nobility.

No State shall, without the Consent of the Congress, lay any Imposts or Duties on Imports or Exports, except what may be absolutely necessary for executing its inspection Laws: and the net Produce of all Duties and Imposts, laid by any State on Imports or Exports, shall be for the Use of the Treasury of the United States; and all such Laws shall be subject to the Revision and Controul of the Congress.

No State shall, without the Consent of Congress, lay any Duty of Tonnage, keep Troops, or Ships of War in time of Peace, enter into any Agreement or Compact with another State, or with a foreign Power, or engage in War, unless actually invaded, or in such imminent Danger as will not admit of delay.

ARTICLE II.

(The Executive)

Section 1. The executive Power shall be vested in a President of the United States of America. He shall hold his Office during the Term of four Years, and, together with the Vice President, chosen for the same Term, be elected, as follows.

Each State shall appoint, in such Manner as the Legislature thereof may direct, a Number of Electors, equal to the whole Number of Senators and Representatives to which the State may be entitled in the Congress; but no Senator or Representative, or Person holding an Office of Trust or Profit under the United States, shall be appointed an Elector.

[The Electors shall meet in their respective States, and vote by Ballot for two Persons, of whom one at least shall not be an Inhabitant of the same State with themselves. And they shall make a List of all the Persons voted for, and of the Number of Votes for each; which List they shall sign and certify, and transmit sealed to the Seat of the Government of the United States, directed to the President of the Senate. The President of the Senate shall, in the Presence of the Senate and House of Representatives, open all the Certificates, and the Votes shall then be counted. The Person having the greatest Number of Votes shall be the President, if such Number be a Majority of the whole Number of Electors appointed; and if there be more than one who have such Majority, and have an equal Number of Votes, then the House of

Representatives shall immediately chuse by Ballot one of them for President; and if no Person have a Majority, then from the five highest on the List the said House shall in like Manner chuse the President. But in chusing the President, the Votes shall be taken by States, the Representation from each State having one Vote; A quorum for this Purpose shall consist of a Member or Members from two thirds of the States, and a Majority of all the States shall be necessary to a Choice. In every Case, after the Choice of the President, the Person having the greatest Number of Votes of the Electors shall be the Vice President. But if there should remain two or more who have equal Votes, the Senate shall chuse from them by Ballot the Vice President.][7]

The Congress may determine the Time of chusing the Electors, and the Day on which they shall give their Votes; which Day shall be the same throughout the United States.

No Person except a natural born Citizen, or a Citizen of the United States, at the time of the Adoption of this Constitution, shall be eligible to the Office of President; neither shall any Person be eligible to that Office who shall not have attained to the Age of thirty five Years, and been fourteen Years a Resident within the United States.

[In Case of the Removal of the President from Office, or of his Death, Resignation, or Inability to discharge the Powers and Duties of the said Office, the Same shall devolve on the Vice President, and the Congress may by Law provide for the Case of Removal, Death, Resignation or Inability, both of the President and Vice President, declaring what Officer shall then act as President, and such Officer shall act accordingly, until the Disability be removed, or a President shall be elected.][8]

The President shall, at stated Times, receive for his Services, a Compensation, which shall neither be encreased nor diminished during the Period for which he shall have been elected, and he shall not receive within that Period any other Emolument from the United States, or any of them.

Before he enter on the Execution of his Office, he shall take the following Oath or Affirmation:—"I do solemnly swear (or affirm) that I will faithfully execute the Office of President of the United States, and will to the best of my Ability, preserve, protect and defend the Constitution of the United States."

Section 2.   The President shall be Commander in Chief of the Army and Navy of the United States, and of the Militia of the several States, when called into

[7]See Amendment XII.
[8]See Amendment XXV.

the actual Service of the United States; he may require the Opinion, in writing, of the principal Officer in each of the executive Departments, upon any Subject relating to the Duties of their respective Offices, and he shall have Power to grant Reprieves and Pardons for Offences against the United States, except in Cases of Impeachment.

He shall have Power, by and with the Advice and Consent of the Senate, to make Treaties, provided two thirds of the Senators present concur; and he shall nominate, and by and with the Advice and Consent of the Senate, shall appoint Ambassadors, other public Ministers and Consuls, Judges of the supreme Court, and all other Officers of the United States, whose Appointments are not herein otherwise provided for, and which shall be established by Law: but the Congress may by Law vest the Appointment of such inferior Officers, as they think proper, in the President alone, in the Courts of Law, or in the Heads of Departments.

The President shall have Power to fill up all Vacancies that may happen during the Recess of the Senate, by granting Commissions which shall expire at the end of their next Session.

Section 3.   He shall from time to time give to the Congress Information of the State of the Union, and recommend to their Consideration such Measures as he shall judge necessary and expedient; he may, on extraordinary Occasions, convene both Houses, or either of them, and in Case of Disagreement between them, with Respect to the Time of Adjournment, he may adjourn them to such Time as he shall think proper; he shall receive Ambassadors and other public Ministers; he shall take Care that the Laws be faithfully executed, and shall Commission all the Officers of the United States.

Section 4.   The President, Vice President and all civil Officers of the United States, shall be removed from Office on Impeachment for, and Conviction of, Treason, Bribery, or other high Crimes and Misdemeanors.

ARTICLE III.

(The Judiciary)

Section 1.   The judicial Power of the United States, shall be vested in one supreme Court, and in such inferior Courts as the Congress may from time to time ordain and establish. The Judges, both of the supreme and inferior Courts, shall hold their Offices during good Behaviour, and shall, at stated Times, receive for their Services, a Compensation, which shall not be diminished during their Continuance in Office.

Section 2. The judicial Power shall extend to all Cases, in Law and Equity, arising under this Constitution, the Laws of the United States, and Treaties made, or which shall be made, under their Authority;—to all Cases affecting Ambassadors, other public Ministers and Consuls;—to all Cases of admiralty and maritime Jurisdiction;—to Controversies to which the United States shall be a Party;—to Controversies between two or more States; [—between a State and Citizens of another State;—][9] between Citizens of different States,—between Citizens of the same State claiming Lands under Grants of different States, [and between a State, or the Citizens thereof, and foreign States, Citizens or Subjects.][10]

In all Cases affecting Ambassadors, other public Ministers and Consuls, and those in which a State shall be Party, the supreme Court shall have original Jurisdiction. In all the other Cases before mentioned, the supreme Court shall have appellate Jurisdiction, both as to Law and Fact, with such Exceptions, and under such Regulations as the Congress shall make.

The Trial of all Crimes, except in Cases of Impeachment, shall be by Jury; and such Trial shall be held in the State where the said Crimes shall have been committed; but when not committed within any State, the Trial shall be at such Place or Places as the Congress may by Law have directed.

Section 3. Treason against the United States, shall consist only in levying War against them, or in adhering to their Enemies, giving them Aid and Comfort. No Person shall be convicted of Treason unless on the Testimony of two Witnesses to the same overt Act, or on Confession in open Court.

The Congress shall have Power to declare the Punishment of Treason, but no Attainder of Treason shall work Corruption of Blood, or Forfeiture except during the Life of the Person attainted.

ARTICLE IV.

(Interstate Relations)

Section 1. Full Faith and Credit shall be given in each State to the public Acts, Records, and judicial Proceedings of every other State. And the Congress may by general Laws prescribe the Manner in which such Acts, Records and Proceedings shall be proved, and the Effect thereof.

Section 2. The Citizens of each State shall be entitled to all Privileges and Immunities of Citizens in the several States.

A Person charged in any State with Treason, Felony, or other Crime, who shall flee from Justice, and be found in another State, shall on Demand of the executive Authority of the State from which he fled, be delivered up, to be removed to the State having Jurisdiction of the Crime.

[No Person held to Service or Labour in one State under the Laws thereof, escaping into another, shall, in Consequence of any Law or Regulation therein, be discharged from such Service or Labour, but shall be delivered up on Claim of the Party to whom such Service or Labour may be due.][11]

Section 3. New States may be admitted by the Congress into this Union; but no new State shall be formed or erected within the Jurisdiction of any other State; nor any State be formed by the Junction of two or more States, or Parts of States, without the Consent of the Legislatures of the States concerned as well as of the Congress.

The Congress shall have Power to dispose of and make all needful Rules and Regulations respecting the Territory or other Property belonging to the United States; and nothing in this Constitution shall be so construed as to Prejudice any Claims of the United States, or of any particular State.

Section 4. The United States shall guarantee to every State in this Union a Republican Form of Government, and shall protect each of them against Invasion, and on Application of the Legislature, or of the Executive (when the Legislature cannot be convened) against domestic Violence.

ARTICLE V.

(Amending the Constitution)

The Congress, whenever two thirds of both Houses shall deem it necessary, shall propose Amendments to this Constitution, or, on the Application of the Legislatures of two thirds of the several States, shall call a Convention for proposing Amendments, which, in either Case, shall be valid to all Intents and Purposes, as Part of this Constitution, when ratified by the Legislatures of three fourths of the several States, or by Conventions in three fourths thereof, as the one or the other Mode of Ratification may be proposed by the Congress; Provided that no Amendment which may be made prior to the Year One thousand eight hundred and eight shall in any Manner affect the first and fourth Clauses in the Ninth Section of the first Article; and that no State, without its Consent, shall be deprived of its equal Suffrage in the Senate.

[9]See Amendment XI.
[10]See Amendment XI.

[11]See Amendment XIII.

ARTICLE VI.

(Debts, Supremacy, Oaths)

All Debts contracted and Engagements entered into, before the Adoption of this Constitution, shall be as valid against the United States under this Constitution, as under the Confederation.

This Constitution, and the laws of the United States which shall be made in Pursuance thereof; and all Treaties made, or which shall be made, under the Authority of the United States, shall be the supreme Law of the Land; and the Judges in every State shall be bound thereby, any Thing in the Constitution or Laws of any State to the Contrary notwithstanding.

The Senators and Representatives before mentioned, and the Members of the several State Legislatures, and all executive and judicial Officers, both of the United States and of the several States, shall be bound by Oath or Affirmation, to support this Constitution;

but no religious Test shall ever be required as a Qualification to any Office or public Trust under the United States.

ARTICLE VII.

(Ratifying the Constitution)

The Ratification of the Conventions of nine States, shall be sufficient for the Establishment of this Constitution between the States so ratifying the Same.

Done in Convention by the Unanimous Consent of the States present the Seventeenth Day of September in the Year of our Lord one thousand seven hundred and Eighty seven and of the Independence of the United States of America the Twelfth. IN WITNESS whereof we have hereunto subscribed our Names.

Go. WASHINGTON
Presid't. and deputy from Virginia

ATTEST	CONNECTICUT	PENNSYLVANIA	MARYLAND	SOUTH CAROLINA
William Jackson	Wm. Saml. Johnson	B. Franklin	James McHenry	J. Rutledge
Secretary	Roger Sherman	Thomas Mifflin	Dan of St. Thos.	Charles Cotesworth
		Robt. Morris	Jenifer	Pinckney
DELAWARE	NEW YORK	Geo. Clymer	Danl. Carroll	Charles Pinckney
Geo. Read	Alexander Hamilton	Thos. FitzSimons		Pierce Butler
Gunning Bedford jun		Jared Ingersoll	VIRGINIA	
John Dickinson	NEW JERSEY	James Wilson	John Blair	GEORGIA
Richard Basset	Wh. Livingston	Gouv. Morris	James Madison Jr.	William Few
Jaco. Broom	David Brearley			Abr. Baldwin
	Wm. Paterson	NEW HAMPSHIRE	NORTH CAROLINA	
MASSACHUSETTS	Jona. Dayton	John Langdon	Wm. Blount	
Nathaniel Gorbam		Nicholas Gilman	Richd. Dobbs Spaight	
Rufus King			Hu. Williamson	

Articles in addition to, and amendment of the Constitution of the United States of America, proposed by Congress and ratified by the Legislatures of the several states, pursuant to the Fifth Article of the original Constitution.

(The first ten amendments were passed by Congress on September 25, 1789, and were ratified on December 15, 1791.)

Amendment I—Religion, Speech, Assembly, Petition

Congress shall make no law respecting an establishment of religion, or prohibiting the free exercise thereof; or abridging the freedom of speech, or of the press; or the right of the people peaceably to assemble, and to petition the Government for a redress of grievances.

Amendment II—Right to Bear Arms

A well regulated Militia, being necessary to the security of a free State, the right of the people to keep and bear Arms, shall not be infringed.

Amendment III—Quartering of Soldiers

No Soldier shall, in time of peace be quartered in any house, without the consent of the Owner, nor in time of war, but in a manner to be prescribed by law.

Amendment IV—Searches and Seizures

The right of the people to be secure in their persons, houses, papers, and effects, against unreasonable searches and seizures, shall not be violated, and no warrants shall issue, but upon probable cause, supported by Oath or affirmation, and particularly describing the place to be searched, and the persons or things to be seized.

Amendment V—Grand Juries, Double Jeopardy, Self-incrimination, Due Process, Eminent Domain

No person shall be held to answer for a capital, or otherwise infamous crime, unless on a presentment or indictment of a Grand Jury, except in cases arising in the land or naval forces, or in the Militia, when in actual service in time of War or public danger; nor shall any person be subject for the same offence to be twice put in jeopardy of life or limb; nor shall be compelled in any criminal case to be a witness against himself, nor be deprived of life, liberty, or property, without due process of law; nor shall private property be taken for public use, without just compensation.

Amendment VI—Criminal Court Procedures

In all criminal prosecutions, the accused shall enjoy the right to a speedy and public trial, by an impartial jury of the State and district wherein the crime shall have been committed, which district shall have been previously ascertained by law, and to be informed of the nature and cause of the accusation; to be confronted with the witnesses against him; to have compulsory process for obtaining witnesses in his favor, and to have the assistance of counsel for his defence.

Amendment VII—Trial by Jury in Common-law Cases

In Suits at common law, where the value in controversy shall exceed twenty dollars, the right of trial by jury shall be preserved, and no fact tried by a jury, shall be otherwise re-examined in any Court of the United States, than according to the rules of the common law.

Amendment VIII—Bails, Fines, and Punishment

Excessive bail shall not be required, nor excessive fines imposed, nor cruel and unusual punishments inflicted.

Amendment IX—Rights Retained by the People

The enumeration in the Constitution, of certain rights, shall not be construed to deny or disparage others retained by the people.

Amendment X—Rights Reserved to the States

The powers not delegated to the United States by the Constitution, nor prohibited by it to the States, are reserved to the States respectively, or to the people.

Amendment XI—Suits Against the States (Ratified February 7, 1795)

The Judicial power of the United States shall not be construed to extend to any suit in law or equity, commenced or prosecuted against one of the United States by Citizens of another State, or by Citizens or Subjects of any Foreign State.

Amendment XII—Election of the President and Vice-President (Ratified June 15, 1804)

The Electors shall meet in their respective states, and vote by ballot for President and Vice-President, one of whom, at least, shall not be an inhabitant of the same state with themselves; they shall name in their ballots the person voted for as President, and in distinct ballots the person voted for as Vice-President, and they shall make distinct lists of all persons voted for as President, and of all persons voted for as Vice-President, and of the number of votes for each, which lists they shall sign and certify, and transmit sealed to the seat of the government of the United States, directed to the President of the Senate;—The President of the Senate shall, in the presence of the Senate and House of Representatives, open all the certificates and the votes shall then be counted;—The person having the greatest number of votes for President, shall be the President, if such number be a majority of the whole number of Electors appointed; and if no person have such majority, then from the persons having the highest numbers not exceeding three on the list of those voted for as President, the House of Representatives shall choose immediately, by ballot, the President. But in choosing the President, the votes shall be taken by states, the representation from each state having one vote; a quorum for this purpose shall consist of a member or members from two-thirds of the states, and a majority of all the states shall be necessary to a Choice. [And if the House of Representatives shall not choose a President whenever the right of choice shall devolve upon them, before the fourth day of March next following, then the Vice-President shall act as President, as in the case of the death or other constitutional disability of the President.][12]—The person having the greatest number of votes as Vice-President, shall be the Vice-President, if such number be a majority of the whole number of Electors appointed, and if no person have a majority, then from the two highest numbers on the list, the Senate shall choose the Vice-President; a quorum for the purpose shall consist of two-thirds of the whole number of Senators, and a majority of the whole number shall be necessary to a choice. But no person constitutionally ineligible to the office of President shall be eligible to that of Vice-President of the United States.

Amendment XIII—Slavery (Ratified on December 6, 1865)

Section 1. Neither slavery nor involuntary servitude, except as a punishment for crime whereof the party shall have been duly convicted, shall exist within the United States, or any place subject to their jurisdiction.

Section 2. Congress shall have power to enforce this article by appropriate legislation.

[12]Amendment XX.

219

Amendment XIV—Citizenship, Due Process, and Equal Protection of the Laws (Ratified on July 9, 1868)

Section 1. All persons born or naturalized in the United States, and subject to the jurisdiction thereof, are citizens of the United States and of the State wherein they reside. No State shall make or enforce any law which shall abridge the privileges or immunities of citizens of the United States; nor shall any State deprive any person of life, liberty, or property, without due process of law; nor deny to any person within its jurisdiction the equal protection of the laws.

Section 2. Representatives shall be apportioned among the several States according to their respective numbers, counting the whole number of persons in each State, excluding Indians not taxed. But when the right to vote at any election for the choice of electors for President and Vice President of the United States, Representatives in Congress, the Executive and Judicial officers of a State, or the members of the Legislature thereof, is denied to any of the male inhabitants of such State, being twenty-one years of age, and citizens of the United States, or in any way abridged, except for participation in rebellion, or other crime, the basis of representation therein shall be reduced in the proportion which the number of such male citizens shall bear to the whole number of male citizens twenty-one years of age in such State.

Section 3. No person shall be a Senator or Representative in Congress, or elector of President and Vice President, or hold any office, civil or military, under the United States, or under any State, who, having previously taken an oath, as a member of Congress, or as an officer of the United States, or as a member of any State legislature, or as an executive or judicial officer of any State, to support the Constitution of the United States, shall have engaged in insurrection or rebellion against the same, or given aid or comfort to the enemies thereof. But Congress may by a vote of two-thirds of each House, remove such disability.

Section 4. The validity of the public debt of the United States, authorized by law, including debts incurred for payment of pensions and bounties for services in suppressing insurrection or rebellion, shall not be questioned. But neither the United States nor any State shall assume or pay any debt or obligation incurred in aid of insurrection or rebellion against the United States, or any claim for the loss or emancipation of any slave, but all such debts, obligations and claims shall be held illegal and void.

Section 5. The Congress shall have power to enforce, by appropriate legislation, the provisions of this article.

Amendment XV—The Right To Vote (Ratified on February 3, 1870)

Section 1. The right of citizens of the United States to vote shall not be denied or abridged by the United States or by any State on account of race, color, or previous condition of servitude.

Section 2. The Congress shall have power to enforce this article by appropriate legislation.

Amendment XVI—Income Taxes (Ratified on February 3, 1913)

The Congress shall have power to lay and collect taxes on incomes, from whatever source derived, without apportionment among the several States, and without regard to any census or enumeration.

Amendment XVII—Election of Senators (Ratified on April 8, 1913)

The Senate of the United States shall be composed of two Senators from each State, elected by the people thereof, for six years; and each Senator shall have one vote. The electors in each State shall have the qualifications requisite for electors of the most numerous branch of the State legislatures.

When vacancies happen in the representation of any State in the Senate, the executive authority of such State shall issue writs of election to fill such vacancies: *Provided,* That the legislature of any State may empower the executive thereof to make temporary appointments until the people fill the vacancies by election as the legislature may direct.

This amendment shall not be so construed as to affect the election or term of any Senator chosen before it becomes valid as part of the Constitution.

Amendment XVIII—Prohibition (Ratified on January 16, 1919)

Section 1. After one year from the ratification of this article the manufacture, sale, or transportation of intoxicating liquors within, the importation thereof into, or the exportation thereof from the United States and all territory subject to the jurisdiction thereof for beverage purposes is hereby prohibited.

Section 2. The Congress and the several States shall have concurrent power to enforce this article by appropriate legislation.

Section 3. This article shall be inoperative unless it shall have been ratified as an amendment to the Constitution by the legislatures of the several States, as provided in the Constitution, within seven years from the date of the submission hereof to the States by the Congress.[13]

Amendment XIX—Women's Right To Vote (Ratified on August 18, 1920)

The right of citizens of the United States to vote shall not be denied or abridged by the United States or by any State on account of sex.

Congress shall have power to enforce this article by appropriate legislation.

Amendment XX—Terms of Office, Convening of Congress, and Succession (Ratified February 6, 1933)

Section 1. The terms of the President and Vice President shall end at noon on the 20th day of January, and the terms of Senators and Representatives at noon on the 3d day of January, of the years in which such terms would have ended if this article had not been ratified; and the terms of their successors shall then begin.

Section 2. The Congress shall assemble at least once in every year, and such meeting shall begin at noon on the 3d day of January, unless they shall by law appoint a different day.

Section 3. If, at the time fixed for the beginning of the term of the President, the President elect shall have died, the Vice President elect shall become President. If a President shall not have been chosen before the time fixed for the beginning of his term, or if the President elect shall have failed to qualify, then the Vice President elect shall act as President until a President shall have qualified; and the Congress may by law provide for the case wherein neither a President elect nor a Vice President elect shall have qualified, declaring who shall then act as President, or the manner in which one who is to act shall be selected, and such person shall act accordingly until a President or Vice President shall have qualified.

Section 4. The Congress may by law provide for the case of the death of any of the persons from whom the House of Representatives may choose a President whenever the rights of choice shall have devolved upon them, and for the case of the death of any of the persons from whom the Senate may choose a Vice President whenever the right of choice shall have devolved upon them.

Section 5. Sections 1 and 2 shall take effect on the 15th day of October following the ratification of this article.

Section 6. This article shall be inoperative unless it shall have been ratified as an amendment to the Constitution by the legislatures of three-fourths of the several States within seven years from the date of its submission.

Amendment XXI—Repeal of Prohibition (Ratified on December 5, 1933)

Section 1. The eighteenth article of amendment to the Constitution of the United States is hereby repealed.

Section 2. The transportation or importation into any State, Territory, or possession of the United States for delivery or use therein of intoxicating liquors, in violation of the laws thereof, is hereby prohibited.

Section 3. This article shall be inoperative unless it shall have been ratified as an amendment to the Constitution by conventions in the several States, as provided in the Constitution, within seven years from the date of the submission hereof to the States by Congress.

Amendment XXII—Number of Presidential Terms (Ratified on February 27, 1951)

No person shall be elected to the office of the President more than twice, and no person who has held the office of President, or acted as President, for more than two years of a term to which some other person was elected President shall be elected to the office of the President more than once. But this Article shall not apply to any person holding the office of President when this Article was proposed by the Congress, and shall not prevent any person who may be holding the office of President, or acting as President, during the term within which this Article becomes operative from holding the office of President or acting as President during the remainder of such term.

[13]Amendment XXI.

Amendment XXIII—Presidential Electors for the District of Columbia (Ratified on March 29, 1961)

Section 1. The District constituting the seat of Government of the United States shall appoint in such manner as the Congress may direct:

A number of electors of President and Vice President equal to the whole number of Senators and Representatives in Congress to which the District would be entitled if it were a State, but in no event more than the least populous State; they shall be in addition to those appointed by the States, but they shall be considered, for the purposes of the election of President and Vice President, to be electors appointed by a State; and they shall meet in the District and perform such duties as provided by the twelfth article of amendment.

Section 2. The Congress shall have power to enforce this article by appropriate legislation.

Amendment XXIV—Poll Tax (Ratified on January 23, 1964)

Section 1. The right of citizens of the United States to vote in any primary or other election for President or Vice President, for electors for President or Vice President, or for Senator or Representative in Congress, shall not be denied or abridged by the United States or any State by reason of failure to pay any poll tax or other tax.

Section 2. The Congress shall have power to enforce this article by appropriate legislation.

Amendment XXV—Presidential Disability and Vice Presidential Vacancies (Ratified on February 10, 1967)

Section 1. In case of the removal of the President from office or of his death or resignation, the Vice President shall become President.

Section 2. Whenever there is a vacancy in the office of the Vice President, the President shall nominate a Vice President who shall take office upon confirmation by a majority vote of both Houses of Congress.

Section 3. Whenever the President transmits to the President pro tempore of the Senate and the Speaker of the House of Representatives his written declaration that he is unable to discharge the powers and duties of his office, and until he transmits to them a written declaration to the contrary, such powers and duties shall be discharged by the Vice President as Acting President.

Section 4. Whenever the Vice President and a majority of either the principal officers of the executive departments or of such other body as Congress may by law provide, transmit to the President pro tempore of the Senate and the Speaker of the House of Representatives their written declaration that the President is unable to discharge the powers and duties of his office, the Vice President shall immediately assume the powers and duties of the office as Acting President.

Thereafter, when the President transmits to the President pro tempore of the Senate and the Speaker of the House of Representatives his written declaration that no inability exists, he shall resume the powers and duties of his office unless the Vice President and a majority of either the principal officers of the executive department or of such other body as Congress may by law provide, transmit within four days to the President pro tempore of the Senate and the Speaker of the House of Representatives their written declaration that the President is unable to discharge the powers and duties of his office. Thereupon Congress shall decide the issue, assembling within forty-eight hours for that purpose if not in session. If the Congress, within twenty-one days after receipt of the latter written declaration, or, if Congress is not in session, within twenty-one days after Congress is required to assemble, determines by two-thirds vote of both Houses that the President is unable to discharge the powers and duties of his office, the Vice President shall continue to discharge the same as Acting President; otherwise, the President shall resume the powers and duties of his office.

Amendment XXVI—Eighteen-year-old Vote (Ratified on July 1, 1971)

Section 1. The right of citizens of the United States, who are eighteen years of age or older, to vote shall not be denied or abridged by the United States or by any State on account of age.

Section 2. The Congress shall have power to enforce this article by appropriate legislation.

Amendment XXVII—Congressional Salaries (Ratified on May 18, 1992)

Section 1. No law varying the compensation for the services of the Senators and Representatives, shall take effect, until an election of Representatives shall have intervened.

Presidents of the United States

YEAR	PRESIDENTIAL CANDIDATES	POLITICAL PARTY	ELECTORAL VOTE	PERCENTAGE OF POPULAR VOTE
1789	**George Washington**	–	69	–
	John Adams		34	
	Others		35	
1792	**George Washington**	–	132	–
	John Adams		77	
	Others		55	
1796	**John Adams**	Federalist	71	–
	Thomas Jefferson	Democratic-Republican	68	
	Thomas Pinckney	Federalist	59	
	Aaron Burr	Democratic-Republican	30	
	Others		48	
1800	**Thomas Jefferson**	Democratic-Republican	73	–
	Aaron Burr	Democratic-Republican	73	
	John Adams	Federalist	65	
	C. C. Pinckney	Federalist	64	
	John Jay	Federalist	1	
1804	**Thomas Jefferson**	Democratic-Republican	162	–
	C. C. Pinckney	Federalist	14	
1808	**James Madison**	Democratic-Republican	122	–
	C. C. Pinckney	Federalist	47	
	George Clinton	Independent-Republican	6	
1812	**James Madison**	Democratic-Republican	128	–
	De Witt Clinton	Federalist	89	
1816	**James Monroe**	Democratic-Republican	183	–
	Rufus King	Federalist	34	
1820	**James Monroe**	Democratic-Republican	231	–
	John Q. Adams	Independent-Republican	1	
1824	**John Q. Adams**	Democratic-Republican	84	30.5
	Andrew Jackson	Democratic-Republican	99	
	Henry Clay	Democratic-Republican	37	
	W. H. Crawford	Democratic-Republican	41	
1828	**Andrew Jackson**	Democratic	178	56.0
	John Q. Adams	National Republican	83	
1832	**Andrew Jackson**	Democratic	219	55.0
	Henry Clay	National Republican	49	
	William Wirt	Anti-Masonic	7	
	John Floyd	Independent Democrat	11	
1836	**Martin Van Buren**	Democratic	170	50.9
	William H. Harrison	Whig	73	
	Hugh L. White	Whig	26	
	Daniel Webster	Whig	14	
1840	**William H. Harrison***	Whig	234	53.0
	Martin Van Buren	Democratic	60	
	(John Tyler, 1841)			
1844	**James K. Polk**	Democratic	170	49.6
	Henry Clay	Whig	105	
1848	**Zachary Taylor***	Whig	163	47.4
	Lewis Cass	Democratic	127	
	(Millard Fillmore, 1850)			

Note: Presidents are shown in boldface.
*Died in office, succeeding vice president shown in parentheses.

223

YEAR	PRESIDENTIAL CANDIDATES	POLITICAL PARTY	ELECTORAL VOTE	PERCENTAGE OF POPULAR VOTE
1852	Franklin Pierce	Democratic	254	50.8
	Winfield Scott	Whig	42	
1856	James Buchanan	Democratic	174	45.3
	John C. Fremont	Republican	114	
	Millard Fillmore	American	8	
1860	Abraham Lincoln	Republican	180	39.8
	J. C. Breckinridge	Democratic	72	
	Stephen A. Douglas	Democratic	12	
	John Bell	Constitutional Union	39	
1864	Abraham Lincoln*	Republican	212	55.0
	George B. McClellan	Democratic	21	
	(Andrew Johnson, 1865)			
1868	Ulysses S. Grant	Republican	214	52.7
	Horatio Seymour	Democratic	80	
1872	Ulysses S. Grant	Republican	286	55.6
	Horace Greeley	Democratic	**	
1876	Rutherford B. Hayes	Republican	185	47.9
	Samuel J. Tilden	Democratic	184	
1880	James A. Garfield*	Republican	214	48.3
	Winfield S. Hancock	Democratic	155	
	(Chester A. Arthur, 1881)			
1884	Grover Cleveland	Democratic	219	48.5
	James G. Blaine	Republican	182	
1888	Benjamin Harrison	Republican	233	47.8
	Grover Cleveland	Democratic	168	
1892	Grover Cleveland	Democratic	277	46.0
	Benjamin Harrison	Republican	145	
	James B. Weaver	People's	22	
1896	William McKinley	Republican	271	51.0
	William J. Bryan	Democratic	176	
1900	William McKinley*	Republican	292	51.7
	William J. Bryan	Democratic	155	
	(Theodore Roosevelt, 1901)			
1904	Theodore Roosevelt	Republican	336	56.4
	Alton B. Parker	Democratic	140	
1908	William H. Taft	Republican	321	51.6
	William J. Bryan	Democratic	162	
1912	Woodrow Wilson	Democratic	435	41.8
	Theodore Roosevelt	Progressive	88	
	William H. Taft	Republican	8	
1916	Woodrow Wilson	Democratic	277	49.2
	Charles E. Hughes	Republican	254	
1920	Warren G. Harding*	Republican	404	60.3
	James M. Cox	Democratic	127	
	(Calvin Coolidge, 1923)			
1924	Calvin Coolidge	Republican	382	54.1
	John W. Davis	Democratic	136	
	Robert M. LaFollette	Progressive	13	
1928	Herbert C. Hoover	Republican	444	58.2
	Alfred E. Smith	Democratic	87	
1932	Franklin D. Roosevelt	Democratic	472	57.4
	Herbert C. Hoover	Republican	59	

**Horace Greeley died between the popular vote and the meeting of the presidential electors.

(continues)

Presidents of the United States (continued)

YEAR	PRESIDENTIAL CANDIDATES	POLITICAL PARTY	ELECTORAL VOTE	PERCENTAGE OF POPULAR VOTE
1936	**Franklin D. Roosevelt**	Democratic	523	60.8
	Alfred M. Landon	Republican	8	
1940	**Franklin D. Roosevelt**	Democratic	449	54.7
	Wendell L. Willkie	Republican	82	
1944	**Franklin D. Roosevelt***	Democratic	432	53.4
	Thomas E. Dewey	Republican	99	
	(Harry S Truman, 1945)			
1948	**Harry S Truman**	Democratic	303	49.5
	Thomas E. Dewey	Republican	189	
	J. Strom Thurmond	States' Rights	39	
1952	**Dwight D. Eisenhower**	Republican	442	55.1
	Adlai E. Stevenson	Democratic	89	
1956	**Dwight D. Eisenhower**	Republican	457	57.4
	Adlai E. Stevenson	Democratic	73	
1960	**John F. Kennedy***	Democratic	303	49.7
	Richard M. Nixon	Republican	219	
	(Lyndon B. Johnson, 1963)			
1964	**Lyndon B. Johnson**	Democratic	486	61.0
	Barry M. Goldwater	Republican	52	
1968	**Richard M. Nixon**	Republican	301	43.4
	Hubert H. Humphrey	Democratic	191	
	George C. Wallace	American Independent	46	
1972	**Richard M. Nixon†**	Republican	520	60.7
	George S. McGovern	Democratic	17	
	(Gerald R. Ford, 1974)‡			
1976	**Jimmy Carter**	Democratic	297	50.1
	Gerald R. Ford	Republican	240	
1980	**Ronald Reagan**	Republican	489	50.7
	Jimmy Carter	Democratic	49	
	John B. Anderson	Independent	—	
1984	**Ronald Reagan**	Republican	525	58.8
	Walter Mondale	Democratic	13	
1988	**George Bush**	Republican	426	53.4
	Michael Dukakis	Democratic	112	
1992	**Bill Clinton**	Democratic	370	43.0
	George Bush	Republican	168	
	H. Ross Perot	Independent	—	
1996	**Bill Clinton**	Democratic	379	49.2
	Robert Dole	Republican	159	
	H. Ross Perot	Reform	—	
2000	**George W. Bush**	Republican	271	47.8
	Al Gore	Democratic	266	
	Ralph Nader	Green		
	Patrick J. Buchanan	Reform		
2004	**George W. Bush**	Republican	286	50.7
	John Kerry	Democratic	251	
	Ralph Nader	Independent	—	
2008	**Barack Obama**	Democratic	365	52.7
	John McCain	Republican	173	

†Resigned
‡Appointed vice president

Party Control of the Presidency, Senate, and House of Representatives in the Twentieth and Twenty-first Centuries

CONGRESS	YEARS	PRESIDENT	SENATE			HOUSE		
			D	R	OTHER*	D	R	OTHER*
57th	1901–03	McKinley	29	56	3	153	198	5
		T. Roosevelt						
58th	1903–05	T. Roosevelt	32	58	—	178	207	—
59th	1905–07	T. Roosevelt	32	58	—	136	250	—
60th	1907–09	T. Roosevelt	29	61	—	164	222	—
61st	1909–11	Taft	32	59	—	172	219	—
62d	1911–13	Taft	42	49	—	228‡	162	1
63d	1913–15	Wilson	51	44	1	290	127	18
64th	1915–17	Wilson	56	39	1	230	193	8
65th	1917–19	Wilson	53	42	1	200	216	9
66th	1919–21	Wilson	48	48‡	1	191	237‡	7
67th	1921–23	Harding	37	59	—	132	300	1
68th	1923–25	Coolidge	43	51	2	207	225	3
69th	1925–27	Coolidge	40	54	1	183	247	5
70th	1927–29	Coolidge	47	48	1	195	237	3
71st	1929–31	Hoover	39	56	1	163	267	1
72d	1931–33	Hoover	47	48	1	216‡	218	1
73d	1933–35	F. Roosevelt	59	36	1	313	117	5
74th	1935–37	F. Roosevelt	69	25	2	322	103	10
75th	1937–39	F. Roosevelt	75	17	4	333	89	13
76th	1939–41	F. Roosevelt	69	23	4	262	169	4
77th	1941–43	F. Roosevelt	66	28	2	267	162	6
78th	1943–45	F. Roosevelt	57	38	1	222	209	4
79th	1945–47	Truman	57	38	1	243	190	2
80th	1947–49	Truman	45	51‡	—	188	246‡	1
81st	1949–51	Truman	54	42	—	263	171	1
82d	1951–53	Truman	48	47	1	234	199	2
83d	1953–55	Eisenhower	47	48	1	213	221	1
84th	1955–57	Eisenhower	48‡	47	1	232‡	203	—
85th	1957–59	Eisenhower	49‡	47	—	234‡	201	—
86th†	1959–61	Eisenhower	64‡	34	—	283‡	154	—
87th	1961–63	Kennedy	64	36	—	263	174	—
88th	1963–65	Kennedy Johnson	67	33	—	258	176	—
		Johnson						
89th	1965–67	Johnson	68	32	—	295	140	—
90th	1967–69	Johnson	64	36	—	248	187	—
91st	1969–71	Nixon	58‡	42	—	243‡	192	—
92d	1971–73	Nixon	55‡	45	—	255‡	180	—
93d	1973–75	Nixon	57‡	43	—	243‡	192	—
		Ford						
94th	1975–77	Ford	61‡	38	—	291‡	144	—
95th	1977–79	Carter	62	38	—	292	143	—
96th	1979–81	Carter	59	41	—	277	158	—
97th	1981–83	Reagan	47	53	—	243‡	192	—
98th	1983–85	Reagan	46	54	—	269‡	166	—
99th	1985–87	Reagan	47	53	—	253‡	182	—
100th	1987–89	Reagan	55‡	45	—	258‡	177	—
101st	1989–91	Bush	55‡	45	—	260‡	175	—

*Excludes vacancies at beginning of each session. Party balance immediately following election.

†The 437 members of the House in the 86th and 87th Congresses are attributable to the at-large representative given to both Alaska (January 3, 1959) and Hawaii (August 21, 1959) prior to redistricting in 1962.

‡Chamber controlled by party other than that of the president.

D=Democrat   R=Republican

(continues)

Party Control of the Presidency, Senate, and House of Representatives in the Twentieth and Twenty-first Centuries (continued)

CONGRESS	YEARS	PRESIDENT	SENATE			HOUSE		
			D	R	OTHER*	D	R	OTHER*
102ᵈ	1991-93	Bush	56‡	44	—	267‡	167	1
103ᵈ	1993-95	Clinton	57	43	—	258	176	1
104ᵗʰ	1995-97	Clinton	46	54	—	202	232	1
105ᵗʰ	1997-99	Clinton	45	55	—	206	228	1
106ᵗʰ	1999-01	Clinton	45	55	—	211	223	1
107ᵗʰ	2001-03	G. W. Bush	50	49	1	212	221	2
108ᵗʰ	2003-05	G. W. Bush	48	51	1	205	229	1
109ᵗʰ	2005-07	G. W. Bush	44	55	1	202	232	11
110ᵗʰ	2007-09	G. W. Bush	50	49	1	233	202	—
111ᵗʰ	2009-11	Obama	56	42	2	257	178	—

Supreme Court Justices Serving in the Twentieth and Twenty-first Centuries

NAME	NOMINATED BY	SERVICE
John M. Harlan	Hayes	1877–1911
Horace Gray	Arthur	1882–1902
Melville W. Fuller*	Cleveland	1888–1910
David J. Brewer	Harrison	1890–1910
Henry B. Brown	Harrison	1890–1906
George Shiras, Jr.	Harrison	1892–1903
Edward D. White	Cleveland	1894–1910
Rufus W. Peckham	Cleveland	1895–1909
Joseph McKenna	McKinley	1898–1925
Oliver W. Holmes	T. Roosevelt	1902–1932
William R. Day	T. Roosevelt	1903–1922
William H. Moody	T. Roosevelt	1906–1910
Horace H. Lurton	Taft	1910–1914
Edward D. White	Taft	1910–1921
Charles E. Hughes	Taft	1910–1916
Willis Van Devanter	Taft	1911–1937
Joseph R. Lamar	Taft	1911–1916
Mahlon Pitney	Taft	1912–1922
James C. McReynolds	Wilson	1914–1941
Louis D. Brandeis	Wilson	1916–1939
John H. Clarke	Wilson	1916–1922
William H. Taft	Harding	1921–1930
George Sutherland	Harding	1922–1938
Pierce Butler	Harding	1922–1939
Edward T. Sanford	Harding	1923–1930
Harlan F. Stone	Coolidge	1925–1941
Charles E. Hughes	Hoover	1930–1941
Owen J. Roberts	Hoover	1930–1945
Benjamin N. Cardozo	Hoover	1932–1938
Hugo L. Black	F. Roosevelt	1937–1971
Stanley F. Reed	F. Roosevelt	1938–1957
Felix Frankfurter	F. Roosevelt	1939–1962
William O. Douglas	F. Roosevelt	1939–1975

*Boldface type indicates service as chief justice.

227

Frank Murphy	F. Roosevelt	1940–1949
Harlan F. Stone	F. Roosevelt	1941–1946
James F. Byrnes	F. Roosevelt	1941–1942
Robert H. Jackson	F. Roosevelt	1941–1954
Wiley B. Rutledge	F. Roosevelt	1943–1949
Harold H. Burton	Truman	1945–1958
Fred M. Vinson	Truman	1946–1953
Tom C. Clark	Truman	1949–1967
Sherman Minton	Truman	1949–1956
Earl Warren	Eisenhower	1953–1969
John M. Harlan	Eisenhower	1955–1971
William J. Brennan, Jr.	Eisenhower	1956–1990
Charles E. Whittaker	Eisenhower	1957–1962
Potter Stewart	Eisenhower	1958–1981
Byron R. White	Kennedy	1962–1993
Arthur J. Goldberg	Kennedy	1962–1965
Abe Fortas	Johnson	1965–1969
Thurgood Marshall	Johnson	1967–1991
Warren E. Burger	Nixon	1969–1986
Harry A. Blackmun	Nixon	1970–1994
Lewis F. Powell, Jr.	Nixon	1971–1987
William H. Rehnquist	Nixon	1971–1986
John Paul Stevens	Ford	1975–
Sandra Day O'Connor	Reagan	1981–2006
William H. Rehnquist	Reagan	1986–2005
Antonin Scalia	Reagan	1986–
Anthony M. Kennedy	Reagan	1988–
David H. Souter	Bush	1990–
Clarence Thomas	Bush	1991–
Ruth Bader Ginsburg	Clinton	1993–
Stephen G. Breyer	Clinton	1994–
John G. Roberts Jr.	G. W. Bush	2005–
Samuel A. Alito Jr.	G. W. Bush	2006–

GLOSSARY

527 groups Independent groups that seek to influence the political process but are not subject to contribution restrictions because they do not directly seek the election of particular candidates. Their name comes from Section 527 of the federal tax code, under which they are governed. In 2004, 52 individuals gave over a million dollars to such groups, and all told they spent $424 million on political messages.

A

activation. One of three key consequences of electoral campaigns for voters, in which the voter is activated to contribute money or ring doorbells instead of just voting. See also **reinforcement** and **conversion**.

actual group. That part of the **potential group** consisting of members who actually join. See also **interest group**.

Adarand Constructors v. Pena. A 1995 Supreme Court decision holding that federal programs that classify people by race, even for an ostensibly benign purpose such as expanding opportunities for minorities, should be presumed to be unconstitutional. Such programs must be subject to the most searching judicial inquiry and can survive only if they are "narrowly tailored" to accomplish a "compelling governmental interest."

administrative discretion. The authority of administrative actors to select among various responses to a given problem. Discretion is greatest when routines, or **standard operating procedures**, do not fit a case.

advertising. According to David Mayhew, one of three primary activities undertaken by members of Congress to increase the probability of their reelection. Advertising involves contacts between members and their constituents between elections. See also **credit claiming** and **position taking**.

affirmative action. A policy designed to give special attention to or compensatory treatment for members of some previously disadvantaged group.

agenda. See **policy agenda**.

agents of socialization. Families, schools, television, peer groups, and other influences that contribute to **political socialization** by shaping formal and especially informal learning about politics.

Americans with Disabilities Act of 1990. A law passed in 1990 that requires employers and public facilities to make "reasonable accommodations" for people with disabilities and prohibits discrimination against these individuals in employment.

amicus curiae **briefs.** Legal briefs submitted by a "friend of the court" for the purpose of raising additional points of view and presenting information not contained in the briefs of the formal parties. These briefs attempt to influence a court's decision.

Anti-Federalists. Opponents of the American Constitution at the time when the states were contemplating its adoption. They argued that the Constitution was a class-based document, that it would erode fundamental liberties, and that it would weaken the power of the states. See also **Federalists** and **U.S. Constitution**.

antitrust policy. A policy designed to ensure competition and prevent monopoly, which is the control of a market by one company.

appellate jurisdiction. The jurisdiction of courts that hear cases brought to them on appeal from lower courts. These courts do not review the factual record, only the legal issues involved. Compare **original jurisdiction**.

appropriations bill. An act of Congress that actually funds programs within limits established by **authorization bills**. Appropriations usually cover one year.

arms race. A tense relationship beginning in the 1950s between the Soviet Union and the United States whereby one side's weaponry became the other side's goad to procure more weaponry, and so on.

Articles of Confederation. The first constitution of the United States, adopted by Congress in 1777 and enacted in 1781. The Articles established a national legislature, the Continental Congress, but most authority rested with the state legislatures.

authorization bill. An act of Congress that establishes, continues, or changes a discretionary government program or an entitlement. It specifies program goals and maximum expenditures for discretionary programs. Compare **appropriations bill**.

B

balance of trade. The ratio of what is paid for imports to what is earned from exports. When more is imported than exported, there is a balance-of-trade deficit.

balanced budget amendment. A proposed amendment to the Constitution that would instruct Congress to hold a national convention to propose to the states a requirement that peacetime federal budgets be balanced. The amendment has been passed in varied forms by the legislatures of nearly two-thirds of the states.

Barron v. Baltimore. The 1833 Supreme Court decision holding that the **Bill of Rights** restrained only the national government, not the states and cities. Almost a century later, the Court first ruled in *Gitlow v. New York* that state governments must respect some **First Amendment rights**.

beats. Specific locations from which news frequently emanates, such as Congress or the White House. Most top reporters work a particular beat, thereby becoming specialists in what goes on at that location.

bicameral legislature. A legislature divided into two houses. The U.S. Congress and every American state legislature except Nebraska's are bicameral.

bill. A proposed law, drafted in precise, legal language. Anyone can draft a bill, but only a member of the House of Representatives or the Senate can formally submit a bill for consideration.

Bill of Rights. The first ten amendments to the **U.S. Constitution**, drafted in response to some of the **Anti-Federalist** concerns. These amendments define such basic liberties as freedom of religion, speech, and press and offer protections against arbitrary searches by the police and being held without talking to a lawyer.

blanket primaries. Elections to select party nominees in which voters are presented with a list of candidates from all the parties. Voters can then select some Democrats and some Republicans if they like. See also **primaries**.

block grants. Federal grants given more or less automatically to states or communities to support broad programs in areas such as community development and social services. Compare **categorical grants**.

broadcast media. Television and radio, as compared with **print media**.

Brown v. Board of Education. The 1954 Supreme Court decision holding that school segregation in Topeka, Kansas, was inherently unconstitutional because it violated the **Fourteenth Amendment's** guarantee of **equal protection**. This case marked the end of legal segregation in the United States. See also *Plessy v. Ferguson*.

budget. A policy document allocating burdens (taxes) and benefits (expenditures). See also **balanced budget amendment**.

budget resolution. A resolution binding Congress to a total expenditure level, supposedly the bottom line of all federal spending for all programs.

bureaucracy. According to Max Weber, a hierarchical authority structure that uses task specialization, operates on the merit principle, and behaves with impersonality. Bureaucracies govern modern states.

C

cabinet. A group of presidential advisers not mentioned in the Constitution, although every president has had one. Today the cabinet is composed of 14 secretaries and the attorney general.

campaign strategy. The master game plan candidates lay out to guide their electoral campaign.

capitalism. An economic system in which individuals and corporations, not the government, own the principal means of production and seek profits. Pure capitalism means the strict noninterference of the government in business affairs. Compare **mixed economy**.

casework. Activities of members of Congress that help constituents as individuals; cutting through bureaucratic red tape to get people what they think they have a right to get. See also **pork barrel**.

categorical grants. Federal grants that can be used only for specific purposes, or "categories," of state and local spending. They come with strings attached, such as nondiscrimination provisions. Compare **block grants**.

caucus (congressional). A group of members of Congress sharing some interest or characteristic. Most are composed of members from both parties and from both houses.

caucus (state party). A meeting of all state party leaders for selecting delegates to the **national party convention**. Caucuses are usually organized as a pyramid.

censorship. Governmental regulation of media content.

census. A valuable tool for understanding demographic changes. The Constitution requires that the government conduct an "actual enumeration" of the population every ten years. See also **demography**.

Central Intelligence Agency (CIA). An agency created after World War II to coordinate American intelligence activities abroad. It became involved in intrigue, conspiracy, and meddling as well.

chains. See **newspaper chains**.

checks and balances. An important part of the Madisonian model designed to limit government's power by requiring that power be balanced among the different governmental institutions. These institutions continually check one another's activities. This system reflects Madison's goal of setting power against power. See also **separation of powers**.

city manager. An official appointed by the city council who is responsible for implementing and administrating the council's actions. More than one-third of U.S. cities use the council–manager form of government.

civic duty. The belief that in order to support democratic government, a citizen should always vote.

civil disobedience. A form of **political participation** that reflects a conscious decision to break a law believed to be immoral and to suffer the consequences. See also **protest**.

civil law. The body of law involving cases without a charge of criminality. It concerns disputes between two parties and consists of both statutes and **common law**. Compare **criminal law**.

civil liberties. The legal constitutional protections against government. Although our civil liberties are formally set down in the **Bill of Rights**, the courts, police, and legislatures define their meaning.

civil rights. Policies designed to protect people against arbitrary or discriminitory treatment by government officials or individuals.

Civil Rights Act of 1964. The law that made racial discrimination against any group in hotels, motels, and restaurants illegal and forbade many forms of job discrimination. See also **civil rights movement** and **civil rights policies**.

civil rights movement. A movement that began in the 1950s and organized both African Americans and Whites to end the policies of segregation. It sought to establish equal opportunities in the political and economic sectors and to end policies that erected barriers between people because of race.

civil rights policies. Policies that extend government protection to particular disadvantaged groups. Compare **social welfare policies**.

civil service. A system of hiring and promotion based on the **merit principle** and the desire to create a nonpartisan government service. Compare **patronage**.

class action suits. Lawsuits permitting a small number of people to sue on behalf of all other people similarly situated.

Clean Air Act of 1970. The law aimed at combating air pollution.

Clean Water Act of 1972. A law intended to clean up the nation's rivers and lakes. It requires municipal, industrial, and other polluters to use pollution control technology and secure permits from the **Environmental Protection Agency** for discharging waste products into waters.

closed primaries. Elections to select party nominees in which only people who have registered in advance with the party can vote for that party's candidates, thus encouraging greater party loyalty. See also **primaries.**

coalition. A group of individuals with a common interest upon which every political party depends. See also **New Deal Coalition.**

coalition government. When two or more parties join together to form a majority in a national legislature. This form of government is quite common in the multiparty systems of Europe.

coattails. See **presidential coattails.**

Cold War. War by other than military means usually emphasizing ideological conflict, such as that between the United States and the Soviet Union from the end of World War II until the 1990s.

collective bargaining. Negotiations between representatives of labor unions and management to determine acceptable working conditions.

collective good. Something of value (money, a tax write-off, prestige, clean air, and so on) that cannot be withheld from a group member.

command-and-control policy. According to Charles Schultze, the existing system of **regulation** whereby government tells business how to reach certain goals, checks that these commands are followed, and punishes offenders. Compare **incentive system.**

commercial speech. Communication in the form of advertising. It can be restricted more than many other types of speech but has been receiving increased protection from the Supreme Court.

commission government. A form of municipal government in which voters elect individuals to serve as city commissioners who will have legislative responsibilities to approve city policies and executive responsibilities to direct a functional area of city government, such as public safety or public works. See also **mayor-council government** and **council-manager government.**

committee chairs. The most important influencers of the congressional agenda. They play dominant roles in scheduling hearings, hiring staff, appointing subcommittees, and managing committee bills when they are brought before the full house.

committees (congressional). See **conference committees, joint committees, select committees,** and **standing committees.**

common law. The accumulation of judicial decisions applied in civil law disputes.

comparable worth. The issue raised when women are paid less than men for working at jobs requiring comparable skill.

conference committees. Congressional committees formed when the Senate and the House pass a particular **bill** in different forms. Party leadership appoints members from each house to iron out the differences and bring back a single bill. See also **standing committees, joint committees,** and **select committees.**

Congressional Budget and Impoundment Control Act of 1974. An act designed to reform the congressional budgetary process. Its supporters hoped that it would also make Congress less dependent on the president's budget and better able to set and meet its own budgetary goals.

Congressional Budget Office (CBO). A counterweight to the president's **Office of Management and Budget (OMB).** The CBO advises Congress on the probable consequences of budget decisions and forecasts revenues.

Connecticut Compromise. The compromise reached at the Constitutional Convention that established two houses of Congress: the House of Representatives, in which **representation** is based on a state's share of the U.S. population, and the Senate, in which each state has two representatives. Compare **New Jersey Plan** and **Virginia Plan.**

consensus. Agreement. Consensus is reflected by an opinion distribution in which a large majority see eye to eye.

consent of the governed. According to John Locke, the required basis for government. **The Declaration of Independence** reflects Locke's view that governments derive their authority from the consent of the governed.

conservatives. Those who advocate **conservatism.** Compare **liberals.**

constitution. A nation's basic law. It creates political institutions, assigns or divides powers in government, and often provides certain guarantees to citizens. Constitutions can be either written or unwritten. See also **U.S. Constitution.**

constitutional convention. A method of amending a state constitution in which voters may approve the calling of a convention of state citizens to propose amendments to the state constitution; the proposals are submitted to state voters for approval. See also **initiative** and **legislative proposal.**

constitutional courts. Lower federal courts of original jurisdiction created by Congress by the Judiciary Act of 1789. Compare **legislative courts.**

consumer price index (CPI). The key measure of **inflation** that relates the rise in prices over time.

containment doctrine. A **foreign policy** strategy advocated by George Kennan that called for the United States to isolate the Soviet Union, "contain" its advances, and resist its encroachments by peaceful means if possible, but by force if necessary.

continuing resolutions. When Congress cannot reach agreement and pass appropriations bills, these resolutions allow agencies to spend at the level of the previous year.

convention. See **national party convention.**

conversion. One of three key consequences of electoral campaigns for voters, in which the voter's mind is actually changed. See also **reinforcement** and **activation.**

cooperative federalism. A system of government in which powers and policy assignments are shared between states and the national government. They may also share costs, administration, and even blame for programs that work poorly. Compare **dual federalism.**

council-manager government. A common form of government used by municipalities in which voters elect a city council (and possibly an independent mayor) to make public policy for the city. The city council, in turn, appoints a professional city manager to serve as chief executive of the city and to administer public policy. See also **mayor-council government** and **commission government**.

Council of Economic Advisers (CEA). A three-member body appointed by the president to advise the president on economic policy.

council of governments (COG). Councils in many areas of the country where officials from various localities meet to discuss mutual problems and plan joint, cooperative action.

county. A political subdivision of state government that has a set of government officers to administer some local services—often on behalf of the state. Called a *parish* in Louisiana and a *borough* in Alaska. See also **county government**.

county government. A unit of local government that serves as the administrative arm of state government at the local level. It has many social service and record-keeping responsibilities. See also **county**.

court of last resort. The final appeals court in a state, often known as the state "supreme court."

courts. See **constitutional courts, legislative courts, district courts,** and **courts of appeal**.

courts of appeal. Appellate courts empowered to review all final decisions of district courts, except in rare cases. In addition, they also hear appeals to orders of many federal regulatory agencies. Compare **district courts**.

Craig v. Boren. In this 1976 Supreme Court decision, the Court determined that gender classification cases would have a "heightened" or "middle level" of scrutiny. In other words, the courts were to show less deference to gender classifications than to more routine classifications, but more deference than to racial classifications.

credit claiming. According to David Mayhew, one of three primary activities undertaken by members of Congress to increase the probability of their reelection. It involves personal and district service. See also **advertising** and **position taking**.

criminal law. The body of law involving a case in which an individual is charged with violating a specific law. The offense may be harmful to an individual or society and in either case warrants punishment, such as imprisonment or a fine. Compare **civil law**.

crisis. A sudden, unpredictable, and potentially dangerous event requiring the president to play the role of crisis manager.

critical election. An electoral "earthquake" whereby new issues emerge, new coalitions replace old ones, and the majority party is often displaced by the minority party. Critical election periods are sometimes marked by a national crisis and may require more than one election to bring about a new **party era**. See also **party realignment**.

cruel and unusual punishment. Court sentences prohibited by the **Eighth Amendment**. Although the Supreme Court has ruled that mandatory death sentences for certain offenses are unconstitutional, it has not held that the death penalty itself constitutes cruel and unusual punishment. See also *Furman v. Georgia, Gregg v. Georgia,* and *McClesky v. Kemp*.

culture of poverty. Negative attitudes and values toward work, family, and success that condemn the poor to low levels of accomplishment. The view that there is a culture of poverty is most commonly held by **conservatives**.

D

Dartmouth College v. Woodward. The 1819 case in which the Supreme Court held that Dartmouth's charter, as well as the charter of any corporation, is a legal contract that cannot be tampered with by a government.

dealignment. See **party dealignment**.

debate. See **presidential debate**.

debt. See **federal debt**.

Declaration of Independence. The document approved by representatives of the American colonies in 1776 that stated their grievances against the British monarch and declared their independence.

deficit. An excess of federal **expenditures** over federal **revenues**. See also **budget**.

delegate. See **instructed delegate**.

democracy. A system of selecting policymakers and of organizing government so that policy represents and responds to the public's preferences.

democratic theory. See **traditional democratic theory**.

demography. The science of population changes. See also **census**.

Dennis v. United States. A 1951 Supreme Court decision that permitted the government to jail several American Communist Party leaders under the Smith Act, a law forbidding advocacy of the violent overthrow of the U.S. government.

deregulation. The lifting of restrictions on business, industry, and professional activities for which government rules had been established and that bureaucracies had been created to administer.

détente. A slow transformation from conflict thinking to cooperative thinking in **foreign policy** strategy and policymaking. It sought a relaxation of tensions between the superpowers, coupled with firm guarantees of mutual security.

devolution. Transferring responsibility for policies from the federal government to state and local governments.

Dillon's Rule. The idea that local governments have only those powers that are explicitly given them by the states. This means that local governments have very little discretion over what policies they pursue or how they pursue them. It was named for Iowa Judge John Dillon, who expressed this idea in an 1868 court decision.

direct democracy. Procedures such as the initiative, the referendum, and the recall, by which voters can have a direct impact on policymaking and the political process by means of the voting booth.

direct mail. A high-tech method of raising money for a political cause or candidate. It involves sending information and requests for money to people whose names appear on lists of those who have supported similar views or candidates in the past.

direct primaries. Primaries used to select party nominees for congressional and state offices.

district courts. The 91 federal courts of original jurisdiction. They are the only federal courts in which no trials are held and in which juries may be empaneled. Compare **courts of appeal**.

dual federalism. A system of government in which both the states and the national government remain supreme within their own spheres, each responsible for some policies. Compare **cooperative federalism**.

due process clause. Part of the **Fourteenth Amendment** guaranteeing that persons cannot be deprived of life, liberty, or property by the United States or state governments without due process of law. See also *Gitlow v. New York*.

E

earned income tax credit (EITC). A "negative income tax" that provides income to very poor individuals in lieu of charging them federal tax.

efficacy. See **political efficacy**.

Eighth Amendment. The constitutional amendment that forbids **cruel and unusual punishment**, although it does not define this phrase. Through the **Fourteenth Amendment**, this **Bill of Rights** provision applies to the states.

elastic clause. The final paragraph of Article I, Section 8, of the Constitution, which authorizes Congress to pass all laws "necessary and proper" to carry out the enumerated powers. See also **implied powers**.

electioneering. Direct group involvement in the electoral process. Groups can help fund campaigns, provide testimony, and get members to work for candidates, and some form **political action committees (PACs)**.

electoral college. A unique American institution created by the Constitution that provides for the selection of the president by electors chosen by the state parties. Although the electoral college vote usually reflects a popular majority, the winner-take-all rule gives clout to big states.

electoral mandate. A concept based on the idea that "the people have spoken." It is a powerful symbol in American electoral politics, according legitimacy and credibility to a newly elected president's proposals. See also **mandate theory of politics**.

elite. The upper class in a society that utilizes wealth for political power. According to the **elite and class theory** of government and politics, elites control policies because they control key institutions.

elite theory. A theory of government and politics contending that societies are divided along class lines and that an upper-class elite will rule, regardless of the formal niceties of governmental organization. Compare **hyperpluralism, pluralist theory**, and **traditional democratic theory**.

Endangered Species Act of 1973. This law requires the federal government to protect actively each of the hundreds of species listed as endangered—regardless of the economic effect on the surrounding towns or region.

Engel v. Vitale. The 1962 Supreme Court decision holding that state officials violated the **First Amendment** when they wrote a prayer to be recited by New York's schoolchildren. Compare *School District of Abington Township, Pennsylvania v. Schempp*.

entitlement programs. Policies for which expenditures are uncontrollable because Congress has in effect obligated itself to pay X level of benefits to Y number of recipients. Each year, Congress' bill is a straightforward function of the X level of benefits times the Y number of beneficiaries. Social Security benefits are an example.

entrepreneur. See **political entrepreneur**.

enumerated powers. Powers of the federal government that are specifically addressed in the Constitution; for Congress, these powers are listed in Article I, Section 8, and include the power to coin money, regulate its value, and impose taxes. Compare **implied powers**.

environmental impact statement (EIS). A report filed with the **Environmental Protection Agency (EPA)** that specifies what environmental effects a proposed policy would have. The **National Environmental Policy Act** requires that whenever any agency proposes to undertake a policy that is potentially disruptive of the environment, the agency must file a statement with the EPA.

Environmental Protection Agency (EPA). An agency of the federal government created in 1970 and charged with administering all the government's environmental legislation. It also administers policies dealing with toxic wastes. The EPA is the largest federal **independent regulatory agency**.

equal opportunity. A policy statement about equality holding that the rules of the game should be the same for everyone. Most of our **civil rights** policies over the past three decades have presumed that equality of opportunity is a public policy goal. Compare **equal results**.

equal protection of the laws. Part of the **Fourteenth Amendment** emphasizing that the laws must provide equivalent "protection" to all people. As one member of Congress said during debate on the amendment, it should provide "equal protection of life, liberty, and property" to all a state's citizens.

equal results. A policy statement about equality holding that government has a duty to help break down barriers to **equal opportunity**. **Affirmative action** is an example of a policy justified as promoting equal results rather than merely equal opportunities.

Equal Rights Amendment (ERA). A constitutional amendment originally introduced in 1923 and passed by Congress in 1972 and sent to the state legislatures for ratification, stating that "equality of rights under the law shall not be denied or abridged by the United States or by any state on account of sex." Despite substantial public support and an extended deadline, the amendment failed to acquire the necessary support from three-fourths of the state legislatures.

establishment clause. Part of the **First Amendment** stating that "Congress shall make no law respecting an establishment of religion."

European Union (EU). An alliance of the major Western European nations that coordinates monetary, trade, immigration, and labor policies, making its members one economic unit. An example of a regional organization.

exclusionary rule. The rule that evidence, no matter how incriminating, cannot be introduced into a trial if it was not constitutionally obtained. The rule prohibits use of evidence obtained through **unreasonable search and seizure**.

executive agency. See **independent executive agency**.

executive orders. Regulations originating from the executive branch. Executive orders are one method presidents can use to control the bureaucracy; more often, though, presidents pass along their wishes through their aides.

exit poll. Public opinion surveys used by major media pollsters to predict electoral winners with speed and precision.

expenditures. Federal spending of **revenues**. Major areas of such spending are social services and the military.

extradition. A legal process whereby an alleged criminal offender is surrendered by the officials of one state to officials of the state in which the crime is alleged to have been committed.

F

facilitator. According to George Edwards, the effective leader who works at the margin of coalition building to recognize and exploit opportunities presented by a favorable configuration of political forces.

factions. Interest groups arising from the unequal distribution of property or wealth that James Madison attacked in *Federalist Paper No. 10*. Today's parties or interest groups are what Madison had in mind when he warned of the instability in government caused by factions.

federal debt. All the money borrowed by the federal government over the years and still outstanding. Today the federal debt is more than $8 trillion.

Federal Election Campaign Act. A law passed in 1974 for reforming campaign finances. The act created the **Federal Election Commission (FEC)**, provided public financing for presidential primaries and general elections, limited presidential campaign spending, required disclosure, and attempted to limit contributions.

Federal Election Commission (FEC). A six-member bipartisan agency created by the **Federal Election Campaign Act** of 1974. The FEC administers the campaign finance laws and enforces compliance with their requirements.

Federal Regulation of Lobbying Act. Passed in 1946, an act requiring congressional lobbyists to register and state their policy goals. According to the Supreme Court, the law applies only to groups whose "principal" purpose is **lobbying**.

Federal Reserve System. The main instrument for making **monetary policy** in the United States. It was created by Congress in 1913 to regulate the lending practices of banks and thus the money supply. The seven members of its Board of Governors are appointed to 14-year terms by the president with the consent of the Senate.

Federal Trade Commission (FTC). The **independent regulatory agency** traditionally responsible for regulating false and misleading trade practices. The FTC has recently become active in defending consumer interests through its truth-in-advertising rule and the Consumer Credit Protection Act.

federalism. A way of organizing a nation so that two levels of government have formal authority over the same land and people. It is a system of shared power between units of government. Compare **unitary government**.

Federalist Papers. A collection of 85 articles written by Alexander Hamilton, John Jay, and James Madison under the name "Publius" to defend the Constitution in detail. Collectively, these papers are second only to the U.S. **Constitution** in characterizing the framers' intents.

Federalists. Supporters of the U.S. **Constitution** at the time the states were contemplating its adoption. See also **Anti-Federalists** and **Federalist Papers**.

feminization of poverty. The increasing concentration of poverty among women, especially unmarried women and their children.

Fifteenth Amendment. The constitutional amendment adopted in 1870 to extend **suffrage** to African Americans.

Fifth Amendment. The constitutional amendment designed to protect the rights of persons accused of crimes, including protection against double jeopardy, **self-incrimination**, and punishment without due process of law.

filibuster. A strategy unique to the Senate whereby opponents of a piece of legislation try to talk it to death, based on the tradition of unlimited debate. Today, 60 members present and voting can halt a filibuster.

First Amendment. The constitutional amendment that establishes the four great liberties: freedom of the press, of speech, of religion, and of assembly.

fiscal federalism. The pattern of spending, taxing, and providing grants in the federal system; it is the cornerstone of the national government's relations with state and local governments. See also **federalism**.

fiscal policy. The policy that describes the impact of the federal budget—taxes, spending, and borrowing—on the economy. Unlike **monetary policy**, which is mostly controlled by the **Federal Reserve System**, fiscal policy is almost entirely determined by Congress and the president, who are the budget makers. See also **Keynesian economic theory**.

Food and Drug Administration (FDA). The federal agency formed in 1913 and assigned the task of approving all food products and drugs sold in the United States. All drugs, with the exception of tobacco, must have FDA authorization.

foreign policy. A policy that involves choice taking, like domestic policy, but additionally involves choices about relations with the rest of the world. The president is the chief initiator of foreign policy in the United States.

formula grants. Federal **categorical grants** distributed according to a formula specified in legislation or in administrative regulations.

Fourteenth Amendment. The constitutional amendment adopted after the Civil War that states, "No State shall make or enforce any law which shall abridge the privileges or immunities of citizens of the United States; nor shall any state deprive any person of life, liberty, or property, without due process of law; nor deny to any person within its jurisdiction the **equal protection of the laws**." See also **due process clause**.

fragmentation. A situation in which responsibility for a policy area is dispersed among several units within the bureaucracy, making the coordination of policies both time consuming and difficult.

free exercise clause. A **First Amendment** provision that prohibits government from interfering with the practice of religion.

free-rider problem. The problem faced by unions and other groups when people do not join because they can benefit from the group's activities without officially joining. The bigger the group, the more serious the free-rider problem. See also **interest group**.

frontloading. The recent tendency of states to hold primaries early in the calendar in order to capitalize on media attention. At one time, it was considered advantageous for a state to choose its delegates late in the primary season so that it could play a decisive role. However, in recent years, votes cast in states that have held late primaries have been irrelevant given that one candidate had already sewn up the nomination early on.

full faith and credit clause. A clause in Article IV, Section 1, of the Constitution requiring each state to recognize the official documents and civil judgments rendered by the courts of other states.

G

gender gap. A term that refers to the regular pattern by which women are more likely to support Democratic candidates. Women tend to be significantly less conservative than men and are more likely to support spending on social services and to oppose higher levels of military spending.

General Schedule rating. See **GS (General Schedule) rating.**

Gibbons v. Ogden. A landmark case decided in 1824 in which the Supreme Court interpreted very broadly the clause in Article I, Section 8, of the Constitution giving Congress the power to regulate interstate commerce, encompassing virtually every form of commercial activity. The commerce clause has been the constitutional basis for much of Congress' regulation of the economy.

Gideon v. Wainwright. The 1963 Supreme Court decision holding that anyone accused of a felony where imprisonment may be imposed, however poor he or she might be, has a right to a lawyer. See also **Sixth Amendment.**

Gitlow v. New York. The 1925 Supreme Court decision holding that freedoms of press and speech are "fundamental personal rights and liberties protected by the **due process clause** of the **Fourteenth Amendment** from impairment by the states" as well as the federal government. Compare *Barron v. Baltimore.*

government. The institutions and processes through which **public policies** are made for a society.

governmental corporation. A government organization that, like business corporations, provides a service that could be provided by the private sector and typically charges for its services. The U.S. Postal Service is an example. Compare **independent regulatory agency** and **independent executive agency.**

governor. The elected chief executive of state government who directs the administration of state government and the implementation of public policy in the state.

Gramm-Rudman-Hollings. Named for its sponsors and also known as the Balanced Budget and Emergency Deficit Act, legislation mandating maximum allowable deficit levels each year until 1991, when the budget was to be balanced. In 1987, the balanced budget year was shifted to 1993, but the Act was abandoned in 1991.

grandfather clause. One of the methods used by Southern states to deny African Americans the right to vote. In order to exempt illiterate Whites from taking a literacy test before voting, the clause exempted people whose grandfathers were eligible to vote in 1860, thereby disenfranchising the grandchildren of slaves. The grandfather clause was declared unconstitutional by the Supreme Court in 1913. See also **poll taxes** and **White primary.**

grants. See **categorical grants** and **block grants.**

Gregg v. Georgia. The 1976 Supreme Court decision that upheld the constitutionality of the death penalty, stating that "It is an extreme sanction, suitable to the most extreme of crimes." The court did not, therefore, believe that the death sentence constitutes **cruel and unusual punishment.**

gross domestic product. The sum total of the value of all the goods and services produced in a nation.

GS (General Schedule) rating. A schedule for federal employees, ranging from GS 1 to GS 18, by which salaries can be keyed to rating and experience. See **civil service.**

H

Hatch Act. A federal law prohibiting government employees from active participation in partisan politics.

health maintenance organizations (HMOs). Organizations contracted by individuals or insurance companies to provide health care for a yearly fee. Such network health plans limit the choice of doctors and treatments. About 60 percent of Americans are enrolled in HMOs or similar programs.

Hernandez v. Texas A 1954 Supreme Court decision that extended protection against discrimination to Hispanics.

high-tech politics. A politics in which the behavior of citizens and policymakers and the political agenda itself are increasingly shaped by technology.

home rule. The practice by which municipalities are permitted by the states to write their own charters and change them without permission of the state legislature, within limits. Today this practice is widely used to organize and modernize municipal government. See also **local charter.**

House Rules Committee. An institution unique to the House of Representatives that reviews all bills (except revenue, budget, and appropriations bills) coming from a House committee before they go to the full House.

House Ways and Means Committee. The House of Representatives committee that, along with the **Senate Finance Committee,** writes the tax codes, subject to the approval of Congress as a whole.

hyperpluralism. A theory of government and politics contending that groups are so strong that government is weakened. Hyperpluralism is an extreme, exaggerated, or perverted form of **pluralism.** Compare **elite and class theory, pluralist theory,** and **traditional democratic theory.**

I

ideology. See **political ideology.**

impacts. See **policy impacts.**

impeachment. The political equivalent of an indictment in criminal law, prescribed by the Constitution. The House of Representatives may impeach the president by a majority vote for "Treason, Bribery, or other high Crimes and Misdemeanors."

implementation. The stage of policymaking between the establishment of a policy and the consequences of the policy for the people whom it affects. Implementation involves translating the goals and objectives of a policy into an operating, ongoing program. See also **judicial implementation.**

implied powers. Powers of the federal government that go beyond those enumerated in the Constitution. The Constitution states that Congress has the power to "make all laws necessary and proper for carrying into execution" the powers enumerated in Article I. Many federal policies are justified on the basis of implied powers. See also *McCulloch v. Maryland*, **elastic clause**, and **enumerated powers**.

incentive system. According to Charles Shultze, a more effective and efficient policy than **command-and-control**; in the incentive system, market-like strategies are used to manage public policy.

income. The amount of funds collected between any two points in time. Compare **wealth**.

income distribution. The "shares" of the national income earned by various groups.

income tax. Shares of individual wages and corporate revenues collected by the government. The first income tax was declared unconstitutional by the Supreme Court in 1895, but the **Sixteenth Amendment** explicitly authorized Congress to levy a tax on income. See also **Internal Revenue Service**.

incorporation doctrine. The legal concept under which the **Supreme Court** has nationalized the **Bill of Rights** by making most of its provisions applicable to the states through the **Fourteenth Amendment**.

incrementalism. The belief that the best predictor of this year's **budget** is last year's budget, plus a little bit more (an increment). According to Aaron Wildavsky, "Most of the budget is a product of previous decisions."

incumbents. Those already holding office. In congressional elections, incumbents usually win.

independent executive agency. The government not accounted for by **cabinet** departments, **independent regulatory agencies**, and **government corporations**. Its administrators are typically appointed by the president and serve at the president's pleasure. NASA is an example.

independent regulatory agency. A government agency responsible for some sector of the economy, making and enforcing rules supposedly to protect the public interest. It also judges disputes over these rules. Compare **government corporation** and **independent executive agency**.

industrial policy. An economic policy that advocates the federal government's support of key strategic industries, such as the making of computer chips, and protection of these industries from foreign competition by tariffs and other measures.

INF Treaty. The elimination of intermediate range nuclear forces (INF) through an agreement signed by President Reagan and Mikhail Gorbachev during the May 1988 Moscow summit. It was the first treaty to reduce current levels of nuclear weapons.

inflation. The rise in prices for consumer goods. Inflation hurts some but actually benefits others. Groups such as those who live on fixed incomes are particularly hard hit, while people whose salary increases are tied to the **consumer price index** but whose loan rates are fixed may enjoy increased buying power.

initiative. A process permitted in some states whereby voters may put proposed changes in the state constitution to a vote if sufficient signatures are obtained on petitions calling for such a referendum. See also **legislative proposal** and **constitutional convention**.

instructed delegate. A legislator who mirrors the preferences of his or her constituents. Compare **trustee**.

interdependency. Mutual dependency, in which the actions of nations reverberate and affect one another's economic lifelines.

interest group. An organization of people with shared policy goals entering the policy process at several points to try to achieve those goals. Interest groups pursue their goals in many arenas.

intergenerational equity. The issue of the distribution of government benefits and burdens among the generations and over time. Affected groups include children, the working and middle classes, and the elderly, all of whom are beneficiaries of public policies.

intergovernmental relations. The workings of the federal system—the entire set of interactions among national, state, and local governments.

Internal Revenue Service. The office established to collect federal **income taxes**, investigate violations of the tax laws, and prosecute tax criminals.

investigative journalism. The use of in-depth reporting to unearth scandals, scams, and schemes, which at times puts reporters in adversarial relationships with political leaders.

iron triangles. Entities composed of bureaucratic agencies, interest groups, and congressional committees or subcommittees, which have dominated some areas of domestic policymaking. Iron triangles are characterized by mutual dependency, in which each element provides key services, information, or policy for the others.

isolationism. A **foreign policy** course followed throughout most of our nation's history, whereby the United States has tried to stay out of other nations' conflicts, particularly European wars. Isolationism was reaffirmed by the Monroe Doctrine.

issue. See **political issue**.

item veto. The power possessed by 42 state governors to veto only certain parts of a bill while allowing the rest of it to pass into law.

J

Joint Chiefs of Staff. The commanding officers of the armed services who advise the president on military policy.

joint committees. Congressional committees on a few subject-matter areas with membership drawn from both houses. See also **standing committees**, **conference committees**, and **select committees**.

judicial activism. A judicial philosophy in which judges make bold policy decisions, even charting new constitutional ground. Advocates of this approach emphasize that the courts can correct pressing needs, especially those unmet by the majoritarian political process.

judicial implementation. How and whether court decisions are translated into actual policy, affecting the behavior of others. The courts rely on other units of government to enforce their decisions.

judicial interpretation. A major informal way in which the Constitution is changed by the courts as they balance citizens' rights against those of the government. See also **judicial review**.

judicial restraint. A judicial philosophy in which judges play minimal policymaking roles, leaving that strictly to the legislatures. Compare **judicial activism**.

judicial review. The power of the courts to determine whether acts of Congress, and by implication the executive, are in accord with the **U.S. Constitution**. Judicial review was established by

John Marshall and his associates in *Marbury v. Madison*. See also **judicial interpretation**.

jurisdiction. See **original jurisdiction** and **appellate jurisdiction**.

justiciable disputes. A constraint on the courts, requiring that a case must be capable of being settled by legal methods.

K

Keynesian economic theory. The theory emphasizing that government spending and deficits can help the economy weather its normal ups and downs. Proponents of this theory advocate using the power of government to stimulate the economy when it is lagging. See also **fiscal policy**.

Korematsu v. United States. A 1944 Supreme Court decision that upheld as constitutional the internment of more than 100,000 Americans of Japanese descent in encampments during World War II.

L

labor union. An organization of workers intended to engage in **collective bargaining**.

laissez-faire. The principle that government should not meddle in the economy. See also **capitalism**.

leak. See **news leak**.

legislative courts. Courts established by Congress for specialized purposes, such as the Court of Military Appeals. Judges who serve on these courts have fixed terms and lack the protections of **constitutional court** judges.

legislative oversight. Congress's monitoring of the bureaucracy and its administration of policy, performed mainly through hearings.

legislative proposal. A method of state constitutional revision in which the state legislature offers a proposed change to state voters for approval (or may be used to describe a bill proposed by a legislator). See also **constitutional convention** and **initiative**.

legislative turnover. The rate at which incumbent state legislators leave office by choice or by defeat during a bid for reelection.

legislative veto. The ability of Congress to override a presidential decision. Although the **War Powers Resolution** asserts this authority, there is reason to believe that, if challenged, the Supreme Court would find the legislative veto in violation of the doctrine of separation of powers.

legislators. The elected representatives of state citizens who serve in the state legislature and make public policy.

legitimacy. A characterization of elections by political scientists meaning that they are almost universally accepted as a fair and free method of selecting political leaders. When legitimacy is high, as in the United States, even the losers accept the results peacefully.

Lemon v. Kurtzman. The 1971 Supreme Court decision that established that aid to church-related schools must (1) have a secular legislative purpose (2) have a primary effect that neither advances nor inhibits religion and (3) not foster excessive government entanglement with religion.

libel. The publication of false or malicious statements that damage someone's reputation.

liberalism. A **political ideology** whose advocates prefer a government active in dealing with human needs, support individual rights and liberties, and give higher priority to social needs than to military needs.

lieutenant governor. Often the second-highest executive official in state government, who is elected with the governor as a ticket in some states and is elected separately in others. May have legislative and executive branch responsibilities.

limited government. The idea that certain things are out of bounds for government because of the **natural rights** of citizens. Limited government was central to John Locke's philosophy in the seventeenth century, and it contrasted sharply with the prevailing view of the divine rights of monarchs.

line-item veto. The power possessed by 42 state governors to veto only certain parts of a bill while allowing the rest of it to pass into law.

linkage institutions. The channels or access points through which issues and people's policy preferences get on the government's **policy agenda**. In the United States, elections, **political parties**, **interest groups**, and the **mass media** are the three main linkage institutions.

litigants. The **plaintiff** and the **defendant** in a case.

lobbying. According to Lester Milbrath, a "communication, by someone other than a citizen acting on his own behalf, directed to a governmental decisionmaker with the hope of influencing his decision."

local charter. An organizational statement and grant of authority from the state to a local government, much like a state or federal constitution. States sometimes allow municipalities to write their own charters and to change them without permission of the state legislature, within limits. See also **home rule**.

M

majority leader. The principal partisan ally of the Speaker of the House or the party's wheel horse in the Senate. The majority leader is responsible for scheduling bills, influencing committee assignments, and rounding up votes in behalf of the party's legislative positions.

majority rule. A fundamental principle of **traditional democratic theory**. In a democracy, choosing among alternatives requires that the majority's desire be respected. See also **minority rights**.

mandate. See **electoral mandate** and **mandate theory of elections**.

mandate theory of elections. The idea that the winning candidate has a mandate from the people to carry out his or her platforms and politics. Politicians like the theory better than political scientists do.

Mapp v. Ohio. The 1961 Supreme Court decision ruling that the Fourth Amendment's protection against **unreasonable searches and seizures** must be extended to the states as well as the federal government. See also **exclusionary rule**.

Marbury v. Madison. The 1803 case in which Chief Justice John Marshall and his associates first asserted the right of the **Supreme Court** to determine the meaning of the **U.S. Constitution**. The decision established the Court's power of **judicial review** over acts of Congress, in this case the Judiciary Act of 1789.

mass media. Television, radio, newspapers, magazines, and other means of popular communication. They are a key part of **high-tech politics**. See also **broadcast media** and **print media**.

matching funds. Contributions of up to $250 are matched from the Presidential Election Campaign Fund to candidates for the presidential nomination who qualify and agree to meet various conditions, such as limiting their overall spending.

mayor–council government. One of three common forms of municipal government in which voters elect both a mayor and a city council. In the weak mayor form, the city council is more powerful; in the strong mayor form, the mayor is the chief executive of city government. See also **council–manager government**.

McCarthyism. The fear, prevalent in the 1950s, that international communism was conspiratorial, insidious, bent on world domination, and infiltrating American government and cultural institutions. It was named after Senator Joseph McCarthy and flourished after the Korean War.

McCleskey v. Kemp. The 1987 Supreme Court decision that upheld the constitutionality of the death penalty against charges that it violated the **Fourteenth Amendment** because minority defendants were more likely to receive the death penalty than White defendants.

McCulloch v. Maryland. An 1819 Supreme Court decision that established the supremacy of the national government over state governments. In deciding this case, Chief Justice John Marshall and his colleagues held that Congress had certain **implied powers** in addition to the **enumerated powers** found in the Constitution.

McGovern-Fraser Commission. A commission formed at the 1968 Democratic convention in response to demands for reform by minority groups and others who sought better representation.

means-tested programs. Government programs available only to individuals below a poverty line.

media events. Events purposely staged for the media that nonetheless look spontaneous. In keeping with politics as theater, media events can be staged by individuals, groups, and government officials, especially presidents.

Medicaid. A public assistance program designed to provide health care for poor Americans. Medicaid is funded by both the states and the national government. Compare **Medicare**.

Medicare. A program added to the Social Security system in 1965 that provides hospitalization insurance for the elderly and permits older Americans to purchase inexpensive coverage for doctor fees and other expenses. Compare **Medicaid**.

melting pot. The mixing of cultures, ideas, and peoples that has changed the American nation. The United States, with its history of immigration, has often been called a melting pot.

merit plan. A hybrid system of appointment and election used to select judges in 17 states. In this system the governor appoints the state's judges from a list of recommended persons; an appointed judge then serves a short "trial run" term, after which a retention election is held. If voters approve retention by a majority vote, then the judge continues in office for a lengthy term.

merit principle. The idea that hiring should be based on entrance exams and promotion ratings to produce administration by people with talent and skill. See also **civil service** and compare **patronage**.

Miami Herald Publishing Company v. Tornillo. A 1974 case in which the Supreme Court held that a state could not force a newspaper to print replies from candidates it had criticized, illustrating the limited power of government to restrict the **print media**. See *Red Lion Broadcasting Company v. FCC.*

Miller v. California. A 1973 Supreme Court decision that avoided defining obscenity by holding that community standards be used to determine whether material is obscene in terms of appealing to a "prurient interest."

minimum wage. The legal minimum hourly wage for large employers, currently $5.15 per hour.

minority leader. The principal leader of the minority party in the House of Representatives or in the Senate.

minority majority. The emergence of a non-Caucasian majority, as compared with a White, generally Anglo-Saxon majority. It is predicted that, by about 2060, Hispanic Americans, African Americans, and Asian Americans together will outnumber White Americans.

minority rights. A principle of **traditional democratic theory** that guarantees rights to those who do not belong to majorities and allows that they might join majorities through persuasion and reasoned argument. See also **majority rule**.

Miranda v. Arizona. The 1966 Supreme Court decision that sets guidelines for police questioning of accused persons to protect them against **self-incrimination** and to protect their right to counsel.

mixed economy. An economic system in which the government is deeply involved in economic decisions through its role as regulator, consumer, subsidizer, taxer, employer, and borrower. The United States can be considered a mixed economy. Compare **capitalism**.

monetarism. An economic theory holding that the supply of money is the key to a nation's economic health. Monetarists believe that too much cash and credit in circulation produces inflation. See also **monetary policy**.

monetary policy. Based on **monetarism**, monetary policy is the manipulation of the supply of money in private hands by which the government can control the economy. See also the **Federal Reserve System**, and compare **fiscal policy**.

Motor Voter Act. Passed in 1993, this act went into effect for the 1996 election. It requires states to permit people to register to vote at the same time they apply for driver's licenses.

multinational corporations. Large businesses with vast holdings in many countries. Many of these companies are larger than most governments.

municipalities. Another name for *cities*, also known by the legal term *municipal corporations*; denotes a government created by charter granted from the state government or by home rule charter approved by local voters.

N

NAACP v. Alabama. The Supreme Court protected the right to assemble peaceably in this 1958 case when it decided the NAACP did not have to reveal its membership list and thus subject its members to harassment.

238

narrowcasting. As opposed to the traditional "broadcasting," the appeal to a narrow, particular audience by channels such as ESPN, MTV, and C-SPAN, which focus on a narrow particular interest.

national chairperson. One of the institutions that keeps the party operating between conventions. The national chairperson is responsible for the day-to-day activities of the party and is usually selected by the presidential nominee. See also **national committee.**

national committee. One of the institutions that keeps the party operating between conventions. The national committee is composed of representatives from the states and territories. See also **national chairperson.**

national convention. The meeting of party delegates every four years to choose a presidential ticket and write the party's platform.

National Environmental Policy Act (NEPA). The law passed in 1969 that is the centerpiece of federal environmental policy in the United States. The NEPA established the requirements for **environmental impact statements.**

national health insurance. A compulsory insurance program for all Americans that would have the government finance citizens' medical care. First proposed by President Harry S Truman, the plan has been soundly opposed by the American Medical Association.

National Labor Relations Act. A 1935 law, also known as the Wagner Act, that guarantees workers the right of **collective bargaining,** sets down rules to protect unions and organizers, and created the National Labor Relations Board to regulate labor management relations.

national party convention. The supreme power within each of the parties. The convention meets every four years to nominate the party's presidential and vice-presidential candidates and to write the party's platform.

national primary. A proposal by critics of the **caucuses** and **presidential primaries** systems who would replace these electoral methods with a nationwide **primary** held early in the election year.

National Security Council. An office created in 1947 to coordinate the president's foreign and military policy advisers. Its formal members are the president, vice president, **secretary of state,** and **secretary of defense,** and it is managed by the president's national security assistant.

NATO. See **North Atlantic Treaty Organization.**

natural rights. Rights inherent in human beings, not dependent on governments, which include life, liberty, and property. The concept of natural rights was central to English philosopher John Locke's theories about government, and was widely accepted among America's Founding Fathers. Thomas Jefferson echoed Locke's language in drafting the Declaration of Independence.

Near v. Minnesota. The 1931 Supreme Court decision holding that the First Amendment protects newspapers from **prior restraint.**

necessary and proper clause. See **elastic clause.**

New Deal Coalition. A coalition forged by the Democrats, who dominated American politics from the 1930s to the 1960s. Its basic elements were the urban working class, ethnic groups, Catholics and Jews, the poor, Southerners, African Americans, and intellectuals.

New Jersey Plan. The proposal at the Constitutional Convention that called for equal **representation** of each state in Congress regardless of the state's population. Compare **Virginia Plan** and **Connecticut Compromise.**

New York Times v. Sullivan. Decided in 1964, this case established the guidelines for determining whether public officials and public figures could win damage suits for libel. To do so, said the Court, such individuals must prove that the defamatory statements made about them were made with "actual malice" and reckless disregard for the truth.

news leak. A carefully placed bit of inside information given to a friendly reporter. Leaks can benefit both the leaker and the leakee.

newspaper chains. Newspapers published by massive media conglomerates that account for almost three-quarters of the nation's daily circulation. Often these chains control **broadcast media** as well.

Nineteenth Amendment. The constitutional amendment adopted in 1920 that guarantees women the right to vote. See also **suffrage.**

nomination. The official endorsement of a candidate for office by a **political party.** Generally, success in the nomination game requires momentum, money, and media attention.

nonrenewable resources. Minerals and other resources that nature does not replace when they are consumed. Many commonly used energy resources, such as oil and coal, are nonrenewable.

North Atlantic Treaty Organization (NATO). Created in 1949, an organization whose members include the United States, Canada, most Western European nations, and Turkey, all of whom agreed to combine military forces and to treat a war against one as a war against all. Compare **Warsaw Pact.**

O

Office of Management and Budget (OMB). An office that grew out of the Bureau of the Budget, created in 1921, consisting of a handful of political appointees and hundreds of skilled professionals. The OMB performs both managerial and budgetary functions, and although the president is its boss, the director and staff have considerable independence in the budgetary process. See also **Congressional Budget Office.**

Office of Personnel Management (OPM). The office in charge of hiring for most agencies of the federal government, using elaborate rules in the process.

Olson's law of large groups. Advanced by Mancur Olson, a principle stating that "the larger the group, the further it will fall short of providing an optimal amount of a collective good." See also **interest group.**

OPEC. See **Organization of Petroleum Exporting Countries.**

open primaries. Elections to select party nominees in which voters can decide on Election Day whether they want to participate in the Democratic or Republican contests. See also **primaries.**

opinion. A statement of legal reasoning behind a judicial decision. The content of an opinion may be as important as the decision itself.

Organization of Petroleum Exporting Countries (OPEC). An economic organization, consisting primarily of Arab nations, that controls the price of oil and the amount of oil its members produce and sell to other nations. The Arab members of OPEC caused the oil boycott in the winter of 1973–1974.

original intent. A view that the Constitution should be interpreted according to the original intent of the framers. Many **conservatives** support this view.

original jurisdiction. The jurisdiction of courts that hear a case first, usually in a trial. These are the courts that determine the facts about a case. Compare **appellate jurisdiction.**

oversight. The process of monitoring the bureaucracy and its administration of policy, mainly through congressional hearings.

P

PACs. See **political action committees (PACs).**

parliamentary governments. Governments, like the one in Great Britain, that typically select the political leader from membership in the parliament (the legislature).

participation. See **political participation.**

party. See **political party.**

party competition. The battle of the parties for control of public offices. Ups and downs of the two major parties are one of the most important elements in American politics.

party dealignment. The gradual disengagement of people and politicians from the parties, as seen in part by shrinking **party identification.**

party eras. Historical periods in which a majority of voters cling to the party in power, which tends to win a majority of the elections. See also **critical election** and **party realignment.**

party identification. A citizen's self-proclaimed preference for one party or the other.

party image. The voter's perception of what the Republicans or Democrats stand for, such as **conservatism** or **liberalism.**

party machines. A type of political party organization that relies heavily on material inducements, such as patronage, to win votes and to govern.

party platform. A political party's statement of its goals and policies for the next four years. The platform is drafted prior to the party convention by a committee whose members are chosen in rough proportion to each candidate's strength. It is the best formal statement of what a party believes in.

party realignment. The displacement of the majority party by the minority party, usually during a **critical election period.** See also **party eras.**

patients' bill of rights. A controversial proposal before Congress that would give patients certain rights against medical providers, particularly HMOs, including the right to sue.

patronage. One of the key inducements used by political machines. A patronage job, promotion, or contract is one that is given for political reasons rather than for merit or competence alone. Compare **civil service** and the **merit principle.**

Pendleton Civil Service Act. Passed in 1883, an act that created a federal **civil service** so that hiring and promotion would be based on merit rather than **patronage.**

***per curiam* decision.** A court decision without explanation—in other words, without an **opinion.**

Personal Responsibility and Work Opportunity Reconciliation Act (PRWORA). The official name of the welfare reform law of 1996.

Planned Parenthood v. Casey. A 1992 case in which the Supreme Court loosened its standard for evaluating restrictions on abortion from one of "strict scrutiny" of any restraints on a "fundamental right" to one of "undue burden" that permits considerably more regulation.

plea bargaining. A bargain struck between the defendant's lawyer and the prosecutor to the effect that the defendant will plead guilty to a lesser crime (or fewer crimes) in exchange for the state's promise not to prosecute the defendant for a more serious (or additional) crime.

Plessy v. Ferguson. An 1896 Supreme Court decision that provided a constitutional justification for segregation by ruling that a Louisiana law requiring "equal but separate accommodations for the white and colored races" was not unconstitutional.

pluralist theory. A theory of government and politics emphasizing that politics is mainly a competition among groups, each one pressing for its own preferred policies. Compare **elite and class theory, hyperpluralism,** and **traditional democratic theory.**

pocket veto. A veto taking place when Congress adjourns within ten days of having submitted a **bill** to the president, who simply lets it die by neither signing nor vetoing it. See also **veto.**

policy. See **public policy.**

policy agenda. The issues that attract the serious attention of public officials and other people actually involved in politics at any given point in time.

policy differences. The perception of a clear choice between the parties. Those who see such choices are more likely to vote.

policy entrepreneurs. People who invest their political "capital" in an issue. According to John Kingdon, a policy entrepreneur "could be in or out of government, in elected or appointed positions, in interest groups or research organizations."

policy gridlock. A condition that occurs when no coalition is strong enough to form a majority and establish policy. The result is that nothing may get done.

policy impacts. The effects a policy has on people and problems. Impacts are analyzed to see how well a policy has met its goal and at what cost.

policy implementation. See **implementation.**

policymaking institutions. The branches of government charged with taking action on political issues. The U.S. Constitution established three policymaking institutions—the Congress, the presidency, and the courts. Today, the power of the bureaucracy is so great that most political scientists consider it a fourth policymaking institution.

policymaking system. The process by which political problems are communicated by the voters and acted upon by government policymakers. The policymaking system begins with people's needs and expectations for governmental action. When people confront government officials with problems that they want solved, they are trying to influence the government's policy agenda.

policy voting. Electoral choices that are made on the basis of the voters' policy preferences and on the basis of where the candidates stand on policy issues.

political action committees (PACs). Funding vehicles created by the 1974 campaign finance reforms. A corporation, union, or some other interest group can create a PAC and register it with the **Federal Election Commission (FEC)**, which will meticulously monitor the PAC's expenditures.

political culture. An overall set of values widely shared within a society.

political efficacy. The belief that one's **political participation** really matters—that one's vote can actually make a difference.

political ideology. A coherent set of beliefs about politics, public policy, and public purpose. It helps give meaning to political events, personalities, and policies. See also **liberalism** and **conservatism**.

political issue. An issue that arises when people disagree about a problem and a public policy choice.

political participation. All the activities used by citizens to influence the selection of political leaders or the policies they pursue. The most common, but not the only, means of political participation in a **democracy** is voting. Other means include **protest** and **civil disobedience**.

political party. According to Anthony Downs, a "team of men [and women] seeking to control the governing apparatus by gaining office in a duly constituted election."

political questions. A doctrine developed by the federal courts and used as a means to avoid deciding some cases, principally those involving conflicts between the president and Congress.

political socialization. According to Richard Dawson, "the process through which an individual acquires his [or her] particular political orientations—his [or her] knowledge, feelings, and evaluations regarding his [or her] political world." See also **agents of socialization**.

political system. A set of institutions and activities that link together people, politics, and policy.

politics. The process by which we select our governmental leaders and what policies these leaders pursue. Politics produces authoritative decisions about public issues.

poll taxes. Small taxes, levied on the right to vote, that often fell due at a time of year when poor African American sharecroppers had the least cash on hand. This method was used by most Southern states to exclude African Americans from voting registers. Poll taxes were declared void by the **Twenty-fourth Amendment in 1964**. See also **grandfather clause** and **White primary**.

polls. See **exit polls**.

pork barrel. The mighty list of federal projects, grants, and contracts available to cities, businesses, colleges, and institutions available in a congressional district.

position taking. According to David Mayhew, one of three primary activities undertaken by members of Congress to increase the probability of their reelection. It involves taking a stand on issues and responding to constituents about these positions. See also **advertising** and **credit taking**.

potential group. All the people who might be **interest group** members because they share some common interest. A potential group is almost always larger than an actual group.

poverty line. A method used to count the number of poor people, it considers what a family would need to spend for an "austere" standard of living.

power. The capacity to get people to do something they would not otherwise do. The quest for power is a strong motivation to political activity.

precedent. How similar cases have been decided in the past.

presidential approval. An evaluation of the president based on many factors, but especially on the predisposition of many people to support the president. One measure is provided by the Gallup Poll.

presidential coattails. The situation occurring when voters cast their ballots for congressional candidates of the president's party because they support the president. Recent studies show that few races are won this way.

presidential debate. A debate between presidential candidates. The first televised debate was between Richard Nixon and John Kennedy during the 1960 campaign.

Presidential Election Campaign Fund. Money from the $3 federal income tax check-off goes into this fund, which is then distributed to qualified candidates to subsidize their presidential campaigns.

presidential primaries. Elections in which voters in a state vote for a candidate (or delegates pledged to him or her). Most delegates to the **national party conventions** are chosen this way.

press conferences. Meetings of public officials with reporters.

press secretary. The person on the White House staff who most often deals directly with the press, serving as a conduit of information. Press secretaries conduct daily press briefings.

primaries. Elections that select candidates. In addition to **presidential primaries**, there are **direct primaries** for selecting party nominees for congressional and state offices and proposals for **regional primaries**.

print media. Newspapers and magazines, as compared with **broadcast media**.

prior restraint. A government's preventing material from being published. This is a common method of limiting the press in some nations, but it is usually unconstitutional in the United States, according to the **First Amendment** and as confirmed in the 1931 Supreme Court case of *Near v. Minnesota*.

privacy. See **right to privacy**.

privileges and immunities clause. A clause in Article IV, Section 2, of the Constitution according citizens of each state most of the privileges of citizens of other states.

probable cause. The situation occurring when the police have reason to believe that a person should be arrested. In making the arrest, police are allowed legally to search for and seize incriminating evidence. Compare **unreasonable searches and seizures**.

progressive tax. A tax by which the government takes a greater share of the income of the rich than of the poor—for example, when a rich family pays 50 percent of its income in taxes and a poor family pays 5 percent. Compare **regressive tax** and **proportional tax**.

project grants. Federal grants given for specific purposes and awarded on the basis of the merits of applications. A type of the **categorical grants** available to states and localities.

proportional representation. An electoral system used throughout most of Europe that awards legislative seats to political parties in proportion to the number of votes won in an election. Compare with **winner-take-all system**.

241

proportional tax. A tax by which the government takes the same share of income from everyone, rich and poor alike—for example, when a rich family pays 20 percent and a poor family pays 20 percent. Compare **progressive tax** and **regressive tax**.

protectionism. Economic policy of shielding an economy from imports.

protest. A form of **political participation** designed to achieve policy change through dramatic and unconventional tactics. See also **civil disobedience**.

public goods. Goods, such as clean air and clean water, that everyone must share.

public interest. The idea that there are some interests superior to the private interest of groups and individuals, interests we all have in common. See also **public interest lobbies**.

public interest lobbies. According to Jeffrey Berry, organizations that seek "a collective good, the achievement of which will not selectively and materially benefit the membership or activities of the organization." See also **lobbying** and **public interest**.

public opinion. The distribution of the population's beliefs about politics and policy issues.

public policy. A choice that **government** makes in response to a political issue. A policy is a course of action taken with regard to some problem.

R

random digit dialing. A technique used by pollsters to place telephone calls randomly to both listed and unlisted numbers when conducting a survey. See also **random sampling**.

random sampling. The key technique employed by sophisticated survey researchers, which operates on the principle that everyone should have an equal probability of being selected for the sample. See also **sample**.

rational-choice theory. A popular theory in political science to explain the actions of voters as well as politicians. It assumes that individuals act in their own best interest, carefully weighing the costs and benefits of possible alternatives.

realignment. See **party realignment**.

reapportionment. The process of reallocating seats in the House of Representatives every 10 years on the basis of the results of the census.

recall. A procedure that allows voters to call a special election for a specific official in an attempt to throw him or her out of office before the end of his or her term. Recalls are only permitted in 17 states, are seldom used because of their cost and disruptiveness, and are rarely successful.

reconciliation. A congressional process through which program authorizations are revised to achieve required savings. It usually also includes tax or other revenue adjustments.

Red Lion Broadcasting Company v. FCC. A 1969 case in which the Supreme Court upheld restrictions on radio and television broadcasting, such as giving adequate coverage to public issues and covering opposing views. These restrictions on the **broadcast media** are much tighter than those on the **print media** because there are only a limited number of broadcasting frequencies available. See *Miami Herald Publishing Company v. Tornillo.*

Reed v. Reed. The landmark case in 1971 in which the Supreme Court for the first time upheld a claim of gender discrimination.

referendum. A state-level method of direct legislation that gives voters a chance to approve or disapprove legislation or a constitutional amendment proposed by the state legislature.

Regents of the University of California v. Bakke. A 1978 Supreme Court decision holding that a state university could not admit less qualified individuals solely because of their race. The Court did not, however, rule that such **affirmative action** policies and the use of race as a criterion for admission were unconstitutional, only that they had to be formulated differently.

regional primaries. A proposal by critics of the **caucuses** and **presidential primaries** to replace these electoral methods with a series of primaries held in each geographic region.

registration. See **voter registration**.

regressive tax. A tax in which the burden falls relatively more heavily on low-income groups than on wealthy taxpayers. The opposite of a **progressive tax**, in which tax rates increase as income increases.

regulation. The use of governmental authority to control or change some practice in the private sector. Regulations pervade the daily lives of people and institutions.

regulatory agency. See **independent regulatory agency**.

reinforcement. One of three key consequences of electoral campaigns for voters, in which the voter's candidate preference is reinforced. See also **activation** and **conversion**.

relative deprivation. A perception by a group that it is doing less well than is appropriate in relation to a reference group. The desire of a group to correct what it views as the unfair distribution of resources, such as income or government benefits, is a frequent motivator for political activism.

representation. A basic principle of **traditional democratic theory** that describes the relationship between the few leaders and the many followers.

republic. A form of government that derives its power, directly or indirectly, from the people. Those chosen to govern are accountable to those whom they govern. In contrast to a direct democracy, in which people themselves make laws, in a republic the people select representatives who make the laws.

responsible party model. A view favored by some political scientists about how parties should work. According to the model, parties should offer clear choices to the voters, who can then use those choices as cues to their own preferences of candidates. Once in office, parties would carry out their campaign promises.

retrospective voting. A theory of voting in which voters essentially ask this simple question: "What have you done for me lately?"

revenues. The financial resources of the federal government. The individual income tax and Social Security tax are two major sources of revenue. Compare **expenditures**.

right to privacy. The right to a private personal life free from the intrusion of government. The right to privacy is implicitly protected by the **Bill of Rights**. See also **Privacy Act**.

right-to-work law. A state law forbidding requirements that workers must join a union to hold their jobs. State right-to-work laws were specifically permitted by the Taft-Hartley Act of 1947.

Roe v. Wade. The 1973 Supreme Court decision holding that a state ban on all abortions was unconstitutional. The decision forbade state control over abortions during the first trimester of pregnancy, permitted states to limit abortions to protect the mother's health in the second trimester, and permitted states to protect the fetus during the third trimester.

Roth v. United States. A 1957 Supreme Court decision ruling that "obscenity is not within the area of constitutionally protected speech or press."

S

sample. A relatively small proportion of people who are chosen in a survey so as to be representative of the whole.

sampling error. The level of confidence in the findings of a public opinion poll. The more people interviewed, the more confident one can be of the results.

Schenck v. United States. A 1919 decision upholding the conviction of a socialist who had urged young men to resist the draft during World War I. Justice Holmes declared that government can limit speech if the speech provokes a "clear and present danger" of substantive evils.

School District of Abington Township, Pennsylvania v. Schempp. A 1963 Supreme Court decision holding that a Pennsylvania law requiring Bible reading in schools violated the **establishment clause** of the **First Amendment**. Compare *Engel v. Vitale*.

school districts. Units of local government that are normally independent of any other local government and are primarily responsible for operating public schools.

Scott v. Sandford. The 1857 Supreme Court decision ruling that a slave who had escaped to a free state enjoyed no rights as a citizen and that Congress had no authority to ban slavery in the territories.

search warrant. A written authorization from a court specifying the area to be searched and what the police are searching for.

secretary of defense. The head of the Department of Defense and the president's key adviser on military policy; a key **foreign policy** actor.

secretary of state. The head of the Department of State and traditionally a key adviser to the president on **foreign policy**.

Securities and Exchange Commission (SEC). The federal agency created during the New Deal that regulates stock fraud.

select committees. Congressional committees appointed for a specific purpose, such as the Watergate investigation. See also **joint committees, standing committees,** and **conference committees.**

selective benefits. Goods (such as information publications, travel discounts, and group insurance rates) that a group can restrict to those who pay their yearly dues.

selective perception. The phenomenon that people often pay the most attention to things they already agree with and interpret them according to their own predispositions.

self-incrimination. The situation occurring when an individual accused of a crime is compelled to be a witness against himself or herself in court. The **Fifth Amendment** forbids self-incrimination. See also *Miranda v. Arizona*.

Senate Finance Committee. The Senate committee that, along with the **House Ways and Means Committee,** writes the tax codes, subject to the approval of Congress as a whole.

senatorial courtesy. An unwritten tradition whereby nominations for state-level federal judicial posts are not confirmed if they are opposed by the senator from the state in which the nominee will serve. The tradition also applies to courts of appeal when there is opposition from the nominee's state senator, if the senator belongs to the president's party.

Senior Executive Service (SES). An elite cadre of about 11,000 federal government managers, established by the Civil Service Reform Act of 1978, who are mostly career officials but include some political appointees who do not require Senate confirmation.

seniority system. A simple rule for picking **committee chairs,** in effect until the 1970s. The member who had served on the committee the longest and whose party controlled Congress became chair, regardless of party loyalty, mental state, or competence.

separation of powers. An important part of the **Madisonian model** that requires each of the three branches of government—executive, legislative, and judicial—to be relatively independent of the others so that one cannot control the others. Power is shared among these three institutions. See also **checks and balances.**

Shays' Rebellion. A series of attacks on courthouses by a small band of farmers led by revolutionary war Captain Daniel Shays to block foreclosure proceedings.

single-issue groups. Groups that have a narrow interest, tend to dislike compromise, and often draw membership from people new to politics. These features distinguish them from traditional **interest groups.**

Sixteenth Amendment. The constitutional amendment adopted in 1913 that explicitly permitted Congress to levy an **income tax.**

Sixth Amendment. The constitutional amendment designed to protect individuals accused of crimes. It includes the right to counsel, the right to confront witnesses, and the right to a speedy and public trial.

social policies. Policies that manipulate opportunities through public choice. They include policies related to income and policies related to opportunity.

Social Security Act. A 1935 law passed during the Great Depression that was intended to provide a minimal level of sustenance to older Americans and thus save them from poverty.

social welfare policies. Policies that provide benefits to individuals, particularly to those in need. Compare **civil rights policies.**

socialized medicine. A system in which the full cost of medical care is borne by the national government. Great Britain and the former Soviet Union are examples of countries that have socialized medicine. Compare **Medicaid** and **Medicare.**

soft money. Political contributions earmarked for party-building expenses at the grass-roots level (or for generic party advertising). Unlike money that goes to the campaign of a particular candidate, such party donations are not subject to contribution limits.

solicitor general. A presidential appointee and the third-ranking office in the Department of Justice. The solicitor general is in charge of the appellate court litigation of the federal government.

sound bites. Short video clips of approximately 15 seconds, which are typically all that is shown from a politician's speech or activities on television news.

Speaker of the House. An office mandated by the Constitution. The Speaker is chosen in practice by the majority party, has both formal and informal powers, and is second in line to succeed to the presidency should that office become vacant.

special districts. Limited-purpose local governments called *districts* or *public authorities* that are created to run a specific type of service, such as water distribution, airports, public transportation, libraries, and natural resource areas.

standard operating procedures. Better known as SOPs, these procedures are used by bureaucrats to bring uniformity to complex organizations. Uniformity improves fairness and makes personnel interchangeable. See also **administrative discretion**.

standing committees. Separate subject-matter committees in each house of Congress that handle **bills** in different policy areas. See also **joint committees, conference committees,** and **select committees**.

standing to sue. The requirement that **plaintiffs** have a serious interest in a **case**, which depends on whether they have sustained or are likely to sustain a direct and substantial injury from a party or an action of government.

stare decisis. A Latin phrase meaning "let the decision stand." Most cases reaching appellate courts are settled on this principle.

statutory construction. The judicial interpretation of an act of Congress. In some cases where statutory construction is an issue, Congress passes new legislation to clarify existing laws.

Strategic Defense Initiative (SDI). Renamed "Star Wars" by critics, a plan for defense against the Soviet Union unveiled by President Reagan in 1983. SDI would create a global umbrella in space, using computers to scan the skies and high-tech devices to destroy invading missiles.

street-level bureaucrats. A phrase coined by Michael Lipsky, referring to those bureaucrats who are in constant contact with the public and have considerable **administrative discretion**.

subgovernments. A network of groups within the American political system which exercise a great deal of control over specific policy areas. Also known as iron triangles, subgovernments are composed of interest group leaders interested in a particular policy, the government agency in charge of administering that policy, and the members of congressional committees and subcommittees handling that policy.

subnational governments. Another way of referring to state and local governments. Through a process of reform, modernization, and changing intergovernmental relations since the 1960s, subnational governments have assumed new responsibilities and importance.

suffrage. The legal right to vote, extended to African Americans by the **Fifteenth Amendment**, to women by the **Nineteenth Amendment**, and to people over the age of 18 by the **Twenty-sixth Amendment**.

Super Tuesday. Created by a dozen or so Southern states when they held their **presidential primaries** in early March 1988. These states hoped to promote a regional advantage as well as a more conservative candidate.

superdelegates. National party leaders who automatically get a delegate slot at the Democratic **national party convention**.

Superfund. A fund created by Congress in the late 1970s and renewed in the 1980s to clean up hazardous waste sites. Money for the fund comes from taxing chemical products.

supply-side economics. An economic theory, advocated by President Reagan, holding that too much income goes to taxes and too little money is available for purchasing and that the solution is to cut taxes and return purchasing power to consumers.

supremacy clause. Article VI of the Constitution, which makes the Constitution, national laws, and treaties supreme over state laws when the national government is acting within its constitutional limits.

Supreme Court. The pinnacle of the American judicial system. The Court ensures uniformity in interpreting national laws, resolves conflicts among states, and maintains national supremacy in law. It has both **original jurisdiction** and **appellate jurisdiction**, but unlike other federal courts, it controls its own agenda.

symbolic speech. Nonverbal communication, such as burning a flag or wearing an armband. The Supreme Court has accorded some symbolic speech protection under the **First Amendment**. See *Texas v. Johnson*.

T

Taft-Hartley Act. A 1947 law giving the president power to halt major strikes by seeking a court injunction and permitting states to forbid requirements in labor contracts forcing workers to join a union. See also **right-to-work law**.

talking head. A shot of a person's face talking directly to the camera. Because this is visually unappealing, the major commercial networks rarely show a politician talking one-on-one for very long. See also **sound bites**.

tariff. A special tax added to imported goods to raise the price, thereby protecting American businesses and workers from foreign competition.

tax. See **proportional tax, progressive tax,** and **regressive tax**.

tax expenditures. Defined by the 1974 Budget Act as "revenue losses attributable to provisions of the federal tax laws which allow a special exemption, exclusion, or deduction." Tax expenditures represent the difference between what the government actually collects in taxes and what it would have collected without special exemptions.

tax incidence. The proportion of its income a particular group pays in taxes.

Temporary Assistance for Needy Families (TANF). Once called "Aid to Families with Dependent Children," the new name for public assistance to needy families.

Tenth Amendment. The constitutional amendment stating that "The powers not delegated to the United States by the Constitution, nor prohibited by it to the states, are reserved to the states respectively, or to the people."

term limits. Laws to restrict legislators from serving more than a fixed number of years or terms in office.

Texas v. Johnson. A 1989 case in which the Supreme Court struck down a law banning the burning of the American flag on the grounds that such action was **symbolic speech** protected by the **First Amendment**.

third parties. Electoral contenders other than the two major parties. American third parties are not unusual, but they rarely win elections.

Thirteenth Amendment. The constitutional amendment passed after the Civil War that forbade slavery and involuntary servitude.

ticket splitting. Voting with one party for one office and with another party for other offices. It has become the norm in American voting behavior.

town meeting. A special form of direct democracy under which all voting-age adults in a community gather once a year to make public policy. Now only used in a few villages in upper New England, originally many municipalities in the United States were run by town meeting. The growth of most cities has made them too large for this style of governance.

township. A political subdivision of local government that is found in 20 states and often serves to provide local government services in rural areas. It is a particularly strong form of local government—comparable to a municipality—in the Northeast.

traditional democratic theory. A theory about how a democratic government makes its decisions. According to Robert Dahl, its cornerstones are equality in voting, effective participation, enlightened understanding, final control over the agenda, and inclusion.

transfer payments. Benefits given by the government directly to individuals. Transfer payments may be either cash transfers, such as Social Security payments and retirement payments to former government employees, or in-kind transfers, such as food stamps and low-interest loans for college education.

transnational corporations. Businesses with vast holdings in many countries—such as Microsoft, Coca-Cola, and McDonald's—many of which have annual budgets exceeding that of many foreign governments.

trial balloons. An intentional **news leak** for the purpose of assessing the political reaction.

trial courts. The lowest tier in the trial court system, in which the facts of a case are considered. These courts hear both civil and criminal matters.

trustee. A legislator who uses his or her best judgment to make policy in the interests of the people. This concept was favored by Edmund Burke. Compare **instructed delegate**.

Twenty-fifth Amendment. Passed in 1967, this amendment permits the vice president to become acting president if both the vice president and the president's cabinet determine that the president is disabled. The amendment also outlines how a recuperated president can reclaim the job.

Twenty-fourth Amendment. The constitutional amendment passed in 1964 that declared **poll taxes** void.

Twenty-second Amendment. Passed in 1951, the amendment that limits presidents to two terms of office.

U

uncontrollable expenditures. Expenditures that are determined not by a fixed amount of money appropriated by Congress but by how many eligible beneficiaries there are for some particular program or by previous obligations of the government. Three-fourths of the federal **budget** is uncontrollable. Congress can change uncontrollable expenditures only by changing a law or existing benefit levels.

unemployment rate. As measured by the Bureau of Labor Statistics (BLS), the proportion of the labor force actively seeking work but unable to find jobs.

unfunded mandates. When the federal government requires state and local action but does not provide the funds to pay for the action.

union shop. A provision found in some collective bargaining agreements requiring all employees of a business to join the union within a short period, usually 30 days, and to remain members as a condition of employment.

unitary government. A way of organizing a nation so that all power resides in the central government. Most national governments today, including those of Great Britain and Japan, are unitary governments. Compare **federalism**.

United Nations (UN). Created in 1945, an organization whose members agree to renounce war and to respect certain human and economic freedoms. The seat of real power in the UN is the Security Council.

United States v. Nixon. The 1974 case in which the Supreme Court unanimously held that the doctrine of executive privilege was implicit in the Constitution but could not be extended to protect documents relevant to criminal prosecutions.

unreasonable searches and seizures. Obtaining evidence in a haphazard or random manner, a practice prohibited by the Fourth Amendment. Both **probable cause** and a **search warrant** are required for a legal and proper search for and seizure of incriminating evidence.

unwritten constitution. The body of tradition, practice, and procedure that is as important as the written constitution. Changes in the unwritten **constitution** can change the spirit of the Constitution. **Political parties** and **national party conventions** are a part of the unwritten constitution in the United States.

urban underclass. The poorest of the poor in America. These are the Americans whose economic opportunities are severely limited in almost every way. They constitute a large percentage of the Americans afflicted by homelessness, crime, drugs, alcoholism, unwanted pregnancies, and other endemic social problems.

U.S. Constitution. The document written in 1787 and ratified in 1788 that sets forth the institutional structure of U.S. government and the tasks these institutions perform. It replaced the Articles of Confederation. See also **constitution** and **unwritten constitution**.

V

veto. The constitutional power of the president to send a **bill** back to Congress with reasons for rejecting it. A two-thirds vote in each house can override a veto. See also **legislative veto** and **pocket veto**.

Virginia Plan. The proposal at the Constitutional Convention that called for *representation* of each state in Congress in proportion to that state's share of the U.S. population. Compare **Connecticut Compromise** and **New Jersey Plan**.

voter registration. A system adopted by the states that requires voters to register well in advance of Election Day. A few states permit Election Day registration.

Voting Rights Act of 1965. A law designed to help end formal and informal barriers to African American **suffrage**. Under the law, federal registrars were sent to Southern states and counties that had long histories of discrimination; as a result, hundreds of thousands of African Americans were registered and the number of African American elected officials increased dramatically.

W

War Powers Resolution. A law passed in 1973 in reaction to American fighting in Vietnam and Cambodia that requires presidents to consult with Congress whenever possible prior to using military force and to withdraw forces after 60 days unless Congress declares war or grants an extension. Presidents view the resolution as unconstitutional. See also **legislative veto**.

Watergate. The events and scandal surrounding a break-in at the Democratic National Committee headquarters in 1972 and the subsequent cover-up of White House involvement, leading to the eventual resignation of President Nixon under the threat of **impeachment**.

wealth. The amount of funds already owned. Wealth includes stocks, bonds, bank deposits, cars, houses, and so forth. Throughout most of the last generation, wealth has been much less evenly divided than **income**.

whips. Party leaders who work with the **majority leader** or **minority leader** to count votes beforehand and lean on waverers whose votes are crucial to a **bill** favored by the party.

White primary. One of the means used to discourage African American voting that permitted political parties in the heavily Democratic South to exclude African Americans from primary elections, thus depriving them of a voice in the real contests. The Supreme Court declared White primaries unconstitutional in 1944. See also **grandfather clause** and **poll taxes**.

winner-take-all system. An electoral system in which legislative seats are awarded only to the candidates who come in first in their constituencies. In American presidential elections, the system in which the winner of the popular vote in a state receives all the electoral votes of that state. Compare with **proportional representation**.

World Trade Organization (WTO). International organization that regulates international trade.

writ of certiorari. A formal document issued from the **Supreme Court** to a lower federal or state court that calls up a case.

writ of habeas corpus. A court order requiring jailers to explain to a judge why they are holding a prisoner in custody.

writ of mandamus. A court order forcing action. In the dispute leading to *Marbury v. Madison*, Marbury and his associates asked the **Supreme Court** to issue a writ ordering Madison to give them their commissions.

Z

Zelman v. Simmons-Harris. The 2002 Supreme Court decision that upheld a state providing families with vouchers that could be used to pay tuition at religious schools.

Zurcher v. Stanford Daily. A 1978 Supreme Court decision holding that a proper **search warrant** could be applied to a newspaper as well as to anyone else without necessarily violating the **First Amendment** rights to freedom of the press.